Developing EJB™ 2.0 Components

PRAVIN V. TULACHAN

Sun Microsystems Press
A Prentice Hall Title

ISBN 0-13-034863-5

9 780130 348630

Prentice Hall PTR
Upper Saddle River, NJ 07458
www.phptr.com

The publisher offers discounts on this book when ordered in bulk quantities.
For more information, contact Corporate Sales Department, Prentice Hall PTR ,
One Lake Street, Upper Saddle River, NJ 07458. Phone: 800-382-3419; FAX: 201- 236-7141.
E-mail: corpsales@prenhall.com.

Editorial/production supervision: *Faye Gemmellaro*
Cover design director: *Jerry Votta*
Cover designer: *Nina Scuderi*
Art director: *Gail Cocker-Bogusz*
Manufacturing manager: *Alexis R. Heydt-Long*
Marketing manager: *Debby vanDijk*
Executive editor: *Gregory G. Doench*
Associate editor: *Eileen Clark*
Editorial assistant: *Brandt Kenna*
Sun Microsystems Press publisher: *Michael Llwyd Alread*

10 9 8 7 6 5 4 3 2 1

ISBN 0-13-034863-5

Sun Microsystems Press
A Prentice Hall Title

This book is dedicated to my parents —
Rudra Vilas and Bishnu Kumari Tulachan.

Contents

PART 1
OVERVIEW

PART 2
DEVELOPING EJBs

7   DEVELOPING STATEFUL SESSION BEANS. 166

PART 3
ADVANCED TOPICS

Preface

What Are Enterprise JavaBeans (EJB)?

If you've picked up this book and are reading this page, it's probably because you're curious about or interested in Enterprise JavaBeans (EJB), Java 2 Enterprise Edition, or Java. Or perhaps you just liked the cute giraffe on the cover with its backdrop of Mt. Kilimanjaro and wondered what a giraffe was doing on a cover of a J2EE book.

This book is about Enterprise JavaBeans 2.0. EJB is a component model for building scalable, reusable, portable, transactional, and distributed enterprise business applications. Well-designed EJBs encapsulate discrete business logic, and EJBs that encapsulate different kinds of business logic can be assembled to form a complete business application. For example, one could take discrete EJBs that implement user authentication, credit card authorization, shopping cart, order fulfillment, inventory management, and customer relationship management tasks and assemble them into one integrated application, then add the Web front end and ... presto! You have an e-commerce application, are ready for an IPO (well, that *was* true back in 1999 and early 2000), and can afford to buy a two-bedroom mansion in Silicon Valley. We'll worry about profitability later.

Why Should You Buy This Book?

There are several good books on EJBs, and I'm sure there will be more in the future. Most current EJB books fall into two basic categories—standalone EJB books that focus solely on EJB and do a good job at it but usually lack context, and books that attempt to cover everything—all the J2EE technologies, CORBA, and even (in some cases) COM/DCOM, in one humongous tome. These latter books have plenty of breadth but usually lack depth.

This book, *Developing EJB 2.0 Components*, the first book in a three-book series, focuses exclusively on the practical aspects of how to implement EJB 2.0. It is an attempt to bring the right balance between depth and breath within the broader context of the Java 2 Enterprise Edition platform. The book incorporates a unique perspective from my experience as a J2EE developer and as an instructor who teaches Java programmers—nationally, internationally for Netscape, and currently for Sun—how to develop J2EE applications. The second book in the series, *Developing Web Components and Web Services*, will focus exclusively on the presentation and user-interaction aspects of the J2EE technologies. The third (as yet untitled) book will focus exclusively on the J2EE infrastructure technologies. Together, these three titles will provide the audience with the necessary practical knowledge, depth, and breadth to write robust J2EE applications.

So you must be wondering, "Why should I buy this book?" Following are some good reasons (my reasons, of course), but you be the judge.

Go the Whole Nine Yards

Let's face it: EJB has a steep learning curve. Implementing EJB applications can be complex, and knowing how to write an EJB component is just half of the challenge. After coding and compiling the EJB components, you need to package, assemble, and then deploy them—no trivial tasks for a beginning EJB developer. Unlike most EJB books, *Developing EJB 2.0 Components* not only has chapters that discuss the theory, the APIs, and the rules on writing various types of EJBs and their methods, but it also has a separate chapter that discusses step-by-step implementation details followed by packaging and deployment steps and information on how to run the sample application. This information is complete with a copious number of diagrams and screen captures of the steps to guide you to a successful completion for each type of EJB. If my instructor-lead training experience is any indication, most rookie EJB developers will appreciate my effort to show you how to "go the whole nine yards" (to borrow an expression from American football), or in other words, to implement a complete solution.

Respect Your Intelligence

One of the hardest tasks in writing a book like this is setting the level at which to write the sample applications. On one hand, they shouldn't be so long and complicated that they distract the attention of the audience from fundamental EJB concepts in the process of trying to figure out complicated and nifty algorithms. At the other extreme, the sample applications shouldn't be so simple that they add little or no value to the learning process. My view is that I respect your intelligence and don't need to impress you with complex examples, so I've taken the middle path. The sample applications are not too complicated and not too long, so you can focus on the fundamentals of EJB without being too simplistic. Once you've mastered the concepts, you can take the sample application and use it to add real-world business complexity to your own applications. Most of the examples implement discrete business logic per EJB, and the last chapter takes all the EJBs you've implemented in the previous chapters and assembles them into an integrated EJB application, applying EJB design patterns and best practices. I hope I've been successful with this approach.

Advanced EJB Concepts...When You're Ready for Them

I've purposely deferred discussing advanced and complex issues such as transactions, security, and design patterns in Part 3 of the book so as to focus on the fundamentals of EJBs. Once you've mastered the fundamentals of EJB 2.0, you can then dive into more advanced concepts in Part 3. In that section, we concentrate on how to implement EJB transactions, EJB security, EJB design patterns, and strategies for migrating from EJB 1.1 to EJB 2.0, with complete code examples.

Repetition is the Key to Learning

The approach this book takes is first to discuss the concepts, characteristics, APIs, and rules on how to write specific EJB in an introductory chapter and then follow up with an implementation chapter that repeats the key concepts and rules during step-by-step implementation of a sample code example. I believe the discussion of the EJB fundamentals, followed by reinforcement through repetition of key concepts with example code, helps reduce the learning curve.

What This Book Doesn't Cover

I've told you all the great reasons why you *should* buy this book, so in the interest of fairness, I'll be up front and tell you that in some cases, you might *not* want to buy it. Here's why.

Vendor Neutrality

This book doesn't discuss packaging, assembling, and deploying using BEA's Weblogic, IBM's Websphere, Sun's iPlanet, or any other brand-name application server. The EJB implementation details are standard, so they're applicable to all application servers. This book focuses on packaging, assembling, and deploying EJB applications using Sun's J2EE Reference Implementation's deployment tool (deploytool), so the instructions are specific to that tool. The main reason I chose J2SDKEE RI is the resource requirements—it requires less than 15 MB of drive space, features ease of installation, runs with 128 MB of RAM, and is *free*. Most brand-name application servers require 100 MB of disk space and a minimum of 256 MB of RAM (or more), and installations can be challenging.

Not a Java Programming Book

This book doesn't teach you Java programming—only how to write business applications using EJBs.

Servlet, JSP, SQL, JDBC, UML, or CORBA Not Covered

This book assumes that the reader has real-world Java programming experience and also has familiarity with HTML, servlet, JSP, SQL, JDBC, and CORBA. I use UML diagrams and assume you have basic familiarity with such diagrams.

Audience for This Book

This book is primarily geared toward helping new EJB programmers and existing EJB 1.1 programmers learn how to write business logic in EJB 2.0. The ideal reader should have at least one year of Java programming experience and be familiar with HTML, servlet, JSP, SQL, rmi, and JDBC.

How the Book Is Organized

The book consists of eighteen chapters and is organized in three parts.

Part 1: Overview

The first part of this book consists of two introductory chapters that give an introductory, non-technical overview of the Java 2 Enterprise Edition and Enterprise JavaBeans 2.0. Audiences who will benefit from this section are novice Java programmers and nonprogrammers (such as technical managers, project managers, and so forth) who can read these two chapters and get a good grasp of the fundamentals of J2EE (1.3) and EJB (2.0) technologies. The information in these chapters will help them communicate effectively with EJB programmers.

- *Chapter 1: Introduction to Java 2 Enterprise Edition 1.3*—This chapter is a basic, nontechnical introduction to Java 2 Enterprise Edition. It discusses the various Java technologies required by the J2EE 1.3 specification and how they all fit together.

- *Chapter 2: Introduction to Enterprise JavaBeans 2.0*—This chapter is an introduction to Enterprise JavaBeans 2.0 and discusses the basics of Enterprise JavaBeans without overwhelming the reader with technical details.

Part 2: Developing EJBs

The second part of this book is geared toward Java programmers and EJB programmers who are interested in learning how to implement EJB 2.0. The chapters in this section deal with theory, followed by a step-by-step guide to implementing, packaging and deploying session, entity, and message-driven beans.

- *Chapter 3: Overview of Sample Applications*—This chapter offers a high-level implementation overview of sample applications of stateless and stateful session beans, bean-managed persistent and container-managed persistent entity beans, and message-driven beans.

- *Chapter 4: The EJB Client View*—This chapter discusses the local and remote client view of EJB and rules for implementing remote and local interfaces and their advantages and disadvantages.

- *Chapter 5: Introduction to Session Beans*—Here, you'll be introduced to characteristics, APIs, and details of session beans.

- *Chapter 6: Developing Stateless Session Beans*—This chapter covers the life cycle of stateless session beans and provides a step-by-step guide to implementing, packaging, assembling, and deploying a stateless session bean sample application.

- *Chapter 7: Developing Stateful Session Beans*—This chapter describes the life cycle of stateful session beans and provides a step-by-step guide to implementing, packaging, assembling, and deploying a stateful session bean sample application.

- *Chapter 8: Introduction to Entity Beans*—This chapter discusses the basic characteristic of entity beans, their life cycle, API, and rules for writing entity beans.

- *Chapter 9: Developing Bean-Managed Entity Beans*—This chapter povides a step-by-step guide to implementing, packaging, assembling, and deploying a BMP entity bean sample application.

- *Chapter 10: CMP 2.0: Abstract Persistence Model and EJB QL*—This chapter helps you understand the concepts behind the abstract persistence schema and the EJB Query language.

- *Chapter 11: Developing CMP 2.0 Entity Beans*—These pages offer a step-by-step guide to implementing, packaging, assembling, and deploying a CMP entity bean sample application.

- *Chapter 12: Java Message Service*—This chapter discusses the JMS API, messaging models, and how to use JMS APIs.

- *Chapter 13: Developing Message-Driven Beans*—This chapter is a step-by-step guide to implementing, packaging, assembling, and deploying a message-driven bean sample application.

Part 3: Advanced Topics

The final section in the book discusses advanced EJB concepts, including transaction, security, EJB design patterns, and migration issues.

- *Chapter 14: Transactions*—This chapter discusses how to implement programmatic and declarative transactions in different types of EJBs.

- *Chapter 15: Enterprise JavaBean Security*—This chapter discusses security concepts and how to implement programmatic and declarative security in EJBs.

- *Chapter 16: EJB Design Patterns, Interoperability, and Performance*—This chapter discusses common EJB design patterns and issues with performance and interoperability in EJB 2.0.

- *Chapter 17: Migrating EJB 1.1 Applications to the EJB 2.0 Container*—This chapter discusses issues involved in migrating EJB 1.1 beans to EJB 2.0 containers. It includes details and steps for migration of a sample application.

- *Chapter 18: Assembling the J2EE Online Registration Application*—The final chapter takes some of the discrete EJBs components developed in

Part 2 of the book, refactors them if necessary, applies appropriate design patterns, and creates a complete application. It also discusses some of the implementation issues.

Appendix

At the back of the book, you will find instructions on how to download, install, and set up Sun's J2SDKEE 1.3 Reference Implementation. For the latest updates, please go to the companion Web site at http://www.J2EEBootCamp.com and download Appendix.pdf.

Companion Web Site

To keep the book within reasonable number of pages, the book lists no examples in their entirety but instead takes code snippets from the sample examples to elucidate key concepts during the discussion. The complete source code, along with compiled classes and deployable ear files, are available for download from the companion Web site, http://www.J2EEBootCamp.com. I encourage you to return here for the latest on bug fixes, new articles, new sample examples, and my public speaking engagements.

Feel free to send comments and suggestions to pvt@j2eebootcamp.com, and I'll do my best to respond within few days.

What's a Giraffe Doing on the Front Cover of an EJB Book?

I'm an avid adventure traveler, and as a server-side Java consultant working in Silicon Valley, I've been able to travel two months a year for the past several years, thanks to the Internet boom (ah, those good old days!). I always had a vague notion of writing a Java book someday, and it became a real-life goal during a long trip across East Africa—to be precise, at the top of Mt. Kilimanjaro on January 1, 2000 at the first sunrise of the millennium. So the picture on the cover of the book is my tribute to the majestic Mt. Kilimanjaro (the highest mountain in Africa), its amazing wildlife, and the diverse cultures and peoples of Africa.

Acknowledgments

To put it positively (and mildly), writing this book has been one of the most challenging experiences of my life. I know you've read such statements by other authors—and so have I—but it really is a challenge, trust me. Even though the book has only my name on it, there are many talented people who've played significant roles in making this book possible. Without their assistance, this book would not have become a reality.

At Prentice Hall, I would like to express my gratitude to executive editor Greg Doench for accepting the J2EE book series proposal and bringing it to fruition. My thanks also go to marketing manager Debby vanDijk and acquisition editor Eileen Clark for all their efforts toward the completion of the book. I would also like to thank developmental editor Jim Markham for helping me with the development and structure of the book.

Thanks also go to production coordinator, editor, and compositor Sybil Ihrig of Helios Productions, technical reviewer Rob Gordon, and editors Casey Andrysiak and Elizabeth Hayes for their meticulous reviews and suggestions regarding the content and style of the book. At Sun Press, I wish thank Michael Alread and Rachel Borden for their efforts in expediting production of the book.

I would also like to express my thanks to three excellent authors—Phillip Heller (*The Complete Java Certification*), Marty Hall (*Core Servlet and JavaServer Pages*), and Peter Haggar (*Practical Java Programming Guide*) for their initial encouragement with my book. The acknowledgment list would be incomplete without expressing my deep appreciation to Jason Fish, business development manager at Sun Educational Services, for introducing me to Greg Doench at Prentice Hall and thus starting the ball rolling on the this book. Thanks, Jason.

—*Pravin Tulachan*

Part 1

OVERVIEW

INTRODUCTION TO JAVA 2 ENTERPRISE EDITION 1.3

Topics in This Chapter

- The Evolution of Enterprise Computing
- Considerations of Enterprise Computing
- Enterprise Computing Platforms
- Technologies Required by J2EE 1.3
- The J2EE Architecture
- Technical Advantages of the J2EE Architecture
- Business-Related Advantages of the J2EE Architecture
- J2EE Development and Deployment Roles
- Developing a J2EE Application
- J2EE Disadvantages

Chapter 1

To understand and appreciate the benefits of Enterprise JavaBeans technology for implementing portable and scalable business logic, one first needs to understand the Java 2 Enterprise Edition (J2EE) platform. This chapter provides a high level introduction to Java 2 Enterprise Edition (hereafter referred to as J2EE) version 1.3, including

- the requirements for highly scalable and available enterprise computing platforms and some of the competing platforms in the market today
- brief explanations of all the Java technologies required by the J2EE 1.3 specification and their function within J2EE architecture
- roles an individual might play in the development and deployment of a J2EE application

The Evolution of Enterprise Computing

In the 1970s, information technology (IT) consisted of mainframes running monolithic applications. Computing resources were expensive, centralized, and accessible only to a handful of data processing personnel and high-level managers. Programmers used batch jobs to run programs, and the few users able to access the mainframe application did so via slow character-based terminals. Loads on the computing resources were predictable and controlled. The security was rudimentary and not a major issue because the applications were accessible only to a few select people in the corporation.

The development of client-server computing in the 1980s equipped departments with affordable computing resources such as minicomputers. Applications were written in two parts: The server consisted of departmental minicomputers that handled business and data access logic, while the client consisted of desktop PCs that handled client-side logic and user interface. Programmers and employees in the department used desktop computers (now graphical user interface [GUI] enabled) connected to their local area networks (LANs) to access client-server applications. The number of client installations ensured a controlled impact on the computing resources. The security was one of the concerns and was addressed by a basic user authentication scheme, but it was not a high-level concern because access to the computing resources was localized at the departmental level.

The controlled computing environments of the 1970s and 1980s gave way to the distributed multitiered computing era in the 1990s (which still reigns today). Multitier computing enables anytime/anywhere access to relatively inexpensive distributed computing resources by anyone who can access a network with a Web browser. Today, users can access applications on the Internet at any time from anywhere in the world using devices such as desktop computers, Internet appliances, and personal digital assistants (PDAs) such as PalmPilots. Because access is now so unlimited and geographically dispersed, businesses cannot consistently and accurately predict the number of simultaneous users or loads on computing resources. To deal with this unpredictability, established businesses must choose scalable, available, and secure computing platforms. In the Internet era, with pervasive access to the corporate network, security has become a critical issue, and users accessing the corporate data must be not only authenticated but also authorized for access to specific resources.

Considerations of Enterprise Computing

To understand the impact of this unlimited access to computing resources, let's review the basic requirements for a fictitious startup scenario in the Silicon Valley. John Doe, an entrepreneur and avid golfer, has a simple business-to-consumer (B2C) business plan to develop an e-commerce site, get his site funded by a notable venture capitalist firm, have a successful initial public offering (IPO), and then sell his valuable shares, move to Bali, and retire to play golf.

The first step is to design and build an application that lets him sell golf supplies over the Internet—the application that will enable e-commerce. John, his Chief Technology Officer (CTO), and the core technology team have a brainstorming session to come up with application architecture and infrastructure issues for e-commerce application requirements. The result of the brainstorming session is the following list:

- application related issues
  - an e-commerce Web site with a shopping cart that lets customers track their items and purchase them on-line with credit card payments
  - a way to process, fulfill, ship, and track customer orders
  - the ability to manage warehouse inventory and to interface to a supplier's legacy system (IBM mainframes, for example)
  - customer notification functionality, such as e-mail notifications of shipped orders
- infrastructure-related issues
  - programming language (Perl, C, C++, VB, and/or Java)
  - operating system (Windows, MacOS, UNIX, Solaris, AIX, or Linux)
  - hardware (Intel, Sun, HP, and/or IBM)

As a self-funded startup company with limited funding, the group adopts a low-cost approach to the hardware and operating system requirements and decides to use the Intel/Windows platform. Because the engineering team has extensive experience in the Perl and C programming languages, the engineers decide to write the Web portion of the application in Perl and the business logic portion in C.

The team of talented engineers works furiously for months but soon realizes that the tasks are more complicated than the list of requirements they had originally compiled. Besides the core e-commerce application requirements, the team also has to write low-level system utilities (such as thread management and input/output control logic software) to manage their applications. It must also write code to handle infrastructure issues (such as low-level security logic implementation and transaction services) and additional code to access proprietary legacy applications.

Six months behind schedule, the e-commerce application is finally complete and is presented to the venture capital firm. The venture capitalists are impressed with the application and are willing to fund the company but are concerned about the following issues:

- Is the e-commerce application scalable enough to handle millions of customers and fault-tolerant enough so that the application can process customer orders without crashing during peak load times?
- Can the e-commerce application also run on highly available UNIX servers?

John's visualization of golfing in Bali diminishes once he realizes that the application was written using the proprietary Windows-only API in C and Perl. Thus, the application isn't portable to highly scalable, available, and fault-tolerant UNIX servers. And, to enable the application to run on UNIX servers, John decides that it's much easier to rewrite the application using UNIX APIs than to attempt to migrate the application to UNIX. As a technologist, John knows that he has months of work ahead for this engineering team.

But what if John instead had used one of several enterprise-computing platforms or, better yet, the J2EE platform to develop his dream application? Before we discuss enterprise-computing platforms, let's first look at the characteristics of an enterprise application, which are as follows:

- *Interoperability*—This is the ability of the enterprise application to communicate with other applications regardless of the language in which it was written or the type of operating system and hardware platform on which it's executing. Interoperability is essential for enterprise applications because businesses have collections of incompatible computing systems as a result of business acquisitions or mergers. This economic fact requires that new computing platforms be interoperable with existing systems. Interoperability gives businesses the flexibility to pick and choose the best-of-breed products (for example, one of the twenty application servers in the market) that will enhance the business' goals without the computing isolation that the use of a single-vendor platform causes. Certain features are necessary for interoperability. One example is cross-language support—the ability of the computing platform to support several different programming languages, such as COBOL, Fortran, C, C++, VB, and Java. Another important feature is cross-platform support—the ability to interoperate with applications written in different languages running on different platforms such as Windows, UNIX, and IBM's MVS. A third important interoperability feature is support for multiple standard network protocols such as TCP/IP, HTTP, and HTTPS.
- *Integration with legacy systems*—Most businesses have technologically outdated *legacy* systems where historical business data is stored.

Businesses require the ability to integrate the new enterprise application seamlessly with existing legacy applications and provide access to the data using standard multivendor-supported interfaces.

- *Programming productivity*—Programming productivity equates to faster application development that requires few programmers, reduced time-to-market, and fewer bugs. Factors contributing to programming productivity include choice of the right object-oriented programming language and software component model.

- *Reliability and performance*—A customer's perception of performance and reliability equates to the responsiveness of the application and the availability and consistency of the application's behavior when a customer accesses it. An enterprise application must be reliable and perform well under heavy load.

- *Security*—Whenever sensitive business data is exposed to the Internet, security becomes a critical issue. The computing platform has to provide standard security features that are easy to implement, easy to enforce, and hard to compromise. Enterprise application must support a flexible security model that is easy to implement.

Enterprise Computing Platforms

Several popular competing enterprise application development platforms currently in use promise to meet the challenges just outlined. These platforms include CORBA, .NET, and Java 2 Enterprise Edition (J2EE).

CORBA

The Common Object Request Broker Architecture (CORBA) platform comes to us from the Object Management Group. The Object Management Group is made up of more than 800 members and has been around since the early 1970s. CORBA is a vendor-independent, language-neutral, and operating system-agnostic platform for developing enterprise applications. The CORBA differentiator is the Interface Definition Language (IDL), which defines the contractual interface with potential clients. Components written using the IDL specification are portable across languages and operating systems. There are four elements to CORBA architecture—ORB, CORBAservices, CORBAfacilities, and the business application objects. The Object Request Broker (ORB) is the object bus, which enables objects to transparently make requests to and receive response from other local or remote objects. The CORBAservices element consists of collections of system-level services that are packaged according to the IDL specification and are available to objects. The CORBAfacilities are application frameworks intended to be used directly by business objects. Finally, the business application objects encapsulate the business logic and use the CORBA services and frameworks. Two major drawbacks with CORBA platform thus far have been the complexity of writing CORBA applications and the overall performance of CORBA applications.

.NET

.NET is the latest architecture from Microsoft for building distributed enterprise applications. Although .NET is language independent, it's still a platform-dependent architecture. Programmers have a choice of several languages as long as they use the Windows platform. The .NET architecture is a new and evolving computing platform; industry analysts don't expect significant numbers of third-party applications that support the .NET architecture to become available until late 2002. The .NET platform supports applications written in 27 languages, including the Java-like language, C#. The applications are compiled to Microsoft Independent Language (MSIL) code, which is a low-level compiled language format. At runtime, MSIL code is executed within the IL Common Language Runtime (ILCLR) virtual machine. Even though .NET is a new and evolving platform, the fact that it originates from Microsoft ensures that it eventually will occupy a prominent place in the enterprise computing platform space.

Refer to www.microsoft.com/net (Microsoft) and www.omg.org (CORBA) for further information.

J2EE

The Java 2 computing platform comes in three separate editions, each one targeted for specific product types:

- *Java 2 Platform, Micro Edition (J2ME)* is targeted to consumer product markets such as cell phones, PDAs, set-top boxes that enable access to cable services, and other devices with limited connectivity, memory, and user-interface capabilities. J2ME enables manufacturers and content creators to write portable Java applications geared for the consumer market.
- *Java 2 Platform, Standard Edition (J2SE)* is targeted to desktop applications that incorporate rich GUIs, sophisticated logic, and fast performance. J2SE supports standalone Java applications or client-side applications interacting with servers.
- *Java 2 Platform, Enterprise Edition (J2EE)* is targeted to enterprise applications for providing mission-critical services, which must be highly

scalable and available. It's based on modular, reusable software components written in the Java language. J2EE runs on top of J2SE.

The Java 2 computing platforms are Java language-centric but have a platform-independent architecture so that, for example, J2EE can run on different platforms such as Sun Solaris, Microsoft Windows, HP HP/UX, and IBM AIX, just to name a few. J2EE is a standard multitier architecture for developing and deploying distributed component-based enterprise applications that are highly available, secure, scalable, reliable, and easily manageable.

The J2EE specification is an industry-supported standard specification available through the Java Community process that defines the J2EE architecture and its functions. The Java Community Process is an organization of Java developers and licensees who are involved in the development and revision of Java technology specifications, reference implementations, and technology compatibility kits. As of December 2001, 36 companies have licensed J2EE from Sun Microsystems. The goals of the J2EE architecture are to reduce the complexity and the cost of developing distributed applications and to simplify the processes of development and deployment. Application services are portable, can be rapidly deployed, and are easy to enhance.

The J2EE platform is multitiered. As Figure 1-1 shows, it encompasses the architecture and the programming model for building a standard Java enterprise application that spans from customer user interface at the client tier to data storage at the Enterprise Information System (EIS) tier.

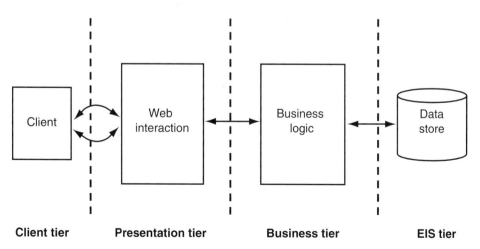

Figure 1-1 Simple multitier architecture

The J2EE platform guarantees the portability of enterprise applications across varying vendor implementations of the J2EE certified application servers. To encourage application portability, Sun Microsystems has provided a set of four guidelines:

- *The Java 2 Enterprise Edition Specification*—This specification defines the standard Java technologies requirements that all J2EE vendors must implement in their application server and make available to the enterprise applications. It specifies which required technologies must be implemented, but not how they must be implemented. Individual vendors are free to optimize the implementation and include additional value-added services and other technologies to differentiate their products from other vendors' products in the marketplace. The most recent J2EE specification, version 1.3, defines 15 Java technologies and their APIs that must be available on all J2EE certified application servers.

- *J2EE BluePrints*—It's possible for developers to use all the appropriate J2EE APIs and still end up writing enterprise applications that are neither scalable nor portable. The J2EE BluePrints is a standard programming guideline for developers on how to develop, package, and deploy scalable and portable multitiered standard enterprise applications using J2EE APIs.

- *J2EE Reference implementation*—To demonstrate the capabilities of the J2EE platform APIs, Sun has implemented the technologies in a J2EE Reference implementation server and has made it available to the Java community. Any applications that run on the reference implementation will be able to run unmodified on any J2EE certified application server.

- *J2EE Compatibility Test Suites (CTS)*—Because the J2EE specification mentions only which APIs must be included and not how they must be implemented, it's possible for vendors to implement all of the Java technologies required by the J2EE 1.3 specification in their products in a nonstandard way. As a result, J2EE applications written in accordance with the J2EE BluePrints guidelines on an application server from one vendor might not be portable to another application server from a different vendor. The J2EE Compatibility Test Suites, which consist of more than 5,000 tests, are used for verifying that a J2EE product complies with the J2EE platform standard. To be certified as J2EE compliant, products must pass the J2EE CTS. This certification assures customers that any J2EE application developed with standard J2EE APIs on a J2EE certified application server will be portable across all J2EE certified application servers.

Technologies Required by J2EE 1.3

To appreciate the J2EE architecture fully, we need to look at each of the 15 Java technologies that the J2EE 1.3 specification requires and understand their respective roles and how they complement the J2EE architecture. Some of these Java technologies such as servlet, JDBC, and JMS can be and are used in standalone applications. These technologies, when used within a J2EE context, enable businesses to develop and deploy portable distributed component applications that are extensible, highly scalable, and available. To delineate these 15 Java technologies, I have classified them into five functional groups of enabling technologies: communication, security, presentation, business application, and enterprise information system enabling technologies. Table 1-1 provides a listing of the Java technologies, their acronyms, and the current version number of each. A discussion of each Java technology and its function within the J2EE architecture follows.

Table 1-1 J2EE 1.3 Technologies

No.	Java 2 Enterprise Edition Specification	Acronym	Version
1	Java Message Service	JMS	1.0
2	Java Mail	JavaMail	1.2
3	JavaBean Activation Framework	JAF	1.0
4	Java Interface Definition Language (part of J2SE 1.3)	JavaIDL	1.3
5	Remote Method Invocation—Internet Inter-ORB Protocol	RMI-IIOP	1.0
6	Extensible Markup Language	XML	1.0
7	Java Naming and Directory Interface	JNDI	1.2
8	Java Authorization and Authentication Service (NEW)	JAAS	1.0
9	Java Servlet	Servlet	2.3
10	JavaServer Pages	JSP	1.2
11	Java API for XML Parsing (NEW)	JAXP	1.1
12	Enterprise JavaBeans	EJB	2.0
13	Java Database Connectivity Extension	JDBC	2.0
14	Java Transaction API	JTA	1.0
15	J2EE Connector Architecture (NEW)	Connector or JCA	1.0

Communication-Enabling Technologies

The six Java technologies in the communication-enabling technology group—JMS, JavaMail, JAF, RMI-IIOP, Java IDL, and JNDI—enable the clients to communicate with the business components by providing the necessary infrastructure. Let's look at each of them more closely.

Java Message Service (JMS) 1.0.2

Most business enterprise systems need to reliably exchange messages such as status reports, invoices, and notifications among business applications, independent of platform considerations. Prior to the adoption of JMS, businesses developed proprietary messaging formats, which made the integration of application services with applications from other businesses tedious, time consuming, unreliable, and expensive. For example, imagine the case of a small company that supplies widgets to five large companies. To improve business efficiency and save cost, each of these five large companies has implemented its own proprietary message systems and decreed that anyone doing business with them must conform to their message format for exchanging business information. The small business, with its limited IT staff and tight budget, now has to make its application able to process and generate five different proprietary message formats. Each time one of the large companies modifies its message format, the small company has to change its application to handle the new format—this is a maintenance nightmare above and beyond any consideration of costs.

JMS solves this problem by providing a single standard, unified message API for five different message formats (including XML) to encapsulate and exchange asynchronous messages reliably between enterprise Java applications regardless of the operating systems, platform, architecture, and computer languages being used. The JMS API supports two types of messaging—point-to-point and publish-subscribe. In J2EE 1.3, complete implementation of the JMS API is mandatory. (See Chapter 12 for further details about JMS.)

Java Mail (JavaMail) 1.2

E-mail is the Internet "killer" application and is used daily by net-savvy users. An e-mail consists of two parts—the client portion (the messaging front with which we're familiar) and the backend, which is vendor specific. Prior to JavaMail, Java programmers had to write e-mail applications to specific APIs and protocols, a requirement that crippled the portability of e-mail applications. But in a J2EE application, the JavaMail API framework provides a standard way to create, send, and access e-mail from a Java application in a platform- and protocol-independent manner.

JavaBean Activation Framework (JAF) 1.0.1

As popular data formats evolve and new data formats are adopted, there's a need for a smart framework that can take arbitrary data, discover and abstract its useful operations, and make it available to other components. The JavaBean Activation Framework provides these functionalities, and JavaMail relies on the JAF API to support various multipurpose Internet mail extension (MIME) types.

Remote Method Invocation and Internet Inter-ORB Protocol (RMI-IIOP) 1.0

Java objects on a computer communicate with remote Java objects on a different computer using the standard Remote Method Invocation (RMI), which relies on the Java Remote Method Protocol (JRMP) for communication. RMI is a simple and powerful way to write distributed applications, but it works only in a Java environment. The Internet Inter-ORB protocol (IIOP) is a CORBA-based standard, which is independent of the underlying protocol. Because one of the goals of J2EE is interoperability with non-Java and CORBA clients, RMI and IIOP were merged to enable cross-platform communication. The RMI-IIOP is a portable version of the RMI and supports both Java Remote Method Protocol (JRMP) and the Internet Inter-ORB Protocol (IIOP). So RMI-IIOP gives Java objects the *remoteability* feature—the ability to invoke methods on objects located on different computers as easily as invoking a method on objects on the same computer, regardless of the programming languages or operating systems involved.

Java Interface Definition Language (Java IDL) 1.3

Most businesses have legacy applications that might need to be integrated with Java applications. In the past, this was a difficult and expensive, if not impossible, task. The Java IDL is an Object Request Broker (ORB) that is included with Java 2 Standard Edition (J2SE), and it allows J2EE components to invoke requests to external CORBA objects using the IIOP protocol. J2EE applications can use Java IDL to act as clients to CORBA services and also use Java IDL to present CORBA services to others.

Extensible Markup Language (XML) 1.0

Prior to XML, businesses used proprietary data formats tied to applications to exchange data between businesses. Obviously, this was a difficult and expensive process. XML, a popular meta-markup language, is used to define and exchange data in a system-independent format. XML has gained popularity because it enables businesses to define data independently from the application and thus offers data portability and reusability across different platforms and devices. In the J2EE application, XML is used to define behavior, transaction, and security characteristics of components and data. XML enables exchanges of messages and data in a vendor- and application-neutral format.

Java Naming and Directory Interface 1.2 (JNDI)

In a distributed computing model, services and objects can reside on any number of servers on the network, a reality that requires a uniform and transparent mechanism for locating objects and services. JNDI is the standard API for naming and directory access, and it enables applications to access resources transparently in the network. For example, JNDI APIs are used by applications to look up database access objects, security objects, and objects to locate business applications from a repository on the network. A J2EE application uses JDNI, along with the RMI-IIOP, and executes the logic on J2EE objects transparently.

Security-Enabling Technology

Security-enabling technology allows the J2EE application to implement, authenticate, and authorize user access to enterprise resources in a standard and portable manner. The primary representative of this technology is Java Authentication and Authorization Service (JAAS).

Java Authentication and Authorization Service (JAAS) version 1.0

JAAS defines a standard way to authenticate users and authorize access by extending the security model in Java 2 Standard Edition (J2SE) version 1.3. JAAS simplifies and standardizes the implementation and enforcement of security in J2EE applications for developers; notably, there's no U.S. export control restriction. Businesses enforce security by controlling user authentication and authorization to their enterprise applications. Previous versions of the J2EE specification did not explicitly address authentication and authorization services, so developers and vendors implemented security in a proprietary manner that hindered application portability.

Presentation-Enabling Technologies

This group consists of the three technologies that are involved with the presentation-related logic. They mediate the client's request to the business tier and the output from the business tier to the client.

Java Servlet (Servlet) 2.3

Servlets are server-side, network-aware Java objects that interact with Web clients via the HTTP request/response paradigm. Servlets extend the functionality of the Web server—for example, for those familiar with CGI programming, servlets perform the same functions as CGI programs. In the J2EE application model, the servlet application usually implements the presentation logic and mediates requests from the Web browsers to the business tier.

JavaServer Pages (JSP) 1.2

A JSP is a servlet extension that is optimized for building dynamic presentation-centric applications. A JSP page can consist of HTML or XML interlaced with Java code snippets. JSP provides functionality in the J2EE platform that is similar to Active Server Pages (ASP) in a Windows environment. In the J2EE architecture, the JSP pages are used mainly for dynamic page generation, but can also interact with the business tier.

Java API for XML Parsing (JAXP) 1.1

Because XML use has becomes more pervasive in enterprise applications, an XML parser, JAXP, was included in the latest J2EE specification. JAXP is used for reading and transforming XML documents into appropriate output using the standard Java APIs. JAXP supports the Simple API for XML (SAX 2.0), Document Object Model (DOM 2.0), and XSLT.

Business Application-Enabling Technology

Enterprise JavaBeans (EJB) 2.0 is the central focus of the J2EE platform. It's a component technology that implements business logic. Prior to EJBs, business logic was implemented as Java objects. These Java objects were not portable because they did not follow any standard framework, and they were tedious to develop because programmers also had to write complex system services such as security, transaction, and thread managements using system-specific APIs. Enterprise JavaBeans provide the standard framework for implementing complex business logic.

Enterprise JavaBeans (EJB) 2.0

Enterprise JavaBeans are software components designed to encapsulate business logic and simplify programming. The EJB container manages the life cycle, security, and transaction for the EJB. This allows programmers to implement only the business logic and to let the container handle low-level, system-related services. There are three types of Enterprise JavaBeans designed to implement specific types of business logic—session, entity, and message-driven beans. In Chapter 2, we'll discuss EJBs in greater detail.

Enterprise Information System-Enabling Technologies

The three technologies in this group enable communication with the Enterprise Information Tier, which could include databases or enterprise resource planning (ERP) applications such as PeoplesSoft and SAP and a third technology that helps manage transactions.

Java Database Connectivity (JDBC) 2.1

Prior to the advent of JDBC, Java programmers were forced to use proprietary APIs from the database vendor, which hindered the portability of applications. The JDBC API provides a standard and uniform way to access relational databases from Java applications. Java applications using the standard JDBC API calls to an Oracle database will also be able to make calls to an IBM DB2 database without any modifications.

J2EE Connector Architecture (JCA or Connector) 1.0

Like the JDBC, the Connector API enables applications to access enterprise resource planning (ERP) systems in a consistent and portable manner. Prior to Connector API, vendors provided access to their ERP systems using proprietary APIs.

Java Transaction API (JTA) 1.0

Transactions are an important part of most business exchanges. Applications using the Java Transaction API will employ the Java Transaction Service (JTS) to manage transactions between components in an application. See Chapter 14 for a more detailed discussion of transaction.

Putting It All Together

Figure 1-2 is an illustration of the multitier Java 2 Enterprise Edition (J2EE) version 1.3 platform. The boxes labeled Thin, Fat, and Non-Java apps on the left side of the figure represent the client tier, which handles the presentation tier. The

middle tier (depicted by the dashed rectangle in the middle of the figure) encloses
a Web container. Together, the Web container and the EJB container represent the
J2EE application server, which handles the presentation and business logic layer.s,
respectively. The Web container consists of two ovals labeled Servlet and
JavaServer pages —this group collectively represents the Web tier. The EJB
container, representing the business tier, encloses three ovals depicting session,
entity, and message-driven beans. The EIS tier at the right side of the figure
represents the data layer, labeled RDBMS and ERP, respectively.

The J2EE Architecture

The J2EE architecture is a multitier, end-to-end solution spanning from the client
tier to the presentation tier to the business tier and, finally, to the enterprise
information system tier. The J2EE architecture clearly separates the presentation,
business, and data layers of an enterprise application as illustrated in Figure 1-2.
These layers are mapped into four distinct tiers that handle specific functions

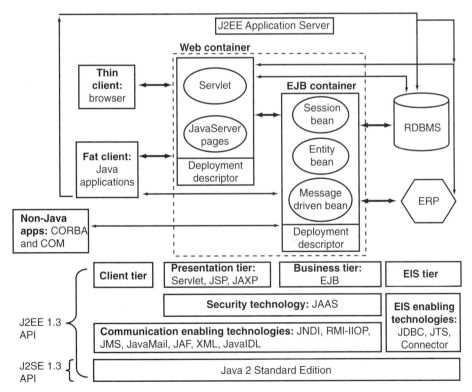

Figure 1-2 The Java 2 Enterprise Edition (J2EE) 1.3 architecture

within a J2EE architecture implementation. A client tier—commonly a desktop computer—consists of a GUI that customers use to interact with the application. The middle tier consists of one or more application servers; the application servers process client requests, execute complex presentation and business logic, and then return the results to the client tier. The enterprise information systems (EIS) tier, also called the data tier, is where all the business data resides. The EIS is accessed by the middle tier while processing business logic. Figure 1-2 illustrates a simple J2EE architecture with all of the J2EE technologies. Most J2EE applications usually span all four tiers and use some or all of the Java technologies specified in the J2EE specification. Let's take a closer look at the client tier, presentation tier, business tier, and the enterprise information system tier.

Client Tier

This tier handles the client presentation and user-interface of a J2EE application. The client tier can be represented in the physical world by a desktop computer, Internet device, or a wireless device. There can be two types of clients—thin clients and fat clients.

Thin Clients

Thin clients are Web based or browser based and use HTTP/HTTPS to interact with the Presentation tier. We can further divide Web-based clients into plain HTML or applet-based clients.

In HTML-based clients, Web browsers use HTTP/HTTPS to interact with servlets and JSPs at the web tier. The Web browsers download static or dynamic Hypertext Markup Language (HTML), Extensible Markup Language (XML), and/or Wireless Markup Language (WML) for the appropriate device from the Web tier and render the page. HTML clients have a simple user interface and are the most common type of clients for Web applications.

Applets are small Java client applications that are downloaded from the Web tier and execute within the constraint of the Java Virtual Machine (JVM) installed in the Web browser. Applets can also execute on any device that supports an applet programming model. Applets provide a much richer user GUI interface for J2EE applications than HTML-based clients can. Applets are classified as thin clients because they use HTTP and usually execute within the Web browser.

Fat Clients

Also known as rich clients, fat clients are non-Web clients (such as standalone applications with their own GUI) that execute outside of a browser but within a client container. Rich clients interact with the business tier using the Remote Method Invocation and Internet Inter-ORB Protocol (RMI-IIOP). Fat clients can use HTTP and XML to interact with the Web tier, but this rarely occurs. One can further divide rich clients into two types—Java- and non-Java-based standalone applications.

Standalone Java client applications are used when a much richer GUI and/or application with complex logic is required on the client side. Rich clients use RMI-IIOP to interact with the business tier and usually are inside the firewall on an intranet.

Non-Java applications can be CORBA or COM clients that use RMI-IIOP to interact with the business tier. Non-Java clients are used in a legacy environment where JVM isn't available, and they are forced to use CORBA or COM clients.

The application server illustrated in Figure 1-2 represents the middle tier that is responsible for handling the server-side presentation logic and the business logic of the J2EE application. J2EE Application Server provides two types of application framework and the network infrastructure, which are termed containers. Containers provide the runtime environment for two types of components supported in the J2EE platform—the Web container and the Enterprise JavaBeans container.

Presentation Tier

The Presentation tier, also referred to as the Web tier, is represented by the Web container and handles thin-client HTTP requests and responses. The Web container provides the runtime environment for the Web components. Web components consist of two related Java technologies, the Servlet and JavaServer pages. The Servlet, along with JSPs, handles requests from the clients, processes presentation logic that can include making a request to the business tier, and then creates dynamic content presentations, which are sent back to the clients. The Web components execute within the Web container environment.

Business Tier

The business tier consists of EJB container, which provides the runtime environment for the Enterprise JavaBeans (EJB). EJBs are software components that typically encapsulate business logic and execute on the server-side within an EJB container. The business components service requests from the clients (servlets, JSPs, or Java and/or CORBA applications) and may access the enterprise information system tier when processing requests. There are three different kinds of enterprise beans: session, entity, and message-driven beans.

These enterprise beans have been designed to solve different aspects of business processes and help to implement complex business logic easily and quickly. Chapter 2 and the remainder of this book will discuss Enterprise JavaBeans 2.0 in detail.

Enterprise Information System Tier (EIS)

The EIS tier separates data—including database, enterprise resource planning (ERP), mainframe transaction processing, and other legacy information—from the business and client tiers. To provide standard portable access to the EIS tier, the J2EE specifies two technologies: Java Database Connectivity (JDBC) and Connector.

Figure 1-3 illustrates another perspective of the J2EE architecture with components and communication protocols.The double-headed arrows in Figure 1-3 depict various inter- and intra-tier communications. The thin clients communicate using HTTP/HTTPS with Web tier, while the fat and non-Java clients communicate using RMI-IIOP with the business tier. The Web tier communicates with the business tier using RMI-IIOP and a vendor proprietary protocol. The HTML container (browser) and standalone Java and non-Java application containers represent the client presentation tier. The Web container supporting servlet and JSP components represents the server-side presentation tier. The business tier is illustrated by the EJB container located in the business logic tier. The cylinder labeled RDBMS represents the EIS tier or the data layer. Note that the application servers must support RMI-IIOP communication protocol and that vendors are free to implement additional optimized proprietary protocols.

Technical Advantages of the J2EE Architecture

The computing industry has embraced the J2EE architecture as a popular standard for developing and deploying enterprise applications. The J2EE platform provides many technical advantages, a summary of which follows.

Interoperability

The enterprise applications are written in Java, which makes them *write once, run anywhere* applications. JavaIDL and RMI-IIOP provide cross-language and cross-platform support for non-Java applications and CORBA clients. The J2EE platform also supports standard Internet protocols such as TCP/IP, HTML, XML, HTTPS, and HTTP. The J2EE platform will continue to support emerging standards supported by Web services, such as Simple Object Access Protocol (SOAP), Web Service Description Language (WSDL), and Universal Description, Discovery, and Integration (UDDI).

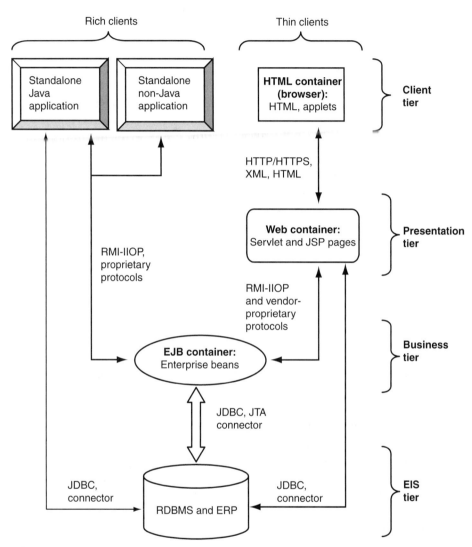

Figure 1-3 J2EE 1.3 component containers and standard protocols

Standard Integration with Legacy Systems

JDBC and Connector provide a standard way to access popular databases and ERP systems. The JTA enables local and distributed transaction management. Java IDL and RMI-IIOP support interoperability with legacy applications.

Programming Productivity

Programmers able to program using Java are able to participate in all aspects of J2EE development, from the client tier to the EIS tier. Businesses can leverage their existing Java programming resources to write Web and EJB components. The J2EE platform also provides a rich set of existing J2SE and J2EE APIs, which help programmers become productive more quickly. In the J2EE architecture, programmers implement business logic using EJBs and implement presentation logic using Web components; the respective containers handle system-level resource management logic, thus simplifying and accelerating the development process. Well-designed components can be reused in different applications. When developing Web and EJB components, the developer can choose to implement complex features such as security and transaction either programmatically or declaratively. If the developer elects the declarative option, he or she can defer the setting of transaction and security to the application assembler or the deployer, and the container will implement the security and transaction logic based on the setting in the deployment descriptor. In this way, the declarative option enhances portability and flexibility in the process of implementing J2EE applications.

Distributed Components

The multitier component architecture of the J2EE platform naturally translates to the development of distributed applications. The EJB and Web components can be deployed among several application servers to load-balance user requests. The JNDI and RMI-IIOP give the J2EE application component location transparency, which means that it enables clients to invoke methods on EJB components without having to worry about the components' location. Because the components are distributed among multiple servers, there's no single point of failure; as a result, applications are scalable and highly available. This component model encourages EJB component vendors to develop and sell off-the-shelf components so that other businesses can either buy these pre-built components or choose to develop their own EJB components as necessary to build their business applications. Either way, the distributed components architecture saves time and money in the software development cycle.

Reliability and Performance

The J2EE platform supports local and distributed transactions through the standard Java Transaction APIs (JTA) and the Java Transaction Services. Because components are distributed among multiple servers, servers can be added as loads increase. Increased performance and reliability are achieved as single points of failure are eliminated. J2EE product vendors such as BEA (Weblogic), IBM (Websphere), Sun (iAS), and Oracle (OAS) sell application servers that are optimized for performance and high availability, enabling businesses that run these J2EE applications to inherit the performance and high availability features automatically.

Security

The J2EE platform defines an enterprise-wide security mechanism by mandating Java Authentication and Authorization (JAA) APIs. These APIs enable a consistent and portable security mechanism that all vendors can implement and support.

Minimized Development and Deployment Complexity

The J2EE facilitates the use of off-the-shelf components and the reuse of existing components, which result in reduced coding efforts and simplified development. A related advantage of using the J2EE platform is the standard application packaging and deployment architecture used across vendors, which likewise reduces the complexity of developing and deploying distributed enterprise applications.

Business-Related Advantages of the J2EE Architecture

In addition to technical advantages, the use of the J2EE platform for developing enterprise applications offers specific business-related benefits.

Simplified Application Development

The J2EE platform simplifies distributed application development by defining standard component model and container APIs. Programmers have only to concern themselves with implementing business logic in EJB and Web components. The container provided by the vendor handles all the system-level logic.

Freedom to Choose

Because 36 vendors have licensed the J2EE specification, businesses can select the J2EE product that best suits their needs. The freedom to choose among J2EE application servers and J2EE components that are guaranteed to interoperate ultimately provides more cohesive and transparent services to a business' customers.

Faster Time to Market

The component model accelerates development, as programmers only need to write business logic and can leave the system-level services to the container vendor. Businesses can also buy ready-made business components from third parties and customize them, thus reducing development time.

Lower Development Cost

Shortening the development effort, reusing components, and providing the ability to buy off-the-shelf business components all contribute to reducing the cost of software development.

Application Manageability

Vendors can provide add-on services and tools to help businesses manage their applications in a distributed environment.

Application Portability

Businesses are not locked into a specific vendor. J2EE applications developed on J2EE-certified application servers are portable across all other J2EE-certified products. Customers can purchase a J2EE application and then customize the application behavior to meet their business criteria by modifying the security, transaction, and resources elements in the deployment descriptors during deployment. (Deployment descriptors are XML-based files that contain property information about the Web and EJB components. The EJB container reads the deployment descriptor properties to control the behavior of the Web and EJB instances during execution.)

J2EE Development and Deployment Roles

The J2EE architecture is an end-to-end solution, encompassing different Java technologies that require multiple skill sets and varying degrees of knowledge in the development and deployment of J2EE applications. To accommodate the diverse skill requirements and to simplify the processes of development and deployment, the J2EE specification defines several roles and responsibilities, including the following:

- *Application component providers*—Programmers and businesses that provide J2EE application components are known as application component providers. There are two types of application component providers: Web component providers and EJB component providers.

- *Web component providers*—HTML designers, Servlet and JSP programmers, or software vendors with expertise in user-interface and client-side logic. Web component providers encapsulate their client-side logic expertise to create and sell Web components, which might include HTML, applets, servlets, JSP, graphics images, and audio files, all packaged into a portable ZIP format known as *war files* (Web archive files). Web component provider tasks may include development of servlet programs, JSP and HTML, .gif, .jpeg, and audio files; specifying the appropriate deployment descriptors (DD) for the Web component; and packaging Java classes, JSPs, HTML, graphics images, audio files, and deployment descriptors files into a war file.

- *EJB component providers*—Software developers and software vendors with expertise in specific business rules and processes. EJB providers encapsulate and implement business logic in Enterprise JavaBean components and package them into Enterprise JAR files, called ejb-jar files. Their specific tasks may include development of EJB source code that encapsulates business logic; specifying the deployment descriptors (DD) for the EJBs; developing any helper class files and dependent objects; and packaging Java class files and deployment descriptor files into a portable ZIP format called an *ejb-jar file.*

- *Application assemblers*— J2EE application architects or value-added software application vendors with business domain expertise who understand how various components must work together in an application to meet the business objectives. An assembler takes existing Web components and EJB components developed by the application component provider, assembles them into a complete J2EE application, and packages them into an *enterprise archive* (ear) file. Assemblers customize components by modifying the deployment descriptor file; they might also write some wrapper code to glue various components together and provide assembly instructions describing the external dependencies of the application, such as security roles, data source names, and transaction attributes. Assemblers use the vendor-provided assembly tool to read the war and ejb-jar files and package them into an ear file. Application assembler tasks include

  - taking the previously developed Web component (the war file) and business component (the ejb-jar file) and packaging the application as an enterprise application archive (ear) file

  - modifying and resolving external dependencies in the deployment descriptors (DD) for the J2EE application

  - verifying the compliance of the ear file

- *Application deployers*—The parties who deploy the ear file on an application server and take the application live. A deployer has expertise in a specific operational environment; he or she is responsible for reading the assembly information in the application deployment descriptor file and then configuring and mapping deployment descriptor requirements to the existing operational environment. An EJB deployer modifies the enterprise application deployment descriptor file using vendor-provided deployment tools. For example, an e-commerce company using an iPlanet or Weblogic application server requires that the deployer have expertise with iPlanet or Weblogic. The company might also require the ability to modify specific operational environment and value-added vendor-specific fields in the deployment descriptor, such as mapping security settings, transaction options, and data access information for the specific environment. A deployer's tasks include

  - taking the enterprise application (ear file) and configuring and customizing the deployment descriptors for the operational environment

  - verifying that the contents of the ear file are well formed and meet the J2EE specification

  - modifying the external dependencies to match the local operational environment in the deployment descriptor; adjusting and implementing for any vendor-specific features

  - deploying the application on the application server

- *System administrators*—Responsible for the configuration and administration of the application servers and the underlying operating systems. A system administrator's responsibilities include

  - monitoring and managing the deployed applications and application servers by using sophisticated tools provided by the vendor or third party

  - maintaining the application servers and the hardware and doing preventative maintenance

- *Tool providers*—Usually, the application vendor provides the necessary packaging and deployment tools, which tend to be proprietary. There are some providers of platform-independent tools such as object-to-relational (O/R) mapping and monitoring tools used with J2EE applications.

- *J2EE product providers*—Vendors who supply the application servers that support all of the Java technologies required by J2EE 1.3 specifications. The platform must implement the J2EE APIs that support containers and mapping of the application components to the network protocols as defined by the specification. These vendors must provide application development, deployment, and management tools and may also provide additional features such as clustering, load balancing, caching, and fail-over.

J2EE product providers typically include companies that sell applications, databases, and hardware such as iPlanet (iPlanet Application Server), BEA (Weblogic), IBM (WebSphere), and Oracle (Oracle App. Server).

Some readers might think that the various roles we just discussed are unnecessary, but if you view application development in the context of one of the goals of J2EE, having such a division of labor makes sense. Keep in mind that when Web or EJB developers are creating their components, they might neither know how the components will be assembled into an application nor be familiar with the operating environment where the application will eventually be deployed. Even the application assembler won't have detailed information of the operating environment where the application will eventually be deployed. For this reason, the developers and assemblers have to specify the requirements in an abstract layer. It's the application deployer who is knowledgeable about details regarding the operating environment that have to be mapped from the abstract to actual setting, such as the type of application server and assigned security roles, data source names, and transactional support.

Developing a J2EE Application

The development and deployment of J2EE applications go through three distinct phases where people with various roles participate, as depicted in Figure 1-4. The three phases of development are

- *Development*—During the development phase, Web component providers develop Web components that encapsulate presentation logic, and they then make those components available as war files. The EJB component providers develop EJB components that encapsulate business logic, and they make those components available as ejb-jar files. The Web and EJB developers can work independently or together in the same company to make their component files available.

- *Assembly*—The assembler takes the war and ejb-jar files developed in-house or purchased from third party vendors and assembles them into a single enterprise archive (ear) file to satisfy the business requirements. If necessary, the assembler might add some code or subclass components to integrate the application and might add features to the components to complete the application. The assembler reviews the Web and EJB components, customizes fields in the deployment descriptor files, and resolves and specifies external dependencies by modifying the deployment descriptor file. The assembler uses the assembly tool supplied by the vendor.

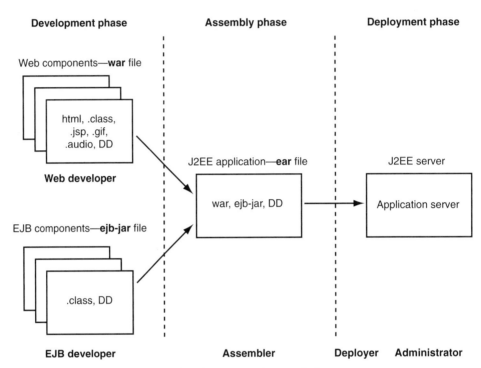

Figure 1-4 J2EE application development roles and phases

- *Deployment*—During this phase, the deployer takes the ear file assembled by the application assembler and examines the deployment descriptor files, resolves any external dependencies, and configures the application to execute and deploy in the operational environment. The deployer uses the vendor-supplied deployment tool to modify, customize, and map the deployment descriptor fields. The administrator is then responsible for monitoring and managing the application and application servers.

J2EE Disadvantages

Thus far, we've discussed the features and advantages of J2EE platform. Before we end this chapter, let's look at some of the drawbacks of the J2EE platform.

Steep Learning Curve

Before a programmer can write J2EE components, he or she must first be well versed in the Java programming language, in addition to having a good understanding of the concepts underlying object-oriented analysis (OOA) and object-oriented design (OOD). Writing Web components additionally requires knowledge of Servlet and JSP API. To write business components, the knowledge of EJB architecture and API are necessary as well. The EJB are powerful and complex components, and one cannot learn how to write EJB components well in a week.

Higher Resource Requirements

Remember, the J2EE platform is designed for highly available and large-scalable applications, so there are certain implicit resource requirements such as larger servers, more memory and disk requirements, and higher-bandwidth networks, all of which translate to higher infrastructure costs.

Expense of J2EE Application Servers (Higher Infrastructure Cost)

There are couple of application servers that are based on open-source technology (and are therefore free), but the majority of J2EE application servers don't come cheap, and you'll need multiple copies of them to benefit from their scalability and availability features. Besides the application servers, there are additional costs associated with required infrastructure related to Web servers, directory servers, and databases.

Higher Maintenance Costs

There are additional costs with running application servers, as well as administrative and maintenance related costs. Someone also has to maintain not only the application servers but also the Web servers, directory servers, and database servers.

When to Avoid J2EE

Because J2EE platforms are designed for running highly scalable and available enterprise applications with high traffic, there's a fair amount of complexity in developing distributed J2EE applications and a fairly high level of infrastructure and maintenance costs associated with running J2EE application servers. For corporations with B2B and B2C e-commerce presence, some complexity and the costs associated with implementing a J2EE platform pale in comparison with the development, maintenance, security, high-availability, and high-performance nightmares they are likely to encounter with home-grown application systems that haven't been well thought out. The J2EE platform, therefore, isn't ideal for companies with the following environments:

- *Where high scalability and availability are not primary concerns*—Why bother with J2EE if you have only a few hundred clients who don't require 24×7 availability? You can get away with a Web server and CGI, but consider servlets and JSP for writing your applications.

- *Low-traffic sites*—If your Web site attracts a low volume of traffic and you don't expect much growth in either the customer base or overall Web traffic, implementing a full J2EE platform is probably overkill.

- *Limited IT budget*—If your company can't afford to invest in the necessary infrastructure costs for application severs and high-end UNIX servers, J2EE might not be for you.

- *Lack of J2EE expertise in-house*—If your current staff has insufficient experience with J2EE and your company doesn't have the training budget to send the IT staff to J2EE training courses, reconsider this development platform.

- *Where higher maintenance costs conflict with long-range goals*—If your company is a startup and your exit strategy is to be acquired by Microsoft, for example, then implementing the J2EE platform might not be prudent for your company's valuation.

If companies are interested in J2EE and the cost is the only issue, then you might want to investigate one or more of the several open-source J2EE-based application servers such as JBOSS (www.jboss.org) and JonAS (www.evidian.com/jonas) that are available for free. A matrix of J2EE application servers is available at http://www.flashline.com/components/appservermatrix.jsp. If your company lacks in-house J2EE expertise and has a limited IT training budget, check out your local colleges and universities for extension courses in Java and J2EE technologies. There are also many fine books that are geared toward helping programmers learn how to write Web and EJB components.

The rest of this book is focused on teaching Java programmers how to write Enterprise JavaBeans 2.0, and my upcoming book, *J2EE Boot Camp: Developing Web Components,* is geared for Web component developers. But just because a company can't afford to implement a complete J2EE architecture at present doesn't mean that it can't benefit from some of the J2EE technologies. For instance, companies can use the Web components, servlet, and JSP instead of CGI or ASP and can use JDBC to write their Web application to access their database. They can use Java Authentication and Authorization (JAA) to enforce security and Java Mail to send e-mail from the application. Learning to write servlet and

JSP applications is much easier than writing EJB applications. So, by using this Web component strategy, companies can at least be J2EE ready, and later, when customers and market demand require higher scalability and availability, the business logic in the Web components can be migrated and implemented as EJB components. This migration strategy has the benefit of phased migration while a company's IT team builds J2EE expertise.

Summary

In this chapter, we discussed the fundamentals of the J2EE architecture, the various Java technologies required by the J2EE 1.3 specification, and their functions within the architecture. We grouped the 15 Java techologies into five different functional groups.

We also looked at the various roles an individual can play in the development-to-deployment cycle and how the Web and EJB developer, Assembler, deployer, administrator, and vendor contribute to the development of a J2EE application. We concluded with a discussion on some of the drawbacks of the J2EE platform.

In this first chapter, we lightly touched upon Enterprise JavaBeans. In Chapter 2 we'll discuss EJB in high-level detail.

INTRODUCTION TO ENTERPRISE JAVABEANS 2.0

Topics in This Chapter

- The Software Component Model
- Enterprise JavaBeans Architecture
- EJB Security
- EJB Advantages
- EJB Disadvantages
- Differences between Enterprise JavaBeans and JavaBeans

Chapter 2

Chapter 1 reviewed the Java technologies required by the J2EE 1.3 specification and their respective functions within the J2EE architecture. This chapter provides a high-level, non-technical introduction to Enterprise JavaBeans (EJB) 2.0 and its significance within the J2EE framework. Topics discussed include the following:

- the software component model and its relationship to EJB
- an introduction to Enterprise JavaBeans 2.0 architecture
- elements of EJB 2.0, including new features
- advantages and disadvantages of using EJB
- comparing Enterprise JavaBeans and JavaBeans

The Software Component Model

Until the mid-1990s, software development projects were slow, tedious, and expensive because most software applications were custom written; standard frameworks and APIs weren't popular.

Today's hyper competitive business world is moving away from custom-designed applications. A business must bring its product to market faster and with lower development costs, while finding qualified software engineers and delivering robust applications that will increase profitability. The software component model satisfies the requirements for software reusability, programming productivity, and application interoperability.

Software components are standard, prebuilt, reusable pieces of application code that encapsulate specific business logic. A software component can be written in any of several languages, such as C++, Java, or Visual Basic. Software components must have the following characteristics:

- *They must be task specific*—A component is designed to perform a specific task or subtask within a large application. For example, a credit card authorization component gathers parameters such as the credit card number, type of card, expiration date, and the submitter's address, and it then executes the card authorization logic to contact a financial institution and either authorizes or denies the request. By itself, the credit card authorization component isn't very useful; however, when it's assembled with other components such as the shopping cart, sales tax, and order shipment components, it becomes an integral part of an e-commerce application.

- *They must feature a standard interface design*—A component model defines a standard interface. Thanks to that standard interface, other components or applications can invoke the component's function to access and manipulate data encapsulated by the component, while hiding the implementation details. The standard interface and its rules for use as defined by the component model make it possible for an application assembler to assemble a business' enterprise application from a collection of components provided by different vendors.

- *They must be customizable without direct modifications to the source code*—Components are reusable and adaptable precisely because their behavior can be customized to work with different business applications. The ability to modify properties through an external text file only—without modifying the source code of the component—is an important characteristic of the component model. For example, the credit card authorization component just described might have many features—such as support for multiple international currency and character sets—that allow it to be used in e-commerce applications in various countries. Support for multiple character sets makes it possible to localize a character set and local currency quickly, simply by specifying the appropriate language setting in a property setup file that's external to the source code. Even though this setting is specified in an external file, the credit card authorization component automatically displays the correct characters and currency at runtime.

- *They must execute in a container with standard APIs*—Components execute within a container. A container provides the runtime environment—such as JVM—along with Java standard class libraries and other libraries to support specific components. The container interacts with the components by way of standard APIs, and it implicitly manages the security transactions, state, and life cycle of the component. The standard APIs allow components from other vendors to be quickly assembled and executed within the container. Because the container handles the low-level system management tasks, programmers are required to write only the business application logic within a component.

Enterprise JavaBeans Architecture

Enterprise JavaBeans (EJB) is a distributed component model for the development and deployment of business applications that are highly scalable, *transactional*, and secure for multiple users. EJB applications can only be written in Java and must adhere to the EJB APIs. Well written EJB applications are portable and interoperable across J2EE-certified application servers without any modification to the source code. The EJB specification clearly outlines its goals and can be viewed online at http://java.sun.com/products/ejb/docs.html.

Note: *A transaction groups multiple subtasks into one task so that if any of the subtasks fails, the entire task fails, and all the changes made by the subtasks are restored to their original states. If all subtasks within a transaction are successfully executed, the task is successful, and the changes made by all the subtasks are saved.*

The EJB architecture consists of EJB components, the EJB container, and packaging and deployment tools.

Enterprise JavaBeans Components

EJB are server-side components that encapsulate business logic, are written in Java, and are designed to run in an EJB container. Because EJB are components, individual EJB can be combined to create an enterprise application. The enterprise application can be further customized and optimized to run in a particular environment during deployment with the aid of a deployment tool provided by the vendor. Developers package the EJB into an ejb-jar file format and provide the deployment descriptor file for the EJB.

Broadly speaking, EJB can be categorized based on communication characteristics (synchronous and asynchronous). The three basic types of Enterprise JavaBeans—session beans (SBs), entity beans (EBs), and message-driven beans (MDB)—are shown in Figure 2-1.

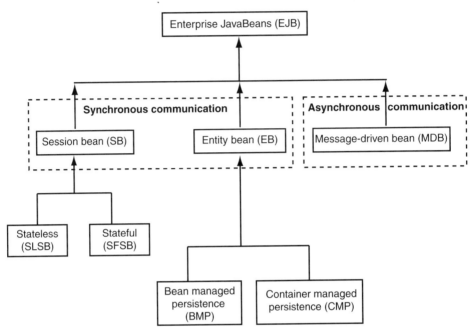

Figure 2-1 Types of Enterprise JavaBeans

Synchronous Communication EJB

Synchronous communication refers to interactions that can occur only if both client and EJB are available simultaneously. The EJB executes client requests, and the client waits for the result of the request from the EJB. The concept of synchronous communication is analogous to having a telephone conversation, where both parties must be available in order to talk. With asynchronous communication, on the other hand, the client and EJB don't have to be available at the same time for the interaction to be successful; the client's message is delivered to the MDB when the EJB server is rebooted.

There are two types of EJB that use synchronous communication: session beans and entity beans.

Session Beans *Session beans* encapsulate business processes by implementing business logic and rules. Session beans are used for modeling *verbs,* which represent workflow logic such as buying items and purchase approval. A session bean performs operations such as computing sales tax or credit card verification on behalf of a single client. A session bean exists only as long as the lifespan of the client session. Session beans cannot be shared and are designed to handle only one client at a time. Session beans can be transactional; they can participate in a transaction, but they don't survive a container or server crash. In short, session beans are transient extensions of the client in the container. (You can find a discussion of how to use session beans with programming APIs in Chapter 5.)

Session beans can further be divided into *stateless* and *stateful* session beans. *Stateless session beans* (SLSB) don't maintain state information between method requests. For this reason, stateless session beans are used to model business processes that can be performed in a single request. For example, a SLSB would be used to implement stock quote lookup logic. (See Chapter 6 for a step-by-step guide to writing SLSBs.)

Stateful session beans (SFSB) maintain state information between method requests and thus are useful for modeling business processes that span multiple interdependent requests. Stateful session beans are conversational. A classic example is the shopping cart on e-commerce sites implemented using SFSB. (See Chapter 7 for a step-by-step guide on writing SFSB.)

Entity Beans The other type of EJB that employs synchronous communication is the entity bean. Entity beans model *nouns,* which can represent entities such as cars, books, invoices, and so forth; they encapsulate the necessary logic to manipulate these entities, which are saved to data store. Entity beans provide an in-memory view of *persistent* data (fields in the bean class that are saved to data store) stored in an enterprise information system such as a database or an enterprise resource planning (ERP) system. An entity bean represents persistent data along with data access logic that the business processes can manipulate. Entity beans are inherently transactional and will therefore survive server crashes. Multiple clients can access a single entity bean. The entity bean is responsible for managing persistence—that is, it synchronizes the in-memory persistent data with the underlying data store. Refer to Chapter 8 to learn more about using entity beans with programming APIs.

Entity beans can be classified into two types—bean-managed persistent entity beans and container-managed persistent entity beans—depending on how the persistence is handled.

Bean Managed Persistent Entity Beans In the case of *bean-managed persistent* (BMP) entity beans, the bean developer is responsible for writing the necessary code to manage persistent operations, such as JDBC calls with SQL statements in the methods of the bean class or the data access helper class. (See Chapter 9 for a step-by-step guide to writing BMP entity beans.)

Container Managed Persistent Entity Beans In the case of *container-managed persistent* (CMP) entity beans, the EJB container is responsible for implementing the persistence management task. The developer is responsible for specifying the container-managed persistent fields and container-managed relationships fields by using the vendor-provided deployment tools or third-party tools. The persistent and relationship fields, along with other information, are saved in the deployment descriptor. The container reads the deployment descriptor file at runtime and implicitly performs all the data storage and retrieval and synchronization operations on behalf of the CMP entity bean. The developer doesn't need to write any code for managing persistence. (See Chapter 11 for a step-by-step guide to writing CMP entity beans.)

Asynchronous Communication EJB

Synchronous communication is essential in the vast majority of interactive applications between clients and EJB, and for that purpose, session and entity beans are ideal. On the other hand, certain non-interactive applications, such as shipping an order from the warehouse and sending the tracking number, are better suited for asynchronous communication. It would be ridiculous to implement the warehouse processing logic as a synchronous application, in which a client would be *blocked* until the items are packed and the shipping company has picked up the order and assigned a tracking number. (A blocked client must wait until it receives a response to its request, and it cannot execute any of its logic until that request is received.) Under real-world conditions, this could take quite some time, and it would be poor application design to make the client wait until the tracking number can be returned. With asynchronous communication, the client can send its request to ship an order from the warehouse and forward the tracking number as a message and then continue with the rest of the application. When the shipping company eventually generates the tracking order, it's sent to the application based on that message. The key point here is that the client isn't blocked when communication is asynchronous.

Message-driven beans are the only type of EJB that uses asynchronous communication.

Message-Driven Beans Message-driven beans (MDB) enable asynchronous communication within the EJB architecture. Message-driven beans are called asynchronous message consumers, because when a JMS message arrives, the EJB container automatically routes the message to the MDB instance, which then executes its business logic. MDB are stateless and short-lived and therefore don't survive a server crash. An MDB instance handles only one client message at a time and can be transaction aware. MDB support two messaging models: point-to-point (P2P); and publish/subscribe (Pub/Sub). Both messaging models depend on JMS Provider, which is a server that provides messaging services such as routing messages, persistent message handling, and destination service to both the producer and receiver of a given message.

JMS Provider supports two types of destinations—queue and topic, which are employed in P2P and publish/subscribe messaging, respectively. In P2P messaging, both the sender and receiver write and read messages from the queue destination. Because P2P supports one-to-one delivery of messages, there's only one receiver for every message. The sender writes a message to a specific queue, and the receiver reads the message from that particular queue, as illustrated in Figure 2-2.

In pub/sub messaging, on the other hand, the publisher publishes messages to a topic destination, and subscribers consume the message from the topic destination. Unlike P2P messaging, pub/sub messaging provides *one-to-many* delivery of messages. For example, when a message is published to a particular topic destination, all subscribers that have subscribed to the topic automatically receive the message, as illustrated in Figure 2-3. Chapter 13 provides a step-by-step guide on writing MDB with P2P and pub/sub messaging.

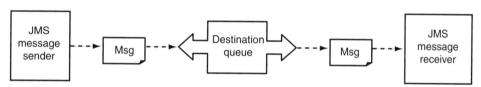

Figure 2-2 Point-to-point messaging model

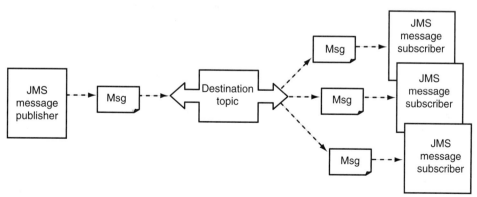

Figure 2-3 Publish-subscribe messaging model

Key EJB Elements

The EJB package file must include certain elements as part of its EJB components. Session and entity bean providers must provide the following:

- interfaces
- bean implementation class
- helper classes
- deployment descriptor
- primary key classes (entity beans only)
- helper classes (optional)

A message-driven bean provider provides only the bean class, optional helper class, and deployment descriptor when they package their components into an ejb-jar file. Table 2-1 lists the elements of EJB that must be included in the ejb-jar file.

Table 2-1 Elements of Enterprise JavaBeans by Bean Type

Element of EJB	Session Bean	Entity Beans	Message-Driven Beans
Interfaces	Yes	Yes	No
EJB class	SessionBean	EntityBean	MessageDrivenBean
Deployment descriptor	Yes	Yes	Yes
Primary key class	No	Yes	No
Helper classes (optional)	Yes	Yes	Yes

EJB Interfaces Enterprise JavaBeans components provide interfaces to expose certain logic to clients. Clients can use these interfaces to execute logic encapsulated by the EJB. Session and entity beans support two types of specialized interfaces, so for each bean class, a bean developer must provide corresponding home and component interfaces. Clients use the home interface to create, remove, and destroy the EJB instances, and they use the component interface to execute the business methods exposed by the EJB instances. On an e-commerce site, for example, a client might use the interface to create a shopping cart for the Web shopper and then use the component interface for adding items to the shopping cart; when the shopping is completed, the client uses the home interface to delete the shopping cart from the memory in the container. Figure 2-4 illustrates a client making a request to a synchronous EJB using the EJB's home and component interfaces.

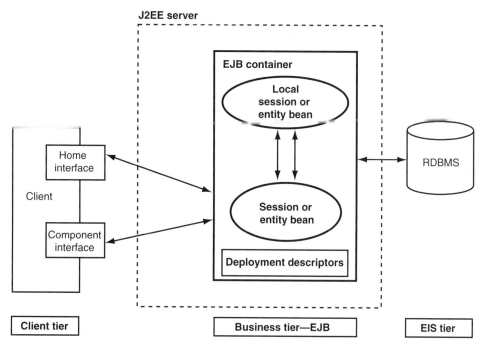

Figure 2-4 Synchronous Enterprise JavaBean interaction between session and entity beans

Message-driven beans have no interfaces, so the client communicates with the MDB by sending and receiving JMS messages asynchronously. This is illustrated in Figure 2-5.

Bean Implementation Classes The bean implementation class contains the implementation of the business logic necessary to provide services to the clients. The implementation bean instance exists within an EJB container, and the container intercepts requests from clients and executes the request in the bean instance on behalf of the client. Different types of EJB have different APIs and life cycles and therefore behave differently. (Note that stateless and stateful session beans, BMP and CMP entity beans, and message-driven bean APIs are discussed in Part 2 of this book.)

Helper Classes For design and efficiency reasons, EJB may depend on helper Java classes or dependent objects to implement low-level business functions. Even though these helper Java classes aren't EJB, they can be an integral part of

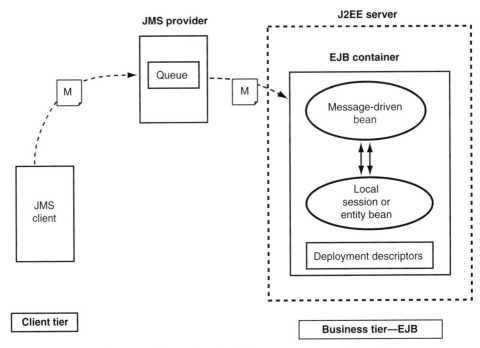

Figure 2-5 Asynchronous Enterprise JavaBeans—message-driven bean

the business logic and must be included in the ejb-jar file. Helper classes allow certain logic to be reused by other EJB. For example, logic to access databases is usually implemented as helper class and can be reused by other EJBs.

Deployment Descriptors A deployment descriptor is an XML file that contains two types of information—structural and assembly. The *structural information* defines the structure of an EJB and its external dependencies, such as its home and component interfaces, which cannot be changed without rendering the EJB's function unusable. The *assembly information* describes how the EJB is associated with other EJB and includes the security and transaction settings. Either the application assembler or the deployer can customize the assembly information. The deployment descriptor is initially created during the development phase by the vendor-provided tool and is used to set various parameters and rules governing life cycle, transaction, security, and persistence of EJB. It must conform to the data type definition (DTD) file (refer to http://java.sun.com/dtd/ejb-jar_2_0.dtd) specified by the EJB 2.0 specification. The deployment descriptor is packaged along with EJB class files in an ejb-jar file. The deployment descriptor file makes it possible for the application assembler and deployer to modify the behavior of the EJB during the assembly and deployment phases of development to resolve external dependencies. This file also makes it possible to customize the behavior of the EJB for the target environment, a process known as *declarative programming*. The EJB container reads the deployment descriptor file to manage the runtime behavior of the EJB.

The EJB Container

The EJB container exists within the J2EE server framework. The current EJB 2.0 specification doesn't define a clear demarcation between the EJB server and the EJB container API; vendors provide both the container and the server in the application server market.

It's likely that a clear separation between the EJB container and server will be specified in future versions of the EJB specification, enabling businesses to choose a container and a server from different vendors. The EJB container provides the runtime environment for the EJB component. The container implements services according to the EJB specification, which defines a contract between an EJB and the container. Because of this contract, EJB can run in any container that meets the EJB specifications. The container reads the deployment descriptor file and uses the information from the deployment descriptor to provide the life cycle management accordingly, enforces security, demarcates transaction, and controls the behavior of the bean instances. Vendors must implement the standard EJB APIs, but they are free to provide value-added features. Common implicit services that a container provides include

- *Life cycle management*—A bean developer doesn't have to explicitly write code to handle low-level tasks such as object activation or destruction, thread management, or process allocation. The EJB container provides these services to manage the lifecycle of the EJB.

- *State management*—The container automatically manages the state of an EJB instance. A developer isn't required to write state management code to explicitly save and restore conversational state information between method calls.

- *Security services*—The container provides user authentication and authorization services on behalf of the EJB based on the security parameters in the deployment descriptor file.

- *Transaction services*—Transactions are an important part of most business exchanges. EJB support both local and distributed transactions via Java Transaction API and Java transaction services. Local transactions involve single relational databases, while distributed transactions can span multiple databases from different vendors on multiple systems coordinated by global transaction managers. The transactions are *atomic* (each one representing one unit of work), consistent, isolated from other transactions, and durable, so that the results are saved and available. Developers can implement EJB transactions programmatically using the transaction APIs, or declaratively by setting appropriate fields in the deployment descriptor file. The declarative implementation offers more flexibility and requires no coding; there may be times, however, when the programmatic option is necessary. (Transactions are discussed in Chapter 14.) Implementing transaction services, especially in a distributed application, can be challenging for programmers. Fortunately, the container can automatically manage services such as start, commit, rollback, and demarcation of transactions on behalf of the EJB. It manages these services based on the information in the deployment descriptor.

- *Persistence*—The task of when and how to store or retrieve persistent object data from enterprise information systems (such as databases) can be relegated to the container.

- *Location transparency*—Because the container supports the Remote Method Invocation with Internet Inter-ORB Protocol (RMI-IIOP) and also provides support for the Java Naming and Directory Interface (JNDI), it helps provide location transparency in a distributed environment. The client uses JNDI and RMI-IIOP to locate the EJB interface and execute the business logic.

- *Remote multiclient accessibility*—The container provides the support for access from multiple clients, such as Web components, EJB, or standalone Java or CORBA clients. The thin clients use HTTP/HTTPS (Hypertext Transport Protocol/Secure Hypertext Transport Protocol) to make requests to the Web components, and the Web components may use RMI-IIOP or other low-level, vendor-proprietary protocols to make requests to the EJB. Rich clients depend on RMI-IIOP but may also use other proprietary protocols to make requests directly to the EJB. In addition, J2EE vendors are free to provide additional nonspecified proprietary features in their application servers to differentiate their products in the market. Such features might include load balancing, failover, clustering, integration with legacy systems, and COM/DCOM support. The container intercepts all requests from clients and delegates to the bean instance any security checks and appropriate transactions applied prior to the request.

Packaging and Deployment Tools

Because packaging and deploying EJB applications can be a complex and daunting task, the EJB specification defines a standard way to package EJB and related files into a single ZIP file format, known as an *ejb-jar file*. The ejb-jar file is assembled with other J2EE components to form an application and is packaged into an enterprise application archive (known as an *ear file*) before the application can be deployed.

The EJB container vendor provides tools to simplify the packaging and deployment process. These tools are usually GUI-based and simplify the tasks of configuring, modifying, and deploying EJB applications in a distributed environment. Besides the required standard support for EJB, the tools may support additional proprietary features specific to the container.

For entity beans, the bean developer is required to provide only the entity bean class, the home and component interfaces, a primary key class, and the deployment descriptor file (see Chapter 8 for more information about the primary key class and helper class). Still other classes that are necessary to implement persistence, security, transaction, and other low-level infrastructure must be generated before the EJB can be executed. The vendor-provided deployment tool uses the information in the deployment desciptor, while the container generates the container-specific classes necessary to handle persistence, security, transaction, and so forth during deployment.

After EJB instances are developed, debugged, and tested, they are assembled and packaged for deployment. The EJB specification defines a standard Java file-packaging format for EJB, the *ejb-jar file*, which is based on the popular ZIP file format. The ejb-jar file consists of the interfaces, the bean implementation class, the deployment descriptor, and optional helper classes. Because MDB don't have interfaces, MDB ejb-jar files consist of the bean implementation class, the deployment descriptor file, and any helper class.

Figure 2-6 shows the different types of EJB packaged in an ejb-jar file. The session bean includes interfaces, session bean class, optional helper class, and deployment descriptor. The entity bean includes interfaces, entity bean class, primary key class, helper class, *dependent value class* (a helper class for container-managed persistent entity beans), and the deployment descriptor. The message-driven bean includes only the MDB class and helper class and the deployment decriptor. Each of the EJB can be packaged individually or together as one jar file.

EJB Security

Security is extremely important in a distributed enterprise application, and EJB use the security features built into the Java 2 platform to enforce security implicitly in an EJB application. Security can also be implemented explicitly via the API, or declaratively via the deployment descriptors. (We discuss EJB security features at length in Chapter 15.)

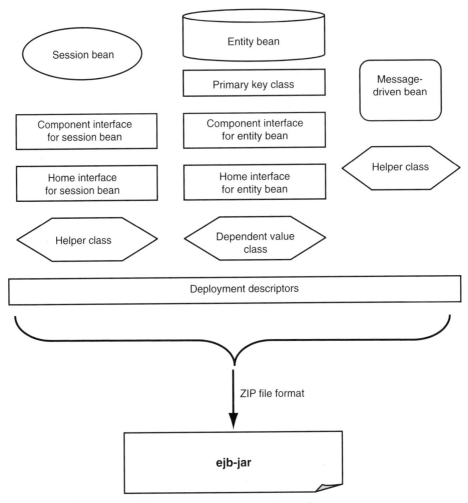

Figure 2-6 Packaging EJB components in an ejb-jar file

EJB Advantages

EJB have become the *de facto* standard for developing and deploying distributed component applications in a multivendor environment due to many advantages. Here are some of the major ones:

- *Reusability*—EJB components encapsulate discrete business logic and can be assembled in various applications that may require a given logic implementation. The reusability saves development time and reduces time to market.

- *Portability*—Enterprise JavaBeans applications are written in Java using the standard EJB API and are therefore portable across different EJB containers and operating systems.

- *Declarative programming*—The ability to alter the behavior of EJB by modifying only the parameters in the deployment descriptors gives businesses the flexibility to customize their applications to meet changing customer demands.

- *Faster time to market*—Portability and reusability, combined with declarative programming, make it possible to assemble and customize enterprise applications without modifying the application code.

- *Simpler to develop*—Because the EJB container takes care of most low-level, system-related interactions, component developers can concentrate on implementing the business logic.

- *Higher quality software*—EJB component development makes it possible for bean developers to concentrate their efforts on implementing business logic (their area of expertise) so they don't have to write low-level system utilities to support their business logic. Allowing bean developers to concentrate on implementing the business logic results in higher-quality software.

- *Ability to use off-the-shelf EJB*—The standard EJB APIs encourage developers and software vendors with business expertise and experience to build and sell higher-quality EJB components in the open market. The result is greater flexibility for businesses application development.

- *Implicit services by the container*—The implicit services provided by the EJB container simplify and reduce development and deployment time.

EJB Disadvantages

Even though there are many benefits of using EJB, there are some drawbacks of which you should be aware:

- *Steep learning curve*—There's a fairly steep learning curve for Java programmers to learn how to write EJB applications: Because EJB applications are distributed component-based applications, Java programmers must not only have Java programming expertise but must also understand the complexity of distributed architecture and learn the EJB APIs. To be a good EJB developer takes time.

- *Higher infrastructure costs*—Running EJB applications requires application servers, which tend to be expensive. In turn, application servers require high-end servers with lots of memory and disk space as well as industrial-strength database servers, directory servers, and a reliable and fast network infrastructure. All these add to the bottom line.

- *Higher resource requirements*—EJB applications are distributed among several high-end servers to ensure reliability, and they require specialized application server administrators to manage and administer the servers.

Differences between Enterprise JavaBeans and JavaBeans

The terms *JavaBeans* and *EJB* are frequently used interchangeably, which is incorrect. Although both JavaBeans and EJB are written in Java and based on the component model, they differ in terms of architecture, function, and complexity. The EJB component architecture is far more complex than the simple *getter* and *setter* JavaBean methods. EJB components are designed for implementing complex server-side business logic that requires life cycle management, transaction support, and sophisticated persistence management. On the other hand, JavaBeans are components with setter and getter methods which, in general, encapsulate simplet logic and lack support for sophisticated persistence, transaction, and life cycle management. Finally, JavaBeans are intended to be developed and modified using visual design tools, whereas it's illegal to invoke any graphical packages (such as Swing) when developing EJB.

Summary

In this chapter, we discussed the software component model as an aid to understanding Enterprise JavaBeans. Enterprise JavaBeans are used to implement business logic, and there are three types of EJB—session, entity, and message-driven beans. Session beans implement workflow business logic (such as purchase order approvals), while entity beans are used to implement business data access and management logic (such as managing an inventory of books). Message-driven beans can implement asynchronous business logic. A bean developer must provide, as a minimum, the bean class, interfaces, and deployment descriptor for session beans and additionally a primary key class for entity beans. For message-driven beans, the bean developer provides only the bean class and JMS message class.

EJB depends on the EJB container to provide the runtime environment and necessary framework support for its execution. A vendor-provided proprietary deployment tool is used to package and deploy the EJB application to the application servers. EJB offers many advantages, among which code reusability, portability, and declarative programming stand out. Keep in mind, however, that there's a steep learning curve to becoming an EJB developer and that there are additional costs associated with EJB infrastructure and resource requirements.

In the next chapter, we'll provide an overview of and discuss the design of all the EJB applications we'll be presenting throughout the book.

Part 2

DEVELOPING EJBs

OVERVIEW OF SAMPLE APPLICATIONS

Topics in This Chapter

- Naming Conventions
- Locating Example Source Code
- Database Tables
- Sample Application Descriptions

Chapter 3

This chapter provides a high-level overview of the sample applications provided in Part 2 of this book. You'll receive background information regarding the schema, design goals, and approaches for the sample applications as well as highlights of various components that we develop throughout the book. Details about implementing the EJB components will be discussed in the respective chapters of Part 2. This chapter also will review the database tables for all of the applications in the examples.

Naming Conventions

The component naming schemes vary from company to company and among developers. This book attempts to follow standard naming schemes for EJBs and their components. For the EJB class name, the class name (followed by the postfix `EJB`) is used for synchronous EJBs (for example, `StudentEJB`). The postfix `MDB` is used for asynchronous EJBs (for example, `RosterMDB`). The naming scheme for the home interface is the class name followed by the postfix `Home`—for example, `ScheduleHome`. Local home interfaces are named using the example syntax `LocalScheduleHome`. For the component interface, the class name is followed without any postfix or prefix—for example, `Schedule` (and for the local component interface, `LocalSchedule`). The postfix `DAO` is used for data access Java class, and `VO` represents value object Java class.

Locating Example Source Code

Throughout the book, we use code fragments to discuss key points. The complete source code of the sample application, including compiled code and deployable sample application components, are available for download from the companion Web site http://www.J2EEBootCamp.com. We'll be using Sun's J2EE Reference Implementation version 1.3 for packaging, deploying, and testing the sample applications. The information on disk space requirements and instructions for downloading, installing, and setting up the development environment are located in the Appendix to this book.

Database Tables

The components in the examples use six tables—ScheduleTable, CourseTable, LocationTable, InstructorTable, StudentTable, and RosterTable. Details for setting up these tables are supplied in the Appendix. Note that these tables hold the persistent data.

ScheduleTable consists of information that students need to search and register for courses. It contains the following fields related to course descriptions

- SID—schedule primary key
- CourseID—course ID
- StartDate—the start date for the course
- EndDate—the end date for the course
- LocationID—ID of the training location
- MaxEnrollment—maximum number of students allowed
- CurrentEnrollment—current enrollment
- Status—open, closed, cancelled, or pending
- InstructorID—ID of the instructor delivering the course

CourseTable consists of data related to descriptions of a course. The fields include

- ID varchar(10)—primary key
- Title—title of the course
- Price—cost of the course per student
- Description—description of the course, including prerequisites

`LocationTable` consists of information regarding the training site. The fields include

- `ID varchar(20)`—primary key
- `BizName`—name of the company conducting the training
- `BuildName`—building name
- `Address`—address of the location
- `City`—city name
- `State`—state name
- `Zip`—zip code
- `Country`—country
- `MainPhone`—contact phone number
- `ContactPerson`—contact person
- `Email`—contact person's e-mail address

`InstructorTable` contains information regarding the instructor's name and contact information as well as details about the courses the instructor is certified to teach. The fields include

- `ID varchar`–primary key
- `Password`–password for students to log in
- `FirstName`–instructor's first name
- `LastName`–instructor's last name
- `Email`–e-mail address
- `Phone`–contact phone number
- `CertfiedToTeach`–course(s) the instructor is certified to teach
- `CreateDate`–record create date

`StudentTable` consists of student contact information. Its fields include

- `ID varchar`–primary key
- `Password`–password for students to log in
- `FirstName`–student's first name
- `LastName`–student's last name
- `Email`–student's e-mail address
- `Phone`–student's phone number
- `CompanyName`–sponsoring company's name

- `CreditCardNo`–payment method
- `CreateDate`–record create date

`RosterTable` is responsible for keeping track of students and the courses for which they are registered. Its fields include

- `RosterID`–primary key for the roster
- `ScheduleId`–schedule ID of the course
- `StudentId`–student's login ID
- `CreateDate`–record create date

The Schedule schema is an aggregation of data from the `CourseTable`, `InstructorTable`, and `LocationTable`. The Roster schema consists of `scheduleID` and `studentID` from `ScheduleTable` and `StudentTable`.

Sample Application Descriptions

The sample applications are categorized by EJB type. Of the seven projects discussed in Part 2, five consist of single EJBs, and two consist of multiple EJBs. Each example in a project highlights the following:

- overview of the application design
- use case
- main function
- interaction diagram
- UML class diagram
- database dependency

Stateless Session Bean Examples (Chapters 4 and 6)

In Chapters 4 and 6, `HelloEJB` and `SearchScheduleEJB` are implemented as stateless session beans. The main goal of `HelloEJB` is to introduce the readers to the most simple possible EJB so we can discuss the interfaces and the basic structure and workings of an EJB. `HelloEJB` has one business method; `sayHelloEJB()` takes an argument and echoes back text that illustrates the interfaces and how they are used by the clients. (This interaction provided by the bean is called a *use case* in object-oriented analysis and object-oriented design (OOA/OOD); it states what the bean should do.)

Echo Back a String

Figure 3-1 illustrates a use case. Figure 3-2 illustrates the standalone Java client `HelloClient` invoking a method on stateless session bean `HelloEJB`, and the bean instance echoes back the string from the client. The stateless session bean `HelloEJB` does not access the database.

The `SearchScheduleEJB` bean is a stateless session bean that implements logic to search for available Java courses in the `ScheduleTable`. The example focuses on the implementation details, life cycle, related APIs, and packaging and deployment details for the stateless session bean class. Figure 3-3 shows the use-case diagram for `SearchScheduleEJB`. Figure 3-4 shows the object interaction diagram, and Figure 3-5 shows the class diagram.

The `SeachScheduleEJB` component searches for Java courses by course title or course number according to the following steps:

1. The `SearchCourse.html` form is the entry point to the application. It provides search options based on entry strings containing words like "Java" or "J2EE" as well as search options for a particular course based on the schedule number.

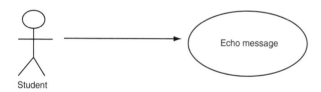

Figure 3-1 `HelloWorld` echoing back a string

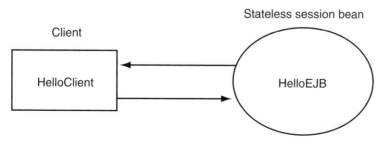

Figure 3-2 Interaction diagram—`HelloEJB`

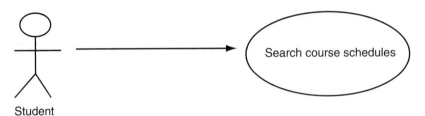

Figure 3-3 Search schedule use case

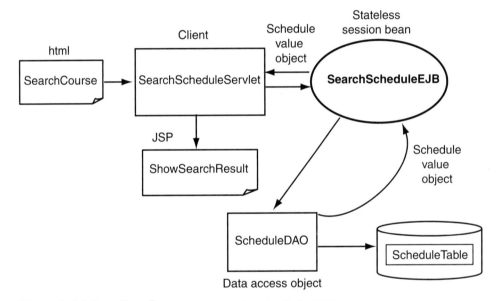

Figure 3-4 Interaction diagram—`SearchScheduleEJB`

2. The search results are displayed as tables by `ShowSearchResult.jsp`.

3. `SearchScheduleServlet` accepts the HTML form request and, depending on the request type, invokes either the `searchCourseByTitle()` or the `searchByScheduleID()` method on the remote interface of the instance.

4. The `SearchScheduleEJB` instance delegates the database access call to the Java helper object, `ScheduleDAO`. The data access object, `ScheduleDAO`, separates the data access logic from the business logic of the EJB. `ScheduleDAO` accesses the database table, `ScheduleTable`.

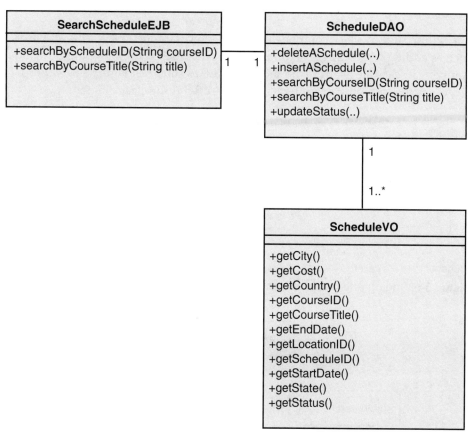

Figure 3-5 Class diagram—`SearchScheduleEJB`

5.   `ScheduleDAO` performs the JDBC call using the `SELECT` statement and, depending on the search criteria, returns a collection of schedule value objects, a single schedule value object, or a zero schedule value object.

6.   The `SearchScheduleEJB` instance returns the schedule results to the `SearchScheduleServlet`. The servlet then dispatches the result to `ShowSearchResult.jsp`.

Stateful Session Bean Example (Chapter 7)

The `ShoppingCartEJB` component described in Chapter 7 takes advantage of the conversational feature of stateful session beans to track items the user is adding to or deleting from the shopping cart. In this example, `ShoppingCartClient` is responsible for presenting the schedules to the end-user; the shopping cart manages the items in the list.

Shopping Cart

The ShoppingCartEJB component manages several functions for the end user, such as adding or deleting schedules, listing schedules in the shopping cart, and emptying a schedule list from the shopping cart, as shown in Figure 3-6. Figure 3-7 illustrates the shopping cart interaction; Figure 3-8 is the class diagram.

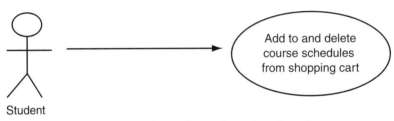

Figure 3-6 Adding and deleting items from the shopping cart

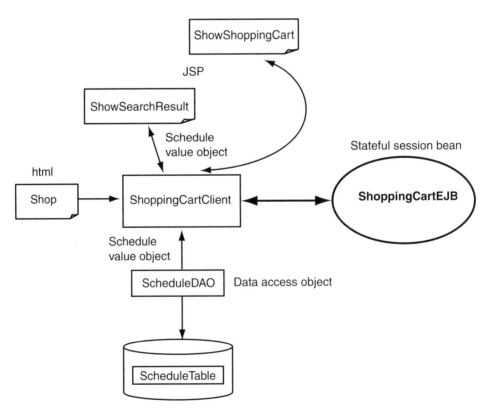

Figure 3-7 Interaction diagram—ShoppingCartEJB

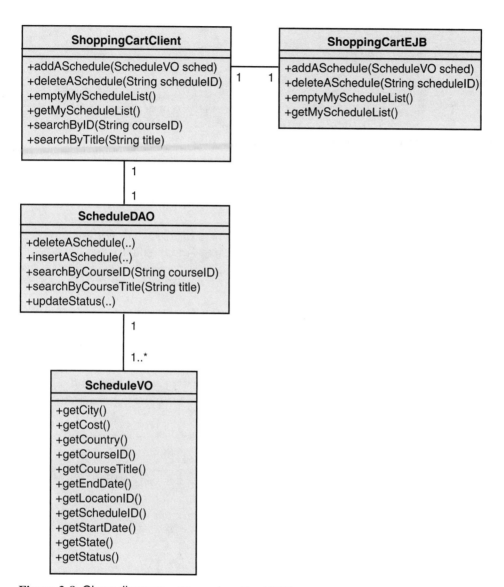

Figure 3-8 Class diagram—ShoppingCartEJB

The ShoppingCartEJB component provides the following functions:

- It adds a course to the shopping cart.
- It shows the list of the courses in the shopping cart.
- It removes a course from the shopping cart.

- It empties the shopping cart.
- It gets the total cost.

The application executes according to the following steps:

1. The `ShoppingCartClient` servlet accepts the request from `Shop.html` form and performs the search with the help of `ScheduleDAO`. It then delegates the presentation of the result to the `ShowSearchResult.jsp`.

2. `ScheduleDAO` provides access to `ScheduleTable` in the database.

3. The end user clicks the Add button to add the course to the shopping cart.

4. The `ShoppingCartClient` servlet directs any output of the interaction with the shopping cart to the `ShowShoppingCart.jsp`. Notice that `ShoppingCartEJB` only implements the business logic, such as adding and deleting items, and is not involved with accessing the database.

Bean-Managed Persistence Entity Bean Example (Chapter 9)

`StudentEJB` implements the logic to manage the bean-managed persistence fields related to the student entity. The bean instance depends on the container to synchronize the persistent data with the underlying database. To access the database, it relies on the helper class `RosterDAO` and on the data access logic that is embedded in the `StudentEJB` class. Embedding data access logic in the bean class has undesirable effects on the readability of the business logic, maintenance of the code, and the portability of the bean class.

Use Case: Creating a Student Account

The use case shown in Figure 3-9 performs functions such as creating a student account, modifying personal information for students, and registering or dropping courses. Figure 3-10 illustrates the interaction between the participating objects. Figure 3-11 is the class diagram.

`StudentEJB` provides the functions of

- creating a student account
- updating student attributes such as name, phone, and e-mail address
- registering for a course
- dropping a course
- listing all courses

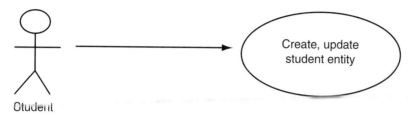

Figure 3-9 Creating and modifying a student account

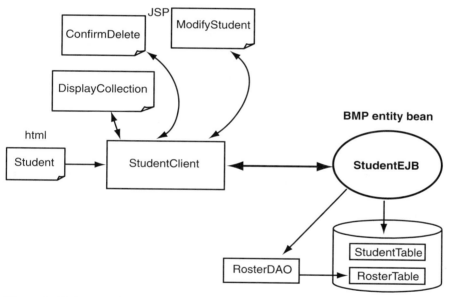

Figure 3-10 Interaction diagram—StudentEJB

The application executes according to the following steps:

1.   The bean instance directly accesses StudentTable but relies on Roster-
      DAO to access RosterTable.

2.   The StudentClient servlet accepts requests from the Student.html
      form and forwards the requests to the bean instance, StudentEJB.

3.   The response from the bean instance is delegated to the one of the following
      files: DisplayCollection.jsp, ConfirmDelete.jsp, or ModifyStu-
      dent.jsp.

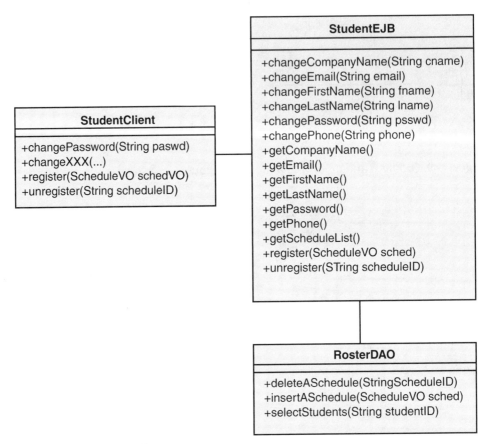

Figure 3-11 Class diagram—`StudentEJB`

Container-Managed Persistence Entity Bean Example (Chapter 11)

The sample application discussed in Chapter 11 consists of three CMP 2.0 entity beans—`StudentEJB`, `AddressEJB`, and `RosterEJB`, which allow students to create a student account, enter one or more addresses, and register for classes. General users also can query for student information such as first name, last name, list of addresses, and courses for which specific students are registered.

Creating a User Account

Using the sample application, a student can create a user account, enter addresses, and register for Java classes. The application also allows users to query a given student account to obtain a listing of the student's addresses and classes for which the student is registered. Figure 3-12 shows the main features of the application.

Figure 3-13 illustrates the interaction among the various objects in the application and the relationships among the three entity beans. Figure 3-14 shows the class diagrams for the EJBs and their interrelationships.

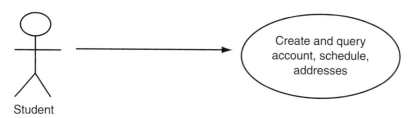

Figure 3-12 Student creating an account and enrolling in a class

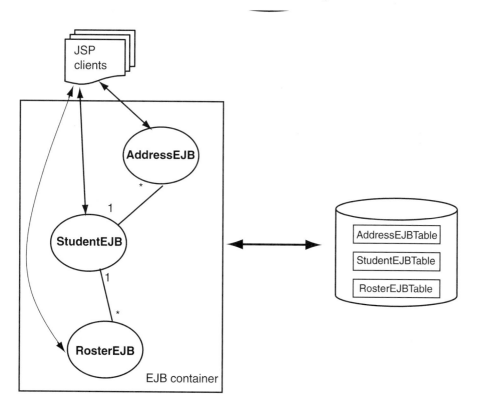

Figure 3-13 The CMP 2.0 entity beans

The clients in this example are JavaServer pages that invoke the `create` method on the `StudentEJB` bean to create a student account. This step is necessary before the student can have an address or be enrolled in classes. The client can call `AddressEJB` to create one or more addresses and `RosterEJB` to enroll the student in one or more classes. The student information can be searched by the student's ID, first name, or last name. Search results can include student first name, last name, and a list of addresses and classes for which the student is registered. Searches can also be performed directly on each of these entity beans. The `StudentEJB` bean has one-to-many relationships with both `AddressEJB` and `RosterEJB`, which means that a student can have one or more addresses and be registered for zero or more classes. The `AddressEJB` and `RosterEJB` beans are dependent on `StudentEJB`, so if the student account is removed, the address and enrolled information for the student are deleted as well.

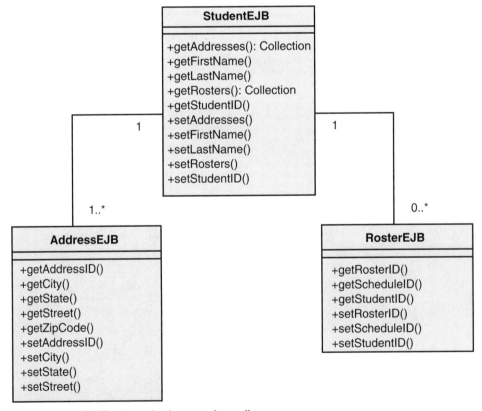

Figure 3-14 CMP 2.0 entity beans class diagram

Message-Driven Bean Implementation Example (Chapter 13)

The `RosterMDB` instance discussed in Chapter 13 is implemented as an asynchronous EJB, which receives a JMS message from a queue. The bean extracts the `studentID`, `scheduleID`, and data stamp and then enrolls the student by inserting the information into a roster table. The bean then extracts the list of all the students registered for a particular schedule and publishes the message to the topic destination.

The bean instance uses the `RosterDAO` object to access the `RosterTable`. This example application illustrates how to send and receive JMS messages using the Point-to-Point and Publish-Subscribe messaging models.

Asynchronous Student Registration

Figure 3-15 shows a use case in which students use messaging to register for Java courses asynchronously and obtain listings of students enrolled in the classes.

Figure 3-16 illustrates the interaction between objects in the sample application, in which a `MessageSender` client creates a JMS message and sends it to the queue destination. When the message arrives, the container automatically notifies the `RosterMDB` bean. Figure 3-17 shows the class diagram.

`RosterEJB` provides these functions:

- It extracts the student and schedule ID from the message.
- It then inserts these fields into the Roster table with the help of data access object `RosterDAO`.
- It then uses the `scheduleID` to extract all the students registered for the schedule.
- Finally, it creates a JMS text message that encapsulates the student's list and publishes it to the `Topic` destination.

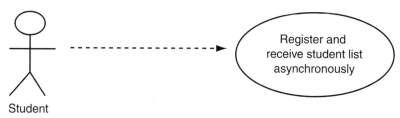

Figure 3-15 Asynchronous registration

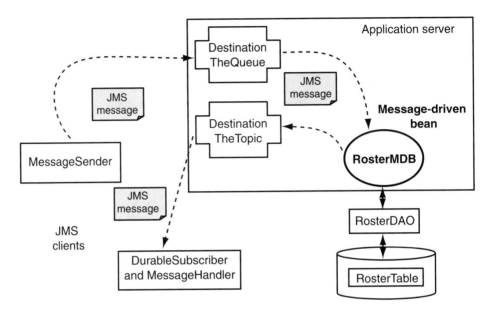

Figure 3-16 Interaction diagram—`RosterMDB` receiving and sending JMS messages

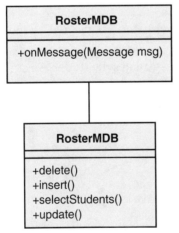

Figure 3-17 Class diagram—roster message-driven bean application

The application executes as follows:

1. `RosterDAO` provides access to `RosterTable`.

2. The administrator is responsible for providing the destinations `TheQueue` and `TheTopic`.

3. When the `MessageSender` client Java program (a servlet client) is executed, it creates a JMS message and uses the `Send` method to forward messages to the `TheQueue` destination.

4. When a message arrives, the container passes the message to a `RosterMDB` instance, which inserts fields into `RosterTable`, then retrieves a list of students registered for a class and publishes that information.

5. The `DurableSubscriber` client is executed using the receive option to retrieve a JMS message from the `TheTopic`. It passes the message to `MessageHandler`, which prints messages to the screen.

Summary

In this chapter, we've provided several sample applications that employ stateless session beans, stateful session beans, bean-managed persistence entity beans, container-managed persistence entity beans, and message-driven beans, all built around the theme of student registration. You've seen examples of use cases for each one.

There are two additional example applications from Part 3 of the book that we haven't covered in this chapter because those applications cover more advanced information concerning EJB design patterns and require knowledge of EJB version 2.0. After you've gone through the chapters in Part 2, read Chapter 16 before tackling Chapters 17 and 18.

The examples in the book use only a subset of the table information, and I've implemented only a few of the possible business logic instances in the EJBs. This was deliberate so we could focus on understanding the fundamentals of implementing EJBs rather than on writing complicated business logic. Once you get the sample application working, I encourage you to take the base code and have fun implementing sophisticated business logic with it.

THE EJB CLIENT VIEW

Chapter 4

In this chapter, we focus on the EJB client view and discuss the requirements and the mechanics of how a client accesses services provided by the EJB in a container. In this chapter, you will learn

- what distributed objects are as well as some of their characteristics
- JNDI and its importance in EJB applications
- RMI-IIOP and how it benefits EJBs
- characteristics of local and remote interfaces, their APIs, and how they are used
- how to write a simple Java client application to highlight the EJB client view implementation

Distributed Objects

To better understand and write client applications, you need an understanding of distributed objects, JNDI, and RMI-IIOP technology and how they relate to EJBs.

With *centralized computing*, monolithic applications ran on big expensive mainframes. This was a simple solution that worked when the number of users on the system could be predicted and controlled. However, this approach had two drawbacks: a single point of failure and limited scalability.

Today, it's difficult to predict the load on the system when users are accessing enterprise applications from anywhere at any time from Internet-connected devices. To handle this unpredictability, businesses have migrated toward *distributed computing* platforms. In distributed computing, applications are written using the component model and compiled into component objects that are then executed in a cluster of servers connected by high-speed networks. The clients don't need to know where the objects reside, or on what operating system they execute, or how the components implement the business logic. Rather, remote clients need to be able to locate the interface to the server object and invoke business methods via the remote interface. This approach has several advantages: high availability with no single point of failure, high scalability made possible by the ability to quickly add inexpensive servers to the server mix, and faster response through the use of either load balancing or distributing user requests across several servers as illustrated in Figure 4-1.

Challenges Associated with Distributed Objects

There are three main challenges with distributed objects. First, distributed applications are far more complex and tedious to develop and deploy than traditional monolithic applications. This is a result of programmers having to work with low-level APIs for transaction and state management details as well as dealing with multi-threaded and resource pooling issues. In addition, programmers also have to factor the complexities of different operating system calls, interoperability between different communication protocols, and interoperability among their programming implementations. Second, a remote client has to be able to locate a server object on a network easily and transparently. This can be difficult because server objects are created and destroyed as needed, making it hard for clients to track the dynamic server objects. Furthermore, a remote client could be in Tokyo, making requests on server objects in New York. Third, once a client locates a server object, the client must be able to execute methods in a seamless and consistent manner, regardless of the language in which the system is written, and regardless of operating system or network protocol.

Solutions

The J2EE platform solves the first issue in two ways. Because EJBs are written in Java, they are portable across platforms. In the EJB architecture, the EJB container (rather than the programmer) handles low-level transaction and statement management details, multi-threaded and resource pooling issues, and also hides

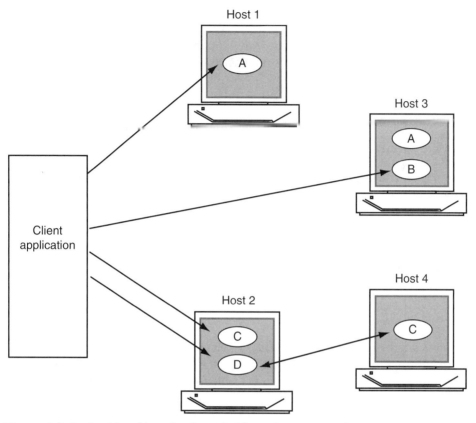

Figure 4-1 A client invoking distributed objects in a server cluster

the complexities of different operating system calls and interoperability inconsistencies with different communication protocols. As a result, the bean developer is free to concentrate on implementing the business logic.

The J2EE platform and the Java Naming and Directory Interface (JNDI) API handle remote clients, providing a standard way to locate distributed objects on the network.

The third issue associated with distributed objects is *accessibility*. Accessibility refers to the ability of a client to seamlessly invoke methods on remote objects without concerning itself with serializing objects and sending them across the network and with low-level transport protocols' compatibility with distributed objects running on different operating system platforms. In the J2EE platform, RMI-IIOP technology and the JNDI enable object accessibility. Java relies on Java Remote Method Invocation (RMI) to support distributed objects, but because RMI is Java specific, Java clients cannot access objects in non-Java environments. Internet Inter-ORB Protocol (IIOP) is a protocol used by CORBA objects to communicate in a heterogeneous environment; therefore, the RMI-IIOP protocol supports communication with Java and CORBA objects. (CORBA is a standard for writing platform, language, and vendor-independent distributed applications. CORBA uses IIOP to achieve interoperability with other applications written in different languages and running on different platforms.)

Introduction to JNDI

The JNDI APIs provide Java applications with vendor-agnostic access to naming and directory services. This *naming service* provides names to object bindings so clients can find distributed objects by names. Directory services, such as the Lightweight Directory Access Protocol (LDAP), manage the directory of entries that can refer to people, objects, or data sources. Similar to using JDBC APIs to write database-agnostic Java applications, programmers can use JNDI APIs to locate distributed objects in any directory server.

Naming Service

A good analogy of a naming service is phone directory assistance and Domain Name Service (DNS). One can call phone directory assistance and get a listed phone number of a person or a business for that particular area by giving the person's first and last name or name of the business. In the case of DNS, an application can retrieve the IP address (for example, 192.18.97.71) by just giving a fully qualified host name (for example, java.sun.com).

For a naming service to function seamlessly, it has to define and follow a specific naming convention. The naming convention defines an *atomic name* and *compound name*. An atomic name is an indivisible component of a name, while a compound name consists of zero or more atomic names composed according to specific naming conventions defined by the naming service. For example, DNS is a naming service where the compound name java.sun.com consists of the atomic names "java," "sun," and "com," separated by the dot character (.).

The naming service also provides a *context* within which an atomic name is associated with, or bound to, an object. A context represents a set of bindings within a naming service that all share the same naming convention. Therefore, a context object provides methods for looking up objects by name, for binding names to objects, for unbinding names from objects, for renaming objects, and for listing bindings. For example, given a name, the lookup operation will return the object associated with that name. Some naming services such as JNDI also provide *subcontext* functionality. A subcontext is a context within a context, analogous to subdirectory within a directory of a hierarchical file system. A context that supports a subcontext also provides methods for creating and destroying subcontext. A subcontext is useful for organizing objects in a hierarchical fashion.

Naming Conventions

Every context has a naming convention. A *naming system* is a connected set of contexts that have the same naming convention and provide a common set of operations, for example, the naming system with DNS (java.sun.com) and the Windows file system (C:\com\javacamp\bin). A naming system provides a naming service for performing name-related operations such as host name to IP address mapping in DNS and filenames to files and directories mapping in a file system.

A naming service consists of the *namespace*, which is a set of names. A name can be atomic or compound. A compound name consists of two or more atomic names that have the same naming convention and are bound in a hierarchical fashion. Consider the Windows directory file system, C:\com\javacamp. The compound name consists of the root context C: with the subcontext as com and javacamp—ordered from left to right and separated by the back-slash character(\). As in this example, a naming system is a connected set of contexts of the same type of naming conventions that provide the same set of operations. To further illustrate, note how one can execute several commands (such as list the contents of the directory, or delete a file or sub-directory and/or create another sub-directory) in the com and javacamp subcontexts.

NameSpace

The namespace is the set of all the names and composite names in a naming system—a namespace can consist of different namespaces spanning multiple naming systems. For example, the URL http://java.sun.com/j2ee/whitepaper.pdf is a composite name that consists of three naming systems including the URL (http://), the DNS (java.sun.com), and the file system namespace (/j2ee/whitepaper.pdf).

Directory Service

A *directory* is a repository for objects, and a *directory object* represents an object that can represent an employee, a computer, or a Java object. These directory objects can have attributes, which in turn have attribute identifiers and a set of attribute values. For example, an employee directory object can have an attribute identifier such as name, title, e-mail, and corresponding attribute values such as John Doe, J2EE Architect, johndoe@yahoo.com. Therefore, a directory provides a connected set of directory objects, and the naming service relies on the directory service to provide the association of names to objects and operations for adding, removing, and modifying the attributes of the associated objects in the directory.

To sum up, a directory service organizes directory objects in a hierarchical manner and provides the mapping between recognizable names and directory objects using the naming system.

The Need for Naming and Directory Services

So why are we interested in naming and directory services? If you recall, one of the challenges in a distributed application is for a client to be able to locate the distributed server object easily and transparently. In J2EE architecture, the directory service is used as a centralized repository for the deployed EJB objects, and clients rely on naming services to locate a desired object by using a name and then making requests.

JNDI APIs are used in Java client application environments to access naming and directory services in a portable manner. The vendors of the naming and directory products provide the service provider interface (SPI) for their product. The JNDI manager's task is to map the JNDI API to the JNDI SPI. Client applications written using JNDI APIs are guaranteed to be compatible with existing and future directory servers. Figure 4-2 illustrates the Java client, the JNDI API, the JNDI managers, and the JNDI SPI. A developer only has to worry about the client application and the JNDI APIs as illustrated by the dashed box.

JNDI in a Client Application

JNDI provides location transparency to a client; in JNDI, there is no concept of absolute names, and every name is relative to a context. As such, before a lookup will return the correct object, the client must provide the context within which the name-object binding is valid. For a client application to perform any naming or directory service operation, the JNDI must first establish a root context. This is done by obtaining the initial context.

To set the initial context for JNDI, use the `javax.naming.InitialContext` class, which has several constructors and methods of interest, including

- initialContext(Hashtable env) constructor
- lookup(String name) method
- static final fields for setting environment properties

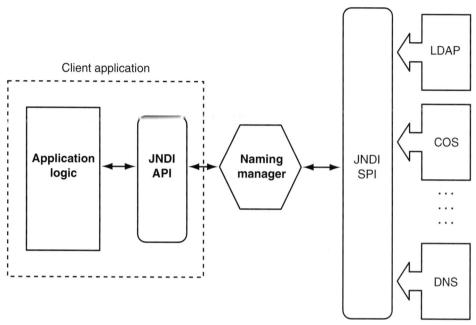

Figure 4-2 JNDI architecture—the naming manager mapping JNDI API to JNDI SPI

Accessing Remote Objects

Before you can access remote objects, you must bootstrap JNDI and execute the lookup method to get the initial context. This is analogous to the way that the Windows operating system associates the floppy drive to drive A: and the primary hard drive to drive C: when you boot a PC.

Bootstrapping JNDI

First, create a hash table to hold and pass the necessary initial fields:

```
Hashtable env = new Hashtable();
```

Then, you must set the environment properties that are specific to the directory server before a valid context can be created. The number and types of environment properties are vendor and server dependent. We will use Sun's LDAP directory server and show the minimum properties required to create the context, namely the context factory and the provider's URL. Remember, JNDI supports different types of directories, and you will need to tell it to create a context that is valid for a particular directory server. To do so, use the context factory object (`com.sun.jndi.ldap.LdapCtxFactory`) provided by the directory vendor (Sun) to tell the JNDI how to create a context that is valid for Sun's LDAP directory server.

`INITIAL_CONTEXT_FACTORY` is used to specify the initial context factory. The value should be the fully qualified class name that will be used to create an initial context for the directory server. Attempting to call the `InitialContext` without setting this value will result in `NoInitialContextException` being thrown. In this case, the value is set to the Sun-provided LDAP server `com.sun.jndi.ldap.LdapCtxFactory`. `PROVIDER_URL` is used to specify the configuration information for the server provider. In this example, the root context is javacamp on an LDAP directory server at ldap://ldap.javacamp.com:389/o=javacamp; the default standard LDAP port is 389. If this value is not specified, a default configuration specified by the service provider is used. After setting the environment parameters, instantiate the `InitialContext` class and pass the environmental parameters set in the hash table to the `InitialContext(env)` constructor. The JNDI will then use the context factory to create the initial context and initialize it. At this point, the JNDI has a starting point into the LDAP namespace.

```
Context ctx = new InitialContext(env);
```

Performing Lookup Service

After creating the context, search for necessary objects on the network as follows:

```
ctx.lookup("MyObject");
```

Once you retrieve the object, you can then perform pertinent operations on the object. Now, put the two steps together:

```
Hashtable env = new Hashtable(4);
env.put(Con-
text.INITIAL_CONTEXT_FACTORY,"com.sun.jndi.ldap.LdapCtxFactory");
env.put(Context.PROVIDER_URL,"ldap://ldap.javacamp.com:389/o=java-
camp");
Context ctx  = new InitialContext(env);
Object obj = (MyObject) ctx.lookup("MyTestObject");
   ........ .
```

Setting JNDI Environment Properties

One simple way to set environment properties for the initial context is to hard code the environment parameters as shown above, but it's obviously not portable. Fortunately, there are other ways to set environment properties in an application that uses JNDI APIs, including the command line, the application resource file, and using default parameters.

The Command Line

This option is flexible because you can change the properties at runtime; however, it's typing intensive for setting multiple and complex properties. For example:

```
java -Djava.naming.factory.initial=com.sun.jndi.ldp.LdapCtxFac-
tory \ -Djava.naming.provider.url=ldap://localhost:389 ejbClient
```

The Application Resource File

Use the %J2EE_HOME%lib/classes/jndi.properties file for J2SDKEE 1.3 implementation (or your application server-specific location) to set the parameters for the JNDI initial context interface. This is simpler than the command line and centralized to one file.

```
#
# jndi.proper ties file for Sun's J2SDKEE 1.3 Ref. implementation
#
java.naming.factory.initial=com.sun.enterprise.naming.SerialInit-
ContextFactory
java.naming.factory.url.pkgs=com.sun.enterprise.naming
```

Preset During Installation

The exact setup procedure is vendor-specific, but during the installation of the application server, the administrator can specify the environmental parameters for the LDAP server by specifying the context factory, provider URL, user name, password, and so forth. Then, when the `initialContext()` method is invoked, the server automatically supplies the parameters. This option is used often in examples where the environment properties aren't explicitly passed. This option enables the administrator to set the LDAP server properties during installation. Programmers can then set the initial context for their objects via the deployment descriptor. This method is popular because it assures the program will be set to the right root context.

JNDI and EJBs

In most J2EE application environments, the LDAP server is often used as a centralized repository for network resources. The JNDI API provides a common way to access directory server resources from Java clients. Although there are many types of objects that can be stored in the LDAP server, we're primarily interested in accessing EJB home objects, data source, security, transaction, JMS, mail, and JCA objects using the JNDI.

Accessing Data Source Using JNDI

When you write a Java program to access the database using JDBC, you need to specify the username, password, database instance name, and the table names. In a distributed application, the information necessary to access the database is stored in a central repository (such as an LDAP directory) as data source objects and clients access the data source information using the JNDI API. For example, in the following code snippet, notice that the InitialContext constructor takes no environment properties—this implies that the information is being passed from the initial system setup. The client used the lookup method to download the JCampDS data source object from the java:comp/env/jdbc/ context and then cast it to the correct object type, DataSource.

```
InitialContext ctx = new InitialContext();
DataSource = (DataSource) ctx.lookup ("java:comp/env/jdbc/JCampDS");
```

Context Naming Conventions

Neither the J2EE nor the EJB specifications specify how to set the naming context in a J2EE application. Because using different naming context hierarchy conventions could compromise the portability of applications, vendors have agreed upon context name conventions. For example, java:comp is the initial root context in J2EE applications—an env context binds environment objects and subcontexts such as jdbc. A jdbc context binds data source objects. In the above example, the JCampDS is a data source object binding within the java:comp/env/jdbc/ context. Another popular binding in the ejb subcontext is the EJB home interface—helloHome in the java:comp/env/ejb/ context. Here are other common JNDI subcontexts used in J2EE applications:

- *data sources*—java:comp/env/jdbc
- *Enterprise JavaBeans*—java:comp/env/ejb
- *JMS*—java:comp/env/jms
- *transaction*—java:comp/env/transaction
- *JCA*—java:comp/env/eis
- *mail*—java:comp/env/mail

Introduction to RMI-IIOP

RMI enables programmers to write distributed applications in Java. RMI applications consist of the RMI client that uses the remote interface to execute methods on the RMI server (executing on a remote host).

After compilation of the RMI application, a *stub* and a *skeleton* are created. The client code uses a stub to *marshal* a request to the remote host where a skeleton *un-marshals* the request and delivers it to the server code. The server code processes the request and returns the results back to the client using the skeleton and stub in reverse order. (*Marshaling* and *un-marshaling* describe the process of serializing and de-serializing and sending the request object across the network.) Note that this process has high overhead and is slow. Figure 4-3 illustrates an RMI client-server application.

Advantages of RMI Over RPC

Unlike traditional Remote Procedure Call (RPC) programming, the RMI uses the Java Remote Method Protocol (JRMP) to hide all the low-level networking intricacies and automatically manage underlying data translation. This simplifies distributed programming in the Java environment because the programmer does not need to differentiate between a local and/or remote call. The RMI client code uses an RMI registry to find the RMI server located on a remote host. RMI simplifies distributed programming in Java; however, RMI works only in a Java

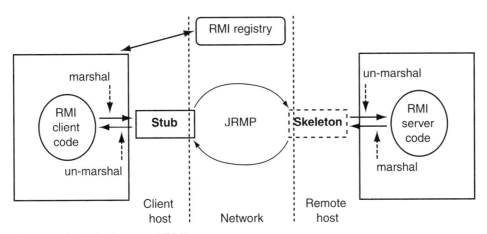

Figure 4-3 RMI client and RMI server

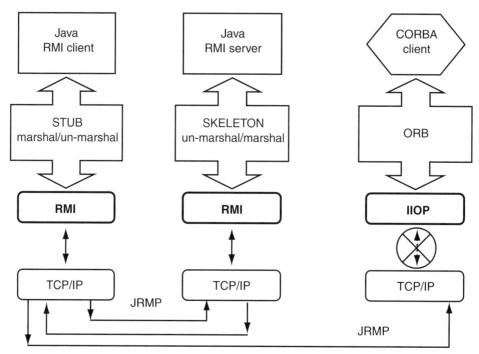

Figure 4-4 A client using JRMP to communicate with an RMI server and CORBA client

environment. Figure 4-4 illustrates this case; the RMI client is communicating to the RMI server using the JRMP, but is unable to communicate with CORBA client due to lack of IIOP support.

Advantages of RMI-IIOP Over Native RMI

One of the goals of EJBs is interoperability with non-Java and CORBA clients. The RMI-IIOP is a marriage of RMI and IIOP, resulting in simple Java RMI programming (EJBs are based on RMI-IIOP) and interoperability with CORBA. Figure 4-5 illustrates an RMI-IIOP client supporting both JRMP and IIOP, communicating with an RMI-IIOP server via JRMP/IIOP, and communicating with CORBA via the IIOP protocol.

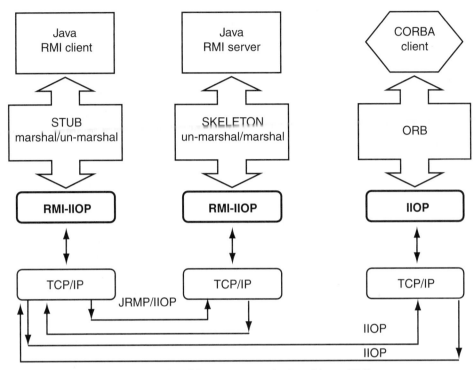

Figure 4-5 A client using RMI-IIOP to communicate with an RMI server and CORBA client

Casting Requirements to Use RMI-IIOP

Prior to the introduction of RMI-IIOP support, programmers would cast a reference to the more specific object type, as in the JNDI lookup in EJB 1.0. For example:

```
RemoteHome remoteHome = (RemoteHome) jndiContext.lookup
("java:comp/env/ejb/remhome");
```

This method worked in a Java-only environment because all objects inherit from a root Java Object; however, when using IIOP with multi-language support, there is not a root object type that is common to all languages. In addition, neither IIOP nor some other languages support casting. To accommodate different languages in an object-oriented programming environment, there must be a way of converting remote objects from a general to a more specific type. RMI-IIOP provides support for explicitly narrowing a general reference type to a desired specific type with a `javax.rmi.PortableRemoteObject.narrow()` method.

Because other protocols besides IIOP may also require explicit narrowing, the `PortableRemoteObject` abstracts the narrowing process, making it protocol agnostic. The narrow method takes two arguments: the remote reference to be narrowed and the type to be narrowed to after the method is executed. If the `narrow()` method is successful, it returns a stub that implements the remote interface type. Then the `narrow(ref.HelloHome.class)` method is applied to the returned `stub(ref)` to make it conform to the desired remote home interface (`HelloHome.class`) type. Finally, it is cast to the remote home interface (`HelloHome`) type. This is shown in the following lines:

```
Object ref  = ctx.lookup ("java:comp/env/ejb/MyHelloHome");
HelloHome helloHome = (HelloHome) PortableRemoteObject.narrow(ref,
HelloHome.class);
```

The `ClassCastException` is thrown if the home object encounters problems with the narrowing process. The `PortableRemoteObject.narrow()` method is required only when the remote reference to an EJB home or EJB Object is returned without a specific remote interface type. This method is not required when the methods return the correct EJB object type, but it's a best practice to always use narrow.

The EJB Client View

This section discusses the client view of EJBs and how the client depends on JNDI and RMI-IIOP to provide location transparency and accessibility. The EJB instances execute within EJB containers; in the case of session and entity beans, the clients can only access them indirectly via their interfaces. The message-driven beans don't have interfaces but instead use messages (MDBs are discussed in Chapter 13). Because the client view of the bean instance is accessed through their interfaces, you need to understand the EJB interfaces to understand a client view.

Session and entity beans have two categories of interface, remote and local, and each category has two types of interfaces that provide specific functionality:

- *Home interface*—The home interface is used to manage the life cycle of the bean instance, which can include the create, the remove, and the find methods.

- *Component interface*—The component interface consists of the business methods that clients can invoke to execute business logic on bean instances in the container.

A bean developer is responsible for providing both the remote home interface and remote component interface, or local home interface and local component interface, or both, in some rare cases, along with bean implementation class, deployment descriptor, and optional helper classes for synchronous EJBs.

Remote and Local Client Views

A client for an EJB instance can be a servlet, a JSP, a standalone Java or CORBA application, or even another EJB. Let us get a deeper understanding of remote and local interfaces by looking at the steps involved in a request. Prior to EJB 2.0, all clients used remote interfaces to invoke methods on the bean instance. Similar to the RMI remote calls discussed earlier, the EJB remote interface calls require marshaling and un-marshaling objects.

Let us look at the steps involved during a remote business method invocation from a client.

1. When the client calls a business method in a remote component interface and passes an object as a parameter, the remote component interface stub marshals the parameter before sending it over to the EJBObject, its proxy at the container. The EJBObject skeleton has to un-marshal the argument at the container.

2. The container then performs security, transaction, and life-cycle services before the Java object is passed to the matching business method and executed on the bean instance.

3. The result of the business method is passed back to the EJBObject.

4. The EJBObject then marshals the result and sends it back to the remote component interface. The remote component interface then un-marshals the object before the client receives the result of the method call.

Remote calls have high overhead, increase network traffic, security checks, transaction propagation, and so forth, and are slow as a result. Prior to EJB 2.0, every method call was potentially a remote call. For example, a Java client invoking a business method on a session bean instance on the same host and on a remote host (from a different JVM) were equivalent because the client had to use remote interfaces and bear the overhead of the remote call. The actual implementation was vendor dependent; some vendors' implementations were optimized to differentiate between the two types of calls and to make local calls whenever appropriate. EJB 2.0 introduced the concept of local home and local component interfaces to provide support for efficient and lightweight access to EJBs when both the EJB instance and the client are co-located in the same JVM. With EJB 2.0, when the client session-bean instance invokes business methods on an entity bean instance located in the same JVM, it can use local interfaces and avoid the inefficiencies associated with the remote calls. Figure 4-6 illustrates a

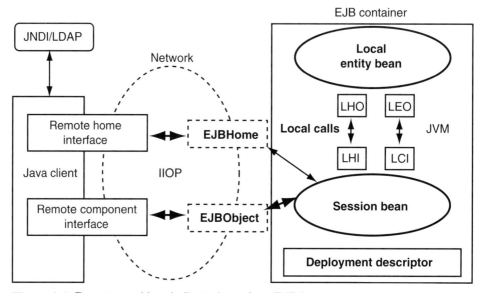

Figure 4-6 Remote and local client view of an EJB instance

client making a remote request to the session bean using the remote home and component interfaces and the session bean making a local home and component interface to an entity bean.

Remote and Local Interfaces

The main difference between the remote and local interfaces is that with a remote interface the caller and callee objects can be distributed across the network, but with local interface the caller and the callee objects must reside in the same JVM. The following are some of the other important characteristics of the two interfaces.

Remote Interfaces

- Remote interfaces provide a remote, location-independent view of EJBs.
- They must implement RMI interfaces (parameters and results of the methods in the home and component interface must support RMI-IIOP).

- Arguments and results are passed by value.
- Remote Java objects implement the remote home and component interface and are generated by the container at deployment time. They are required to throw `RemoteException`.
- When accessing remote home and remote object references, programmers may be required to use the `PortableRemoteObject.narrow()` method before casting to a desired Java object type.

Local Interfaces

- They can only be used by clients if they are co-located in the same JVM as the bean instance. The local client view of a bean is location dependent.
- The objects that implement local home and component interfaces don't have to support RMI-IIOP, nor are they not required to use the narrow method.
- Arguments and results of local methods are passed by reference.
- The objects that implement the local home and component interface are local Java objects generated by the container at deployment time and aren't required to throw `RemoteException`.

Local and Remote Interface APIs

Although a session bean class must implement the `javax.ejb.SessionBean` interface and an entity bean class must implement the `javax.ejb.EntityBean` interface, the home and remote interfaces for both session and entity beans extend the same *superinterfaces*. To write EJB interfaces, review the following APIs for local and remote interfaces.

Remote Home Interfaces

The remote home interface provides a remote client with life-cycle operations and metadata for the bean instance. Every bean type has one home interface as follows:

```
public interface javax.ejb.EJBHome extends java.rmi.Remote {
    public EJBMetaData getEJBMetaData() throws RemoteException;
    public HomeHandle getHomeHandle() throws RemoteException;
    public void remove(Handle handle)
    throws RemoteException, RemoveException;
    public void remove(Object primaryKey)
    throws RemoteException, , RemoveException;
    }
```

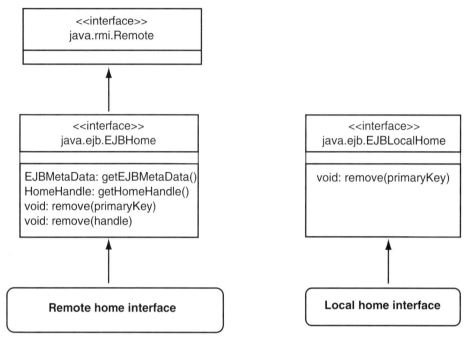

Figure 4-7 Remote and local home interface

Figure 4-7 illustrates the remote and local home interface hierarchy. All EJB remote home interfaces must extend the `javax.ejb.EJBHome` interface and must throw a `RemoteException`.

The following methods are declared in the home interface:

- The `getEJBMetaData()` method returns the enterprise JavaBean's `EJBMetaData` interface, which can be used by the clients to access information about the enterprise bean. This method is used mostly by a vendor's tools such as the deployment tool.

- The `getHomeHandle()` method returns a home handle, which is a reference to a remote home object of the bean instance. The handle can be saved and reused later or passed to another client on a different JVM and later used to reobtain access to the remote home object.

- The `remove(Object primaryKey)` method is used to remove an instance of an entity bean identified by the primary key. This is only applicable to entity beans.

- The `remove(Handle handle)` method can be used to remove a bean instance identified by its handle. Unlike the previous remove `(Object` `primaryKey)`, this remove is applicable for both the entity and session beans. Note that in the case of a stateful bean instance, the handle will cease to exist if the container crashes or if the bean instance is removed by the container upon time out.

- Using the `getEJBMetaData()` and `getHomeHandle()` methods requires programmers to narrow the returned `EJBMetaData` and `HomeHandle` by using the `PortableRemoteObject.narrow()` method

Local Home Interfaces

The local home interface also provides life-cycle operations for the local bean instance. Unlike the remote home interface, local interface is simpler:

```
public interface javax.ejb.EJBLocalHome extends {
    public void remove(Object primaryKey)
        throws RemoveException, EJBException;
    }
```

All local home interfaces must extend the `javax.ejb.EJBLocalHome` interface, which defines a single `remove(Object primaryKey)` method. This method is valid for entity beans. Attempting to call this method to remove a session bean instance will result in the `RemoveException` method being thrown; also note that if the method fails due to system-level failure, `EJBException` is thrown. Only local clients can call local home interfaces.

Remote Component Interfaces

A client uses the remote component to execute business methods implemented in the bean class. All EJB remote component interfaces must extend the `javax.ejb.EJBObject` interface and must throw a `RemoteException`.

```
public interface javax.ejb.EJBObject extends java.rmi.Remote {
    public EJBHome getEJBHome() throws RemoteException;
    public Object getPrimaryKey() throws RemoteException;
    public void remove() throws RemoteException, RemoveException;
    public Handle getHandle() throws RemoteException;
    public Boolean isIdentical(EJBObjct obj) throws RemoteException;
    }
```

Figure 4-8 illustrates a remote and local component interface hierarchy.

The remote component interface declares the following methods:

- The `getEJBHome()` method returns a reference to an EJB's home interface, which can be used to create, find, and remove the bean instance.

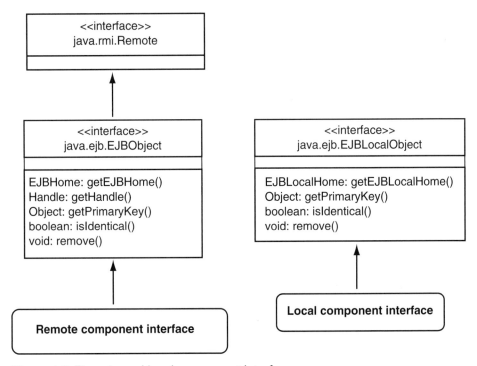

Figure 4-8 Remote and local component interface

A client can pass the reference to the home interface to another client, which can then invoke a lifecycle method.

- The `getPrimaryKey()` method returns a primary key of the bean instance—note that this applies only to entity beans. This method will throw a remote exception if used on a session bean.

- The `getHandle()` returns a handle for the bean instance so it can be used for both session and entity bean instances. The handle can be saved and used at a later time or passed to another client in a different JVM. The handle can then be used to find the EJB object and directly execute business methods. The handle becomes invalid if the stateful session instance has been removed due to a time out or container crash.

- The method `isIdentical (EJBObject obj)` can be used by a client to test whether the remote EJB object is identical—it returns a boolean.

- The `remove()` method is used to remove the EJB object.

- If `getEJBHome ()` and `getHandle ()` methods are used to obtain the EJBHome and Handle respectively, and the `PortableRemote-Object.narrow()` method must be applied to EJBHome and Handle objects before they can be used.

Local Component Interfaces

The local component interface exposes business methods that can only be called by local clients (i.e., clients co-located in the same JVM).

```
public interface EJBLocalObject {
    public EJBLocalHome getEJBLocalHome() throws EJBException;
    public Object getPrimaryKey() throws EJBException;
    public boolean isIdentical() throws EJBException;
    public void remove() throws EJBException, RemoveException;
    }
```

All local component interfaces must extend the `javax.ejb.EJBLocalObject` interface —note that if the method fails due to system-level failure, the `EJBException` will be thrown. Only local clients can invoke business methods in the local component interface. The following methods are declared in the local component interface:

- The `getEJBLocalHome` method returns an `EJBLocalHome` interface, the enterprise bean's local home interface to a local client. The `EJBLocalHome` can pass an interface to another local client.

- The `getPrimaryKey` method returns an object's primary key, which is valid only for a local entity bean; attempting to call this method with the session bean instance will result in an `EJBException` being thrown.

- The `remove()` method is used to remove a reference to a local `EJBObject`. Remember it's the container that actually removes the bean instance. If, for some reason, the container cannot remove the local component object, it will throw `RemoveException`.

- The `isIdentical()` method is useful to verify if two local objects are identical. It returns a boolean.

- These EJB objects - `EJBHome`, `EJBObject`, `EJBLocalHome` and `EJBLocalObject` are automatically generated by the EJB container during deployment phase.

Exceptions

Two types of exceptions to remember when using interfaces include:

- `EJBException`—This exception is thrown by the EJB to its container if the business methods or callback methods fail to complete due to an unexpected error (such as being unable to open network or database resources).

- `RemoteException`—On the other hand, the container throws a `RemoteException` when it encounters system level or network failure errors. Only remote interfaces are required to throw `RemoteExceptions`.

An EJB instance may also throw application-specific exceptions defined by the bean provider. Other sub-classes of these exceptions are discussed in subsequent chapters.

Rules for Writing Remote and Local Interfaces

Table 4-1 is a summary of general rules in writing both local and remote interfaces. Remember that remote interfaces offer the ability to distribute EJBs at the cost of performance, while local interfaces offer better performance at the cost of not being able to distribute EJBs.

Creating a Remote Client Application

You're now ready to write a client application. The first example illustrates a simple `helloworld` EJB example to allow us to focus on the details of how to write a client application without the distraction of complex business logic. A bean developer provides a remote home interface (`HelloHome`), a remote component interface (`Hello`), a stateless session bean class (`HelloEJB`), and a deployment descriptor. In this example, a standalone remote client (`HelloClient`) needs to be written. The remote client will use the remote component interface to invoke methods on the SLSB instance. Let's begin with `HelloEJB` as follows:

1. Create the remote home interface—`HelloHome`
2. Create a component interface—`Hello`
3. Create the remote client application, `HelloClient`, using the remote home and component interface to access an existing `HelloBean` running in the container.

Creating the Remote Home Interface

The home interface for a session bean allows clients to create, find, and remove bean instances. The `HelloHome` is a remote home interface for a stateless session bean, `HelloBean`. The `HelloHome` interface extends `EJBHome` and has only one mandatory method, `create`, defined; it returns a remote component interface for the `HelloBean`, `Hello`. It throws the required `RemoteException` and `CreateException`. The listing for `HelloHome.java` follows.

```
HelloHome.java
    import java.io.Serializable;
    import java.rmi.RemoteException;
    import javax.ejb.EJBHome;
    import javax.ejb.CreateException;

    public interface HelloHome extends EJBHome
    {
        public Hello create() throws CreateException, RemoteException;
    }
```

Table 4-1 Rules for Writing Remote and Local Interfaces

Applicable to...	Rule(s)
Both local and remote home interfaces	For every `create` method declared in the home interface, there must be a matching `ejbCreate` method implemented with an `ejb` prefix in the bean class. The matching `create` method must take identical arguments and must throw `javax.ejb.CreateException`. The return type for the `create` method declared in the home interface must be the bean's component interface. For every finder and home business method declared in the home interfaces, there must be matching `ejbFinder` and `ejbHome` methods implemented in the bean class. The matching methods must take identical arguments and must throw `javax.ejg.FinderException`. The return type for these methods must be the bean's component interface or a collection of them.
Both local and remote component interfaces	For every business method declared in the component interface, a matching business method must be implemented in the bean class with exactly the same method name, the same number and types of arguments, and the same return type. All exceptions defined in the `throw` clause of the method in the component interface must match the `throw` clause defined in the matching method in the bean class.
Remote interfaces only (both home and component)	The arguments and return type for methods declared in the remote interfaces must conform to the RMI-IIOP rules and must throw `java.rmi.RemoteException`. Remote calls involve pass-by-value. In cases where a client with the remote interface is invoking methods on container-managed entity beans with the local interface, the remote interface methods must not expose the local home interface or the local component interface to the remote client. In addition, the remote interface must not expose collections of local interfaces and local results to the remote client. Type narrowing of object references with `PortableRemoteObject.narrow(...)` is required.
Remote home interfaces only	All remote home interfaces must extend `javax.ejb.EJBHome` interface.

Table 4-1 Rules for Writing Remote and Local Interfaces (continued)

Applicable to...	Rule(s)
Remote component interfaces only	All remote component interfaces must extend `javax.ejb.EJBOb-ject` interface.
Local interfaces only (both home and component)	Arguments and return values are pass-by-reference in methods declared in local interfaces. Arguments and return types don't have to conform to RMI-IIOP types, and they must not throw `RemoteException`. Methods on local interfaces can be invoked only by clients located in the same JVM.
Local home interfaces only	All local home interfaces must extend the `javax.ejb.EJBLocal-Home` interface.
Local component interfaces only	All local component interfaces must extend `javax.ejb.EJBLo-calObject`.

Creating a Remote Component Interface

A component interface exposes public business methods implemented in the bean class. The remote component interface for the `HelloBean` class is the `Hello.class`. It extends the `EJBObject` interface and defines one business method, `sayHelloEJB`, which takes a single parameter and returns a string. The method throws a required `RemoteException`.

```
Hello.java
    import java.io.Serializable;
    import java.rmi.RemoteException;
    import javax.ejb.EJBObject;

    public interface Hello extends EJBObject
    {
        public String sayHelloEJB(String name) throws RemoteException;
    }
```

Creating a Remote Client Application

Now that you've created the remote home interface, `HelloHome`, and remote component interface, `Hello`, you can now write the remote EJB client application, `HelloClient`. An EJB client must first perform the following tasks:

1. Import both the remote interfaces—`HelloHome` and `Hello`.

2. Use the JNDI lookup() method to locate and download the `HelloHome` object from the network.

3. Narrow the object and cast it to the correct object type—`HelloHome` in this case.

4. Invoke the create () method defined in the `HelloHome` interface to get access to the `EJBObject`.

5. Use the returned `EJBObject` handle to execute the business methods defined in the `Hello` interface.

6. Finally, before exiting, invoke the `remove` () method.

Here's the implementation of the remote client, `HelloClient`:

```
HelloClient.java
import javax.naming.Context;
import javax.naming.InitialContext;
import javax.rmi.PortableRemoteObject;

import Hello;
import HelloHome;

public class HelloClient {

    public static void main(String[] args) {

        try {
    // Statement 0: Set up the initial context and
        Context initctx = new InitialContext();

    //Statement 1: use JNDI lookup for remote home interface
        Object objref =initctx.lookup("java:comp/env/ejb/HomeRef");

    //Step 2 narrow the home interface and then cast to correct type.
        HelloHome helloHome = (HelloHome)PortableRemoteObject.nar-
row(objref, HelloHome.class);

    //Statement 3: now create home object - which returns a
    //Hello, a reference to the EJBObject
        Hello hello = helloHome.create();

    //Statement 4: now execute business method on the component
reference.
        String fromEJB = hello.sayHelloEJB("What's up!");

    // output the results returned from the HelloEJB
        System.out.println("\n\n HelloEJB returned ==>"+fromEJB+"\n\n");

    //Statement 5: done so call remove
        hello.remove();
        } catch (Exception ex) {
            System.err.println("Caught an unexpected exception!");
            ex.printStackTrace();
```

```
        }

    }
}
```

The following is an implementation of the stateless session bean, HelloEJB:

```
HelloEJB.java
/*
 * HelloEJB - a simple SLSB example
 *
 */

import java.rmi.RemoteException;
import javax.ejb.SessionBean;
import javax.ejb.SessionContext;

public class HelloEJB implements SessionBean
{

    private javax.ejb.SessionContext m_ctx = null;

// call back methods
    public void setSessionContext(javax.ejb.SessionContext ctx)
    {
        m_ctx = ctx;
    }

// empty call back methods.
    public void ejbRemove()
    {
    System.out.println("*** HelloEJB -- ejbRemove() called --");
    }

    public void ejbActivate()
    {
    System.out.println("*** HelloEJB -- ejbActivate() called --");
    }

    public void ejbPassivate()
    {
    System.out.println("*** HelloEJB -- ejbPassivate() called --");
    }

    public HelloEJB()
    {
    System.out.println("*** HelloEJB -- HelloEJB() called --");
    }
```

```
public void ejbCreate()
{
System.out.println("*** HelloEJB -- ejbCreate() called --");
}

//business method ----------
public String sayHelloEJB(String name)
{
    System.out.println("*** HelloEJB -- sayHelloEJB() called --
");
    String theString = "From HelloEJB --\n HelloClient's request
"+name+"\n and HelloEJB's response:\n"+msg;
    return theString;
}

} //;-)
```

Compiling and Executing `HelloWorld`

To compile `Hello.java`, `HelloHome.java` and `HelloEJB.java`, ensure that the computing environment has J2SE 1.3 and J2SDKEE 1.3 installed correctly. (You can find the installation steps in the Appendix to this book.) It's fairly simple to compile these programs once the correct path to the libraries is identified. Change the directory to APPHOME\chapter4 and execute the compileHello batchfile, which will generate the `HelloHome.class`, `Hello.class`, and `HelloEJB.class` files.

Once the Hello application is compiled, you'll need to package the application and then deploy it. To compile `HelloClient`, execute the `compileClient` batchfile, which will generate the `HelloClient.class` file.

Packaging the `HelloWorld` Application

Once you've started the J2EE server and the deployment tool (explained in the Appendix), you can deploy the application.

1. On the deployment tool GUI, select File | New | Application as shown in Figure 4-9.

2. When the New Application menu appears, click the Browse button and choose the directory where the compiled classes are located. (APPHOME\chapter4).

3. Then enter `HelloApp.ear` in the File name box and click the New Application button.

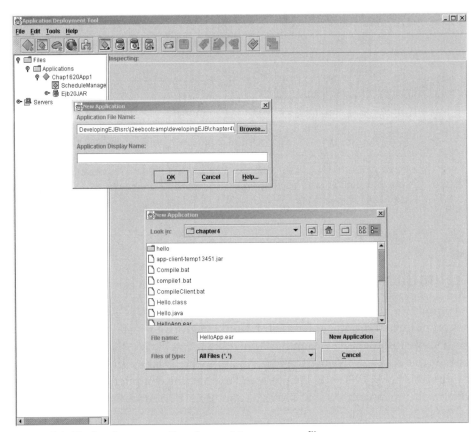

Figure 4-9 Packaging—creating the `HelloApp.ear` file

4. Click OK (as shown in Figure 4-10). The deployment tool creates the `HelloApp` under the Files icon. The `HelloApp.ear` will hold the EJB and client jar files.

Packaging the Files

Now, package the `Hello.class`, `HelloHome.class` and `HelloEJB.class` into ejb-jar file.

1. To create a jar file, select File | New | Enterprise Bean. The New Enterprise Bean Wizard window should appear, which will help you create the ejb-jar file.

2. Click the Next button. The wizard displays an EJB JAR option. Make sure that the Create New JAR File in Application radio button is selected. The pull-down menu will display `HelloApp`.

3. Enter `HelloJAR` under the Jar Display Name and then click the Edit button, which causes another Edit Contents of `HelloJAR` window to pop up.

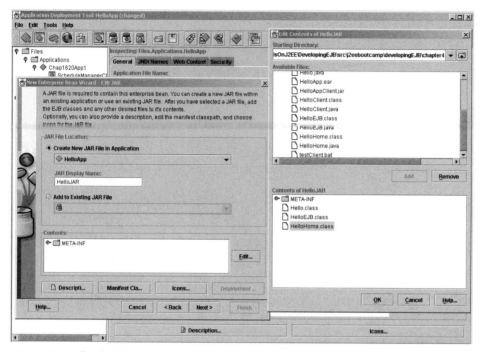

Figure 4-10 Packaging—creating a `HelloJAR` file to package the Hello bean

4. In the Edit Contents of `HelloJAR` window, make sure that Starting Directory points to …\chapter4, and then click the Add button to select `Hello.class`, `HelloHome.class`, and `HelloEJB.class`. They should be displayed in the Content of the `HelloJAR` sub-window.

5. Click OK. The result is depicted in Figure 4-10.

You've now added the necessary class files to ejb-jar file. Next, you must declare the name of the home and component interface, the bean class name, and the type of bean for the deployment descriptor.

6. Click the Next> button to display the General pop-up window.

7. Click the Session radio button and then the Stateless radio button under Bean Type.

8. Use the pull-down menu under the Enterprise Bean class: label and select `HelloEJB`. Leave `HelloEJB` under the Enterprise Bean Name: label.

9. In the lower-right section of the window, use the pull-down menu to select `HelloHome` under the Remote Home Interface: label and Hello under the Remote Interface: label, as shown in Figure 4-12.

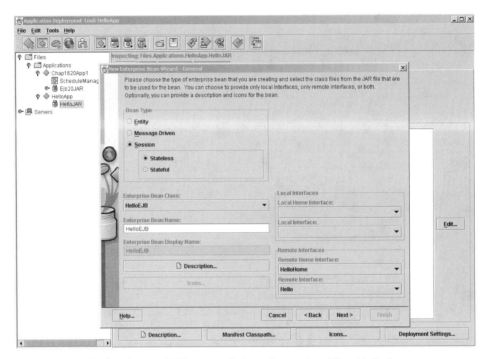

Figure 4-11 Packaging an EJB—specifying elements of the Hello bean

10. You've finished declaring the type of the bean, the name of the bean class, and its remote home and component interfaces. Click the Next> button and then the Finish button.

The EJB application is now packaged, and the following deployment descriptor has been created. Note the <home>, <remote>, and <ejb-class> elements that define the HelloHome, Hello, and HelloEJB elements of the Enterprise JavaBeans. Also notice the <session-type> element that designates this bean as a stateless session bean.

```
<?xml version="1.0" encoding="UTF-8"?>

<!DOCTYPE ejb-jar PUBLIC '-//Sun Microsystems, Inc.//DTD Enterprise
JavaBeans 2.0//EN' 'http://java.sun.com/dtd/ejb-jar_2_0.dtd'>

<ejb-jar>
  <display-name>HelloJAR</display-name>
  <enterprise-beans>
    <session>
```

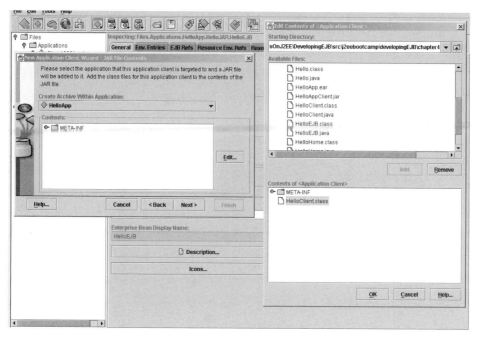

Figure 4-12 Packaging a client—adding `HelloClient.class`

```
      <display -name>HelloEJB</display-name>
      <ejb-name>HelloEJB</ejb-name>
      <home>HelloHome</home>
      <remote>Hello</remote>
      <ejb-class>HelloEJB</ejb-class>
      <session-type>Stateless</session-type>
      <transaction-type>Bean</transaction-type>
      <security-identity>
        <description></description>
        <use-caller-identity></use-caller-identity>
      </security-identity>
    </session>
  </enterprise-beans>
</ejb-jar>
```

Packaging the Client: `HelloClient`

Next, you need to package the client, `HelloClient`, which is a much simpler
process.

1.   Select File I New I Application Client. A New Application Client Wizard
     should appear.

2. Click the Next button and make sure that `HelloApp` appears under the Create Archive Within Application label. Click the Edit button.

3. Make sure that the Starting Directory label points to APPHOME\chapter4, and then click the Add button to select `HelloClient.class` from the Available Files subwindow. It should appear in the contents of the <Application Client> subwindow, as shown in Figure 4-12. Click OK.

4. You still need to let the client know how to access the `HelloEJB`, so click the Next> button three times. The Enterprise Bean Reference wizard window should appear.

5. Click the Add button, and in the Coded Name area, enter **ejb/HelloRef** under the Home Interface label and **HelloHome** under the Local/Remote Interface label.

6. Use the pull-down menu to select Session under the Type label and Remote under the Interface label.

7. Click the Enterprise Bean Name radio button, and then enter **HelloEJB** as shown in Figure 4-13.

8. Click the Finish button.

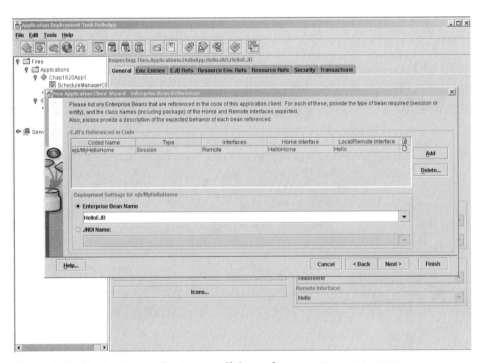

Figure 4-13 Packaging a client—specifying references to `HelloEJB`

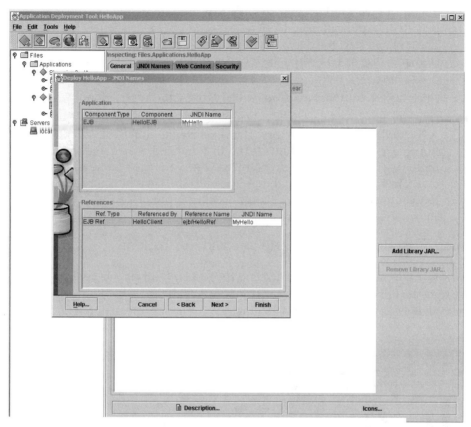

Figure 4-14 Deployment—specifying the JNDI name

Now you're ready to deploy the `HelloApp.ear` application.

1.   First, ensure that `HelloApp` is highlighted under the Files icon in the deployment GUI.

2.   Under Tools in the deployment GUI, click Deploy; the Deploy `HelloApp` window should appear. Make sure that `HelloApp` is displayed under the Object to Deploy: label and that localhost (or your host name) appears under the Target Server label.

3.   Checkmark the Return Client Jar option and browse to select the desired directory. It should save the `HelloAppClient.jar` file in your `..\chapter4` directory by default.

4.   Click the Next> button.

5. You must give a JNDI name, so enter **MyHello** under the JNDI Name label in both the Application and Reference sections. Then click the Finish button. The tool will start the deployment process, and you should see the output shown in Figure 4-14 when the tool has successfully deployed the `HelloApp.ear` file.

6. Click the OK button. Now you're ready to test the application.

7. Open a command window to execute the client and go to the APPHOME\chapter4 directory. Then execute the **runclient –client HelloApp.ear –class HelloClient –textauth** command. When you're prompted for the username/password, enter **j2ee/j2ee** (your site's name and password may vary), and you should the see the output shown in Figure 4-16. In the j2ee command window, you should see the output of the `HelloEJB` bean as shown in Figure 4-17.

Interaction Between `HelloClient` and `HelloBean`

Now that the client code is compiled and the `HelloBean` class is deployed, let us see how the EJB client, `HelloClient`, interacts with the `HelloBean` instance in the container as follows. Figure 4-18 illustrates a client's interaction with an EJB

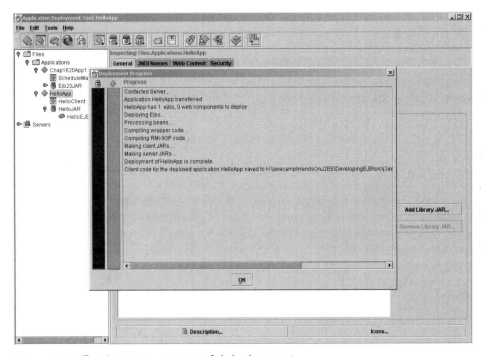

Figure 4-15 Deployment—successful deployment

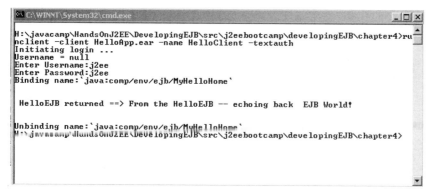

Figure 4-16 Output of `HelloClient`

Figure 4-17 Output of the `HelloEJB` instance

instance, `HelloEJB`. We will refer to this figure and the `HelloClient` source
code to explain the interaction.

The standalone Java client, `HelloClient`, must create a context object using
the `InitialContext()` method. This is shown by `statement 0` in the
`HelloClient` source code.

The client then uses the context object to find the `HelloHome` object by its name,
`MyHelloHome`. This is accomplished by the `lookup("java:comp/env/ejb`
`/HomeRef` in statement 2 in the client code and illustrated by action 1 in Figure 4-18.

Once the client retrieves the `HelloHome` object, it narrows the object using the
`PortableRemoteObject.narrow()` method and casts it to the remote home

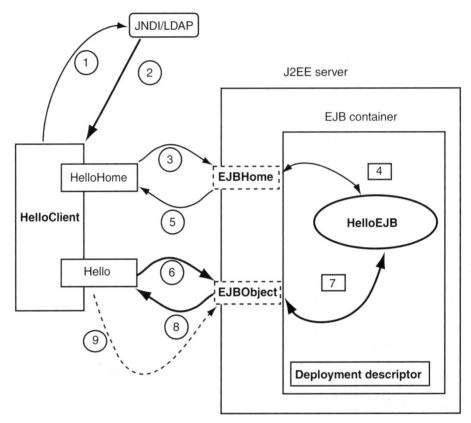

Figure 4-18 Client view and the interaction between a client and an EJB instance

object type. The statement 3 of the client code corresponds to this step and is illustrated by action 3 in the figure.

The container where the `HelloEJB` is deployed is transparent to the client. The client now has the remote home object and executes the `create()` method. The `create()` request is marshaled and sent to the `EJBHome` proxy at the EJB container. Depending on whether the security requirements have been met, the container will create an `EJBObject` instance, assign a `HelloEJB` instance to it, and return a reference to `EJBObject` back to the client. This is indicated by arrows 3, 4, and 5 in the figure and by statement 3 in the client code.

Note the container returns `Hello` object as a reference to the `EJBObject` back to the remote client.

The client now has the reference and uses the business method, `sayHelloEJB(String str)`, defined in the remote component interface, `Hello`. The client calls `sayHelloEJB("EJB World!")` on the remote component interface, `Hello`, which is sent to the `EJBObject` at the container. The `EJBObject` delegates the request to the `HelloEJB` instance where the concrete method, `sayHelloEJB()` is executed and the result is returned to the `EJBObject`, which then returns the result back to the client. The client's request and the EJB instance's response are marshaled and un-marshaled by the client and the container. This is depicted by arrows 6, 7, and 8 in the figure and statement 4 in the client code. Steps 6, 7, and 8 can be repeated until the client is complete.

Before exiting, the client calls the remove method to inform the EJB container that it no longer needs the `HelloBean` instance. This is depicted by arrow 9 in the figure and statement 5 in the client code. The reference to `EJBObject` is removed by the container. Note that removal of the bean instance is at the container's discretion.

Using the Local or the Remote Interface

The decision of whether to use the local or the remote interface when developing EJB applications depends on the application design and deployment environment. In summary, you should use the remote interface when an EJB needs location transparency, coarse-grained component access, and loose coupling. Use local interface when an EJB requires speed, tighter coupling and fine-grained component access. In reality, your application will use a combination of EJBs with remote and local interfaces depending on the business logic design and application requirements. We will discuss design issues in Chapter 16.

Application Performance

To optimize performance (frequently an issue with distributed software applications), consider the following to reduce network traffic, localize calls, and reduce making remote methods calls:

- Keep remote calls granular. For example, instead of executing individual setter methods for street, city, and zip from a client, use a single method for all.

- Consider using design patterns such as the value object and value list handler when passing data from server to a client. (J2EE design patterns and performance are discussed further in Chapter 16.)

- The EJB2.0 specification has added local home and component interfaces for fast, lightweight access from a local client to a bean instance co-located in the same JVM.

Summary

In this chapter, we discussed that EJBs depend on RMI-IIOP protocol to enable EJB instances to interact with other Java and non-Java objects on the network. The EJB clients rely on JNDI to easily locate distributed EJBs instances on the network by using names.

Developers have a choice between remote and local interfaces and should choose the one that best satisfies their business requirements. Remote interfaces are ideal for course-grained business logic and when the ability to distribute the EJBs takes precedence. Local interfaces are appropriate for implementing fine-grained business logic with tightly coupled entity beans where there is no need to separate and distribute these tightly coupled entity beans in different containers.

We'll look at session beans in depth in the next chapter.

INTRODUCTION TO SESSION BEANS

Topics in This Chapter

- Session Bean Characteristics
- Types of Session Beans
- Session Bean Elements
- Writing Session Beans: Rules and Requirements
- Roles of the Deployment Tool in Implementing Session Beans
- Packaging a Session Bean
- Deployment

Chapter 5

In Chapter 4, we discussed the client view of Enterprise JavaBeans and both local and remote interfaces. This chapter examines session bean APIs without getting into specific-coding-level detail, which is a topic we cover in Chapters 6 and 7. We do, however, cover the following subject matter here:

- types of session beans and their characteristics
- session bean APIs
- rules and requirements for writing local and remote interfaces for session beans
- rules and requirements for writing sessions, business methods, and `ejbCreate` methods
- session bean deployment descriptors and packaging
- choosing between the use of stateless and stateful session beans

Session Bean Characteristics

The architects of EJB have devised different types of EJB to satisfy varying business requirements. Specifically, session beans are designed to model rules, workflow processes, and control processes that are common in business—for example, purchase authorization, payment processing, stock quote lookup, or customer order fulfillment. Session beans are also used for coordinating processes and interaction between objects, such as interaction among several entity beans.

Session beans are transient and have relatively short lifespans. A session bean exists within a container to service a client, enabling a session bean to function as a remote extension of a client. As such, the client controls the lifespan of the session bean. In effect, the lifetime of a session bean instance is equivalent to the client's session lifespan. When the client's session ends, the container automatically removes the reference to the session bean's instance. For example, when a customer interacting with a session bean instance logs off from the application, the session bean instance is automatically removed by the container. Alternatively, a client can explicitly request that the container remove the reference to a session bean instance.

Session beans are transient; they're in-memory objects that don't survive a container or server crash. Although session beans are inherently nonpersistent—they don't represent data in the database—they can read and write to the database nonetheless.

A session bean instance cannot be shared among clients. At any given instance, a session bean interacts with only one client at a time, and the container serializes all method calls to the bean instance.

Session beans are *transaction aware,* which means that they can participate and control transactions only when transaction APIs are programmatically implemented.

Session beans are typically used for modeling business processes or control logic that interacts with multiple EJB, especially entity beans. Note that in object-oriented analysis and design phraseology, session beans are generally used for modeling "verbs."

Types of Session Beans

There are two types of session beans: stateless and stateful. A *state* consists of client- and business logic-related information saved in memory by a session bean instance during method invocation; this information may be used in subsequent invocations. For example, to determine applicable sales tax, an EJB component's first method might retrieve a customer's state, county, and city information. The second method might then use this information to retrieve applicable tax rates, and the third method might apply the taxes to the purchase price and return the total amount to the client to be displayed to the customer. The state, county, and city data and their corresponding tax rate information are state-related information and need to be available so that subsequent methods can execute successfully.

Stateless Session Beans (SLSB)

Stateless session beans don't maintain state information between method invocations, so all the necessary arguments must be passed during a method invocation. In another words, a stateless session bean executes a request and returns a result without saving any client-specifc state information. Note that stateless session beans can have an internal state (for example, bean-specific instance variables, such as the references to a data source or connection pool). They also can hold a reference to a database that's maintained during method invocation but that is neither part of the business logic nor is visible to the client.

Because stateless session beans don't maintain state, they're similar to HTTP requests. Stateless session beans are generally fast and efficient and ideal for modeling business processes when the parameters to execute the business logic can be passed in a single method call. A good example of a stateless session bean implementation is a stock quote lookup application. Three or four letters representing a stock symbol are passed as a parameter to a method call. The method in a stateless session bean then executes the applicable business logic and returns the current stock price. Online credit card processing components are also good examples of when to use stateless session beans. On an e-commerce site, a customer makes a credit card payment by filling out an HTML form with a credit card number, the issuer's name, the expiration date, and the owner's name and address. Once the form is submitted, the information entered into the HTML form is passed to a method in a credit card verification stateless session bean. This bean follows specific business rules and executes the credit card processing logic. Stateless session beans can also be used to provide database search logic for nontransactional read-only data.

Stateful Session Beans (SFSB)

In contrast, stateful session beans do maintain state between method invocations and are therefore referred to as *conversational*. Stateful session beans maintain client information between method invocations and so are well suited for business processes that require ongoing conversations between the client and the stateful session bean instance to complete the business task. The shopping cart on e-commerce sites is a good example of a stateful session bean implementation. The shopping cart maintains a list of items while the online customer shops, and it calculates the total price when the customer checks out. The stateful session bean modeling the shopping cart uses state to keep track of items added to the cart during the conversation with the client. A stateful session bean can also be used to coordinate processes between entity beans. For example, a business logic in a stateful bean might depend on several different entity beans to return persistent data.

Although both stateful and stateless beans implement the same interface, `javax.ejb.SessionBean`, they have different life cycles and characteristics and are designed to model different types of business processes. Processes that typically require several sequenced interdependent steps to complete a business task (depending upon the process policies) are generally well suited for stateful session beans.

Session Bean Elements

From a Bean developer's perspective, the only difference between implementing stateful session beans and stateless session beans is the type of business logic employed. In consequence, developers are required to provide the following session bean elements:

- session bean implementation class
- remote or local component interface
- remote or local home interface
- deployment descriptor
- optional helper class

Figure 5-1 illustrates the session bean and its key elements.

The Session Bean Implementation Class

All session bean classes are required to implement the `javax.ejb.SessionBean` interface. The `javax.ejb.SessionBean` interface extends EJB superinterface `javax.ejb.EnterpriseBean`, which in turn extends `java.io.Serializable`. Both `EnterpriseBean` and `Serializable` interfaces are *marker interfaces* that declare no methods or fields. The class hierarchy of the SessionBean and the SessionContext interfaces are illustrated in Figure 5-2 and the EnterpriseBean and EJBContext interfaces are common to all EJBs.

The `SessionBean` interface provides several life cycle management methods, including the `javax.ejb.SessionContext` interface; the container implicitly provides the session bean instance. Figure 5-1 depicts the methods provided by a `SessionBean` interface and those provided by `SessionContext` interface.

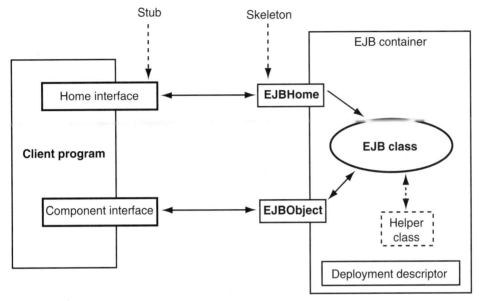

Figure 5-1 Elements of a session bean

SessionBean Interface

A session bean class encapsulates the implementation details of the business logic and algorithm necessary to complete specific business processes. A *bean provider* (a bean developer or a vendor that sells prebuilt EJBs for third parties) is required to implement the `javax.ejb.SessionBean` interface for both stateless and stateful session beans. The `SessionBean` interface, in turn, extends the `javax.ejb.EnterpriseBean`, a base EJB interface. The `EnterpriseBean` interface is a marker interface (an empty interface that has no methods declared) and extends the `java.io.Serializable` interface, thus enabling serialization of session objects.

To understand session beans better, let's examine the `SessionBean` interface in the code that follows. Notice that it declares four methods and extends the `EnterpriseBean` interface. These methods are also referred to as *callback methods* because the container automatically calls them as needed to manage the session bean instance life cycle.

```
public interface javax.ejb.SessionBean extends EnterpriseBean {
    public void ejbSessionContext(SessionContext ctx)
throws EJBException, RemoteException;
    public void ejbActivate() throws EJBException, RemoteException;
    public interface javax.ejb.SessionBean extends EnterpriseBean {
```

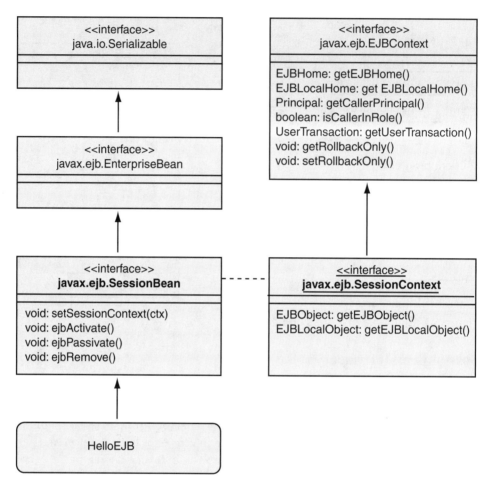

Figure 5-2 SessionBean class hierarchy

```
public void ejbSessionContext(SessionContext ctx)
   throws EJBException, RemoteException
public void ejbActivate()throws EJBException, RemoteException;
public void ejbPassivate()throws EJBException, RemoteException;
public void ejbRemove()throws EJBException, RemoteException;
}
```

The SessionBean interface defines several callback methods, including setSessionContext(),ejbActivate(),ejbPassivate(),and ejbRemove(). Using callback methods, the container provides the infrastructure and manages the life cycle of the session bean instance. Prior to executing a particular life cycle management action, callback methods defined in the SessionBean interface are automatically called by the container to inform the session bean instance of the impending action. A discussion of these methods follows.

The setSessionContext() method associates the bean instance to the container session context; setSessionContext() is called when the session bean instance is initially created. It passes a SessionContext interface as a parameter. Note that the session context is valid throughout the lifespan of the session bean instance.

The container manages the system resources. For example, when the system is low on memory, the container can take session instances from memory, serialize them, and save them to secondary storage. This process is called *passivation*. The container can later de-serialize the session bean from the secondary storage and recreate the session object in memory. This process is known as *activation*. The use of passivation and activation are similar to operating system *swapping*. The ejbPassivate() method is called before passivation occurs; ejbActivate() is called after activation. Note that a container cannot remove or passivate a bean instance in the middle of a business method transaction. To remove the session instance from the container, the ejbRemove() method is called. The session instance may be removed when the client calls the remove method or when the container needs system resources.

I should clarify that it's the container that creates, passivates, activates, and removes the bean instance. Think of callback methods as notices from the container to the bean instance concerning impending container action. This enables the use of ejbPassivate() and ejbActivate() to write and read information to the database and the use of ejbRemove() to close database and network connections.

Note: ejbPassivate() and ejbActivate() are callback methods and called throughout the bean's life cycle. On the other hand, setSessionContext(arg) and ejbRemove() methods are called only once in a bean's lifetime. The setSessionContext() method is called when the bean is first created, and ejbRemove() is called when the bean is removed.

SessionContext Interface

As part of the process of creating a session bean instance, the container creates and passes a SessionContext interface to the session bean instance. The SessionContext interface gives the session bean instance in the container access to the runtime session context. The session context remains associated with the bean instance throughout its lifetime. The SessionContext interface methods—getEJBObject() and getEJBLocalObject()—return EJBObject and EJBLocalObject, respectively, and throw an IllegalStateException if they encounter an error.

The `SessionContext` interface extends the `EJBContext` interface. The `EJBContext` interface contains interface access, security, and transaction-related methods (see Figure 5-2). The `getEJBObject()` and `getEJBHome()` methods return the session bean's remote component and home interface. Similarly, `getEJBLocalObject` and `getEJBLocalHome` return the session bean's local component and home interfaces.

A detailed discussion on security and transaction appears in Chapters 14 and 15, respectively. In general, to identify the client invoking the bean instance's EJB object, use the `getCallerPrincipal()` method. To test if the bean instance caller has a particular role, use the `CallerInRole()` method.

Normally, the `setRollbackOnly` method forces the transaction outcome to *rollback* (meaning that all changes previously made are undone), while the `getRollbackOnly` method determines whether the transaction is marked for rollback. Both of these methods apply to container-managed transaction session beans. Finally, the `getUserTransaction` method returns the `javax.transaction.UserTransaction` interface that's used to obtain the transaction status.

Helper Classes

The helper class is an external Java program that helps EJBs complete a business task by performing low-level functions; one example might be a Java program that enables database access using the JDBC calls for the session bean. Although helper classes are not mandated by the EJB specification, using them makes it possible to separate low-level detail from business logic, and this separation encourages reusability of the session bean.

Deployment Descriptor

A deployment descriptor is an XML document that contains information describing the EJBs' management, life-cycle, home and component interfaces, class name, bean type, persistence, and transaction and security requirements. The EJB container can read the deployment descriptor information at runtime and use it to manage the life cycle and services of the EJB instances. The deployment descriptor file is included when the ejb-jar file is packaged. A deployment descriptor contains two basic kinds of information—structural information and application assembly information.

Structural information describes the structure of the EJB and declares its external dependencies. The bean developer is responsible for initially providing the structural information in the deployment descriptor, and the EJB's structural information cannot be changed without breaking its functionality. The structural information describes the EJB's home and component interfaces, class names, management fields, life cycle requirements, and persistence requirements, depending on the type of EJB. For example, it can specify the EJB's class name, its home and component interface name, bean type, session management type, and so on.

Application assembly information describes the transaction and security requirements and how the EJBs in the ejb-jar file are assembled into a larger deployable application unit. For example, it might describe the security roles, method permission, or transaction attributes of the EJB. The bean developer is not required to provide the application assembly information, which is therefore optional. The developer should provide pertinent information, however, to aid the application assembler and the deployer in their respective tasks.

The content of the deployment descriptor in XML format must conform to the rule specified in the data type definition (DTD), which is available at http://java.sun.com/dtd/ejb-jar_2_0.dtd. This standard deployment descriptor must be supported by all J2EE-compliant application servers. In addition to the standard deployment descriptor, there is a vendor-specific deployment descriptor whose DTDs are defined by the individual vendor. The vendor-specific descriptor specifies proprietary features of the application server that aren't critical to the functioning of the EJBs.

Because both stateless and stateful session beans implement the same `javax.ejb.SessionBean` interface, the container differentiates between the two with the help of a deployment descriptor file. A bean developer must provide a deployment descriptor with the bean component and explicitly specify the bean persistence, transaction, and security requirements using XML syntax. (For those with a Visual Basic background, a deployment descriptor file is similar to a property sheet; for those with a UNIX shell programming background, it's similar to a configuration file like .cshrc.) The container reads the deployment descriptor file during execution and uses it to manage EJB instances.

A developer must declare the mandatory structural information for the session bean—names and paths of the home and remote interfaces and the session bean class and life cycle management parameters, such as whether or not the session bean is stateless or stateful. An assembler or a deployer can later modify the application assembly information in the deployment descriptor files.

The standard J2EE deployment descriptor shown in Example 5-1, `ejb-jar.xml`, is from the `hello world` example in Chapter 4. Notice the `<ejb-jar>` element that encloses the rest of the element and the structural information enclosed by the `<home>`, `<remote>`, and `<ejb-class>` elements that declare `HelloHome` as the remote home interface, `Hello` as the remote component interface, and

HelloEJB as the bean class. The <session-type> element encloses stateless, indicating the type of session bean to the container.

In Example 5-1, the <transaction-type> element indicates that the transaction is bean managed and <security-identity> elements are left empty. All of these elements are enclosed by the <session> element, which identifies the bean type as a session bean. The <ejb-name> element can enclose any arbitrary name, a feature that enables the bean developer to provide a level of indirection to the bean class (HelloEJB) that is specified by the <ejb-class> element. There must be a unique name in the ejb-jar file that maps to the HelloEJB bean. Clients can reference HelloWorldEJB and it will be able to access the HelloEJB class; if, in the future, the HelloEJB bean class is replaced by a new and improved NewHelloEJB bean class, the client will be immune to the changes because the client still references HelloWorldEJB. The session is enclosed by <enterprise-beans> element. This is a simple deployment descriptor file; we'll discuss more complex deployment descriptors as we present more challenging EJB applications.

Example 5-1 The deployment descriptor file ejb-jar.xml

```
<?xml version="1.0" encoding="UTF-8"?>
<!DOCTYPE ejb-jar PUBLIC '-//Sun Microsystems, Inc.//DTD Enterprise
JavaBeans 2.0//EN' 'http://java.sun.com/dtd/ejb-jar_2_0.dtd'>

<ejb-jar>
  <display-name>HelloEJBJAR</display-name>
  <enterprise-beans>
    <session>
      <display-name>HelloWorldEJB</display-name>
      <ejb-name>HelloWorldEJB</ejb-name>
      <home>HelloHome</home>
      <remote>Hello</remote>
      <ejb-class>HelloEJB</ejb-class>
      <session-type>Stateless</session-type>
      <transaction-type>Bean</transaction-type>
      <security-identity>
        <description></description>
        <use-caller-identity></use-caller-identity>
      </security-identity>
    </session>
  </enterprise-beans>
</ejb-jar>
```

So far, whenever we have discussed deployment descriptors, we have implied the standard J2EE deployment descriptor that conforms to the DTD at http://java.sun.com/dtd/ejb-jar_2_0.dtd. There is, however, a second vendor-specific deployment descriptor. Remember, one of the goals of EJB 2.0 was to make EJBs portable across different vendors' product lines while still allowing individual vendors to implement value-added features. The standard J2EE deployment descriptor, when packaged with a vendor-specific deployment descriptor, enables EJBs to be both portable and able to take advantage of vendor-specific features. The vendor-specific deployment descriptor usually has a vendor name prefix to differentiate it from the standard deployment descriptor. Because we are using Sun's Java 2.0 Software Development Kit, Enterprise Edition 1.3 Reference Implementation (J2SDKEE 1.3 RI), the deployment descriptor file is named sun-j2ee-ri.xml.

In Example 5-2, Sun's J2SDKEE RI references the implementation-specific deployment descriptor file, sun-j2ee-ri.xml. This deployment descriptor has quite a few elements, most of which I will ignore because they aren't immediately pertinent. Here, I'll focus on some key elements. Notice that the DTD line points to the file sun-j2ee-ri_1_3.dtd, indicating that this deployment descriptor is vendor specific. The <jndi-name> element with java:comp/env/ejb/HelloRef actually maps to the HelloWorldEJB class enclosed by the <ejb-name> element, and the HelloWordEJB object references the HelloEJB in the ejb-jar.xml file. If you recall from Chapter 4, the HelloClient client application performed a JNDI look up for java:comp/emv/ejb/HelloRef, which maps to the <jndi-name> element in this deployment descriptor and is thus able to execute the sayHelloEJB() method on the HelloEJB stateless session bean instance.

We mentioned earlier that the deployment tool creates concrete classes during deployment based on the EJB classes. The <gen-classes> element includes two elements: the <remote-home-impl> element, which encloses HelloHome_RemoteHomeImpl, and the <remote-impl> element, which encloses HelloEJB_EJBObjectImpl. These two classes are generated by Sun's J2SDKEE 1.3 RI deployment tool and container. We are using them to emphasize that these elements and generated classes in vendor-specific deployment descriptors can vary widely among vendors.

In most cases, bean developers have to deal with only the standard J2EE deployment descriptor. The application deployer, on the other hand, will need to customize the standard deployment descriptor—and especially the vendor's deployment descriptor—to optimize the application settings so they can benefit from the specific application server. Because the bean developer, assembler, and deployer work with a GUI deployment tool, it's not always apparent which of the deployment descriptors is being modified.

Example 5-2   The sun-j2ee-ri.xml file

```
<?xml version="1.0" encoding="UTF-8"?>
<!DOCTYPE j2ee-ri-specific-information PUBLIC '-//Sun Microsystems
Inc.//DTD J2EE Reference Implementation 1.3//EN' 'http://local-
host:8000/sun-j2ee-ri_1_3.dtd'>
<j2ee-ri-specific-information>
  <server-name></server-name>
  <rolemapping />
  <enterprise-beans>
    <module-name>ejb-jar-ic.jar</module-name>
    <unique-id>-2032273522</unique-id>
    <ejb>
      <ejb-name>HelloWorldEJB</ejb-name>
      <jndi-name>java:comp/env/ejb/MyHelloHome</jndi-name>
      <ior-security-config>
        <transport-config>
          <integrity>supported</integrity>
          <confidentiality>supported</confidentiality>
          <establish-trust-in-target>supported</establish-trust-in-
target>
          <establish-trust-in-client>supported</establish-trust-in-
client>
        </transport-config>
        <as-context>
          <auth-method>username_password</auth-method>
          <realm>default</realm>
          <required>true</required>
        </as-context>
        <sas-context>
          <caller-propagation>supported</caller-propagation>
        </sas-context>
      </ior-security-config>
      <gen-classes>
        <remote-home-impl>HelloHome_RemoteHomeImpl</remote-home-
impl>
        <remote-impl>HelloEJB_EJBObjectImpl</remote-impl>
      </gen-classes>
    </ejb>
  </enterprise-beans>
</j2ee-ri-specific-information>
```

Writing Session Beans: Rules and Requirements

To write session beans correctly, Bean developers must follow certain rules and requirements necessary for implementing session beans. We will now discuss the rules and requirements on writing session bean class `ejbCreate` and business methods.

Rules and Requirements for Writing Session Bean Classes

A session bean class must be declared `public`. It must have a public constructor that takes no parameter and that is used by the container to create instances of session bean class. Session bean classes must implement one or more `ejbCreate` methods, and there must be one default `ejbCreate` method that takes no argument—for example, the `ejbCreate()` method.

Session bean classes may implement the `javax.ejb.SessionSynchronization` interface to participate in transactions programmatically. Session bean classes may also implement a session bean's remote component interface but are strongly discouraged from doing so because no real benefit results, and one could accidentally pass `this` (referring to the current object) as a method argument or result in a potential remote method call to distributed objects, and "this" references a local JVM, which results in an error.

Session beans can consist of zero or more business methods and can invoke other methods in helper classes besides the callback methods declared by the bean class. Business methods, `ejbCreate` methods, the `SessionBean` interface, and the `SessionSynchronization` interface can be defined in the session bean class or any of its superclasses. This makes it possible for a developer to buy off-the-shelf session beans, subclass them, and add new functionality to meet a business' requirements.

Session bean class must not be defined as `final` or `abstract` because these designations conflict with the container's ability to extend the bean class to create other proprietary support classes during deployment phase. Declaring session bean class as `final`, then, means that the container cannot extend the session bean class. The container manages the life cycle, the threads, and garbage collection tasks, so session bean class must not define the `finalize()` method, as it would interfere with the container's responsibility.

Rules for Writing `ejbCreate<Method>(...)` Methods

In the process of instantiating a session bean instance, the container invokes the `newInstance()` method, followed by `setSessionContext()` and then `ejbCreate()`. Developers must follow certain rules when writing `ejbCreate<METHOD>`.

A session bean class must define one or more `create` methods. If only one `create` method is defined, it must be a default, no-argument method—`ejbCreate()`. The `ejbCreate` methods must be `public`, the return type must be `void`, and the method arguments must conform to RMI-IIOP standards for remote interfaces.

For every `create` method declared in the session bean's home interface, there must be a matching `ejbCreate` method with a mandatory `ejb` prefix implemented in the session bean class with identical arguments. For example, if the bean developer declares a `createPlatinumLevel(id, preferences, maxLimit)` `create` method in the home interface, there must be an implementation of the `ejbCreatePlatinumLevel(int id, List preferences, double maxLimit) {...}` method in the bean class. Note the addition of `ejb` and the capitalization of the letter `C` in the method name `createPlatinumLevel(..)`. The create method must throw `javax.ejb.CreateException` in addition to any arbitrary application exception.

The `ejbCreate` methods must not be declared `final` or `static`, because doing so would cause them to conflict with the container's ability to create concrete class at deployment phase. The create methods must not throw `java.rmi.RemoteException`.

Rules for Writing Business Methods

Developers use business methods to encapsulate business logic in their applications, and these methods also require that certain rules be followed. A session bean can declare zero or more business methods. For every business method declared in the session bean's component interface, there must be an identical business method implemented in the bean class. The business methods must be declared `public` and can have any arbitrary name. The arguments and return value type of the business methods declared in the remote component interface must conform to RMI-IIOP standards, and the throw clause may define arbitrary application exceptions.

Even though business methods may have arbitrary names, they must not begin with the `ejb` prefix, which could cause conflicts with `SessionBean`'s callback methods used by the container. The business methods must not be declared as `final` or `static` and must not throw a `java.rmi.RemoteException`, but may throw any application-specific exceptions.

Roles of the Deployment Tool in Implementing Session Beans

An EJB container transparently provides transaction and security management, network distribution of remote clients, and management of resources for EJBs. The fact that the business logic implementation is separate from the low-level infrastructure service implementation enhances the portability of EJBs and makes the EJBs independent of container implementation. This implicit separation between EJB and container also means that the concrete infrastructure service classes must be created at deployment time. The container/deployment tools must generate the necessary classes to implement these services.

Let's take the `HelloEJB` example from Chapter 4 to illustrate the responsibilities of the container:

- The container implements the developer-provided session bean and its remote home and component interfaces and generates the `EJBHome` concrete class that implements the session bean's remote home interface. In our `HelloEJB` example, the deployment tool implements the methods of the `EJBHome` interface and the `create` method declared in the `HelloHome` remote interface. So when the `create` method is invoked on `HelloHome`, the matching `ejbCreate()` method is executed in the `HelloEJB` bean class.

- The `EJBObject` class implements the session bean's remote component interface. In our example, the deployment tool implements all the methods in `jaax.ejb.EJBObject` and the business methods declared in the `HelloEJB`'s remote component interface, `Hello`. As a result, when the `HelloEJB` method is invoked on the `Hello` interface, it activates the `sayHelloEJB()` method in the `HelloEJB` instance.

- The deployment tool implements the `Handle` and `HomeHandle` classes for the session bean's remote home and remote component interfaces.

- The deployment tool is also responsible for implementing the `EJBMetaData` class for the remote home interface. The metadata information is intended primarily for use by the GUI development tools.

- The container must implement the `SessionContext.getEJBObject()` method so that the session bean instance can access the runtime session context provided by the container.

- The deployment tool also must implement the local home or remote home interface at deployment time. But the bean developer must implement the `javax.ejb.EJBLocalObject` as the local home interface and `EJBLocalObject` as the local component interface.

- The container must also provide services such as the enforcement of a single-threaded model and transaction, security, and exception support.

Table 5-1 summarizes the elements of the `Hello` session bean that a bean developer must provide and the corresponding elements provided by the deployment tool during deployment.

Table 5-1 Deployment-Time Session Bean Elements Provided by Developers and Generated by the J2SDKEE 1.3 Deploytool

Session Bean Element	Local or Remote Client	Implemented By
Local home interface	Local	Bean developer
Local component interface	Local	Bean developer
Session	Local	Bean developer
Deployment descriptor	Local	Bean developer
Deployment descriptor helper class (optional)	Local	Bean developer
EJBLocalHome class, local home interface	Local	Deployment tool
EJBLocalObject class, local component interface	Local	Deployment tool
Wrapper for SessionBean class	Local	Deployment tool
SessionContext class	Local	Deployment tool
Remote home interface	Remote	Bean developer
Remote component interface	Remote	Bean developer
Session and entity bean	Remote	Bean developer
Deployment descriptor	Remote	Bean developer
Deployment descriptor helper class (optional)	Remote	Bean developer
EJBHome class, remote home interface	Remote	Deployment tool
EJBObject class, remote component interface	Remote	Deployment tool
Wrapper for SessionBean class	Remote	Deployment tool
Handle class	Remote	Deployment tool
EJBMetaData class	Remote	Deployment tool
SessionContext class	Remote	Deployment tool

Figure 5-3 depicts one possible class hierarchy and the respective responsibilities of the bean developer and the container and the deployment tool. The figure illustrates the dependency of EJB APIs on J2SE APIs. The bean developer either extends EJB APIs (shown by the solid arrows) or implements them (shown by the broken arrows). The deployment tool takes the developer-provided classes and generates vendor-proprietary Hello implementation classes and support classes that make it possible to run the HelloEJB application. Note that the exact implementation of and demarcation line between the responsibilities of the container and deployment tool are vendor dependent. Figure 5-3 illustrates the Hello implementatin classes generated by J2SDKEE 1.3 at deployment time.

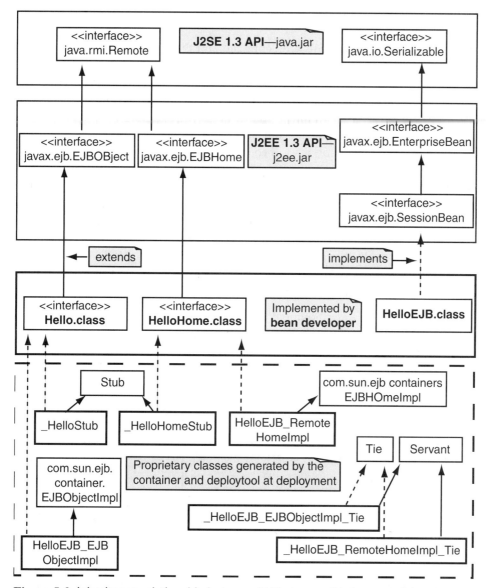

Figure 5-3 Inheritance relationship between EJB classes (Hello example)

Note that the bean developer is required to provide only the `Hello.class`, `Hello.Home.class`, and `HelloEJB.class` classes (enclosed by a dark box) at deployment time, while the deploytool generates the required classes, which are shown in solid boxes enclosed by the large broken box.

Packaging a Session Bean

After the session bean elements are debugged and the deployment descriptors have been correctly specified, the session bean is ready for deployment. The components, however, must first be packaged in a standard format that's portable across J2EE application servers. The standard EJB format is an ejb-jar file. A JAR (Java Archive) file is based on the popular ZIP file format that's commonly used for packaging Java files. This file is normally accessed and read using the deployment tool provided by the EJB container vendor. For this reason, an ejb-jar file must include the session bean class, remote and home interfaces, any helper classes, and the deployment descriptor file packaged into a single, standard JAR-format file. A vendor-provided assembly tool is typically used for this task, but you can also use the **jar** command line utility to package the beans manually. See Figure 5-4 for an illustration of the `hello world` example ejb-jar file. The standard deployment descriptor file, `ejb-jar.xml`, is in the META-INF subdirectory. The META-INF directory also contains the MANIFEST.MF file, which is empty and retained for purposes of backward compatibility.

The Sun J2SDKEE 1.3 RI deployment tool packages the `Hello` application as the ejb-jar-ic.jar file. Its contents are illustrated in Figure 5-4.

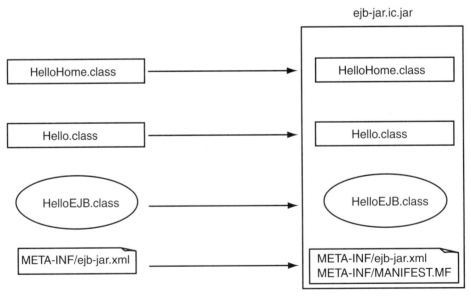

Figure 5-4 Packaging the `Hello` application

Deployment

A sophisticated J2EE application should consist of several types of EJBs encompassing different types of business logic, parts of which were purchased from multiple bean providers and parts of which were developed in-house. These EJBs are assembled using the servlet and JSP to create a complete application. The application is then packaged into a standard enterprise application archive (.ear file), which is a type of .zip file format. Before making the enterprise application available to customers, a deployer will take the .ear file, use the vendor-provided tool to customize the deployment descriptor file to the target environment of the application server, and then deploy the application. In Chapter 4, we packaged the `Hello` component (`ejb-jar-ic.jar`) with a standalone client (`app-client-ic.jar`) and created a HelloApp.ear application file as illustrated in Figure 5-5 before we finally deployed it.

Summary

In this chapter, our focus of discussion was the session bean. Session beans are a type of Enterprise JavaBeans ideal for implementing workflow logic, business processes, and process control logic, such as making ticket reservations or purchasing items. Session beans are relatively short-lived and don't survive a container crash. Session beans are transient. Session beans don't represent

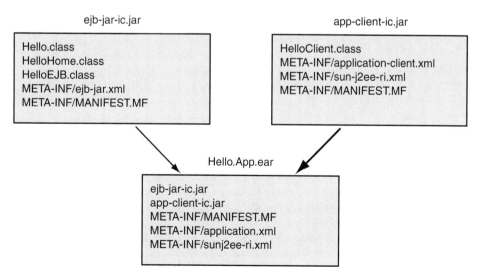

Figure 5-5 Creating a `HelloApp.ear` file

persistent data, but they can access databases nevertheless and are transaction aware. Session beans execute on behalf of a single client and their lifespans are dependent on the client session's lifespan.

There are two types of session beans: stateless and stateful. Stateless session beans don't maintain client information between method calls, so a request must include all the parameters necessary for it to execute the business logic. After the result of the request is returned, stateless session beans retain no request information. They are often pooled and are ideal for providing frequent but brief requests. A common implementation of the stateless session bean is the stock quote lookup service. Stateful session beans retain state information between method invocations and so are conversational.

We also examined various elements of session beans and rules about how to write session bean implementation classes, the `ejbCreate()` method, and business methods. We discussed the standard J2EE deployment descriptor that all J2EE application servers must support, as well as proprietary deployment descriptors that allow deployers to customize the performance of the EJBs. We concluded with a discussion of packaging EJBs into standard jar files and then assembling them with other EJB and Web components to create a deployable ear file.

DEVELOPING STATELESS SESSION BEANS

Topics in This Chapter

- Characteristics and Features of Stateless Session Beans
- Stateless Session Bean Life Cycles
- A Stateless Schedule Bean Application

Chapter 6

Thus far, session beans have been discussed in general, along with the rules and requirements for writing session beans and their interfaces. This chapter focuses on the details of implementing a stateless session bean application and covers the following topics:

- the characteristics and features of SLSBs
- the life cycles of SLSBs
- writing SLSBs and implementing data access objects
- writing servlet clients to invoke business methods in SLSBs

Characteristics and Features of Stateless Session Beans

EJB architects design SLSBs to handle brief and discrete types of business logic in an efficient manner. The SLSB stateless nature presupposes the following:

- As the instances of a type of SLSB are identical, SLSB instances can be pooled and recycled after each invocation. As SLSB instances are pooled, the client does not incur the overhead of creation and destruction associated with the instance's life cycle.
- Compared with stateful and entity beans, SLSBs are comparatively fast, efficient, and can handle relatively larger numbers of client requests with relatively fewer SLSBs in the pool.

Consider the following when designing and implementing EJBs:

- Use SLSBs to model generic business logic that can provide common services to different types of clients and don't require maintaining client-specific state information.
- Use SLSBs if the business logic is discrete and self-contained and can pass all necessary information for the bean instance to execute the business logic and return a result.
- Use SLSBs when desiring higher performance, nonconversational EJBs to implement business logic.
- Use SLSBs for providing a shared view of the data when the data is read-only and not time sensitive.

Stateless Session Bean Life Cycles

Although both stateful and stateless session beans extend the same super interface, `javax.ejb.SessionBean`, their life cycles are very different. An SLSB's life cycle consists of three phases: *initialization, method-ready,* and *destruction.* Figure 6-1 shows a state diagram of the SLSB life cycle.

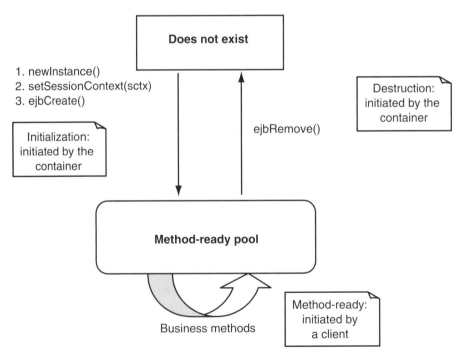

Figure 6-1 The life cycle of a stateless session bean instance

Because the container is in charge of creating and destroying SLSB instances, the container initiates the initialization phase once in the lifetime of the SLSB instance. During this initialization process, the container invokes three methods:

1. A `newInstance()` method initiates the start of the bean instance.

2. Next, the container must set a session context and attach the bean instance to the container by invoking the `setSessionContext()` method and passing a `SessionContext` object as argument.

3. Finally, the container invokes the create method `ejbCreate()` without any argument, which completes the initialization of the bean instance. At the end of the `ejbCreate()` method, the SLSB instance is available in the method-ready pool. (Figure 6-2 illustrates the sequence diagram just discussed.) Notice that the container first creates the `SessionContext` object even before executing `newInstance()` method, so it can pass the `SessionContext` object as parameter to `setSessionContext()` method.

When the SLSBs are in the method-ready pool, they can service client requests. Because SLSB instances are identical, the container assigns a bean instance to a client for the duration of the method call. After the completion of the method call, the bean instance is released back to the method-ready pool so it can be assigned to another prospective client. Figures 6-3 and 6-4 illustrate this scenario by providing a snapshot of the pooling mechanism and showing a pool of `ScheduleEJB` instances and two clients, `ScheduleClient`, making requests.

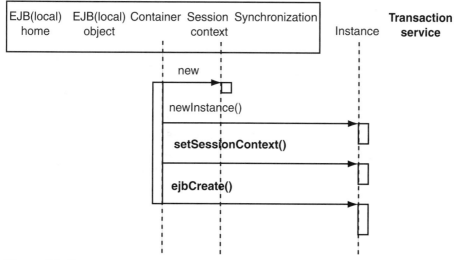

Figure 6-2 Sequence
diagram—creation of an SLSB instance method-ready pool

Specifically, Figure 6-3 depicts a client, (`ScheduleClient1`), executing a business method, `searchCourseByID()`, and the container taking instance `ScheduleEJB1` from the method-ready pool and assigning it to service this request for `ScheduleClient1`; another instance, `ScheduleEJB3`, is being released back to the method-ready pool after having completed executing `searchCourseByTitle()` request for `ScheduleClient2`.

Figure 6-4 is another snapshot of the interaction showing the `ScheduleClient1` making the same request again and the container selecting `ScheduleEJB2` from the method-ready pool and assigning to service this request. The `ScheduleClient2` is also making the same request, and the container assigns `ScheduleEJB1` to service this request. (To avoid clutter, the home and component objects aren't shown in Figures 6-3 and 6-4.)

Because the SLSB instance is in ready state, it can quickly service requests without the overhead of initialization. Because the bean instance is tied up for the duration of the method call and then released back in the pool, the bean instance can service many clients. The SLSB instances are then recycled or put back to the method-ready pool after each method call from client. Note that the exact algorithm for how SLSB instances are assigned to clients isn't specified in the EJB 2.0 specification; however, a container assigns a client an SLSB instance from a pool or creates one if needed.

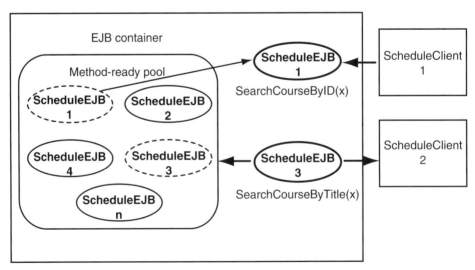

Figure 6-3 Snapshot of an SLSB instance pooling and interacting with clients

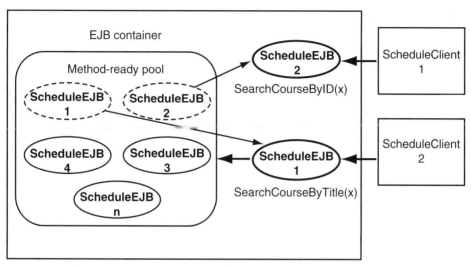

Figure 6-4 Another snapshot of an SLSB instance pooling and interacting with clients

When the container decides to destroy the SLSB instance in the pool, it invokes the `ejbRemove()` method on the bean instance to end its life cycle and evict it from memory. The container may decide to evict the SLSB instance if it needs more memory resources or based on parameters set by the container or by the administrator. Figure 6-5 depicts the container-initiated `ejbRemove()` method.

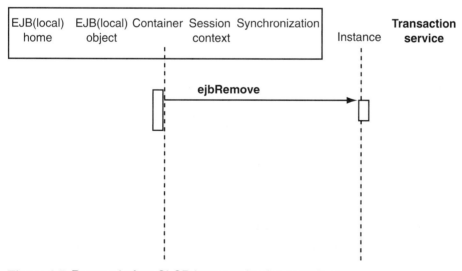

Figure 6-5 Removal of an SLSB instance by the container

A Stateless Schedule Bean Application

A J2EE application consists of EJBs that encapsulate the business logic and a client that invokes the business methods. The following sample schedule bean application consists of an SLSB, `ScheduleEJB`, which encapsulates the logic to search for Java courses in an online Java training site. The Web client consists of a Java servlet, `ScheduleClient`, which invokes the two business methods on the SLSB. The `ScheduleEJB` enables a client to search for courses either by course title or course number. This example application consists of two parts, including the EJB and client parts. We'll discuss the implementation of the EJB component and won't dwell on the client part of the application because a background on servlet, JSP, and html are presumed. Specifically, the EJB part consists of:

- the stateless session bean—`ScheduleEJB`
- the remote home and component interfaces—`ScheduleHome` and `Schedule`
- helper class—`ScheduleDAO`, `ScheduleModelVO`

The client part consists of

- a servlet client—`SearchScheduleServlet`
- an HTML form page—`SearchCourse.htm`

We'll follow these 13 steps to build and test our schedule bean application:

1. Implement the remote home interface: `ScheduleHome`.
2. Implement the remote component interface: `Schedule.java`.
3. Implement the SLSB class: `ScheduleEJB`.
4. Implement a helper class: `ScheduleDAO`, `ScheduleVO`.
5. Compile `ScheduleHome`, `Schedule`, `ScheduleEJB`, `ScheduleVO`, and `ScheduleDAO`.
6. Write the servlet client, `SearchScheduleServlet`, and compile it.
7. Create the JSP: `ShowSearchResult` and `SearchCourse` HTML.
8. Create the search schedule application archive file.
9. Package the EJB element into an ejb-jar file.
10. Package the servlet, JSP, and HTML files as Web archive files.
11. Deploy the search schedule application.
12. Review the deployment descriptor.
13. Run the application.

The following sections provide a guide for writing and compiling an SLSB and its elements and for writing a servlet client to invoke methods on the stateless bean.

Step 1: Implementing the SLSB Remote Home Interface

The first step is to implement the remote home interface, ScheduleHome, which enables clients to manage the life cycle of an EJB. The example that follows shows the ScheduleHome interface extending the EJBHome interface for the SLSB; the ScheduleHome interface declares one method, a mandatory create method that takes no argument. The create method must be declared public and must throw the RemoteException and the CreateException. The create method must return the Schedule, the remote component interface for the ScheduleEJB.

```
public interface ScheduleHome extends EJBHome
{
    public Schedule create() throws CreateException, RemoteException;
}
```

Step 2: Implementing the SLSB Remote Component Interface

The remote component interface, Schedule, must extend the EJBHome interface and can define zero or more business methods. Two business methods, searchByCourseTitle, which returns Vector, and searchCourseID, which returns ScheduleVO, are defined public and throw RemoteException. The SchedueVO is a serializable object used to transfer data efficiently; we'll discuss this design pattern in Chapter 16.

```
public interface Schedule extends EJBObject
{
    public Vector searchByCourseTitle(String title) throws RemoteException;
    public ScheduleVO searchByCourseID(int id) throws RemoteException;
}
```

Step 3: Implementing the SLSB Class

The stateless session bean class, ScheduleEJB, must implement the javax.ejb.SessionBean interface and must be declared public. Only one mandatory default ejbCreate() method that takes no arguments can be implemented in the SLSB class.

```
public class ScheduleEJB implements SessionBean
{
    .....................
```

The ejbCreate method must return type void. As a point of clarification, the create() method defined in the home interface of SLSB only creates and returns a reference to an EJBObject for the client and does not actually create a particular SLSB instance in the pool. In the case of SLSB, it's the container's job to create a pool of SLSB instances and have them ready to service client requests. The ejbCreate() method can contain any initialization routine, but in our example it's left empty because we don't need a special initialization.

```
public void ejbCreate()
{
}
```

ScheduleEJB is an SLSB search application and implements two business methods (searchByCourseTitle and searchByCourseID) enclosed in the try-catch block. The ScheduleByCourseTitle() method takes a string argument and depends on the helper class, ScheduleDAO to delegate the searchByCourseTitle() method. The searchByCouseID() method also uses the ScheduleDAO helper class to execute the searchByCourseID() method. Figure 6-6 illustrates a sequence diagram of the client, SearchSchedule-Servlet, invoking the searchByCourseID() and searchByCourseTitle() business methods and each of the methods being executed by two different ScheduleEJB instances from the pool. Notice that the bean delegates responsibility for search to the data access, which returns a vector as shown by the scheduleDAO.searchByCourseTitle(courseTitle) statement. Similar logic is repeated in the searchByScheduleID(String.scheduleID) method.

```
public Vector searchByCourseTitle(String courseTitle) throws Sched-
uleDAOException
{
    Vector schedList = new Vector(20);

    System.out.println("In ScheduleEJB -- searchByCourseTitle ");
    try
    {
        ScheduleDAO scheduleDAO = new ScheduleDAO();

        schedList = scheduleDAO.searchByCourseTitle(courseTitle);
        System.out.println("In ScheduleEJB- after calling scheduleDAO ");

    }catch(ScheduleDAOException se) {
      throw new  ScheduleDAOException("SearchByCourseTitle exception
="+se.getMessage());
    }

    System.out.println("ScheduleBean -- searchByCourseTitle return-
ing Vector ");
    return schedList;
}

public ScheduleModel searchByScheduleID(String scheduleID) throws Sched-
uleDAOException
{
    System.out.println("In ScheduleBean -- searchByCourseID ");
```

```
    ScheduleModel schedule = null;

    try
    {
        ScheduleDAO scheduleDAO = new ScheduleDAO();
    System.out.println("In ScheduleBean - after calling scheduleDAO ");

        schedule = scheduleDAO.searchByScheduleID(scheduleID);
        System.out.println("In ScheduleBean - got schedule ");

    }catch(ScheduleDAOException se) {
        throw new  ScheduleDAOException("SearchByCourseID exception  ="+se.get-
Message());
    }
    System.out.println("ScheduleBean -- searchByCourseID returning schedule ");

    return schedule;
}
```

The ScheduleEJB bean inherits several callback methods from the SessionBean interface, which are used to manage the life cycle of bean instances. In our example code, we'll leave the ejbActivate() and ejbPassivate() methods empty and are not shown in the code snippet.

The setSessionContext() method is called by the container during the initialization steps of the SLSB instance and is used to set the session context for the bean instance. The container invokes ejbRemove() to evict the SLSB instance when it needs more resources. Note that when a client invokes the inherited remove method in the home and component interfaces of the SLSB, it only removes the EJBObject and does not remove the bean instance in the pool, as shown in Figure 6-6.

Step 4: Implementing Helper Classes

The ScheduleDAO is a Java class with JDBC logic to perform search operations on the database table. It enables database search logic to be isolated from the rest of the SLSB implementation, enabling code reuse. The ScheduleDAO separates the data access logic from the business logic of the EJB and provides a simple interface to it, which simplifies the EJB logic and enhances portability and code maintenance. In the ScheduleDAO constructor, the helper class uses JNDI to look up the datasource object and then uses it to establish connection to the database.

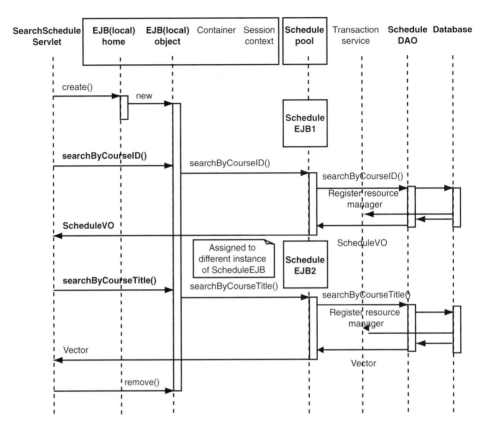

Figure 6-6 Sequence diagram—`ScheduleClient`, `ScheduleEJB`, and `ScheduleDAO` interaction

```
public class ScheduleDAO
{
//private Connection connection = null;
private DataSource dataSource = null;

public ScheduleDAO() throws ScheduleDAOException
{
    try
    {
//Comment 1: JNDI look up for data source
        InitialContext ictx = new InitialContext();
        dataSource = (DataSource)
ictx.lookup("java:comp/env/jdbc/JCampDS");
        System.out.println("ScheduleDAO jcampDataSource lookup OK!");
```

```
      } catch (NamingException ne) {
          throw new  ScheduleDAOException("NamingException while
  looking up datasource connection ="+ne.getMessage());
      }
  }
```

Two methods—searchByCourseTitle() and searchByCourseID()—are
implemented in the data access object class. The searchByCourseTitle() takes
a string argument and uses it to search for Java courses available in the database
table. It uses the JDBC API and creates a SQL query statement, queryString, and
then executeQuery(queryString) to make a JDBC call. A successful query
returns a ResultSet. Each row in the result set is retrieved, a ScheduleVO
object is created from the fields extracted from the result set by the
newSchedule(reset.getString"sid"),
rset.getString("courseID")...) and then added to the vector list
scheduleList by the scheduleList.addElement(schedule) statement.
The method returns a vector of schedule objects, scheduleList, to the
ScheduleEJB, which returns it to the client.

```
  public Vector searchByCourseTitle(String courseTitle) throws Sched-
  uleDAOException
  {
      Statement stmt = null;
      ResultSet rset = null;
      Vector scheduleList = new Vector(20);

      Connection conn = this.getConnection();

      String queryString ="SELECT schedule.id, courseid, locationid, city,
  state, country, region, startdate, enddate, status, title, trainer,
  price, maxenroll, currentenrolled, waitlist FROM schedule, course,
  location  where courseid = course.id AND locationid = location.id AND
  title LIKE '%"+courseTitle+"%'";

System.out.println("ScheduleDAO  - searchByCourseTitle ");
System.out.println("queryString = "+queryString);
      try
      {
          stmt = conn.createStatement();
          System.out.println(" stmt creation OK");

          rset = stmt.executeQuery(queryString);
          System.out.println(" got the resulset rset ");

          while(rset.next())
```

```
        {
            ScheduleModel schedule = new ScheduleVO (
                rset.getString("sid"), rset.getString("courseid"),
    rset.getString("locationid"),
                rset.getString("city"), rset.getString("state"),
    rset.getString("country"),
                rset.getDate("startdate"), rset.getDate("enddate"),
                rset.getString("status"),rset.getString("title"),
                rset.getFloat("price"), rset.getInt("maxenroll"),
    rset.getInt("currentenrolled"),
                rset.getInt("waitlist")
                );

            System.out.println("ScheduleDAO - created schedule item,
    before adding to a vector");

            scheduleList.addElement(schedule);
        }
    } catch(SQLException se) {
        throw new ScheduleDAOException(" Query exception "+se.get-
Message());
    } finally {
        closeResultSet(rset);
        closeStatement(stmt);
        closeConnection(conn);
    }
   System.out.println("ScheduleDAO  - searchByCourseTitle - returning
Vector ");
    return scheduleList;
}
```

The `searchByScheduleID` method is similar to the previous one, but it either
returns zero or one row because it searches on a primary key, `ScheduleID`. It
extracts the fields of the `ResultSet` and creates a `ScheduleVO` and returns it to
the calling SLSB.

```
public ScheduleVO searchByScheduleID(String ScheduleID) throws
ScheduleDAOException
{
    Statement stmt = null;
    ResultSet rset = null;
    ScheduleModel schedule = null;

    Connection conn = this.getConnection();
```

```
    String queryString ="SELECT schedule.id, courseid, locationid,
title, city, state, country, region, startdate, enddate, price, trainer,
status, maxenroll, currentenrolled, waitlist  FROM schedule, course,
location  where courseid = course.id AND locationid = location.id AND
courseid = '"+courseID+"'";
  System.out.println("queryString = "+queryString);

    try
    {
        stmt = conn.createStatement();
        System.out.println(" stmt creation OK");

        rset = stmt.executeQuery(queryString);
        System.out.println(" got the resulset rset ");

        while(rset.next())
        {
            schedule = new ScheduleVO(
            rset.getString("sid"), rset.getString("courseid"),
rset.getString("locationid"),
            rset.getString("city"), rset.getString("state"),
rset.getString("country"),
            rset.getDate("startdate"), rset.getDate("enddate"),
            rset.getString("status"),rset.getString("title"),
            rset.getFloat("price"),rset.getInt("maxenroll"),
rset.getInt("currentenrolled"),
            rset.getInt("waitlist")
            );
        }
    } catch(SQLException se) {
        throw new ScheduleDAOException(" Query exception "+se.get-
Message());
    } finally {
        closeResultSet(rset);
        closeStatement(stmt);
        closeConnection(conn);
    }
    System.out.println("ScheduleDAO  - searchByCourseID - returning
schedule ");
    return schedule;
}

}
```

We've used `ScheduleVO` to encapsulate the fields from the `ResultSet` to pass
the result of the search from the `ScheduleEJB` to the servlet client easily and
efficiently. The servlet takes the results and displays them to the end user with the
help of JSP.

The ScheduleVO is a serializable Java class and has only getter methods, so the client can only use this object to read data. Following is the code snippet.

```
public class ScheduleVO implements Serializable
{
    private int scheduleID;
    private int courseID;
    private int locationID;
..............................

    public ScheduleVO (int aScheduleID, int aCourseID, int aLocationID,
String aCity, String aState, String aCountry, Date aStartDate, Date
aEndDate, String aStatus, String aCourseTitle, float aCost, int
aMaxEnroll, int aCurrentEnrolled, int aWaitList)
    {
        scheduleID = aScheduleID;
        courseID = aCourseID;
        locationID = aLocationID;
        city = aCity;
        state = aState;
        country = aCountry;
        startDate = aStartDate;
        endDate = aEndDate;
        status = aStatus;
        courseTitle = aCourseTitle;
        cost = aCost;
        maxEnroll = aMaxEnroll;
        currentEnrolled = aCurrentEnrolled;
        waitList = aWaitList;
    }


    public int getScheduleID()
    {
        return this.scheduleID;
    }

    public int getCourseID()
    {
        return this.courseID;
    }

    public int getLocationID()
    {
        return locationID;
    }
```

Step 5: Compiling `ScheduleHome`, `Schedule`, `ScheduleEJB`, `ScheduleDAO`, and `ScheduleVO`

To compile the `Schedule` bean source program:

1. Go to the APPHOME\chapter6\search directory and run **compileSchedule.bat**, which produces the class files `ScheduleHome.class`, `Schedule.class`, `ScheduleEJB.class`, `ScheduleDAO.class`, and `ScheduleDAOException.class`.

2. Next, change directory to APPHOME\model and run **compile.bat**, which compiles and produces `ScheduleVO.class`.

Step 6: Writing and Compiling a Servlet Client

The `SearchScheduleServlet` is a simple servlet program that executes within a Web container and uses the `ScheduleHome` and `Schedule` interfaces to access the `ScheduleEJB` in the EJB container. It accepts the requests from the HTML form and invokes an appropriate method on the remote interface, `Schedule`. The results from the `ScheduleEJB` are then forwarded by the servlet to the `ShowSearchResult.jsp`, which displays the result in the browser. By changing the directory to APPHOME\chapter6\web\servlets and executing **compile**, you'll compile `SearchScheduleServlet.java`.

Step 7: Creating an HTML Form Page

Next, you need to create an HTML form page to enable end users to enter a course title or course number to search for a particular course availability: The `ShowSearchResult.jsp` accepts the request from the `SearchScheduleServlet` and then generates the output.

Step 8: Creating the Schedule Application as an Enterprise Archive

Enterprise applications running on the J2EE platform are packaged as enterprise archive files (in ZIP file format with an .ear extension). To package the schedule enterprise application, create an .ear file and then include the EJB package and Web package.

Packaging and deployment tools in the J2EE platform are vendor specific. The following example uses the deploytool that comes with Sun's J2EE Reference Implementation. After ensuring that the J2EE server is running, start the deploytool and then create a `ScheduleApp.ear`. (See the Appendix for information on how to install and set up the `j2sdkee1.3` reference implementation.) Package the schedule application according to the steps on the next page.

1. Start the J2EE server and the deploytool, which should bring up the Application Development Tool GUI.

2. To create the `ScheduleApp.ear` package file to hold the EJB component jar file and Web component war file, go to the Application Deployment GUI Tool and select File | New | Application. A pop-up menu is displayed with an Application File Name and Application Display Name. Using the browse option, select the target destination for saving the archive file. This example uses the APPHOME\chapter6 directory. Enter **ScheduleApp.ear** as the file name and click the New Application button, as shown in Figure 6-7.

3. The Application Display Name should display ScheduleApp—click OK. You'll then see `ScheduleApp` displayed under the Application folder (under the Files folder on the left side of the Deployment tool GUI as shown in Figure 6-8). To the right of the GUI tool, there are several files under the content META-INF, such as `application.xml` and `sun-j2ee-ri.xml`. The `application.xml`

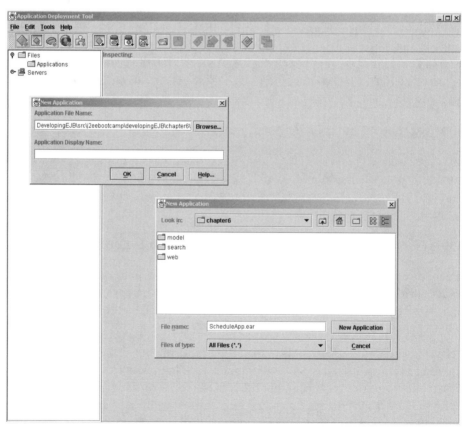

Figure 6-7 Creating the enterprise application archive file—`ScheduleApp.ear`

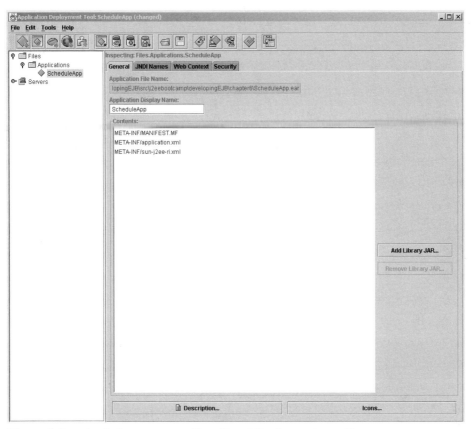

Figure 6-8 `ScheduleApp.ear` file without the jar and war files

is the standard application deployment descriptor, portable across other J2EE application servers. The `sun-j2ee-ri.xml` is the Sun RI specific deployment descriptor.

Step 9: Packaging the SLSB ScheduleEJB as an ejb-jar File

Package the SLSB Schedule into an ejb-jar file as follows:

1. Go to the Deploytool GUI and select File | New | Enterprise Bean. It should display the New Enterprise Bean Wizard. Go to the bottom of the wizard and click Next.

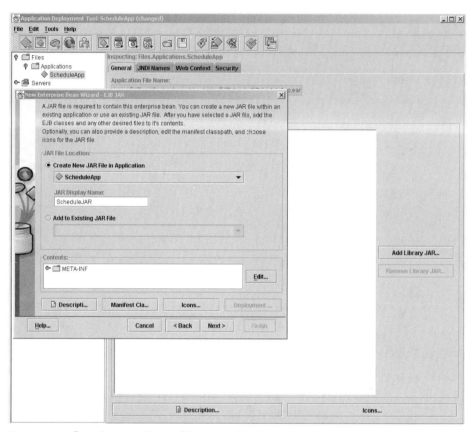

Figure 6-9 Creating an ejb-jar file named `ScheduleJAR`

2. Beneath the Create New JAR File in Application label, you should see `ScheduleApp` already selected. If not, use the pull-down menu to select `ScheduleApp`, and enter `ScheduleJAR` under the JAR Display Name label as shown in Figure 6-9. Click on the Edit button to bring up the Edit Contexts of `ScheduleJAR` window.

3. Use the pull-down menu under the Starting Directory label to go to APPHOME\chapter6\ directory. Click on the folder icon to the left; it should display three folders—search, web. and model. You should also see the `ScheduleApp.ear` file if you had chosen to save the ear file under this directory. After selecting the Search folder, start adding the `Schedule-Home.class`, `Schedule.class`, `ScheduleEJB.class`, `ScheduleDAO.class`, and `ScheduleException.class` by using the

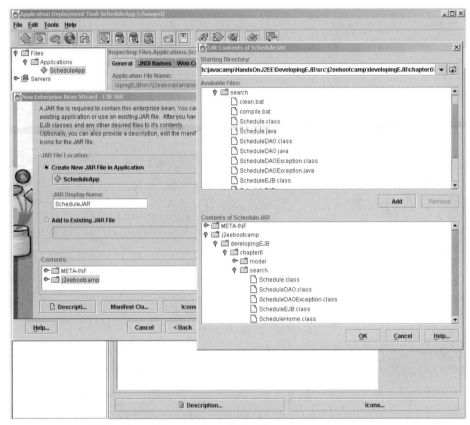

Figure 6-10 Adding class files to the ejb-jar file

Add button. Next, select the Model folder and add the `ScheduleVO.class`. The classes you just added should be visible in the Content of `Schedule-JAR` window as shown in Figure 6-10. Click OK.

4. Now, tell the deployment tool to create an additional deployment descriptor. Click the Next button to go to the General wizard and then change the Bean type to Stateless. Use the pull-down menu to select the `ScheduleEJB.class` as the Enterprise Bean Class. As the Enterprise Bean name, enter **ScheduleEJB**.

5. Under the Remote Interface, use the pull-down menu to select the `ScheduleHome.class` and `Schedule.class` for the Remote Home interface and Remote Interfaces, respectively, as shown in Figure 6-11.

6. Now, click Next. In the Transaction Management wizard, select the Bean-Managed option and then click Next.

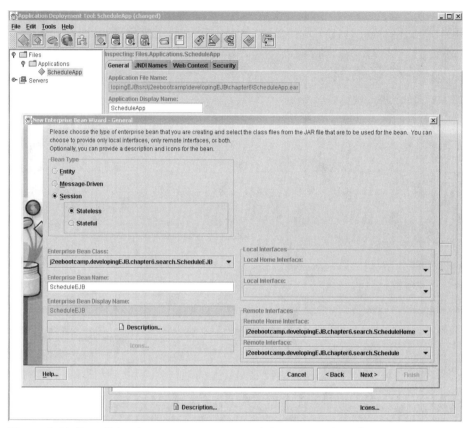

Figure 6-11 Specifying bean name, type, and the remote interfaces

7. Don't set any environmental entries in the Environment Entries wizard; click Next, which brings you to the Enterprise Bean Reference wizard. Because the `ScheduleEJB` isn't invoking any other EJBs, click Next.

8. In the Resource Reference wizard, we need to select Resource Factories Referenced in Code to specify a reference to the data source. The helper class `ScheduleDAO` accesses the database; as such, we need to define an external resource reference. So, first click the Add button, and then under the Coded Name column, enter **jdbc/JCampDS**, select `javax.sql.DataSource` from the pull-down menu under the Type column, and then select Container in the Authentication column. You can also check an icon in the Shareable column. At the bottom of the wizard, select jdbc/Cloudscape as the JNDI name, and enter the user name **j2ee** and password **j2ee**. Note your datasource name, username, and password may vary, so use the one that is valid for your setup. See Figure 6-12 for an illustration. Click Finish, as we don't need to set any other parameters for this example.

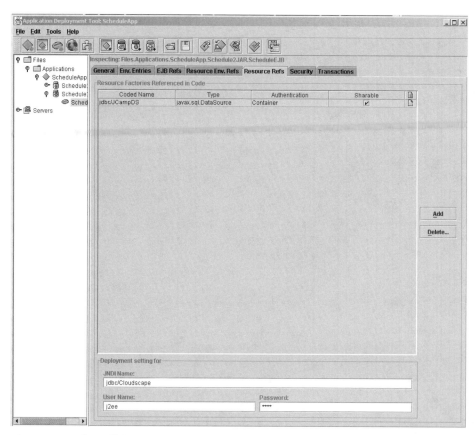

Figure 6-12 Specifying the datasource and the user name and password

We've now completed the necessary steps to package the SLSB schedule into an ejb-jar file. We still need to package the Web component; we'll briefly discuss that next.

Step 10: Packaging the Web Archive Files

Now we need to take the servlet, JSP, and HTML files and package them as a Web component as follows:

1. Select File | New | Web Component in the Application Deployment Tool to pop up a New Web Component wizard. Then click Next. In the WAR File wizard, ensure that the Create New WAR File in Application button is selected and that it displays `ScheduleApp`. Under the WAR Display Name: label, enter **ScheduleWAR**. See Figure 6-13.

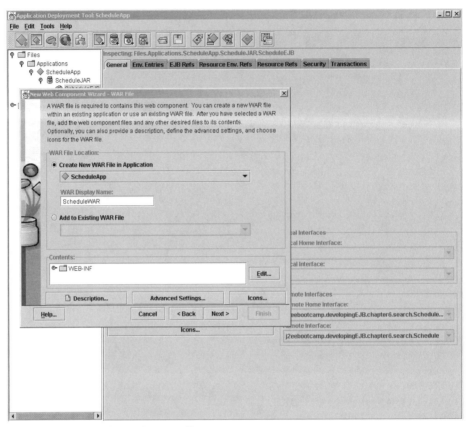

Figure 6-13 Specifying the war file

2.   Click the Edit button to pop up another Edit Contents of the `ScheduleWAR` window and ensure that the Starting Directory: points to the APPHOME\chapter6 directory. Expand the Web folder and further expand the servlet and jsp folders. Select `SearchScheduleServlet.class`, `ShowSearchResult.jsp`, and `SearchCourse.htm`. Use the Add button to include them to the war file, and the selected files should be visible under the Contents of `ScheduleWAR` subwindow as shown in Figure 6-14.

3.   Click OK, and then click Next. In the Choose Component Type wizard, click the Servlet radio button to specify the type of Web component being created, and then click Next.

4.   In the Component General Properties wizard, for the Servlet Class:, select the `SearchScheduleServlet` from the pull-down menu, and enter **Search-ScheduleServlet** as the Web Component Name. Select Load at any time for the startup load sequence. See Figure 6-15 for an illustration. Click Next.

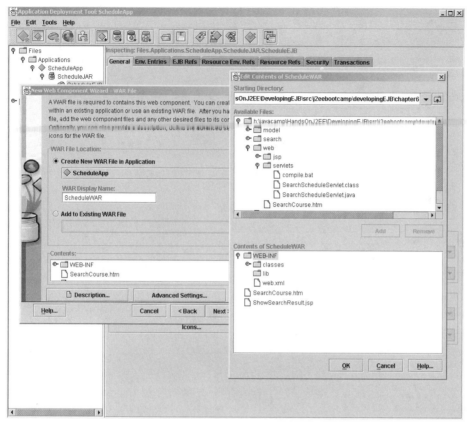

Figure 6-14 Adding servlet, jsp, and html files to the war file

5. Because we're not coding any initial parameters, click Next.

6. In the Aliases wizard, click Add. To give an alias to the Web component, enter **/SearchAlias** for the Web component security, and click Next. Use the default settings, User Caller ID, and click Next.

7. Click Next because we're not setting any WAR file environment variables in this example. We're not setting any context parameters, so click Next again.

8. Because the servlet client, `ScheduleSearchServlet`, uses JNDI to access `ScheduleEJB`, we need to define and specify the necessary parameters. Please note that this mapping information is necessary so the servlet can find the home object via `ejb/MyScheduleRef`, which is referenced in the servlet code and executes business logic in `ScheduleEJB`. Click the Add button, and then enter **ejb/MyScheduleRef** under Coded Name. Then select Session under Type, and Remote under Interface. Enter **ScheduleHome**

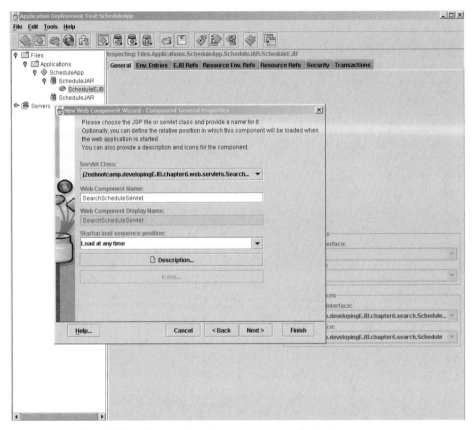

Figure 6-15 Specifying the servlet class, name, and startup sequence

under the Home Interface and **Schedule** under the Local/Remote Interface columns. Also select the Enterprise Bean Name radio button, and then enter **ScheduleEJB**, as shown in Figure 6-16. Click Next.

9. Because we're not setting any resource references, click Next and then, because we're also not specifying resource environment resources, click Next again.

10. Click the Add button under Welcome File in the File Reference wizard menu, and then use the pull-down menu to select SearchCourse.htm, as shown in Figure 6-17. Click Finish because we don't need to specify any additional parameters.

At this point, we've created a deployable enterprise archive file (also known as an ear file) that includes the Web component packaged as war file and enterprise JavaBean packaged as ejb-jar-ic.jar, as shown in Figure 6-18. Notice the left window of the application deployment tool shows the ScheduleApp with two

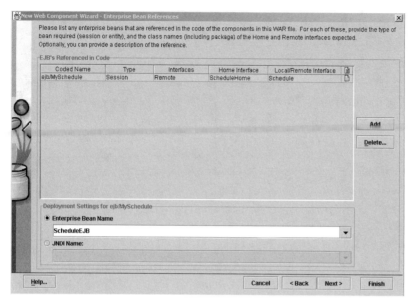

Figure 6-16 Specifying the enterprise bean references

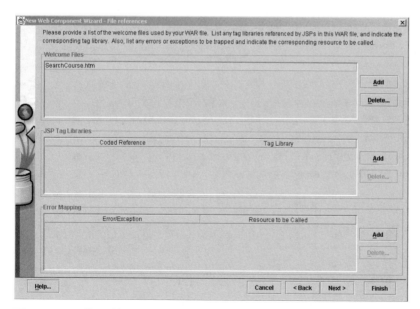

Figure 6-17 Specifying the default html page for the application

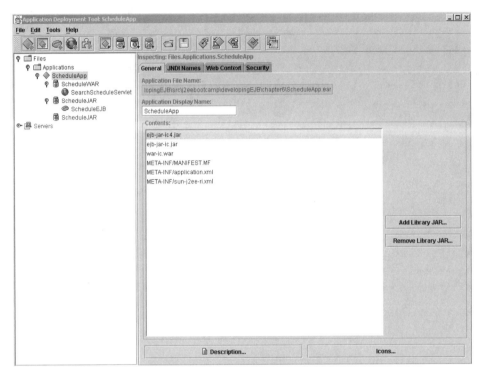

Figure 6-18 ScheduleApp.ear file with the `ScheduleWAR` and
`ScheduleJAR` files

components, `ScheduleWAR` and `ScheduleJAR`. In the middle window under
the Contents label there are five files: the ejb-jar-ic.jar (EJB component), war-ic.war
(Web component), and the various deployment descriptor files application.xml and
sun-j2ee-ri.xml. The MANIFEST.MF file is empty and is there for backward
compatibility with older versions of EJB. We're now ready to deploy.

Step 11: Deploying the Schedule Application

We can now deploy the Web and EJB components using the deployment tool as
follows:

1. In the Deployment Tool GUI, select Tools | Deploy. The Deploy
    `ScheduleApp` GUI window pops up as shown in Figure 6-19.

2. Select `ScheduleApp` in the Object to Deploy drop-down menu; select
    localhost as the Target Server. Select Save object before deploying (see
    Figure 6-19). Click Next.

Figure 6-19 Specifying the deployable file and the target server

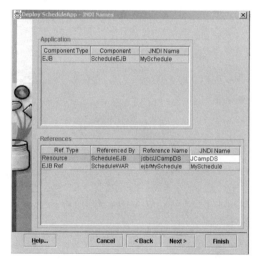

Figure 6-20 Specifying the JNDI name

3. Enter the JNDI name **MySchedule** as the Application and for References (see Figure 6-20), and click Next.

4. Enter the context root for the Web components, **ScheduleRootContext**, as shown in Figure 6-21. Click Next, and then click Finish.

5. The deployment tool deploys the `ScheduleApp.ear` application; it should display the deployment messages as shown in Figure 6-22.

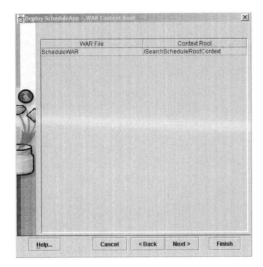

Figure 6-21 Specifying the `ContextRoot` for the Web

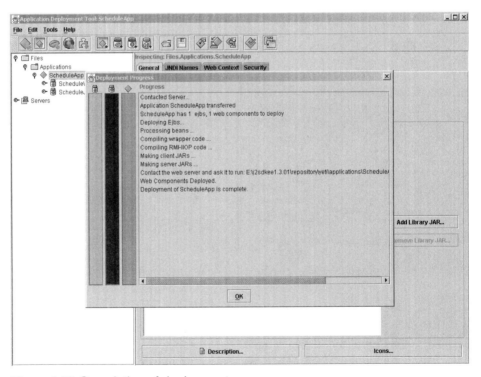

Figure 6-22 Completion of deployment

Step 12: Reviewing the Deployment Descriptor

Let's look at the data source and method description portions of the deployment descriptor generated by the deploytool for ScheduleEJB. This application needs to access database resources, so we specified a resource name, a password, and the information placed between the <resource-ref> element. This contains several elements: a resource type and reference name or <res-ref-name> that encloses jdbc/JCampDS. The resource type identified by <res-type> is javax.sql.DataSource, and the authentication is handled by the EJB container identified by <res-auth>. The <res-sharing-scope> elements imply that this resource is shareable.

```
<ejb-jar>
  <display-name>ScheduleJAR</display-name>
  <enterprise-beans>
    <session>
      <display-name>ScheduleEJB</display-name>
      <ejb-name>ScheduleEJB</ejb-name>
      ................ .
      <resource-ref>
        <res-ref-name>jdbc/JCampDS</res-ref-name>
        <res-type>javax.sql.DataSource</res-type>
        <res-auth>Container</res-auth>
        <res-sharing-scope>Shareable</res-sharing-scope>
      </resource-ref>
```

One of the search methods, searchByCourseTitle(), is identified by the <method-name> element, and its remote interface <method-intf> with a single string argument is identified by the <method-params> and <method-param> elements. The method is contained in the ScheduleEJB bean by the <ejb-name> element. It is similar to the searchByScheduleID() method.

```
............................................. . .
<assembly-descriptor>
    <method>
        <ejb-name>ScheduleEJB</ejb-name>
        <method-intf>Remote</method-intf>
        <method-name>searchByCourseTitle</method-name>
        <method-params>
          <method-param>java.lang.String</method-param>
        </method-params>
    </method>

    ...................... . .
    <method>
        <ejb-name>ScheduleEJB</ejb-name>
        <method-intf>Remote</method-intf>
        <method-name>searchByScheduleID</method-name>
        <method-params>
```

```
        <method-param>java.lang.String</method-param>
        </method-params>
      </method>
 </assembly-descriptor>
 </ejb-jar>
```

Step 13: Running the Schedule Enterprise Application

To run the application, open a browser and enter the URL **http://localhost:8000 /SchedulerRootContext/SearchCourse.htm**. When the HTML form is displayed, select one of the search options. Search by course number or course title, and click on the Submit button as shown in Figure 6-23. The result of the search is shown in Figure 6-24.

Figure 6-23 The default search page of the `ScheduleApp.ear` application

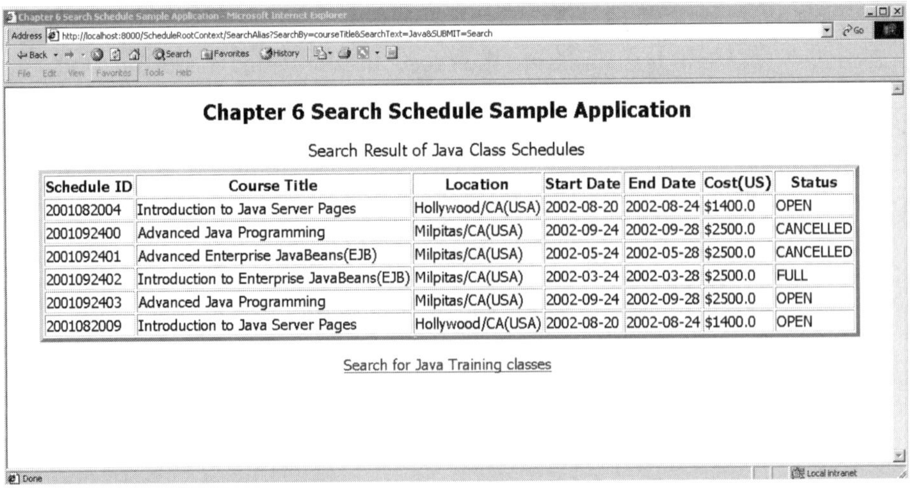

Figure 6-24 The search result

Summary

Stateless session beans don't maintain client state information between method invocation; therefore, they are suited for encapsulating business logic that is brief, frequently called, and that doesn't require saving state between invocation. Because they don't maintain state, stateless session beans can benefit from pooling and caching, resulting in speed and efficiency. In this chapter, you learned how to implement a stateless session bean example.

In the next chapter, you'll learn how to implement a stateful session bean.

DEVELOPING STATEFUL SESSION BEANS

Chapter 7

This chapter focuses on stateful session beans (SFSBs) and includes steps for implementing an SFSB application.

Characteristics of SFSBs

SFSBs maintain client information between method invocations and for this reason are considered conversational. As such, they are ideal for modeling business or workflow processes that span multiple requests, where results from previous requests may be used on subsequent requests to complete business tasks. State maintenance is mandatory to enable this interaction. In the example that follows, note that the methods are dependent on information from previous methods to successfully execute the business logic; the ability to maintain state information makes it easy to manage the process flow.

An e-commerce shopping cart application implemented as an SFSB can have several methods as described next. First, the getAddress() method looks up the shipping address and then passes the address information as a parameter to the getTaxRate() method to look up the applicable local sales and state taxes. The tax information is then passed to the calculateTax() method, which calculates the taxes due before adding the shipping cost. The total price, including the product price and tax information, is displayed to the shopper. The shopper is asked to enter the credit card information and then submits the form.

Stateful session beans are also used for controlling and coordinating interaction with other EJBs, often entity beans. For example, an SFSB that creates purchase orders may have to query several entity beans for product pricing, description, availability, and so forth, before the purchase order is presented to the client.

The life cycle of an SFSB instance is controlled by the client session. The client must explicitly create the SFSB instance before executing business logic. The bean instance is either removed explicitly by the client when it no longer needs to execute business logic on the bean instance, or it is removed implicitly by the container when the client session ends or the bean instance has exceeded its preset timeout value. Throughout its life cycle, an SFSB services only the client that created it and so can be viewed as an extension of the client on the server side.

SFSBs are transaction-aware, meaning they can participate in and manage transactions; however, the bean developer is responsible for writing the code to handle transactions. (SFSB transactions are discussed further in Chapter 14.)

A summary of SFSB characteristics includes the following:

- An SFSB instance is created by a client; its lifespan is controlled by the client, and an SFSB instance services only one client. Note that a client can invoke multiple EJBs.
- SFSBs are conversational—they maintain client specific data between method calls.
- An SFSB instance can be explicitly removed by its client or implicitly by the container when the client session ends or an SFSB times out.
- SFSBs are transactional-aware.
- SFSBs are *transient*—the bean instance and the conversational data last only as long as the session bean's lifespan and are lost if the EJB container or server crashes.

When to Use SFSBs

As a rule of thumb, SFSBs are well suited for business processes or tasks that are made up of several subtasks—some tasks are interrelated and need to be executed in sequence, while others can be executed in parallel. SFSBs are designed to handle business logic that model workflow and business processes that require client information to be saved between interdependent method invocations to complete the business logic. SFSBs are ideal for modeling these types of conversational business processes as they implicitly handle the complexity of state management with help from the container framework. SFSBs are also used for controlling and coordinating a workflow process that involves other objects and EJBs. For example, an SFSB controller bean can manage interaction with an SFSB shopping cart, a credit card verification SLSB, and inventory management entity beans to complete a shopping process.

Some developers avoid stateful session beans and instead use stateless session beans to model conversational business logic because of the stateless bean's speed and efficiency. In general, this approach should be discouraged, because the responsibility for maintaining and managing the state information falls on the client, requiring unnecessary complexity and extra coding in the client development. In most cases, if you need model conversational business logic, use SFSB. Not only will the implementation be simpler, but your component will automatically benefit from the EJB server's features such as session management, load balancing, and transparent fail-over.

The SFSB Life Cycle

SFSB instances have a fairly complex life cycle as illustrated in Figure 7-1. An SFSB exists in the following states: *does not exist*, *method ready*, *passivated*, or *method-ready transaction*. The client and the container directly affect the state and their transition. (See Chapter 14 for a detailed discussion pertaining to transactions.)

ejbCreate<METHOD>()

As shown in Figure 7-1, the initial SFSB state is "does not exist." When a client invokes the `create<METHOD>()` declared in the home interface, it causes the container to do the following:

- create the `EJBObject` and the `SessionContext` object
- create the SFSB instance
- invoke the `setSessionContext()` method
- pass the previously created `SessionContext` followed by a call to the corresponding matching `ejbCreate<METHOD>()` method

The sequence diagram in Figure 7-2 illustrates this action. At the completion of the `ejbCreate<METHOD>()`, the SFSB instance is in "method-ready" state and is able to service the client's requests.

Business Methods

When the SFSB instance is in the "method ready" state, it can execute any nontransactional business methods for the client.

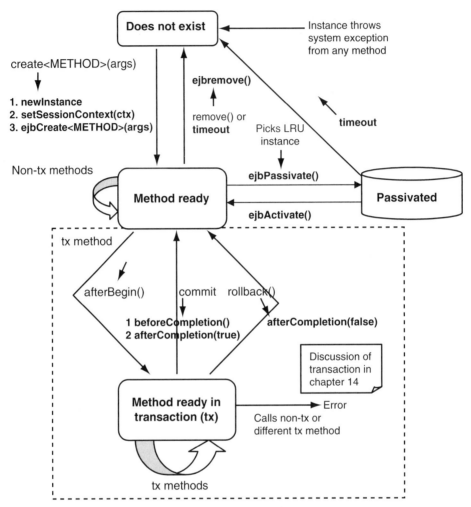

Figure 7-1 Life cycle of a stateful session bean instance

`ejbPassivate()`

Remember that the container is responsible for managing the life cycle of the SFSB instances. Besides the timeout value, the container also sets a *passivation time* for bean instances when it's created. (A passivation time is the maximum time length an SFSB instance can exist in memory continuously between accesses by the client.) The timeout and passivation values enable the container to manage the memory resources efficiently. When the container is low on memory resources, it may use the passivation time and the least recently used (LRU) algorithm to select SFSB instance candidates, serialize them (i.e., save them to secondary storage), and

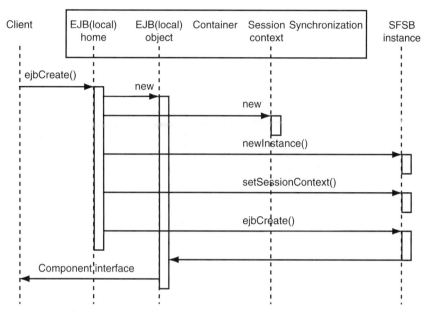

Figure 7-2 Sequence diagram for the creation of an SFSB instance

free up memory. This process is called passivation and is shown in Figure 7-3. A passivated bean instance can transition to "does not exist" if it exceeds the timeout value while in the passivated state. The container invokes the `ejbPassivate()` method before a bean instance is passivated. A container cannot passivate an SFSB instance when it's in the middle of a transaction.

`ejbActivate()`

Note that the client has no knowledge that a bean instance has been passivated. If the client invokes a method on a passivated SFSB, the container implicitly deserializes, recreates the original SFSB instance, and executes the business method. (This process of recreating the bean instance is called activation, previously discussed in Chapter 5.) The container immediately calls the `ejbActivate()` method after the bean instance is activated, as Figure 7-3 shows. A passivated bean instance can transition to a `does not exist` state if it exceeds the timeout value while in the passivated state.

Note that the EJB 2.0 specification does not mandate any specific mechanism for writing and reading bean instances to secondary storage; vendors are free to choose their own mechanism, Java serialization being one such popular mechanism.

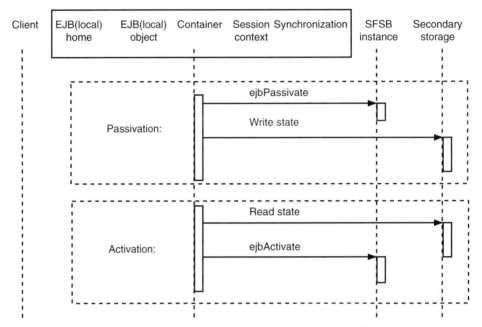

Figure 7-3 Sequence diagram for activation and passivation of an SFSB instance

`ejbRemove()`

When an SFSB instance is created, the container sets a timeout value, which determines the lifespan of the bean instance. There are two ways for the bean instance to transition back to the `does not exist` state:

- First, if the bean instance exceeds the timeout value, the container implicitly removes the bean instance from the memory store by calling the `ejbRemove()` method.

- Second, when the client invokes a `remove()` method on either the home or component interface, the container invokes the `ejbRemove()` method, and the bean instance is removed from memory.

There are two cases when it's possible that the container won't invoke the `ejbRemove()` method when a client calls the remove method:

1. If the EJB container crashes, a system exception is thrown from the bean instance to the container and the bean timeout while in the passivated state.

2. If the client attempts to invoke methods on a session object that no longer exists, the container throws the `java.rmi.NoSuchObjectException` or

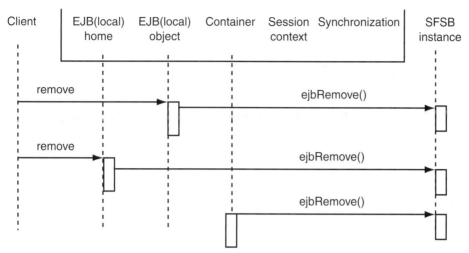

Figure 7-4 Removal of a stateful session bean instance

`javax.ejb.NoSuchObjectLocalException`, depending on whether it was a remote or local call, respectively.

Figure 7-4 shows a state diagram for the removal of a stateful session bean instance.

Implementing a Shopping Cart Application

The following example uses an SFSB to model a shopping cart to enable students to sign up for Java training. Note that the shopping cart bean can be easily adapted for other scenarios.

The shopping cart application consists of two parts:

1.   The enterprise bean, which models the shopping cart concept; it consists of the SFSB and the following interfaces:

   - the SFSB implementation class (`ShoppingCartEJB`)
   - the remote home interface (`ShoppingCartHome`)
   - the component interface (`ShoppingCart`)
   - the deployment descriptor file

2.   A client, comprised of the following:

   - a servlet client (`ShoppingCartServlet`)
   - the HTML form page (`shoppingCart.html`)

We'll use the following steps to build and test the shopping cart sample application:

1. Implement the remote home interface (`ShoppingCartHome`).
2. Implement the component interface (`ShoppingCart`).
3. Implement the SFSB class (`ShoppingCartEJB`).
4. Compile `ShoppingCartHome`, `ShoppingCart`, and `ShoppingCartEJB`.
5. Write and compile a servlet client using the interfaces (`ShoppingCartClient`).
6. Create a JavaServer Page and HTML file.
7. Package the shopping cart into an ejb-jar file and create an enterprise archive (ear) file.
8. Package the shopping cart servlet, JSP, and HTML into a war file.
9. Deploy descriptors.
10. Deploy the ShoppingCart.App.ear.
11. Test the application.

Step 1: Implementing the Remote Home Interface

A remote home interface, `ShoppingCartHome`, must be declared `public` and extend the `javax.ejb.EJBHome` interface. Unlike the stateless session bean home interface, an SFSB home interface can declare more than one `create()` method. This example declares the standard `no argument create()` method and `createCustom(String CustomerID, String CustomerName)` with arguments for the customer ID and name. Both of these create methods must return the remote component interface, `ShoppingCart`; they are also required to declare `RemoteException` and `CreateException`. (Although the `ShoppingCartHome` interface inherits abstract methods from the EJBHome interface, this example focuses on the two interfaces we've declared.) You could declare another `createCustom(String CustomerID, String category)` where the category indicates customer category such as gold, platinum and then provide a different level of service based on the customer category. Invoking one of these methods instantiates a `ShoppingCartEJB` instance and starts its life cycle on the server side.

```
public interface ShoppingCartHome extends EJBHome
{
    public ShoppingCart create() throws CreateException, RemoteExcep-
tion;
    public ShoppingCart createCustom(String customerID, String name)
throws CreateException, RemoteException;
}
```

Step 2: Implementing the Component Interface

The remote component interface, ShoppingCart, is required to extend the javax.ejb.EJBObject interface and must be declared public. There can be zero or more business methods declared in the component interface, which are invoked by a client to execute business logic encapsulated by the SFSB instance. These methods in the ShoppingCart remote component interface must throw RemoteException and any arbitrary exception defined in the bean implementation class. There are several business methods declared in the ShoppingCart interface, which enable a shopper to add (addASchedule) and delete (deleteASchedule) a class schedule from the shopping cart. There is a method (getMyScheduleList) to list all the class schedules and a method (emptyMyScheduleList) to empty the shopping cart of the existing class schedules. Finally, there is a method (getTotalCost) that returns the total cost of classes in the shopping cart. Clients may use methods such as remove() and isIdentical(), inherited from EJBObject, to remove a bean instance or to verify if two references are to the same bean instance in the container.

```
public interface ShoppingCart extends EJBObject
{
    public void addASchedule(int scheduleId) throws RemoteException;
    public void deleteASchedule(int scheduleId) throws RemoteException;
    public Vector getMyScheduleList() throws RemoteException;
    public void emptyMyScheduleList() throws RemoteException;
    public double getTotalCost() throws RemoteException;
    public void checkOut() throws RemoteException;
}
```

Step 3: Implementing the SFSB Class

The ShoppingCartEJB SFSB models the necessary business logic required to implement a simple shopping cart. The ShoppingCartEJB class must be declared public and is required to implement the javax.ejb.SessionBean interface. It also declares several private fields, as shown in the code fragment that follows:

```
public class ShoppingCartEJB implements SessionBean
{
    private SessionContext sctx;
    private String userId;
    private String userName;
    private Vector MyScheduleList;
```

Besides the mandatory SessionContext, we've also declared three additional fields, userId, userName as String, and the MyScheduleList vector, to add to the list of items.

SFSBs have three categories of methods: container-initiated callback methods, client-initiated business methods, and create methods.

Create Methods

The remote home interface, `ShoppingCartHome`, declares `create()` and `createCustom()` methods, so there are two matching `ejbCreate()` and `ejbCreateCustom()` methods implemented in the bean class. Thus, when a client invokes `createCustom()` method on the interface, it causes the container to first create `EJBObject` and `SessionContext` object, followed by creating an instance of `ShoppingCartEJB`. It then invokes the `setSessionContext()` method, passes the `SessionContext` object as parameter, and finally invokes the `ejbCreateCustom()` method. This is illustrated at the top of Figure 7-5. At the end of the `ejbCreateCustom()` method, `ShoppingCartEJB` is in the method-ready state, available to execute business methods for the client. The bean instance retains the session context throughout its lifespan as part of the conversation state.

The `ejbCreate()` method only creates `MyScheduleList Vector` to hold the class schedules. The `ejbCreateCustom(String aUserId, String aName)` also creates `MyScheduleList` vector to hold the schedules and associate the user name and user ID with the bean instance. We can use the user name and user ID to customize the shopping cart for the customer.

```
public void ejbCreate()
{
    MyScheduleList = new Vector(10);
}

public void ejbCreateCustom(String aUserId,  String aUserName)
{
    userId = aUserId;
    userName = aUserName;

    MyScheduleList = new Vector(20);
}
```

Container-Initiated Callback Methods

A container uses several session-bean callback methods to manage the life cycle of an SFSB `ShoppingCartEJB`. In our `ShoppingCartEJB` implementation, we'll leave these callback methods empty because we want the standard behavior. The standard passivation/activation behavior of an SFSB can be described as follows: If its idle time exceeds the passivation timeout value and the container needs

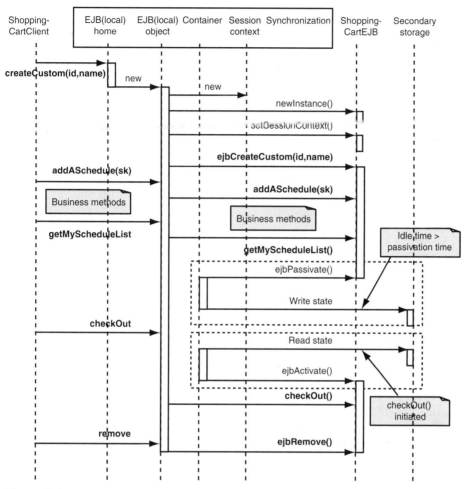

Figure 7-5 `ShoppingCartClient` and `ShoppingCartEJB` interactions

more resources, the bean instance with its shopping list is serialized to a disk, as shown in Figure 7-5. Furthermore, when the session timeout value is exceeded, the bean instance is removed by the container, and the shopping list is deleted. Let us briefly discuss one way we could make the shopping cart persistent. For example, the `ejbPassivate()` method could contain the logic to save the shopping list to a database, and the `ejbActivate()` method could contain the logic to read the shopping list from the database. Then, even if the original `ShoppingCartEJB` instance is removed after passivation, the shopping list is saved in the database. When the customer logs in again at a later time, the shopping cart with its original list can be recreated and presented to the customer.

There is additional logic necessary to save the status of the shopping cart and ensure that abandoned shopping cart lists are periodically removed from the database. The passivated `ShoppingCartEBJ` remains in the secondary storage until it exceeds the timeout value, at which point it becomes garbage collected and is no longer available.

Both `EJBHome` and `EJBObject` declare remove methods; when the client invokes a `remove()` method, the container executes `ejbRemove()`. This removes the `ShoppingCartEJB` instance from memory and transitions it to the "does not exist" state. The `ejbRemove()` method is left empty, and the container implements the removal mechanism. The container throws `NoSuchObjectFound-Exception` to the client if an attempt is made to access a `ShoppingCartEJB` instance after it has been removed.

Developers not wanting to customize the `ejbRemove()` method should be aware that there are three conditions under which `ejbRemove()` methods may not be invoked:

- when the container crashes
- when the container throws an exception to the client due to a logic implementation error when the remove method is invoked
- when the passivated bean instance exceeds its timeout value and expires and is garbage-collected

Note that the container cannot invoke `ejbPassivate()` and `ejbRemove()` methods while the bean instance is executing a business method or while the bean instance is in the middle of transaction.

Client-Initiated Business Methods

For every business method declared in the remote component interface, ShoppingCart, there must be an identical matching `public` method implemented in the `ShoppingCartEJB` class, including the return type.

A *schedule* is an object that encapsulates information about a Java training class. The addASchedule(sched) method adds a schedule value object (`ScheduleVO`) to the vector, `MyScheduleList`, in the shopping cart as shown in the code snippet that follows.

```
public void addASchedule(ScheduleVO schedVO)
    {
    //add a passed ScheduleVO to MyScheduleList
        MyScheduleList.add(schedVO);
        }
```

The deleteASchedule() method deletes a schedule from the MyScheduleList vector by first using the for loop and then using the removeElementAt() method of the vector interface.

```
public void deleteASchedule(String schedID)
    {
    //delete a ScheduleVO from a Vector list
    for( int j=0; j <= MyScheduleList.size(); j++)
    {
        ScheduleVO sched = (ScheduleVO) MyScheduleList.get(j);
        if ( (sched.getScheduleID()).equals(schedID))
            MyScheduleList.removeElementAt(j);
    }
     }
```

The listAllSchedule() method returns all the schedules currently in the MyScheduleList vector of the shopping cart to the client while the removeAllSchedule() method deletes all the schedules currently saved in the shopping cart by calling removeAllElements() on the MyScheduleList vector.

```
public Vector getMyScheduleList() throws ScheduleException
{
//return the updated ScheduleList vector
    return MyScheduleList;
}

public void emptyMyScheduleList() throws ScheduleException
{
//clear the ScheduleList vector
    MyScheduleList.removeAllElements();
}
```

The getTotalCost() method goes through the MyScheduleList vector, retrieves the cost of each of the courses from each schedule, and adds them up. It then applies the tax and returns the total cost for all the training classes in the shopping cart to the client. Notice that this method depends on the getTaxRate() method to retrieve the applicable tax rate.

```
public double getTotalCost()
{
    //add option to local sales tax from the environment.
    double taxRate = getTaxRate();

        // extract cost per schedules from the ScheduleList,
        // add up the total and return
        double total = 0.0;
        double sum = 0.0;
        for (int i=0; i < MyScheduleList.size(); i++)
        {
```

```
        ScheduleVO sched = (ScheduleVO) MyScheduleList.elementAt(i);
        sum =+ (double) sched.getCost();
    }

    total = sum + ( sum * taxRate);
      System.out.println("total cost ="+total);
          return total;
  }
```

`ShoppingCartClient` also invokes the business methods `addASchedule()` and `getMyScheduleList()` on its remote component interface and causes the container to invoke matching `addASchedule()` and `getMyScheduleList()` methods via its proxy `EJBObject`. When there's no interaction with the `ShoppingCartEJB` instance, and if the idle time exceeds the passivation timeout and the system needs more resources, the container invokes the `ejbPassivate()` method on the bean instance to warn of the impending action the container is about to take. It then writes the state information to disk (*serialization*). If `ShoppingCartClient` invokes any business method such as `checkOut()` after the `ShoppingCartEJB` instance is passivated but before the timeout, then the container reads the state information from the disk and recreates the `ShoppingCartEJB` instance with its shopping list intact (*deserialization*). Then, the container executes the `checkOut()` method in the bean instance as expected and transparent to the client.

Step 4: Compiling `ShoppingCartHome`, `ShoppingCart`, and `ShoppingCartEJB`

In order to compile the shopping cart application, change directory to APPHOME\chapter7\shop and then run compile. It will generate `ShoppingCartHome.class`, `ShoppingCart.class`, and `ShoppingCartEJB.class` files.

Step 5: Writing and Compiling the `ShoppingCartClient` Servlet

`ShoppingCartClient` is a servlet that accepts an HTML form request to search for Java course offerings. It accesses the database and then calls JSP to display the results to the browser. When the customer adds the course schedules, it calls the methods in the remote component of the `ShoppingCartEJB` instance.

The `ShoppingCartClient` servlet reuses the `ScheduleDAO` and `ScheduleVO` objects discussed in Chapter 6 to search for available Java courses. When the customer attempts to add the schedule in the shopping cart, the servlet performs a JNDI lookup for the `ShoppingCartHome` object, creates the

`ShoppingCartEJB` instance, and then invokes business methods: `addASchedule()`, `getMyScheduleList()`, `deleteASchedule()`, and `getTotalCost()`.

The servlet code is straightforward and because the focus of this book is EJB and not servlets, we'll keep the servlet code discussion to a minimum. In order to compile the servlet, change directory to APPHOME\chapter7\web\servlet and run the compile batch file; it will generate `ShoppingCartClient.class` file.

Step 6: Creating a JavaServer Page and HTML File

There are two JSP files: `ShowSearchResult.jsp` and `ShowShoppingCart.jsp`. After `ShoppingCartClient` does a search for the Java courses in the database, the servlet calls the `ShowSearchResult.jsp` to display the search results. The `ShowSearchResult.jsp` takes the vector result passed by the servlet and uses the `for` loop to extract and display the individual elements of the schedule in the HTML table format in a form. This JSP page enables an end user to add a class schedule to the shopping cart.

The second JSP page, `ShowShoppingCart.jsp`, takes the `MyScheduleList` vector and then uses the `for` loop to display the contents of the shopping cart and enables the user to add, delete, or empty the schedules from the shopping cart. The code snippet of the `ShowSearchResult.jsp` and `ShowShoppingCart.jsp` are not shown because they are fairly straightforward.

Step 7: Packaging the Shopping Cart

To create the enterprise application archive file:

1. Change to the J2SDKee1.3 bin directory, start the j2ee server, and run the deployment tool.

2. Once in the deployment tool, select the File | New | Enterprise Application option. The New Application window pops up; use the Browse option to locate the file APPHOME\chapter7\. Then enter **ShoppingCartApp.ear** as shown in Figure 7-6, and click OK.

The `ShoppingCartApp.ear` package is now created along with three files: a manifest file, `MANIFEST.MF`, and two application-specific deployment-descriptor xml files, `application.xml` and `sun-j2ee-ri.xml`. The `application.xml` file is a standard J2EE deployment descriptor, while the `sun-j2ee-ri.xml` file is Sun's J2EE Reference Implementation specific application deployment descriptor. Figure 7-6 shows the shopping cart.

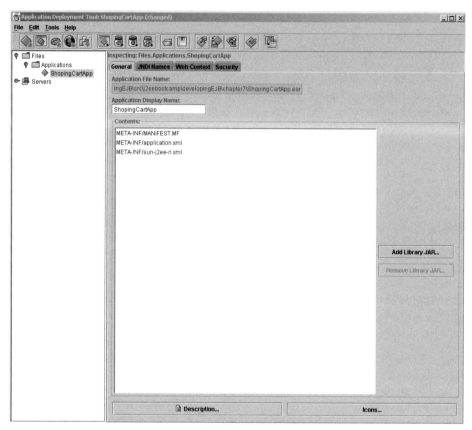

Figure 7-6 Opening a `ShoppingCartApp.ear` file

The `ShoppingCartApp.ear` file can include the EJB and the Web components.
To create the EJB JAR file, follow the steps outlined here.

3. Select the deployment tool and select File | New | Enterprise Bean, which
    pops up a New Enterprise Bean wizard. This wizard prompts you for the
    necessary information to create an EJB JAR file.

4. Now, click Next, and then select the `ShoppingCartApp` from the pulldown
    menu under Create New JAR File in Application. Enter **CartJAR** under
    JARDisplay Name. Then click the Edit button, which brings up the Edit
    Contents of CartJAR window. Use the top half to navigate the directory
    structure.

5. First, go to the APPHOME\chapter7\shop directory and select `Shopping-
    CartHome.class`. Click Add, and do the same for `ShoppingCart.class`
    and `ShoppingCartEJB.class`. Next, navigate to chapter7\model directory

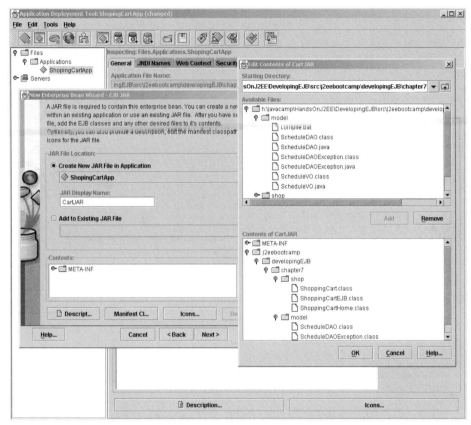

Figure 7-7 Creating the `ShoppingCartJAR` file and adding the `ShoppingCart` class files to it

and add `ScheduleDAO.class`. The added class files are displayed under the Content of the `CartJAR` label as shown in Figure 7-7. After the necessary class files have been selected, click OK and then Next.

6.   Now, specify the type of EJB and its elements. As this is an SFSB, select the Session and Stateful radio buttons, and then select `Shopping-CartEJB.class` under Enterprise Bean class from the pull-down menu. Under Enterprise Bean Name, enter **ShoppingCartBean**, and click Enter. Information about the bean can also be included and associated as an icon.

7.   Next, specify the interfaces by selecting the pull-down menu in the Remote Interfaces; select `ShoppingCartHome` as the Remote Home Interface and `ShoppingCart` as the Remote Interface, as shown in Figure 7-8.

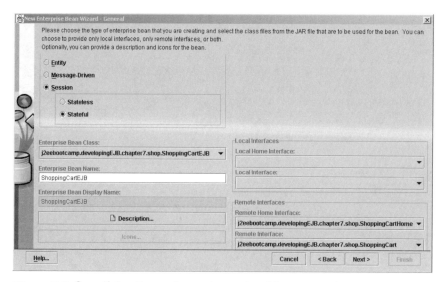

Figure 7-8 Specifying the various elements of the `ShoppingCartApp` and the bean type

8.   Now, click Next, and then select the Bean-Managed transaction management option. Because we don't need to specify any more parameters, click Finish and complete the bean-packing task. A deployment descriptor file for the EJB JAR file is generated and displayed. Note the creation of the ejb-jar-ic.jar file under the Contents and `ShoppingCartJAR` file under `Shopping-Cart-App` in the left section of the window. The deployment descriptor files, `application.xml` and `sun-j2ee-ri.xml`, contain the bean specific descriptors for the container.

Step 8: Packaging the War File

To package the Web components into war file:

1.   Go to the deployment tool and select File | New | Web Component. A New Web Component wizard window pops up. Click Next, and then select Create New war File in Application. Using the pull-down menu, select `Shop-pingCartApp`. Enter **CartWAR** under the war Display Name and click Edit —this action brings up an Edit Contents of CartWAR window with two sections. Use the top part to navigate the directory and select the desired files.

2.   Go to APPHOME\web\servlet and select `ShoppingCartClient.class`; then go to APPHOME\chapter7\web\jsp and select

ShowSearchResult.jsp and ShowShoppingCart.jsp. Finally, go to
APPHOME\chapter7\web and select shop.html.

3. Because the servlet ShoppingCartClient is accessing the database and using
the ScheduleDAO class, include it in the war package. To do this, go to
APPHOME\chapter7\model and select the ScheduleDAO.class,
ScheduleVO, and ScheduleDAOException.class files; click OK. The
files you just added should show up under the Contents of the CartWAR
label. Figure 7-9 shows the selection of the files. Note that the JSP file, Shop-
pingCartClient.class, and the deployment descriptor file, web.xml,
are in the WEB-INF directory. Click Next, and then select Edit on the Web
Component wizard window.

4. Next, specify the type of Web component, as shown in Figure 7-10. Select the
Servlet radio button to indicate that ShoppingCartClient is a servlet
component. Click Next.

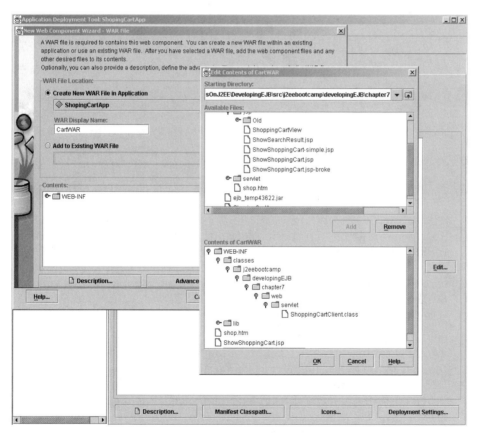

Figure 7-9 Creating the CartWAR and packaging Web components

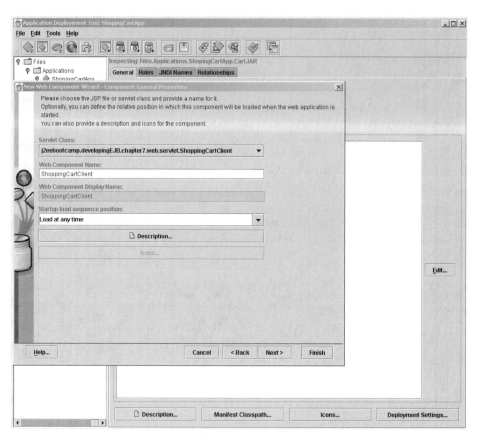

Figure 7-10 Specifying the general Web component properties

5. Specify other items—for the Servlet Class, select `ShoppingCartClient` from the pull-down menu, and leave the default `ShoppingCartClient` as the Web Component Name. The Web Component Display Name also shows `ShoppingCartClient`. You can select the startup load sequence of the servlet. It is recommended to take the default value load at any time. To add any description, use the Description option. (Note that it isn't used in this example.) Click Next.

6. We're not setting any initialization parameters for the component, so skip to the next screen by clicking Next. Use the alias option to map URL to a servlet or JSP. Click Add, and then enter **ShopAlias**. One level of indirection is provided, so the name of the servlet isn't hardcoded to the name in the HTML form. For example, in the HTML form, the action will show that `action=http://www.javacamp.com/ShoppingCartContext/Shop-Alias`. `ShopAlias` is mapped to `ShoppingCartClient`. `ShoppingCart-Client` can be replaced with `PremierCartClient` as long as `ShopAlias`

is mapped to `PremierCartClient`, and the html and JPS files will work normally without the customer being aware of the changes. Click Next.

7. The next screen is security. Ensure that the User Caller ID radio button is selected and click Next. Because we're not setting any environment values or context parameters, click Next twice.

8. `ShoppingCartClient` needs to access `ShoppingCartEJB`, so specify the reference by selecting Add, and under Coded Name, enter **ejb/TheCart**. Under (EJB Bean) Type, select session; under Interfaces, select remote; under Home Interface, enter **ShoppingCartHome**; and under Local/Remote Interface, enter **ShoppingCart**.

9. The java:comp/env/ejb/TheCart lookup parameter maps to ejb/Shop-pingCartHome. Let the Web component know these interfaces map to `ShoppingCartEJB` by specifying the Enterprise Bean Name to **Shopping-CartEJB**, the name given when packing the EJB-JAR file. (See Figure 7-11.) Click Next.

10. Because `ShoppingCartClient` needs to access the database, specify the necessary Reference Factories. Click Add and, under the Coded Name, enter **jdbc/JCampDS**. Under Type, select `javax.sql.DataSource`; under Authentication, select Container and check the Sharable option. Map this to the actual data source defined in the reference implementation by selecting jdbc/Cloud-scape as the JNDI Name. Use j2ee as the user name and password. (See Figure 7-12.) Because we're not specifying any resource environment reference, click Next.

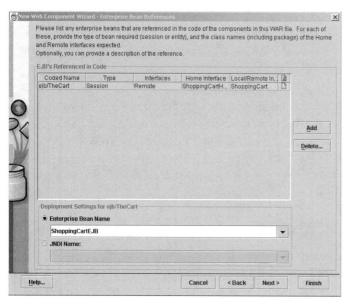

Figure 7-11 Specifying the `ShoppingCartEJB` references to the Web component

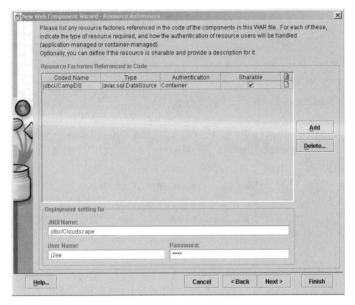

Figure 7-12 Specifying the datasource and JNDI name

11. Specify the startup html page by clicking Add; use the pull-down menu and select `shop.html`. (See Figure 7-13.) This application does not use any JSP tag libraries and does not define any special error pages. Click Next.

12. This example implements no security features, so click Next to display the deployment descriptor. Click Finish, which concludes the Web component deployment steps.

You should see two component icons (`CartWAR` and `CartJAR`) under the `ShoppingCartApp` icon on the left side of the Application Deployment tool. To the right under the Contents label, you'll see the `ejb-jar-ic.jar` that contains the EJB component and the `war-ic.war` file that contains the Web component. There are also two deployment descriptors—`application.xml` and `sun-j2ee-ri.xml`—and an empty `MANIFEST.MF` file under the META-INF directory as shown in Figure 7-14.

Step 9: Deployment Descriptors

The deployment tool generates two types of deployment descriptor files for the enterprise application archive file (the standard J2EE deployment descriptor file and the application server-specific deployment descriptors). The EJB and Web components have their own standard J2EE deployment descriptors. The

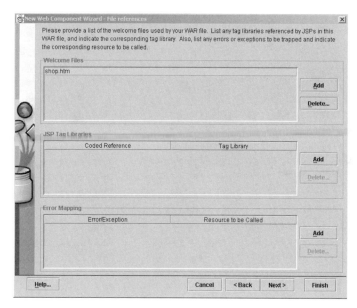

Figure 7-13 Specifying the start-up `shop.htm` file

`application.xml` is an application level deployment descriptor that contains information on various components that make up the enterprise application. The `ejb-jar.xml` and `web.xml` are standard J2EE deployment descriptor files for EJB and Web components, respectively. The `sun-j2ee-ri.xml` is a vendor-specific deployment descriptor. Table 7-1 highlights the component name and applicable deployment descriptors.

Table 7-1 Component Packaging and Deployment Descriptors

Component Name	Standard J2EE Deployment Descriptor	Vendor-Specific Deployment Descriptor
ShoppingCartApp.ear	application.xml	sun-j2ee-ri.xml
ShoppingCartJAR(ejb-jar-ic.jar)	ejb-jar.xml	None
ShoppingCartWAR(war-ic.jar)	web.xml	None

Let's look first at the highlights of the `ejb-jar.xml` deployment descriptor. The main difference from the previous SLSB is the `<session-type>`, which indicates that it's a stateful session bean.

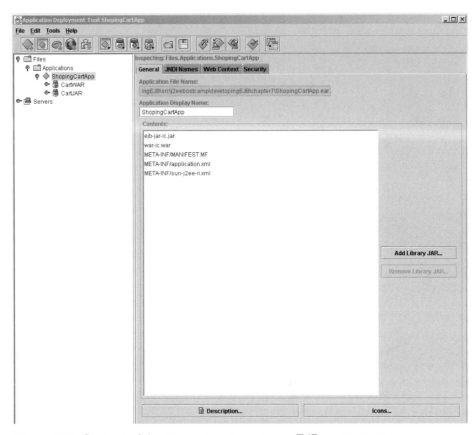

Figure 7-14 Content of the `ShoppingCartApp`—EJB component,
Web components, and the deployment descriptor files

```
<ejb-jar>
    <display-name>CartJAR</display-name>
    <enterprise-beans>
        <session>
            <display-name>ShoppingCartEJB</display-name>
            <ejb-name>ShoppingCartEJB</ejb-name>
            <home>j2eebootcamp.developingEJB.chapter7.shop.Shop-
pingCartHome</home>
            <remote>j2eebootcamp.developingEJB.chapter7.shop.Shop-
pingCart</remote>
            <ejb-class>j2eebootcamp.devel-
opingEJB.chapter7.shop.ShoppingCartEJB</ejb-class>
            <session-type>Stateful</session-type>
            <transaction-type>Bean</transaction-type>
            <security-identity>
```

```
          <description></description>
          <use-caller-identity></use-caller-identity>
          </security-identity>
      </session>
   </enterprise-beans>
```

The deployment descriptor for the Web application, web.xml, contains the information about the servlet and how it maps to ShoppingCartEJB. Most of the tags are quite expressive in their function. Notice the `<servlet-mapping>` tag is used to map an arbitrary name, /Shopalias, enclosed by `<url-pattern>`, to the actual servlet name enclosed by `<servlet-name>` tag. The `<session-timeout>` tag sets the timeout for the servlet session, and the `<welcome-file>` is the default startup file for the Web application. The `<resource-ref>` tag encloses the datasource definition. The `<ejb-ref>` encloses several tags that enable the servlet to find the remote SFSB via the JNDI name enclosed by `<ejb-ref-name>` and the remote home interface, component interface, and ShoppingCartEJB instance.

```
  <web-app>
      <display-name>CartWAR</display-name>
      <servlet>
          <servlet-name>ShoppingCartClient</servlet-name>
          <display-name>ShoppingCartClient</display-name>
          <servlet-class>j2eebootcamp.devel-
opingEJB.chapter7.web.servlet.ShoppingCartClient</servlet-class>
      </servlet>
      <servlet-mapping>
          <servlet-name>ShoppingCartClient</servlet-name>
          <url-pattern>/ShopAlias</url-pattern>
      </servlet-mapping>
      <session-config>
          <session-timeout>30</session-timeout>
      </session-config>
      <welcome-file-list>
          <welcome-file>shop.htm</welcome-file>
      </welcome-file-list>
      <resource-ref>
          <res-auth>Container</res-auth>
      </resource-ref>
      <ejb-ref>
          <ejb-ref-name>ejb/TheCart</ejb-ref-name>
          <ejb-ref-type>Session</ejb-ref-type>
          <home>ShoppingCartHome</home>
          <remote>ShoppingCart</remote>
          <ejb-link>ShoppingCartEJB</ejb-link>
      </ejb-ref>
  </web-app>
```

The `application.xml` file is the deployment descriptor for the enterprise application. It contains information regarding the names of the components that compose the application and their respective package names, as shown next. The packaged Web component file, `war-ic.war`, is enclosed by the `<web-uri>` and the ejb-jar-ic by `<ejb>` tags. It also declares the root context of the application specified by the `<context-root>` tag.

```
<application>
  <display-name>ShopingCartApp</display-name>
  <description>Application description</description>
  <module>
    <web>
      <web-uri>war-ic.war</web-uri>
      <context-root>/ShopNow</context-root>
    </web>
  </module>
  <module>
    <ejb>ejb-jar-ic.jar</ejb>
  </module>
</application>
```

Step 10: Deploying `ShoppingCartApp.ear`

There are two more settings to cover before we can deploy the application. We need to map the JNDI names and specify the Web context.

1. To start, go to the Application Deployment Tool and select the JNDI Names tab. Enter **MyCart** under the JNDI Name under the Application and References section as shown in Figure 7-15. The JNDI name can be any arbitrary name; it gives us another level of indirection and allows us to map any arbitrary name used in the Web component to the EJB component. It helps us link the EJB component reference name to the actual EJB component implementation.

2. Select the Web Context tab in the Deployment tool and enter **/ShopNow** under the Context Root column as shown in Figure 7-16. The Web context is used to specify different application contexts.

3. Next, package both the EJB and Web component into EJB-JAR and war files. To deploy, select Tools and then select Verifier, which checks the files for possible mapping and assignment errors, as shown in Figure 7-17. Then close the window by clicking the Close button.

4. Next, select Tool | Deploy. The Deploy `ShoppingCartApp` window appears. Select `ShoppingCartApp` from the pull-down menu under the Object to Deploy label and then select localhost from the pull-down menu under the Target Server: label. (See Figure 7-18.) Click Next.

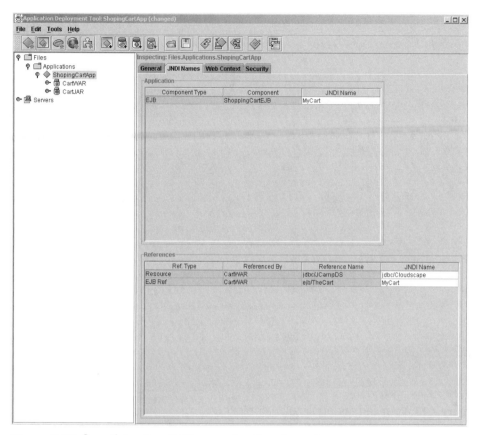

Figure 7-15 Specifying the JNDI name for the `ShoppingCartEJB` component

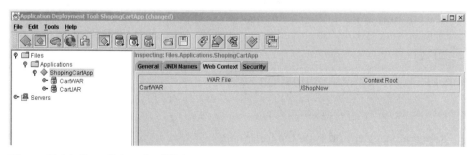

Figure 7-16 Specifying the Web component context root

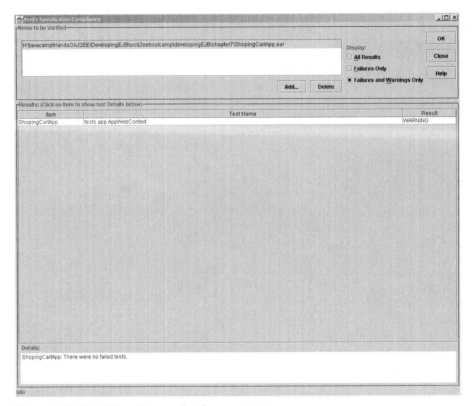

Figure 7-17 Verifying the application context

5. You have another chance to modify or reenter JNDI names at this point, so verify that the names are correct. Select Next and verify that the Context Root name is correct. Select Finish. A successful completion should display the OK button with progress indication as shown in Figure 7-19. Select OK— you've successfully deployed ShoppingCartApp.ear, a J2EE enterprise application.

Step 11: Testing the Application

Now, it's time to test the application.

1. Open a browser and type the following:

```
http://localhost:8000/ShopNow/
```

You should see the search screen shown in Figure 7-20.

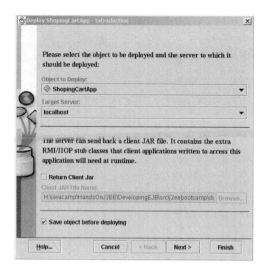

Figure 7-18 Setting the deployment object and target server

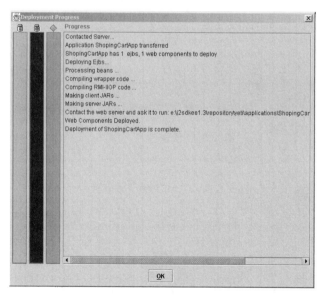

Figure 7-19 Completion of the `ShoppingCartApp` application

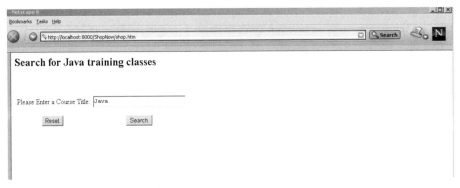

Figure 7-20 HTML search form

Schedule ID	Course Title	Location	Start Date	End Date	Cost	Status	Option
2001082004	Introduction to Java Server Pages	Hollywood/CA(USA)	2002-08-20	2002-08-24	1400.0	OPEN	ADD to Cart
2001092400	Advanced Java Programming	Milpitas/CA(USA)	2002-09-24	2002-09-28	2500.0	CANCELLED	ADD to Cart
2001092401	Advanced Enterprise JavaBeans(EJB)	Milpitas/CA(USA)	2002-05-24	2002-05-28	2500.0	CANCELLED	ADD to Cart
2001092402	Introduction to Enterprise JavaBeans(EJB)	Milpitas/CA(USA)	2002-03-24	2002-03-28	2500.0	FULL	ADD to Cart
2001092403	Advanced Java Programming	Milpitas/CA(USA)	2002-09-24	2002-09-28	2500.0	OPEN	ADD to Cart
2001082009	Introduction to Java Server Pages	Hollywood/CA(USA)	2002-08-20	2002-08-24	1400.0	OPEN	ADD to Cart

Search results of Java courses

Figure 7-21 Result of the search form

2. Next, enter the search text (for example, **java**), and click the Search button. Figure 7-21 is the result of the search.

3. You can use the Add button to add the course to the shopping cart. The result is the addition of the course item to the shopping cart and the display of the running total for the course, as shown in Figure 7-22.

4. When you're finished, empty the shopping card by clicking the Empty button, as shown in Figure 7-23.

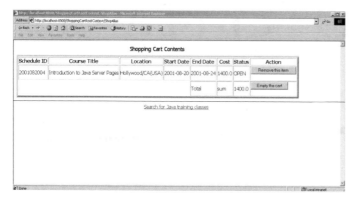

Figure 7-22 Contents of the shopping cart

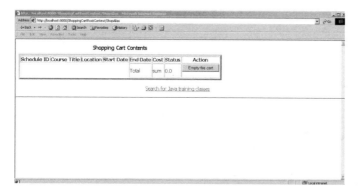

Figure 7-23 Emptying the shopping cart

Summary

Stateful session beans are suited for implementing conversational business logic where state information maintenance is necessary. SFSBs are used for modeling business processes and for controlling and coordinating other objects. In this chapter, we implemented and deployed an SFSB `ShoppingCartEJB`. In the next chapter, we'll look at entity beans and discuss the APIs.

INTRODUCTION TO ENTITY BEANS

Chapter 8

This chapter discusses the general characteristics of entity beans and their functions. Note that hands on coding examples are provided in subsequent chapters. Specifically, this chapter highlights the following:

- the characteristics and features of entity beans
- types of entity beans
- the type of business logic best modeled with entity beans
- the elements of entity beans
- the life cycle of entity beans
- the rules for writing entity beans
- a comparison of bean-managed and container-managed persistence

Overview

Entity beans are a type of Enterprise JavaBean used for modeling persistent data. In the case of EJBs, persistent data are manipulated by methods in the entity bean instance, which are eventually saved to a data store such as a relational database. The entity bean instance encapsulates the persistent data and the business logic that manipulates it. The entity bean instance is responsible for creating, managing, removing, and synchronizing the state of the persistent data with the underlying data store. Persistence can be handled in one of the following ways.

- Java object serialization enables Java objects to suspend the working state of the object from memory, decompose the object state, convert it into byte stream, and write it to secondary storage. Java object serialization is useful for providing persistence for individual Java objects but is neither efficient nor feasible for large-scale data persistence.

- Most business objects are composed of complex data; business objects can be decomposed into individual datum units and stored separately. For example, a customer entity bean could consist of a customer ID, first name, last name, phone number, email, and address. This information would represent persistent data, which are manipulated and saved to a database. This concept, *object/relation (O/R) mapping*, is a highly efficient and scalable way to persist business data by mapping objects to a relational database. The customer entity objects are decomposed into relational data that maps to an individual column of the customer table. Mapping objects to relational data can be done manually in simple cases; complex cases may require sophisticated O/R mapping tools.

- An alternate to mapping objects to a relational database management system (RDBMS) is to use an object database management system (ODBMS) instead. In an ODBMS, the objects are stored directly using the object database API, avoiding the additional step of O/R mapping. Object query language (OQL) is used to query for object properties. Although an ODBMS is a better match for object persistence than an RDMBS, relational databases maintain market share due to legacy data requirements and the slow adoption of ODBMSs.

- Another option is to write a custom protocol for serialization. Depending on your special needs and circumstances, you could write your own special protocol to implement custom serialization with the externalizable interface. The externalizable interface has two methods, `writeExternal()` and `readExternal()`, which are used to custom code the desired protocol to write and read objects. Portability is the main issue with this option.

The most common way to manage persistence in entity beans is to use O/R mapping with a relational database.

Note: Entity beans are agnostic to the underlying data source; their behavior is the same regardless of whether a relational or an object database is used. We'll refer to relational databases throughout the book, though, because they're so pervasive and because the majority of developers understand and have used them.

Entity Bean Characteristics

Entity beans represent business entities and consist of business logic that manipulates business data as well as logic necessary to make the entity bean persistent. This is enabled by writing the data to durable storage such as a database. In an object-oriented design, entity beans are used to model nouns and represent persistent business data, such as cars, books, and widgets that are then stored in the database. In general, an entity bean instance is an in-memory representation of persistent business data in a database; the entity bean instance is responsible for updating and synchronizing the in-memory data with that same data in the database. The database administrator can insert rows directly into the table and create an entity bean representation in the database.

Entity beans have the following characteristics:

- Entity beans are ideal for modeling business concepts that can be expressed as nouns and also referred to as persistent business data. The entity bean, along with the container, provides the necessary framework to simplify and automate the implementation of persistence logic.

- Entity beans are long-lived and survive container crashes. The container and the entity bean instance work together to synchronize the in-memory data with the database, ensuring that if the EJB container or server crashes, the container is able to recreate the entity bean instance from data saved in the database. Entity beans exist in the database until they are explicitly removed.

- Entity beans are identified by primary keys.

- Multiple clients can access an entity bean instance. Unlike the session beans, entity beans can service multiple clients. It's the container's responsibility to serialize the requests.

- Entity beans instances can be pooled. Because entity beans read and write to a database, they are comparatively slow. Pooling adds efficiency and scalability to an entity bean's application.

- Entity beans are inherently transactional; transactions are implemented using the deployment descriptors.

When implementing EJBs, bean developers should consider using entity beans if the business application has the following requirements:

- when the EJB application has to manage persistent business data

- when it's necessary to provide concurrent access to the EJB from multiple clients

- when it's necessary to provide sophisticated and flexible transaction support declaratively
- when the business application logic calls for transparent access to the business data stored in the databases, legacy system, or ERP system
- when the need to provide robust, long-lived, persistent data management and time-to-market is an important criteria

Types of Entity Beans

Entity beans are classified depending on how persistence is managed: bean-managed persistence (BMP) or container-managed persistence (CMP). When using BMP, the EJB developer is responsible for writing the necessary logic to manage the persistence in the entity bean class. The bean developer has to write the necessary database access logic. With CMP, the container is responsible for generating the code necessary for data access and management. The bean developer is responsible for specifying the necessary container-managed persistence fields and container-managed relationship fields in the bean class and declaring abstract persistent schema in the deployment descriptor. The deployment tool uses the deployment descriptor and the CMP entity bean class to generate the concrete classes necessary to manage persistence and the life cycle of the CMP entity bean instance.

The basic differences between CMP and BMP beans are illustrated in Table 8-1.

Table 8-1 Comparison between BMP and CMP Entity Beans

Bean Type	Implemented by Container	Implemented by Developer

CMP	`ejbActivate()`
	`ejbPassivate()`
	`ejbLoad()`
	`ejbStore()`
	abstract getter/setter methods
		Business methods
		Specify abstract methods and abstract persistence schemas

BMP	None	Business methods
		`ejbActivate()`
		`ejbPassivate()`
		`ejbLoad()`
		`ejbStore()`
		`ejbRemove()`

With regard to the entity bean's life cycle, behavior, and APIs, there's essentially no difference between BMP and CMP entity beans.

Life Cycle of an Entity Bean

CMP and BMP entity bean instances have the same life cycle with three possible states: *does not exist*, *pooled*, and *ready*. We'll discuss the various methods that can be implemented in the entity bean class later in the chapter. We'll now focus on the effects of those methods during the entity bean instance's life cycle. We can classify these as *transitional methods* (causing an entity bean instance to change from the current state to another state) and *nontransitional methods* (not affecting the current state of the bean instance). Figure 8-1 illustrates the life cycle of an entity bean instance.

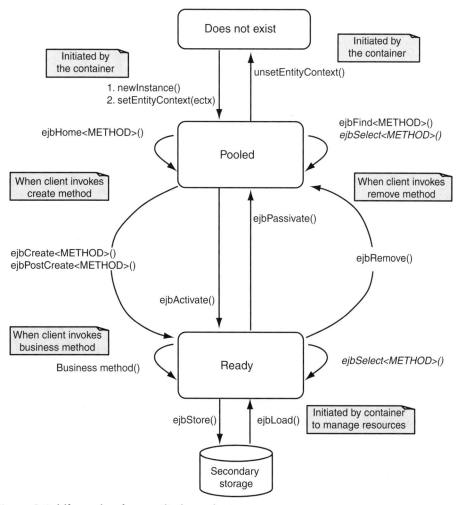

Figure 8-1 Life cycle of an entity bean instance

Does Not Exist State

At initial state, the bean instance is not available. It is in the `does not exist` state. If a client attempts to invoke a method, it will throw `javax.ejb.NoSuchObject-FoundException`. There are two transitional methods invoked by a container to initiate a life cycle of an entity bean instance. First, the container invokes the `newInstance()` method, followed by the `setEntityContext(ectx)` method; it passes the `EntityContext` reference enabling the container to access the bean instance, which (as Figure 8-1 shows) is valid throughout its lifetime. At the end of the `setEntityContext()` method, the entity bean instance transitions from the `does not exist` state to the `pooled` state.

Pooled State

In the `pooled` state, all entity bean instances are considered equivalent because they aren't associated with any particular entity object identity. In addition, they cannot execute any business methods. Each entity bean has its own pool. Entity beans must implement at least one finder method type, `ejbFindByPrimaryKey()`. Optionally, entity beans may have `ejbHome<METHOD>()` implemented.

The CMP beans may have the `ejbSelect<METHOD>()` in addition to the `ejbFind<METHOD>(args)` and the `ejbHome<METHOD>()` method implemented. The `ejbSelect<METHOD>()` method is shown in italics in Figure 8-1 indicating its applicability to CMP beans only. These finder, select, and home methods are nontransitional and implement logic that applies to the entity bean class type.

In the `pooled` state, there are three transitional methods: one is client initiated, while the other two are container initiated. When a client calls a `create` method in the home interface, the container will invoke a matching `ejbCreate` method first, followed by a corresponding `ejbPostCreate` method. The `ejbCreate` method executes the logic to create an entity bean instance. By the end of the `ejbPostCreate` method, the bean instance will have transitioned from `pooled` state to `ready` state.

The container can also move the bean instance from `pooled` state to `ready` state by invoking the `ejbActivate()` method. If the system resources are running low, the container can invoke the `unsetEntityContext()` method and evict the entity bean instance from memory, moving it to the `does not exist` state.

Ready State

When an entity bean instance is in the `ready` state, it is associated with a primary key and can execute business methods for the clients. At this state, there are four nontransitional methods in the case of CMP entity beans and three non-transitional methods in the case of BMP entity beans.

The two nontransitional data access methods are `ejbLoad()` and `ejbStore()`, which execute the SQL code and logic to synchronize the in-memory persistent data with the database. The container automatically invokes these methods, guaranteeing that the persistent data are synchronized with the database.

The two types of nontransitional methods are methods that implement the business methods and, with CMP, the `ejbSelect<METHOD>()`. When a client calls business methods, the container, in most cases, will first invoke the `ejbLoad()` method before executing the business method. After the completion of the business method, the container then invokes `ejbStore()` to synchronize the persistent data. If the bean instance throws RemoteException during the execution of the any business method, the bean instance is evicted from memory and transitions to the `does not exist` state.

Let's look at two transitional methods—one client-initiated and another container-initiated. When a client calls the `remove` method, the container invokes the `ejbRemove()` method, and the bean instance transitions from `the ready` state to the `pooled` state. During `pooled` state, the bean instance isn't associated with a primary key and can be assigned to another client by the container. If the entity bean instance's idle time has exceeded the passivation time or if the system is running low on system resources, the container can invoke the `ejbPassivate()` method and move the bean instance from `ready` to `pooled` state.

Entity Bean Elements

An entity bean developer is responsible for providing the following elements of an entity bean:

- remote home and remote component interfaces (if a remote client view is to be provided)
- local home and local component interfaces (if a local client view is to be provided)
- primary key class
- entity bean implementation class
- deployment descriptor
- dependent and helper classes (optional)

Home and Component Interfaces

Developers can provide either a local client view or remote client view of an entity bean class; in some rare cases both are provided, and the deployer chooses during deployment. When choosing the local client view, both the local home and local component interfaces are implemented, and the entity bean and the client must be colocated in the same JVM. When providing a remote client view, the developer implements the remote home and remote component interfaces, thereby avoiding the colocation restriction. Refer to Chapter 4 for a thorough discussion of the client view.

Primary Key Class

A *primary key* uniquely identifies an entity bean instance. In simple cases, a primary key can be a Java primitive, such as an integer or a string. This integer or string maps to a single field in the entity bean class (such as customer id and purchase order number), representing a table column in the database. In complex cases, a primary key can be a composite of several fields that map to multiple fields in the entity bean class. These fields represent multiple rows of different tables in the database. Every instance of an entity bean is identified by a unique primary key, enabling the container to track the entity bean instance. Below are several rules that must be adhered to when writing a primary key class:

- The primary key class must be declared `public`.
- The primary key class must have a `public` constructor with no parameters.
- Primary key class must be serializable.
- All fields in the primary key class must be declared `public`.
- The primary key class must implement the `hashCode()` method.
- The primary key class must implement the `equals()` method.

Entity Bean Class API

All entity bean classes are required to implement the `javax.ejb.EntityBean` interface. See Figure 8-2, which illustrates an entity bean class hierarchy. Let's discuss the methods declared in the `EntityBean` class.

The `setEntityContext` Method

When instantiating an entity bean instance, the container will invoke the `setEntityContext()` method and pass an entity reference context,

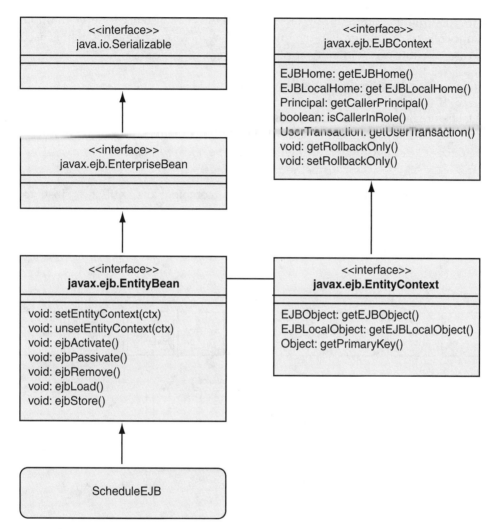

Figure 8-2 Entity bean class hierarchy

EntityContext, as an argument to the entity bean instance (this reference context remains valid throughout the lifetime of the entity bean instance). Using the entity reference context, the container can access and manage the bean instance life cycle.

Bean developers can use the setEntityContext() method to allocate common entity bean class specific resources, which remain valid and accessible throughout the lifetime of all bean instances. Note that this method should not be used to allocate instance-specific resources, because the container can reassign the instance multiple times during the lifetime of the bean instance to serve multiple entity objects' identities. Later in this chapter, we'll discuss a method that is used to assign entity object identity-specific resources.

The `UnsetEntityContext` Method

Just before the entity bean instance is terminated and garbage collected, the container will invoke the `unsetEntityContext()`. All the resources allocated in the `setEntityContext()` method must be released in the `unsetEntityContext()` method.

The sequence diagram in Figure 8-3 shows the container and entity bean instance during the `setEntityContext()` and `unsetEntityContext()` methods.

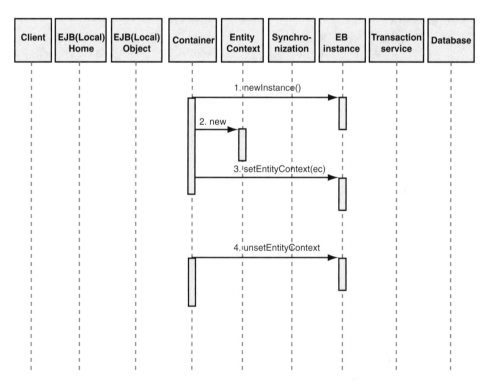

Figure 8-3 Sequence diagram of `setEntityContext()` and `unsetEntityContext()`

The `ejbCreate` Method

Entity beans can have zero or a multiple of `ejbCreate<METHOD>()`. This method creates both a bean instance and a data representation in the database. When a client invokes `create<METHOD>()` on its home interface, the container invokes a matching `ejbCreate<METHOD>()` in the container. In a typical case (see Figure 8-4), `ejbCreate<METHOD>()` validates the client-supplied arguments, inserts a record representing the entity object into the database, and

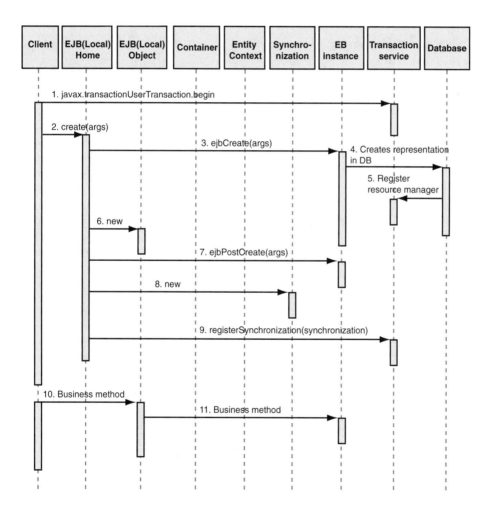

Figure 8-4 Sequence diagram of `ejbCreate()` and `ejbPostCreate()` methods

initializes the bean instance variables before returning the primary key for the created entity object. At that point, `ejbPostCreate<METHOD>()` is invoked.

The `ejbPostCreate` Method

For every `ejbCreate<METHOD>()` method, there must be a corresponding `ejbPostCreate<METHOD>()` with a matching number of arguments, types, and exceptions. After the invocation of `ejbCreate<METHOD>()`, it is followed by the invocation of the corresponding `ejbPostCreate<METHOD>()` method in the bean instance. This is illustrated by the sequence diagram in Figure 8-4.

While the `ejbCreate<METHOD>()` method's return value must be a primary key for the created object, the `ejbPostCreate` method must have return value void. Because the `ejbPostCreate<METHOD>()` method has access to the primary key of the entity instance, this method is useful for applying additional initialization logic prior to the entity bean instance being made available to the client.

These two methods must throw the `CreateException` exception if they encounter any problems while creating the entity bean instance. The `ejbCreate<METHOD>()` may also throw the `DuplicateException` exception if the primary key already exists.

The `ejbRemove` Method

The `ejbRemove()` method contains the necessary logic to remove the entity bean representation from the database. When a client invokes the remove method on the interface, the container initiates the `ejbRemove()` method, deleting a row representing an entity from the database. The container will synchronize the instance's state before invoking the `ejbRemove()` method. At the end of this method, the entity bean's representation of persistent data in the database is deleted and the bean instance is returned to the pool, so it must release any instance-related resources allocated in `ejbActivate()` method. A client can invoke the remove method using the home or the component interface. This method throws the `RemoveException` if it encounters any problem with the removal of the entity bean instance. Refer to Figure 8-5 for the sequence diagram, and note that the client can invoke the `remove()` method via either the home or the component interface.

The `ejbHome` Method

The `ejbHome<METHOD>()` methods are used for implementing bulk updates and aggregator methods that apply to the entity bean class type. The `employee` entity bean class could have a home method called `ejbHomeGiveAllARaise(10)`

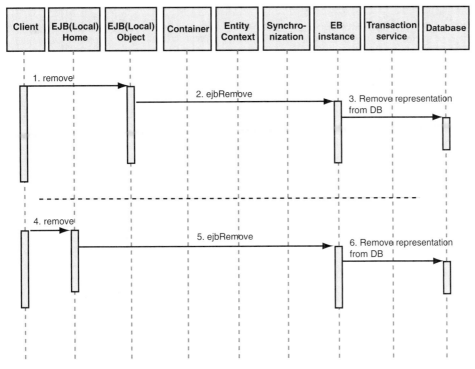

Figure 8-5 Sequence diagram of the `ejbRemove()` method

indicating that all employees, each represented by a row in the database, should be given a 10% raise. The home methods apply to the `entity` class type and not to an instance of the entity bean. The `ejbHome<METHOD>()` implemented in the entity bean class must have a matching `<METHOD>()` method declared in the home interface.

The `ejbFind` Method

The finder methods, those starting with `ejbFind<METHOD>()`, implement the logic to use the method's argument to locate the entity object or a collection of entity objects in the database. Typically, in the case of a relational database, SQL SELECT commands locate specific rows from the database as illustrated in the sequence diagram in Figure 8-6. The finder methods return a primary key or a collection of primary keys depending on the logic. An entity bean class may define one or more finder methods, and every entity bean must implement the `ejbFindByPrimaryKey()` method. There can be other finder methods as well. For example, `ejbFindAccountsWithBalanceGreaterThan(4000)` would return a collection of primary keys satisfying the search criteria. The method

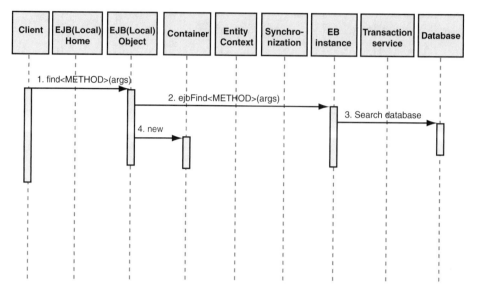

Figure 8-6 Sequence diagram of the `ejbFind` method

`ejbFindByPrimaryKey()` method throws `FinderException` if it cannot find the primary key in the database or `DuplicateException` if it finds duplicate primary keys in the database. Refer to the sequence diagram of `ejbFinder<METHOD>()` in Figure 8-6.

The `ejbActivate` and `ejbPassivate` Methods

The entity bean class has several callback methods that are invoked by the container for managing resources and life cycles of bean instances. For efficiency reasons, entity bean instances are often pooled, and the instances don't have any object identity assigned. When the container invokes the `ejbActivate()` method, it assigns a primary key and object identity to the bean instance and transitions the instance to the `ready` state. It's then ready to execute any business methods. The `ejbActivate()` method is typically used to associate resources that are specific to an entity bean instance. The container also invokes `ejbLoad()` method to synchronize persistent data after `ejbActivate()` method, but before the business method is invoked.

The container calls the `ejbPassivate()` method before the instance is passivated or moved to the pool. All the resources previously allocated in the `ejbActivate()` method for that bean instance must be released in `ejbPassivate()` method. The container invokes `ejbStore()` to save the persistent data before invoking `ejbPassivate()` method. Figure 8-7 illustrates the sequences.

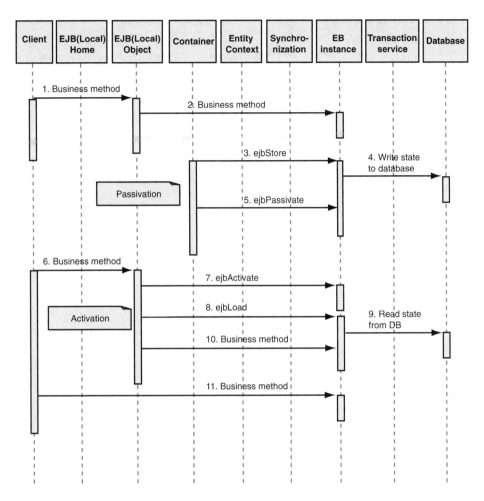

Figure 8-7 Sequence diagram of the `ejbActivate()`,
`ejbPassivate()`, `ejbLoad()`, and `ejbStore()` methods

The `ejbLoad` and `ejbStore` Methods

The container invokes the `ejbLoad()` and `ejbStore()` methods to synchronize in-memory persistent fields with the database. In the case of relational databases, the `ejbLoad()` method contains the necessary SQL SELECT command and the logic to read and translate the persistent data from the database. The `ejbStore()` method consists of the SQL UPDATE command and the logic to save the data to the database. Before a business method is executed, the container first invokes `ejbLoad()`, which loads the data from the database and then executes the business method. After the completion of business method, the container will invoke `ejbStore()` and save the data back in the database. This enables the container to guarantee that the in-memory data is synchronized with the database.

Business Methods

The business methods consist of the business logic that a bean developer implements in the entity bean class and are only executed when the entity bean instance is in `ready` state. For every business method declared in the component interface, there must be an identical matching business method implemented in the entity bean class.

Figure 8-7 illustrates the entity bean methods and the implementation responsibility. As shown, the business methods are always implemented by the bean developers. Callback methods are implemented by the bean developer in the case of BMP and by the container in the case of CMP.

The `EntityContext` Interface

Besides the methods we discussed earlier, there are methods defined in the `EntityBeanContext` interface and its superinterface. These methods can be grouped into three types: *transaction*, *security* and *reference-related*. An entity bean instance may access its primary key by invoking the `getPrimaryKey()` method or its local interfaces by calling the `getEJBLocalHome()` and `getEJBLocalObject()`. It may also access its remote interface by calling the `getEJBHome()` and `getEJBObject()` methods.

The security-related methods, `getCallerPrincipal()` and `isCallerInRole()`, can be used by bean developers to implement EJB security, which we'll discuss in Chapter 15. Not all the methods in the `EntityContext` interface can be invoked within all the methods of the entity bean class. Table 8-2 shows the `EntityContext` methods and the resources that can be accessed within various entity bean methods. The transaction-related methods, `getUserTransaction`, `getRollbackOnly`, and `setRollbackOnly` allow the instance to control the transaction. We'll discuss the details of this in Chapter 14.

One of the differences between CMP and BMP entity beans is that the CMP entity bean can have one optional method, `ejbSelect<METHOD>()`. This method can be used to implement logic to find related entities or dependent values. (This select method will be discussed in detail in Chapter 10.)

Table 8-2 `EntityContext` Methods and Resources Accessible from within an Entity Bean's Methods

Method	Access Allowed	EntityContext Method Operation Allowed
constructor	None	None
getEntityContext, unsetEntityContext	JNDI access to java:com/env	getEJBHome, getEJBEJBLocalHome
ejbActivate, ejbPassivate	JNDI access to java:com/env	getEJBHome, getEJBObject, getEJBLocalHome, getEJBLocalObject, getPrimaryKey
ejbCreate, ejbFind, ejbHome	JNDI access to java:com/env, Resource manager access, Enterprise bean access	getEJBHome, getEJBLocalHome, getCallerPrincipal, getRollbackOnly, isCallerInRole, setRollbackOnly
ejbPostCreate, ejbRemove, ejbLoad, ejbStore, business methods	JNDI access to java:com/env, Resource manager access, Enterprise bean access	getEJBHome, getEJBLocalHome, getCallerPrincipal, getRollbackOnly, isCallerInRole, setRollbackOnly, getEJBObject, getEJBLocalObject, getPrimaryKey

Rules for Implementing the Entity Bean Class

Bean developers must adhere to certain requirements while implementing the entity bean class. The entity bean class must implement, directly or indirectly, the `javax.ejb.EntityBean` interface. The class must be defined as `public`, and it must define a `public` constructor that takes no arguments. The class must not be defined as `abstract` or `final`, and developers cannot define `finalize()` method. The entity bean class must also implement `ejbCreate<METHOD>()`, `ejbPostCreate<METHOD>()`, `ejbFind<METHOD>()`, and `ejbHome<METHOD>()` if the create, finder and home methods are declared in the home interface. At the very least, the home interface must declare the `findByPrimaryKey()` method, and the bean class must implement the `ejbFindByPrimaryKey()` method.

The entity bean class is allowed to have superclasses and/or superinterfaces. If the entity bean has superclasses, then the business methods, the `ejbCreate` and `ejbPostCreate` methods, the finder and home methods, and the `EntityBean` interface methods may be implemented in enterprise bean class or in any of its superclasses. The entity bean class can implement other helper methods besides the methods required by the EJB specification.

Rules for Method Implementation

The specific rules a bean developer must follow to implement the methods discussed in the previous section are elaborated on in the following sections.

Rules for Implementing `ejbCreate` and `ejbPostCreate` Methods

The `ejbCreate<METHOD>()` method consists of the logic to insert data in the database, thereby creating a business entity bean object. Note that there can be zero or more `ejbCreate<METHOD>()` methods implemented in the entity bean class. Additionally, for every `ejbCreate<METHOD>()` method, there must be a matching `ejbPostCreate<METHOD>()` method implemented in the entity bean class. Both methods must follow these rules:

- For every `create<METHOD>()` declared in the entity bean's home interface, there must be identical `create<METHOD>()` methods with `ejb` and `ejbPost` prefixes, that is, `ejbCreate<METHOD>()` and `ejbPostCreate<METHOD>()`, implemented in the entity bean class.

- The method must be declared as `public` and must not be declared as `final` or `static`.

- The return type must be the entity bean's primary key type for the `ejbCreate<METHOD>()` method and type void for the `ejbPostCreate<METHOD>()` method.

- The method argument and return value types must be RMI-IIOP legal for the `ejbCreate<METHOD>()` method, and the method argument in the `ejbPostCreate<METHOD>()` method must be identical to the `ejbCreate<METHOD>()` method.

- Both these methods must throw `javax.ejb.CreateException` and may throw arbitrary application specific exceptions.

- To inform the container of nonapplication exceptions, these `ejbCreate` methods should throw the `javax.ejb.EJBException` or another `java.lang.RuntimeException` but must not throw the `java.rmi.RemoteException`.

Rules for Implementing `ejbFinder` Methods

Finder methods are used to find one or more primary keys in the database. The entity bean class must implement one or more `ejbFind<METHOD>(...)` finder methods, which must adhere to the following rules:

- A finder method must use the `ejbFind` prefix followed by the method name.
- A finder method must be declared `public` and must not be declared as `final` or `static`.
- The method argument types must be RMI-IIOP legal.
- All entity bean classes must implement the `ejbFindByPrimaryKey(arg)` method and must return an entity bean's primary key.
- Single object finder methods may return the entity bean's primary key type while multi-object finder methods return a collection of objects implementing the entity bean's primary key type.
- A finder method may throw `javax.ejb.FinderException` in addition to other application specific exceptions.
- To inform the container of nonapplication exceptions, the ejbFinder method should throw `javax.ejb.EJBException` or another `java.lang.RuntimeException`. The method must not throw the `java.rmi.RemoteException`.
- A single object finder throws `ObjectNotFoundException` if the requested entity object does not exist. The multi-object finder must not throw this exception but instead return an empty collection to indicate that no matching objects were found.
- A remote client program must use the `javax.rmi.PortableRemoteObject.narrow(.)` method to convert object or collection returned by the finder method on the entity bean's remote home interface type. This conversion isn't necessary for local EJBs.

Rules for Implementing `ejbHome` Methods

The home methods implement bulk updates and apply these updates to all the rows that represent a specific entity bean type. There can be zero or more home methods implemented in an entity bean class. The methods must adhere to the following rules:

- The method name must use `ejbHome` as its prefix.
- The method must be declared as `public` but must not be declared as `static`.

- For every <METHOD> method declared in the home interface, there must be a corresponding ejbHome<METHOD> implemented in the entity bean class. The method argument and return types must be RMI-IIOP legal.

- The method may throw arbitrary application specific exceptions but must not throw javax.rmi.RemoteException.

Rules for Implementing Business Methods

There can be zero or more business methods implemented in the bean class. The methods must follow these rules:

- The business method must be declared as public and must not be declared as final or static.

- The method argument and return types must be RMI-IIOP legal.

- The business method name cannot begin with the ejb prefix (to avoid confusing the container with callback methods).

- The business method name, arguments, return type, and exceptions in the bean class must be identical to the method declared in the component interface.

- The throw clause may define arbitrary application-specific exceptions.

- To inform the container of nonapplication exceptions, the business method should throw javax.ejb.EJBException or another java.lang.RuntimeException. It must throw the java.rmi.RemoteException.

The deployment tools are responsible for generating additional proprietary implementation classes that help containers manage the entity bean instances at runtime. The deployment tool can use subclassing, delegation, and code generation that wraps developer-provided classes for further customization.

For local home and remote interfaces provided by the developer, the tool generates the corresponding EJBHome.class and EJBLocalHome.class and implements the methods declared in the interfaces used for managing the life cycle of the entity bean instance. Likewise, for local component and remote component interfaces, the tool creates the EJBLocalObject.class and EJBObject.class and implements the business methods specific to the entity bean. In addition, the tool also implements the serializable Handle.class, which provides for clients a persistent reference to the entity bean instance, the implementation for HomeHandless.class that provides a reference to the home object and for the EJBMetaData.class that provides metadata information about the bean instance to the remote client.

Comparing BMP and CMP Entity Beans

Factors that should be considered when deciding whether to implement application persistence using BMP or CMP include time-to-market, portability of entity bean application, developer expertise using the O/R mapping and deployment tools, standardization of persistence logic, and performance requirements. The advantages of BMP include

- *Complete control of the bean's functionality*—developers have complete control regarding implementation of persistence management.
- *Customized implementation* of BMP coding results in tighter integration with the database, which can result in higher performance depending on the developer's expertise.

BMP disadvantages include

- *Additional coding is required* to implement the persistence logic, which results in a possibly longer time to market and a likely higher number of code defects.
- *BMP may negatively affect* portability due to tighter coupling with schemas in the databases, especially if the code was optimized by using proprietary extensions. Intimate knowledge of the target database and expertise with database design and transactions are required to write efficient BMP entity beans.

CMP advantages include

- Portability.
- Faster time-to-market as container implements the persistence logic.
- CMP may not require extensive database knowledge and experience or expertise with transactions because the deployment tools may handle most of the low-level issues.

CMP disadvantages include

- Developers must learn vendor-specific deployment tools.
- Developers must understand O/R mapping and be able to use the tools.

Concurrent Access in Entity Beans

Entity beans can be re-entrant i.e., they allow *loopback calls*. An example of loopback occurs when a client calls an entity bean instance X , instance X calls another entity bean instance Y, and instance Y calls back instance X in the same transaction context. Although callbacks are supported, developers are discouraged from using them for several reasons. The bean developer providing reentrant entity bean must be careful, because writing robust code to handle loopback calls is difficult, and the container cannot distinguish between loopback calls and concurrent calls from different clients. While entity beans support loopback calls, concurrent calls in the same transaction context targeted at the same entity object are illegal and end with unpredictable results.

In summary, developers should avoid using loopbacks, and entity beans should be marked as nonreentrant in the deployment descriptor.

Differences between Session and Entity Beans

We've discussed session beans in earlier chapters and entity beans in this chapter, so at this point, let's summarize their differences. Session beans represent business processes, while entity beans represent persistent business data. Session beans are transient, short-lived, and don't survive container crashes. Entity beans represent persistent in-memory data of the underlying data saved in the database, and they survive container crashes. While only a single client can access one session bean instance at a time, entity bean instances support multi-client access. While entity beans must have primary keys and be inherently transactional, session beans don't have primary keys and can be transaction aware. Table 8-3 summarizes the comparative characteristics of session and entity beans.

Table 8-3 Characteristics of Session and Entity Beans

Feature	Session Beans	Entity Beans
Purpose	Represents business processes	Represents business data
Access	Single-client access	Multi-client access
State management	Transient; session state lost when client terminates	Persistent; entity state saved in persistent store after client terminates
Transactions	Transaction aware	Inherently transactional
Primary key	None	Required

Object Identity, Handle, and Primary Key

We've mentioned object identity, handle, and primary key earlier in this chapter; in this section we'll illustrate their differences. Every time the container creates a Java object, it's assigned a unique identity at create time and is valid as long as the object is in memory. This we've referred to as object identity. Therefore, whenever an EJB instance is created, it's assigned an object identity and, depending on the type of EJBs, the object identity may or may not be exposed to a client.

A *handle* is an abstraction of a network reference to an EJB object. It uses a persistent reference to a synchronous EJB object, and all session and entity EJB objects support handles. A handle uniquely identifies an object on a network and is serializable. Thus, it can be sent across the network and saved for later reuse.

The primary key uniquely identifies an entity bean instance and its representation in the database and is long-lived. Session beans don't have primary keys.

To sum up, an entity bean can have a primary key, an object identity, and a handle, and its client can access the entity bean instance using either a primary key or a handle. On the other hand, a session bean can have only an object identity and a handle, and its client can access the session bean instance using a handle only.

New Features of CMP 2.0 Entity Beans

The entity bean in the EJB 2.0 specification represents a major upgrade from the previous version. The major changes have been in the container-managed persistence area of the entity bean. Several new features improve the performance and the mechanisms to implement complex relationship logic, including

- *Local interfaces*—The ability to define local and remote interfaces to entity beans has given bean developers the ability to weigh the trade offs between the distribution of objects and performance.
- *Abstract Persistence Schema*—These enable developers to implement sophisticated container-managed fields and container-managed relationships between entity objects and their persistent data and generate optimized code during deployment.
- *EJB Query Language*—This enables developers to use SQL-like querying to manage relationships between CMP entities.

- *Improved association*—This enables developers to implement complex one-to-many and many-to-many associations in business applications among CMP 2.0 entity beans using the local interface.

Summary

This chapter provided an overview of entity beans and discussed how they are used to represent business entities. Entity beans are used to model nouns and represent the in-memory view of the data saved in the database. Entity beans are long-lived and transactional and survive container crashes.

There are two types of entity beans—bean-managed persistent entity beans and container-managed persistent entity beans. With bean-managed persistent entity beans, the bean developer is responsible for implementing persistence management logic, while in container-managed entity beans, the container and deployment are responsible for implementing and managing persistent logic.

We'll discuss BMP entity bean implementation detail in the next chapter.

DEVELOPING BEAN-MANAGED ENTITY BEANS

Topics in This Chapter

- BMP Characteristics
- Bean-Managed Persistence
- BMP Sample Application

Chapter 9

This chapter discusses the characteristics of bean-managed persistence (BMP) entity beans and provides a step-by-step process for implementing, deploying, and running BMP entity beans.

BMP Characteristics

BMP entity beans are used to model persistent data. With BMP entity beans, the bean developer is responsible for implementing the logic necessary to create, delete, retrieve, and save the persistent data to a durable data store, such as a database or ERP system. The bean developer also implements the persistence management logic using the callback methods defined by the `EntityBean` class. At runtime, the container invokes the callback methods to manage persistence. Depending on whether the EIS tier represents a relational database, an object database, or an ERP system, a developer may use JDBC, SQL, OQL, or JCA to implement the data access logic.

When to Use BMP

In Enterprise JavaBeans 2.0, the use of CMP is recommended over BMP entity beans because CMP entity beans make possible greater portability, better flexibility in implementing persistence, and faster time to market. There are, however, situations when BMP entity beans are preferred. Some examples follow.

- when the vendor's deployment tool isn't mature enough to handle complex entity relationships
- when the container cannot satisfactorily implement stringent and fine-grain transaction requirements (i.e., when transaction and security requirements are so unique that they must be implemented programmatically and cannot be implemented declaratively)
- when an experienced bean developer with intimate legacy system knowledge and expertise in transaction and O/R mapping can provide a more efficient custom implementation of BMP to access the legacy system than the container can using CMP entity beans

Keep in mind that vendor-provided deployment tools are proprietary, and their capabilities can vary. So if your deployment tool isn't sophisticated or lacks features required for implanting your CMP entity bean, you might have to use BMP entity beans. This will become less likely as the product matures.

Motivation for BMP

Bean developers aren't restricted from implementing the logic to manage persistent data in a session bean. In fact, before entity bean implementation was widely available on application servers, developers used session beans for persistent data management. The drawback of using session beans for managing persistent data is that developers are required to write not only the business logic but also data access, synchronization logic, and complex management logic to ensure that the persistent management code is executed consistently in the correct sequence. This task is complicated and can lead to implementation errors for inexperienced programmers.

When using BMP entity beans, developers still must implement the data access and synchronization logic in callback methods; however, it's the container that has the responsibility for determining when and how to invoke these callback methods. The Enterprise JavaBeans 2.0 specification contract guarantees that the container will invoke these callback methods appropriately and in the correct sequence. In addition, the specification ensures that the persistent in-memory bean instance data is correctly synchronized with the EIS tier. To appreciate the functionality that the EJB container provides, let's review the methods in the EntityBean class.

Bean-Managed Persistence

With BMP entity beans, the bean developer is required to implement three types of methods—*bean instance life cycle*, *synchronization*, and *pool* methods—in addition to the business methods in the bean class. Let's look at these methods and the rules and requirements for writing them.

Bean Instance Life Cycle Management Method

The life cycle management methods include `ejbCreate<METHOD>()`, `ejbPostCreate<METHOD>()`, `ejbRemove()`, `ejbActivate()`, and `ejbPassivate()`. There are two ways an entity bean instance can transition from pool to the ready state—by invoking `ejbCreate<METHOD>()` or the `ejbActivate()` method.

With `ejbCreate<METHOD>()`, the Bean developer must implement the logic to validate the client-supplied arguments, insert a record representing the entity object into a database, and initialize the instance's variables before returning the primary key for the entity object. In cases with a relational database, the `ejbCreate<METHOD>()` in the bean instance includes a `SQL INSERT` statement, which inserts a row into the database. The invocation of `ejbCreate<METHOD>()` is followed by an invocation of `ejbPostCreate<METHOD>()`, which can include additional business logic that can operate on the entity instance. Business methods can be executed only after completion of the `ejbPostCreate<METHOD>()` method. The `ejbRemove()` method must contain the logic to remove the entity bean representation from the database and release any resources allocated during the `ejbCreate<METHOD>()` and `ejbPostCreate<METHOD>()` methods. In a typical case with a relational database, the `ejbRemove()` method must include `SQL DELETE` statement. At the end of this method, the entity bean instance presentation no longer exists in the database, and the bean instance is returned to the pool.

The entity bean instance transitions from pool to ready state when the container invokes `ejbActivate()` method. The Bean developer must implement the code to associate the instance with the primary key and can also include allocation of instance-specific resources. The `ejbPassivate()` method, on the other hand, must include the logic to dissociate the instance with the primary key and release any resources allocated during the `ejbActivate()` method before the instance can transition back to the pool.

Persistent Data Synchronization Methods

There are two methods that handle persistent data synchronization: `ejbLoad()` and `ejbStore()`. The container automatically invokes `ejbLoad()` at the start of a transaction before the business method is called. The container invokes `ejbStore()` after the business method is called at the end of the transaction. These methods must not be invoked from a client. The bean developer implements the logic to read the persistent data from the database to the entity bean instance using the `ejbLoad()` method. The developer also implements the logic to write the instance data to the database using the ejbStore() method. In a typical environment with a relational database, ejbLoad() method logic consists of the JDBC APIs and the SQL SELECT statement that reads the row from the database. The ejbStore() method code consists of JDBC APIs and the SQL UPDATE statement that updates the persistent fields to the database.

Pool Methods

The pool methods consist of ejbFind<METHOD>(..) and ejbHome<METHOD>(..) in the BMP entity bean class. These methods are executed on bean instances in the pool state. After the method is executed, the bean instance is not assigned an entity object identity but instead is returned to the pool state. In a typical case, the developer must implement the ejbFind<METHOD>() method—which contains the SQL SELECT statement that finds a single entity object or collection of entity objects—and must also return a primary key or a collection that contains primary keys. The optional ejbHome<METHOD>() can consist of code and SQL statements that implement the class specific logic.

BMP Sample Application

The following example uses a BMP entity bean to model a student entity. A student entity in the database is represented by first name, last name, phone number, and e-mail address, as well as by the name of the company for which the student works and a primary key that uniquely identifies each student entity in the database. A client can invoke methods on the StudentEJB instance to add new students, update student information, and register for a class. The BMP used to model a student entity has the following elements:

- remote home interface—StudentHome
- remote component interface—Student
- entity bean implementation using the BMP—StudentEJB
- helper class—RosterDAO
- client that will use the student entity bean—StudentClient

The steps required to implement the BMP entity bean and its client follow:

1. Implement a remote home interface (StudentHome interface).
2. Implement a remote component interface (Student interface).
3. Implement an entity bean class and the associated business logic (StudentEJB).

4. Implement the helper class to handle the data access (RosterDAO).

5. Compile the interfaces, entity bean class, and helper class.

6. Write a servlet client using the remote interfaces (StudentClient).

7. Compile the servlet client.

8. Create an html form to submit the information necessary to create the student identity (Student.htm).

9. Package the enterprise component into an ejb-jar file.

10. Package the Web component into a war file and package the enterprise and Web components into an enterprise archive file (RegistrationApp.ear).

11. Deploy StudentApp.ear onto an application server.

12. Test the BMP entity bean application.

A detailed step-by-step guide for writing the BMP entity bean student application follows.

Step 1: Creating the Home Interface

The StudentHome interface must declare the findByPrimaryKey(PrimaryKey key) method, return the Student interface, and declare two exceptions (RemoteException and FinderException) in the throw clause. In the simplest cases, a primary key class can be represented by Java primitives, usually strings or integers. In other cases, the developer must define the primary key class.

The StudentHome interface extends the EJBHome interface and declares two finder methods and a create method. The required findByPrimaryKey() method takes a primary key as an argument, performs a search, and either returns a component interface (if it finds the primary key in the database) or throws a finderException to indicate that an application-level error has occurred. The findByCompanyName() method takes the company name as an argument, searches for students who share the same company name, and returns a collection.

The create() method takes the arguments, creates a student entity object, returns component interface Student, and throws CreateException to indicate that an error with either the create or initialization operation has occurred. All of these remote methods must throw RemoteException. The following code fragment is the listing of the create(), findByPrimaryKey(), and findByCompanyName() methods of the Student component interface.

```
public interface StudentHome extends EJBHome
{
    public Student findByPrimaryKey(String key) throws FinderExcep-
tion, RemoteException;
```

```
public Collection findByCompanyName(String company) throws Finder-
Exception, RemoteException;

    public Student create(String key, String pw, String firstName,
String lastName, String email, String phone, String company) throws
CreateException, RemoteException;
}
```

Step 2: Creating the Remote Component Interface

The remote component interface `Student` must extend the `javax.ejb.EJBObject`
interface. In the component interface, the developer must declare the public business
methods implemented in the bean class. All of the declared business methods must
throw `RemoteException` in addition to other application-specific exceptions.

The `Student` interface declares several business methods that set and get
persistent data related to student entity. Their functions are self-explanatory. All
of these methods must declare the mandatory `RemoteException`.

The code from the `Student` interface that follows consists of several `get` and `set`
business methods to change student entity values, plus three methods to add and
delete a schedule and get a list of course schedules.

```
Public interface Student extends EJBObject
{
    public void setPassword(String newPassword) throws RemoteException;
    public String getPassword() throws RemoteException;

    public void setFirstName(String first) throws RemoteException;
    public String getFirstName() throws RemoteException;

    public void setLastName(String last) throws RemoteException;
    public String getLastName() throws RemoteException;

    public void setEmail(String email) throws RemoteException;
    public String getEmail() throws RemoteException;

    public void setPhone(String phone) throws RemoteException;
    public String getPhone() throws RemoteException;

    public void setCompanyName(String companyName) throws RemoteEx-
ception;
    public String getCompanyName() throws RemoteException;
    public void addASchedule(String scheduleID) throws RemoteException;
    public void deleteASchedule(String scheduleID) throws RemoteEx-
ception;
    pubic Vector getScheduleList() throws RemoteException

}
```

Step 3: Creating the Entity Bean Implementation Class

StudentEJB, as a BMP entity bean, is required to implement the
java.io.Serializable interface. The StudentEJB class must be defined as
public; it cannot be defined as abstract or final. The entity bean should not
implement the finalize method. The constructor StudentEJB() must be left
empty; don't try to implement JNDI lookup or any other logic

A developer can implement four types of methods in the BMP entity bean class:
the bean instance life cycle management methods, synchronization methods, pool
methods, and optional business methods. These methods are discussed in the text
that follows as implemented in the StudentEJB bean. The following code
snippet shows StudentEJB along with declaration of persistent fields, which are
all declared private.

```
public class StudentEJB implements EntityBean
{
    private EntityContext entityContext;
// persistent fields
    private String primaryKey;
    private String firstName;
    private String lastName;
    private String email;
    private String phone;
    private String password;
    private String companyName;
    private java.sql.Date createDate;
```

The setEntityContext method in the bean instance initializes the entity
context and calls the JNDIlookup method to locate a data source. The
unsetEntityContext method, which is called by the container before the bean
instance is terminated, sets the EntityContext object to null, so it can be
garbage collected.

```
    public void setEntityContext(EntityContext ectx)
    {
        entityContext = ectx;
        try {
            JNDIlookUp();
        } catch (Exception e) {
            System.out.println("Error in setEntityContext() -
="+e.getMessage());
        }
    }

public void unsetEntityContext()
    {
```

```
entityContext = null;
    }

//empty constructor
public StudentEJB()
    {

    }
```

Business Methods

The bean developer must implement the business logic and data access logic in the callback methods to manage persistence data and let the container handle data synchronization. The access control for business methods must be declared public; the arguments and return types must be serializable for remote clients but not for local clients. Business methods cannot be final or static.

There are five set and get methods defined for the password, firstName, lastName, email, phone, and companyName persistent fields. Only a subset of these simple methods are included in the following code snippet.

```
public void setPassword(String newpw)
{
    password = newpw;

}

public void setFirstName(String first)
{
    firstName = first;
}

public String getFirstName()
{
    return firstName;
}

public void setLastName(String last)
{
    lastName = last;
}

public String getLastName()
{
    return lastName;
}

}
```

There are three additional methods that add or delete class schedules and a method to get a list of all classes for which a student is registered. These are implemented in the StudentEJB class as shown in the code fragment that follows. All these methods rely on RosterDAO class to access the database. The addASchedule() method takes the studentID and scheduleID and calls on the insert() method of the RosterDAO to insert the record in the RosterTable. Likewise, the deleteASchedule() method delegates the removal of the row from the RosterTable. The getScheduleList() method delegates the retrieval of all the classes for which the student is registered.

```
public void addASchedule(String scheduleID) throws RosterDAOException
{
    try
    {

    //insert studentID and scheduleID
    rosterDAO.insert(scheduleID, studentID);

    } catch (RosterDAOException re) {
        System.out.println(" StudentEJB - addASchedule() error
="+re.getMessage());
    } catch (Exception e) {
        System.out.println(" StudentEJB - addASchedule() error
="+e.getMessage());
    }

}

public void deleteASchedule(String scheduleID) throws RosterDAOException
{
    try
    {
    //delete   scheduleID
    rosterDAO.delete(scheduleID, studentID);

    } catch (RosterDAOException re) {
        System.out.println(" StudentEJB - addASchedule() error
="+re.getMessage());
    } catch (Exception e) {
        System.out.println(" StudentEJB - addASchedule() error
="+e.getMessage());
    }
}
 public Vector getScheduleList() throws RosterDAOException
{
    Vector classList= new Vector(20);
```

```
    try
    {
    //get list of scheduleID
    classList = rosterDAO.getClassList(studentID);
    } catch (RosterDAOException re) {
        System.out.println(" StudentEJB - addASchedule() error
 ="+re.getMessage());
    } catch (Exception e) {
        System.out.println(" StudentEJB - addASchedule() error
 ="+e.getMessage());
    }
    return classList;
}
```

Note that you can implement additional private business methods that aren't
declared in the component interface. The business methods may throw
application-specific exceptions. The JNDIlookUp() method is one example of a
private business method that encapsulates the logic to look up a datasource so
that the bean instance can perform data access functions.

```
private void JNDIlookUp() throws StudentDAOException
{
try
    {
        InitialContext ictx = new InitialContext();
    System.out.println("********* In StudentEJB -- lookUp() after
initialcontext *****");

        dataSource = (DataSource)
ictx.lookup("java:comp/env/jdbc/JCampDS");
    conn = dataSource.getConnection();

    } catch (NamingException ne) {
        throw new  StudentDAOException("NamingException while look-
ing up datasource connection ="+ne.getMessage());
    } catch(SQLException se) {
          throw new StudentDAOException(" SQL exception while
attempting to OPEN connection ="+se.getMessage());
    }

}
```

Bean Instance Life Cycle Management Methods

The container invokes the ejbCreate(String pk, String pw, String
first, String last, String mailAddr, String phone, String
company) method on behalf of the client, which, in turn, invokes a
corresponding insertStudent() method. The insertStudent() method

uses the JDBC API and the **SQL INSERT** statement and inserts the data into the database. This method returns a primary key. Although mixing business logic with data access logic in the bean class is generally strongly discouraged, we've done just that in the `StudentEJB` bean to illustrate how the inclusion of data access logic affects the portability, maintenance, and readability of the code.

```java
public String ejbCreate(String pK, String pw, String first, String last,
String mailAddr, String aphone, String company) throws CreateException

    {
        primaryKey = pK;
        password = pw;
        firstName = first;
        lastName = last;
        email = mailAddr;
        phone = aphone;
        companyName = company;

    try {

        insertStudent(primaryKey, password, firstName, lastName,
email, phone, companyName);
    }catch (Exception e) {
        System.out.println(" lookUp() error ="+e.getMessage());
    }
        return primaryKey;
    }

public void insertStudent(String pKey, String password, String
firstName, String lastName, String email, String phone, String com-
panyName) throws StudentDAOException
    {
        PreparedStatement pstmt = null;

    Calendar calendar = Calendar.getInstance();
    java.util.Date theTime = calendar.getTime();
    java.sql.Date now = new java.sql.Date(theTime.getTime());

        try
        {
        pstmt = conn.prepareStatement("Insert into Students(id,
password, firstName, lastName, email, phone, companyName, create-
Date) values(?,?,?,?,?,?,?,?)");

        pstmt.setString(1, pKey );
        pstmt.setString(2, password);
        pstmt.setString(3, firstName);
```

```
          pstmt.setString(4, lastName);
          pstmt.setString(5, email);
          pstmt.setString(6, phone);
          pstmt.setString(7, companyName);
          pstmt.setDate(8, now);

             pstmt.executeUpdate();
             System.out.println("  Student inserted");

          } catch(SQLException se) {
             throw new StudentDAOException(" Query exception
   "+se.getMessage());
          } finally {
             closeStatement(pstmt);
          }
    }
```

The matching `ejbPostCreate(String pk, String pw, String first, String last, String mailAddr, String phone, String company)` method is automatically invoked by the container right after executing the `ejbCreate()` method and before any business methods can be invoked. The `ejbPostCreate()` method is available in entity beans to enable the developer to implement additional logic after the entity bean instance is created.

Let's take as an example the case of a `SoccerPlayer` entity bean that has `totalNumberOfGamesPlayed` and `totalGoalsScored` columns in the database table. These columns keep track of player statistics, but the developer might also choose to provide to clients a nonpersistent field, `currentAverageGoalsScoredPerGame`. The value of this field could be calculated in the `ejbPostCreate()` method and made available to the business method without ever being saved in the database. For example, creation of a composite entity object might depend on other entity objects, and the `ejbPostCreate()` method can be used to query dependent entity objects for the information required to complete the creation of the composite entity object (see Chapter 11, which illustrates this principle in the CMP entity bean example). The `ejbPostCreate()` method is usually empty for applications not requiring any postprocessing of the bean instance. Note the matching exceptions, but the return type is `void`. The following listing shows an empty `ejbPostCreate()` method.

```
public void ejbPostCreate(String pK, String pw, String first,
String last, String mailAddr, String phone, String company) throws
CreateException
{
}
```

When a `remove()` method is called by a client, the container will invoke `ejbRemove()` in StudentEJB, which in turn invokes `delete(primaryKey)` to remove the representation of the instance from the database. The `ejbRemove()` method must throw `java.ejb.RemoveExeption` for application errors and must throw `javax.ejb.EJBException` for system-related errors. The following is the listing of the `ejbRemove()` method.

```
public void ejbRemove()
    {
        String pKey = (String)entityContext.getPrimaryKey();

        try     {
            deleteStudent(pKey);
        } catch (Exception e) {
            throw new EJBException( "ejbRemove ="+e.getMessage());
        }

    }
```

The `ejbRemove()` method invokes the `deleteStudent()` method. The `deleteStudent()` method contains the necessary JDBC API and the SQL DELETE statement to remove the object representation from the database, as the following code fragment shows.

```
public void deleteStudent(String pKey) throws StudentDAOException
    {
    PreparedStatement pstmt = null;

    try {
    String updateStatement = "DELETE FROM Students WHERE id = ?";
    pstmt = conn.prepareStatement(updateStatement);

    pstmt.setString(1, pKey);

    int rowCount = pstmt.executeUpdate();
    if (rowCount == 0)
        throw new StudentDAOException("DELETE Failed for Student id
 ="+pKey);

        } catch(SQLException se) {
                throw new StudentDAOException(" SQL exception while
attempting to DELETE ="+se.getMessage());
        } finally {
            closeStatement(pstmt);
        }

    }
```

Synchronization Methods

In the `StudentEJB` class, the `ejbLoad()` and `ejbStore()` methods are
responsible for synchronizing persistent fields. The fragment that follows shows
how the `ejbLoad()` method invokes the `loadStudent()` method, which
contains the logic to read the persistent data from the database.

```
public void ejbLoad()
{
    try      {
        loadStudent();
    } catch (Exception e) {
        throw new EJBException( "ejbStore -- UPDATE ="+e.getMessage());
    }
}
```

The `loadStudent()` method first retrieves the primary key from the entity
instance context and then uses `selectByPrimaryKey()` to read the persistent
data into the instance.

```
private void loadStudent() throws StudentDAOException
{
    ResultSet rs = null;
    primaryKey = (String)entityContext.getPrimaryKey();
    String returnedPK =null;
    try      {
        rs = selectByPrimaryKey(primaryKey);
        int size = rs.getFetchSize();

        if (size == 1) {
          if (rs.next()) {
             returnedPK = rs.getString(1);
             password = rs.getString(2);
             firstName = rs.getString(3);
             lastName = rs.getString(4);
             email = rs.getString(5);
             phone = rs.getString(6);
             companyName = rs.getString(7);
             createDate = rs.getDate(8);
             rs.close();
                 }
          } else {
             throw new StudentDAOException(" ejbLoad() error size
="+size);
          }
    rs.close();
```

```
    } catch (Exception e) {
        throw new EJBException( "ejbStore -- UPDATE ="+e.getMessage());
    }
    primaryKey = returnedPK;
}
```

The `ejbStore()` callback method updates the database and uses the `updateStudent()` method to invoke the SQL UPDATE statement as shown here:

```
public void ejbStore()
{
try    {
    updateStudent(primaryKey, password, firstName, lastName, email,
phone, companyName);
    } catch (Exception e) {
        throw new EJBException( " <<--- ejbStore -- UPDATE
="+e.getMessage());
    }
}
```

The `ejbStore()` method invokes the `updateStudent()` method, which implements the update logic.

```
public void updateStudent(String pKey, String password, String
firstName, String lastName, String email, String phone, String com-
panyName) throws StudentDAOException
   {
     PreparedStatement pstmt = null;


     try {
     String updateStatement = "UPDATE Students set password = ?, firstName
= ?, lastName = ?, email = ?, phone = ?, companyName = ? WHERE id = ?";

     pstmt = conn.prepareStatement(updateStatement);
         pstmt.setString(1, password);
         pstmt.setString(2, firstName);
         pstmt.setString(3, lastName);
         pstmt.setString(4, email);
         pstmt.setString(5, phone);
         pstmt.setString(6, companyName);
         pstmt.setString(7, pKey);

     int rowCount = pstmt.executeUpdate();
     if (rowCount == 0)
         throw new StudentDAOException("Update Failed for Student
primary key ="+pKey);
       } catch(SQLException se) {
```

```
                throw new StudentDAOException(" SQL exception while
   attempting to UPDATE ="+se.getMessage());
        } finally {
                closeStatement(pstmt);
        }
    }
```

The `ejbLoad()` and `ejbStore()` methods are automatically called in a
transaction by the container to synchronize in-memory data with the underlying
database. Then, the container invokes the `ejbActivate()` method to transition
an entity instance from the pool state to the ready state, and the container assigns
a primary key and any instance-specific resources to the instance.

```
public void ejbActivate()
{
        primaryKey = (String)entityContext.getPrimaryKey();
}
```

The container invokes the `ejbPassivate()` method just before the entity
instance is about to be released back to the pool; this method should contain the
code to release the resources allocated during the `ejbActivate()` method.

```
public void ejbPassivate()
{
    primaryKey = null;

}
```

Pool Methods

The methods in the pool method category can be thought of as global—they
apply to all the object representations of a bean type in the underlying database.
Note that at the end of the method, the bean instance is still in the pool state.

The `StudentEBJ` class implements the `ejbFindByPrimaryKey(...)` and
`ejbFindByCompanyName(...)` pool methods. The mandatory
`ejbFindByPrimaryKey(...)` method is a single-object finder method; it takes a
Primary key string as an argument and returns a type `String` primary key. The
`ejbFindByPrimaryKey()` method can throw the following exceptions:
`FinderException`, `DuplicateException`, and `NoSuchEntityException`.
The `selectByPrimaryKey()` method returns a result set, and the code checks
the result set. The `ejbFindByCompanyName(...)` method is a multi-object finder
method that takes a string argument and returns a collection. Note that this
method returns a primary key class. In this case, this is a `String`; on the home
interface, the `findByPrimaryKey()` method returns a component interface.

```
public String ejbFindByPrimaryKey(String pKey) throws FinderException
{
    String primaryKey = null;
    try
    {
        primaryKey = selectByPrimaryKey(pKey) ;
rs.close();
        } catch (SQLException se) {
        throw new EJBException("ejbFindByPrimaryKey  SQL error
="+se.getMessage());
        } catch (Exception e) {
        throw new EJBException("ejbFindByPrimaryKey error ="+e.get-
Message());
        }

        return primaryKey;

    }
```

The selectByPrimaryKey() method implements the SQL SELECT command to search the database with the primary key, and it returns a primary key back to the bean instance.

```
public String selectByPrimaryKey(String pKey) throws StudentDAOException
    {
    PreparedStatement pstmt = null;
    ResultSet rs = null;
    try {
        String selectStatement = "SELECT * from Students where ID = ?";
        pstmt = conn.prepareStatement(selectStatement);
        pstmt.setString(1, pKey);
        rs = pstmt.executeQuery();
            } catch(SQLException se) {
                throw new StudentDAOException(" SQL exception while
attempting to SELECT By Primary Key ="+se.getMessage());
        }
        return rs.getID();
    }
```

StudentEJB implements the multiobject finder method ejbFindByCompany-Name(). This method depends on the selectByCompanyName() method (which consists of primary keys representing students) to return a collection that is then returned to the client.

```
public Collection ejbFindByCompanyName(String company) throws Find-
erException
{
    Collection primaryKeys = null;
```

```
    try
    {
        primaryKeys = selectByCompanyName(company);
    } catch (SQLException se) {
        throw new FinderException(" SQL exception "+se.getMes-
sage());
    } catch (StudentDAOException daoe) {
        throw new FinderException("StudentDAOException ="+daoe.get-
Message());
    } catch(Exception e) {
        throw new FinderException("Exception "+e.getMessage());
    }
    return primaryKeys;
}
```

The `selectByCompanyName()` method implements the SQL SELECT statement to search for all primary keys having the same company name, and it then returns a collection.

```
private Collection selectByCompanyName(String cName) throws Stu-
dentDAOException, SQLException
{
    String selectStatement ="SELECT id FROM students WHERE com-
panyName = ? ";

    PreparedStatement pstmt = conn.prepareStatement(selectState-
ment);

        pstmt.setString(1, cName);
        ResultSet rs = pstmt.executeQuery();
        ArrayList aList = new ArrayList();

        while (rs.next())
        {
          String id = rs.getString(1);
          aList.add(id);
          }
    pstmt.close();
    return aList;
      }
```

Step 4: Implementing a Helper Class

We have implemented data access helper class `RosterDAO` along with `RosterDAOException` and `StudentDAOException` classes to indicate data access errors. The `RosterDAO` class is very similar to other data access objects such as `ScheduleDAO`, which we discussed in Chapter 5. We have included the code to access `StudentTable` with the `StudentEJB` class to illustrate the impact of such inclusion on code readability and portability and to contrast that with the clean separation in the case of `RosterDAO`.

The following code listing shows three methods. The `insert()` method contains the SQL query statement to create a row consisting of `studentID`, `scheduleID`, and current date in the `RosterEJBTable`. The `delete()` method contains the SQL query statement that takes `studentID` and `ScheduleID` to find and delete the matching row. (Remember that a student can be registered in multiple courses, as represented by `ScheduleID`, and that a course can have multiple students.) The last method, `getClassList()`, contains the SQL query statement and logic to retrieve all the `scheduleIDs` associated with the `studentID`, and it returns a vector consisting of `scheduledIDs`. One major point that must not be lost here is if the underlying relational database were to be replaced by an object database, the logic in the `StudentEJB` would not need to be aware of the changes; it still would call the same methods. But the SQL statements in `RosterDAO` would be replaced by equivalent OQL statements, so bugs and testing would be focused primarily on the `RosterDAO` class. The logic to access `StudentEJBTable`, however, is embedded in the `StudentEJB` class, so it must be replaced with equivalent OQL statements, and any changes would affect the `StudentEJB` bean class directly. Any time changes are made, bugs are likely to be introduced, and `StudentEJB` must undergo a new testing and debugging cycle.

```
public void insert(String scheduleID, String studentID) throws Ros-
terDAOException.
  {
    PreparedStatement pstmt = null;
    Connection conn = this.getConnection();

    Calendar calendar = Calendar.getInstance();
    java.util.Date theTime = calendar.getTime();
    java.sql.Date now = new java.sql.Date(theTime.getTime());


    try {
    String updateStatement = "INSERT INTO RosterTable (StudentID,
ScheduleID, RegistrationDate) VALUES (?, ?, ?)";;
    pstmt = conn.prepareStatement(updateStatement);

    pstmt.setString(1, studentID);
    pstmt.setString(2, scheduleID);
    pstmt.setDate(3, now);
```

```
int rowCount = pstmt.executeUpdate();
    if (rowCount == 0)
        throw new RosterDAOException("Update Failed for StudentID
="+studentID+" with ScheduleID ="+scheduleID);

    pstmt.close();
    } catch(SQLException se) {
            throw new RosterDAOException(" SQL exception while
attempting to open connection ="+se.getMessage());
        }
  }

public void delete(String scheduleID, String studentID) throws Ros-
terDAOException
  {
    PreparedStatement pstmt = null;
    Connection conn = this.getConnection();
    try {
    String updateStatement = "DELETE FROM RosterTable WHERE Sched-
uleID= ? AND studentID = ?";
    pstmt = conn.prepareStatement(updateStatement);

    pstmt.setString(1, scheduleID);
    pstmt.setString(2, studentID);


    int rowCount = pstmt.executeUpdate();
    if (rowCount == 0)
        throw new RosterDAOException("DELETE Failed for StudentID
="+studentID+" with ScheduleID ="+scheduleID);


    pstmt.close();
        } catch(SQLException se) {
            throw new RosterDAOException(" SQL exception while
attempting to open connection ="+se.getMessage());
        }

  }

public Vector getClassList(String studentID) throws RosterDAOException
  {
    Vector classList = new Vector(20);
    PreparedStatement pstmt = null;
    Connection conn = this.getConnection();
    ResultSet rset = null;

    try {
```

```
    String updateStatement = "SELECT ScheduleID FROM RosterTable
WHERE studentID= ?";
    pstmt = conn.prepareStatement(updateStatement);

    pstmt.setString(1, studentID);


    rset = pstmt.executeQuery();

    while (rset.next())
    {
        classList.addElement(rset.getString("ScheduleID"));
    }

    pstmt.close();
        } catch(SQLException se) {
            throw new RosterDAOException(" SQL exception while
attempting to open connection ="+se.getMessage());
        }

    return classList;
  }
```

Step 5: Compiling the Interfaces, Entity Bean Class, and Helper Class

Change directory to APPHOME\chapter9\student directory and run
compile.bat, which generates the following classes: `Student.class`,
`StudentHome.class`, `StudentEJB.class`, `ScheduleDAO.class`, and
`ScheduleDAOException.class`. Then, change directory to
APPHOME\chapter9\\roster and run **compile** to generate `RosterDAO.class`
and `RosterDAOException.class`.

Step 6: Writing a Servlet Client Using the Remote Interfaces

The client is a trivial servlet, `StudentClient`, which acts as a controller. It uses
the `Student` and `StudentHome` interfaces to invoke methods on the entity bean.
We provide only a small number of code fragments here, as similar code has been
discussed in previous chapters. The client servlet `StudentClient` does a lookup
for the `StudentHome` object in the `init()` method and uses the home object to
create the bean instance. It then uses the remote component to invoke business
methods. The `findByCompanyName(...)` method is shown in the code fragment
that follows.

```
    public void init()
    {
```

```
    //look up jndi context
        try {
            jndictx = new InitialContext();

            studentHome = (StudentHome) PortableRemoteObject.nar-
    row(jndictx.lookup("java:comp/env/ejb/StudentRef"), StudentH-
    ome.class);

        }
```

The searchByCompany method in the servlet invokes the
findByCompanyName() method declared in the remote home interface and
returns a collection of component interfaces. The collection is forwarded to
DisplayCollection.jsp and displayed to the end user.

```
    public void searchByCompany(HttpServletRequest req, HttpServle-
    tResponse resp)
        {

        company = req.getParameter("Company");

        try
        {
        Collection primaryKeyList = (Collection) studentHome.find-
    ByCompanyName(company);

            Iterator i= primaryKeyList.iterator();

            while (i.hasNext()) {
                Student stud = (Student)i.next();
                String id = (String)stud.getPrimaryKey();

            req.setAttribute("pKeyList", primaryKeyList);
            req.setAttribute("companyName", company);

            RequestDispatcher dispatcher = getServletContext().getRe-
    questDispatcher("/DisplayCollection.jsp");
                dispatcher.forward(req, resp);

        } catch (FinderException fe) {
            System.out.println(" finder exception ="+fe.getMessage());
    . . .  .
```

The code snippet (illustrating a call to a business method in the EJB remote component interface) is used to invoke the `setCompanyName()` method to change the company name in the entity bean. The servlet code then calls `callJSP()` to invoke the JSP page.

```
public void modifyCompanyName(HttpServletRequest req, HttpServlet-
Response resp, String newCompanyName) throws RemoteException
    {
        student.setCompanyName(newCompanyName);
            String changedCompanyName = student.getCompanyName();
            company = changedCompanyName;
            callJSP(req, resp);
}
```

Step 7: Compiling the Servlet Client

Change directory to APPHOME\chapter9\web\servlet, and run **compile.bat**, which will generate the `StudentClient.class` file.

Step 8: Creating an HTML Form and JSP Files

We also need to create `Student.html`, the HTML form, which displays the fields that a student needs to create a Student record in the database and for the presentation, `Confirm.jsp`, `DisplayClassList.jsp`, `DisplayCollection.jsp`, and `ModifyStudent.jsp` files.

Step 9: Packaging the Web Component

To package `StudentEJB` into an ejb-jar file, do the following:

1. Start cloudscape, j2ee, and deploytool (refer to the Appendix for details).
2. To create a StudentApp.ear file, go to deploytool, select the File I New I Application option, and specify the default directory as APPHOME\chapter9 to save the StudentApp.ear file, as shown in Figure 9-1.

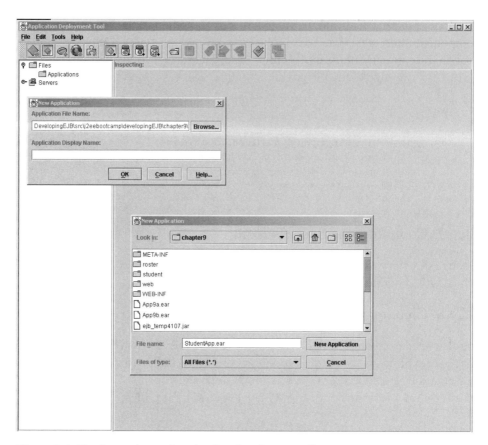

Figure 9-1 Deploytool creating the StudentApp.ear file

3. Create a `StudentJAR` package to include the Student entity bean elements. Select the File | New | Enterprise Bean option; from the pop-up menu, add `StudentEJB.class`, `Student.class`, `Student.class`, `RosterDAO.class`, `RosterDAOException.class`, and `StudentDAOException.class` as shown in Figure 9-2.

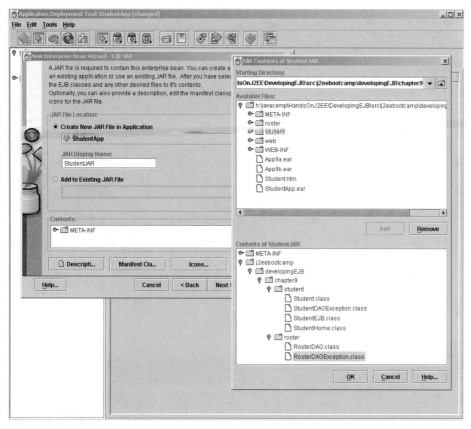

Figure 9-2 Packaging ejb-jar—adding the Student class files

4. Click Next and specify the bean type by selecting Entity; for the Enterprise Bean class, select `StudentEJB.class`. Select the `StudentHome.class` for remote home interface and the `Student.class` for remote interface, as shown in Figure 9-3. Then click Next.

5. Specify the persistence management option by clicking Bean Managed Persistence. Change the default Primary Key Object, `java.lang.Object`, to `java.lang.String` as shown in Figure 9-4. Click Next until Resource Reference appears.

6. Click the Add button to specify the necessary resource factory references, by specifying jdbc/JCampDS for DataSource. Enter jdbc/Cloudscape in the deployment setting for the JNDI name with user name and password set to j2ee as shown in Figure 9-5. Click Finish to complete the ejb-jar file packaging process.

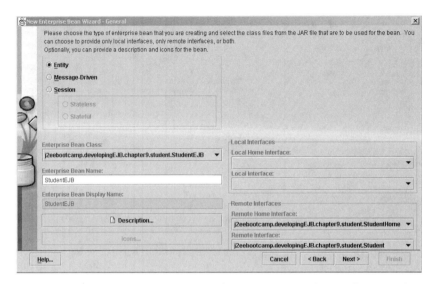

Figure 9-3 Packaging ejb-jar—specifying bean type, bean class, and remote interfaces

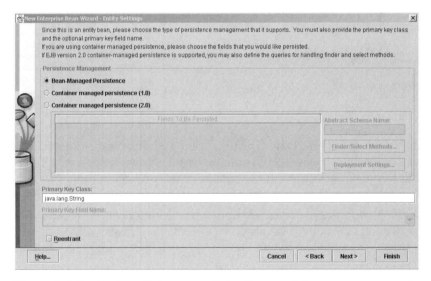

Figure 9-4 Packaging ejb-jar—specifying the persistence management and primary key class

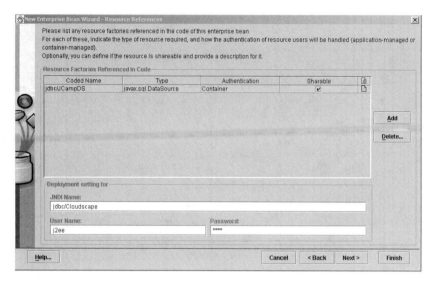

Figure 9-5 Packaging ejb-jar—specifying the database resource reference

Step 10: Packaging the Web and Enterprise Components

Now, package the Web components (consisting of serlvet `StudentClient.class`, `Student.htm`, `ConfirmDelete.jsp`, `DisplayCollection.jsp`, `DisplayClassList,jsp`, and `ModifyStudent.jsp`) into a war file by following these steps:

1.　In deploytool, select the File | New | Web Component option and then click Next.

2.　Click the Create New WAR File in Application radio button to display RegistrationApp beneath it. Select this using the pull-down menu.

3.　Enter **StudentWAR** in the WAR Display Name field.

4.　Use the Edit button to add the `StudentClient.class`, `Student.htm`, `ConfirmDelete.jsp`, `DisplayCollection.jsp`, `DisplayClass-List.jsp`, and `ModifyStudent.jsp` to the war package, as shown in Figure 9-6.

5.　Click OK, and then click Next.

6.　Click Next, and choose the component type Servlet radio button.

7.　Click Next again, and then use the pull-down menu to select StudentClient as the Servlet Class.

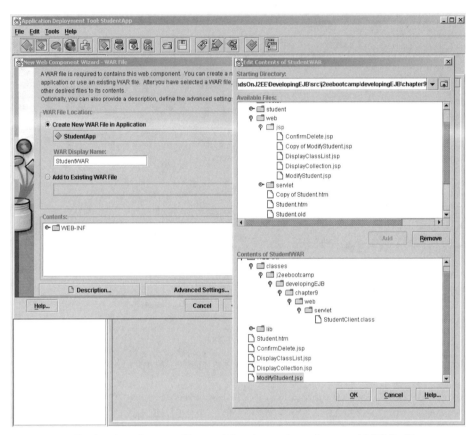

Figure 9-6 Packaging the war file—adding java class, jsp, and HTML files

8. Keep clicking Next until the Aliases window appears. Click the Add button to specify the component alias name that the html form will use to access the servlet component. For this example, enter **StudentAlias**.

9. Click Next four times until the Enterprise Bean Reference screen appears, and then enter **ejb/StudentRef** under Coded Name and enter **StudentHome** and **Student** under Home and Remote Interface. You also need to select Entity for the entity bean in the Type column and choose Remote for remote interfaces under Interface, using the respective pull-down menus shown in Figure 9-7.

10. Then, for the Deployment Setting, click the Enterprise Bean Name button and enter **StudentEJB** as shown in Figure 9-7. Click Next, then Finish.

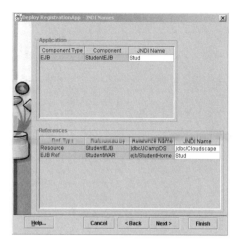

Figure 9-7 Packaging the war file—specifying the Student entity bean references

Figure 9-8 Packaging the war file—specifying the initial HTML file

11. Click Next three times until the File References screen appears, and then click the Add button to specify the Welcome Files by using the pull-down menu to select the Student.htm file, as shown in Figure 9-8.

12. Click Finish to complete the Web archive file.

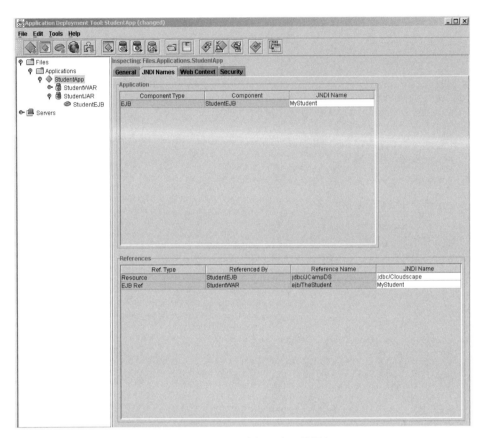

Figure 9-9 Packaging the war file—specifying the JNDI name

13. You still need to specify the JNDI names and the root Web context. To do this, click the JNDI Names tab on the deployment tool and enter **MyStudent** in the JNDI Name column for the Application and References section, as shown in Figure 9-9.

14. Click the Web Context tab on the deployment tool and enter **/StudentContextRoot** in the Context Root field, which specifies the root context of the Web application.

This completes the packaging of the enterprise archive file (ear) file StudentApp.ear, which consists of ejb-jar and Web component war files.

Step 11: Deploying the StudentApp.ear File

1. To deploy the application, highlight the StudentApp.ear file, in the deploytool and click Tool | Deploy. A deploy menu pops up.

2. Ensure that Object to Deploy displays the StudentApp application and that Target Server displays localhost (or the name of your host). Also click the Save Before Deploy button, and then click Next.

3. The next two windows are used for verification; if needed, correct the JNDI names and Web root context. First, verify that the JNDI name for the Component Type EJB is in the Application section and that the References for Ref. Type EJB Ref is set to MyStudent. Ensure that the Resource in the Reference is set to jdbc/Cloudscape, as shown in Figure 9-10, and then click Next.

4. Verify that the Web root context is set to /StudentContextRoot for the StudentWAR as shown in Figure 9-11, and then click Finish. The deployment process should start and successfully deploy the StudentApp.ear, as shown in Figure 9-12.

Step 12: Testing the BMP Entity Bean Registration Application

To test the registration application, open a browser and in the URL, enter **http://localhost:8000/StudentContext-Root/.** The HTML page shown in Figure 9-10 should appear. Figures 9-13 through 9-15 show outputs of interaction with the StudentApp.ear application.

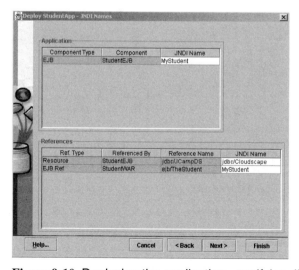

Figure 9-10 Deploying the application—verifying JNDI names

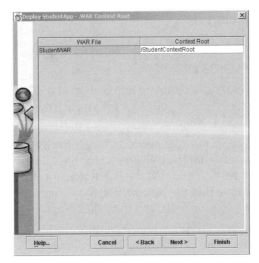

Figure 9-11 Deploying the application—verifying the WAR context root

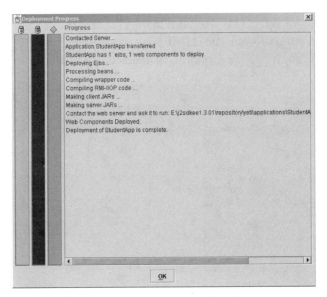

Figure 9-12 Completion of successful deployment

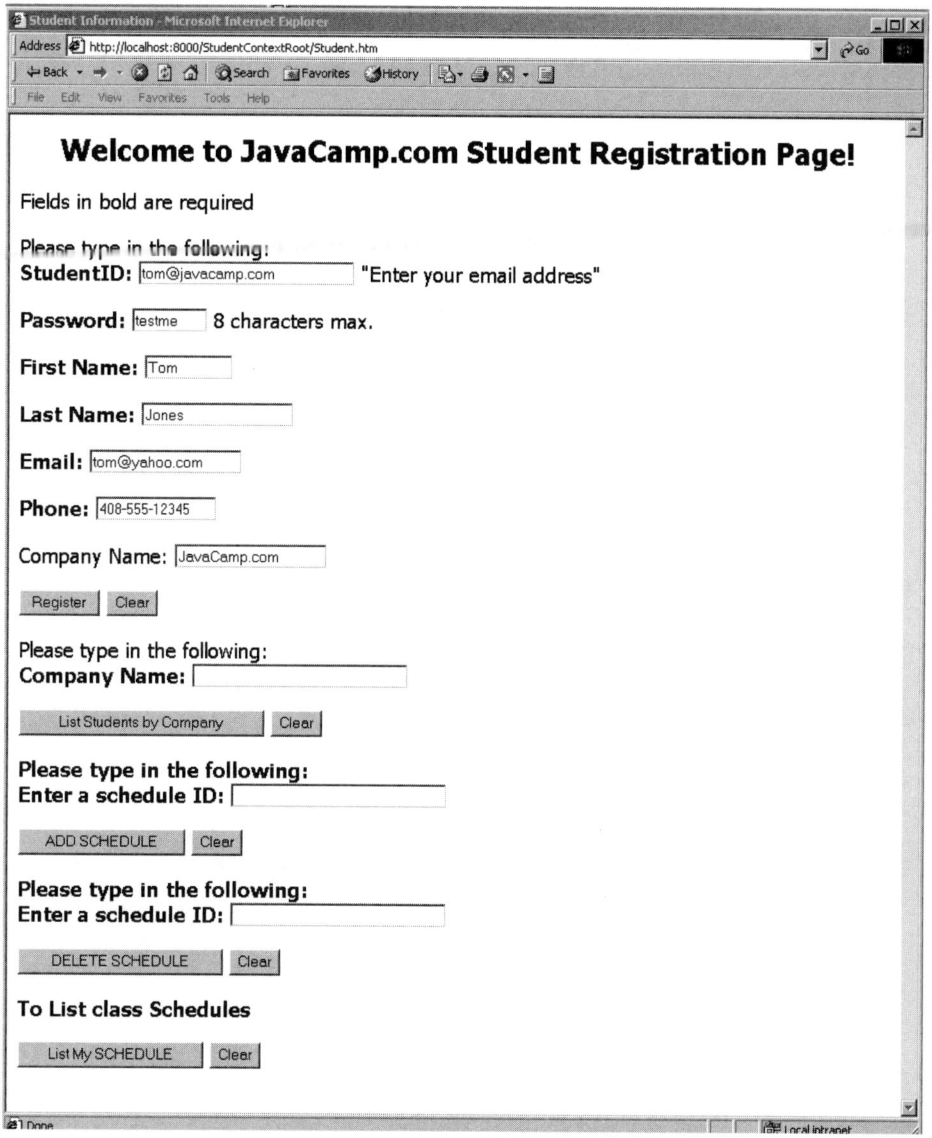

Figure 9-13 Student HTML form

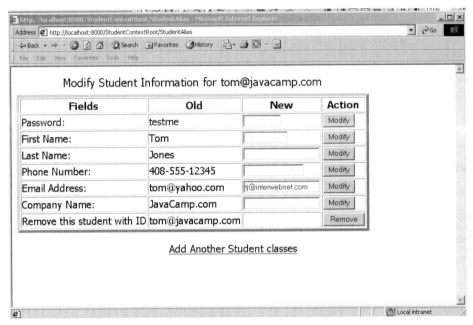

Figure 9-14 The HTML form for modifying student information

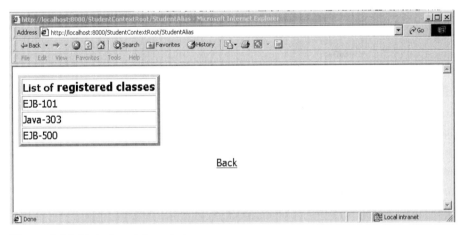

Figure 9-15 List of registered classes

Summary

With bean-managed persistent entity beans, bean developers are responsible for writing the persistent data access logic for the database and the container is responsible for synchronizing the persistent data. BMP entity beans therefore give the bean developer control of data access logic implementation to take advantage of vendor-specific features, but at the expense of portability of the bean class.

In the next chapter, we'll discuss the features of container-managed persistence in Enterprise JavaBeans 2.0, such as the abstract persistence schema and EJB QL.

CMP 2.0: ABSTRACT PERSISTENCE MODEL AND EJB QL

Topics in This Chapter

- CMP 2.0 Entity Bean Architecture
- EJB Query Language
- Rules for Writing CMP 2.0 Entity Bean Classes
- Rules for Writing Abstract Accessor Methods
- Rules for Writing Dependent Value Classes
- Rules for Writing `ejbSelect` Methods
- Responsibilities in CMP Entity Bean Development
- Comparing BMP and CMP Entity Beans
- The Primary Key for CMP 2.0 Entity Beans

Chapter 10

This chapter focuses on the container-managed persistence architecture of entity beans and covers

- the CMP 2.0 entity bean architecture
- an introduction to EJB QL
- the rules for writing CMP 2.0 entity beans and accessor, finder, and ejbSelect methods
- the roles and responsibilities for developing CMP 2.0 entity beans
- a comparison of BMP and CMP entity beans
- the advantages of using CMP over BMP beans

CMP 2.0 Entity Bean Architecture

With *container-managed persistence* (CMP) entity beans, the container is responsible for implementing persistence management. CMP has changed significantly from EJB 1.1 to EJB 2.0. We'll refer to CMP in EJB 1.1 as CMP 1.1 and to CMP in EJB 2.0 as CMP 2.0.

CMP 1.1 entity beans haven't been widely implemented, primarily because of poor performance, lack of support for a sophisticated persistence model, and no standard implementation specification for finder methods.

CMP 2.0 was designed to improve the performance of entity beans, provide implementation for sophisticated persistence models, and provide a standard finder method implementation.

CMP 2.0 entity beans have a clear separation among the client's view of the bean instance, the bean developer's internal view of the bean instance, and the persistent representation in the underlying data stores. As a result, CMP 2.0 entity beans can evolve independently from their clients and be redeployed across different containers and different persistent data stores without requiring redefinition or recompilation. In addition, the data access logic in CMP 2.0 entity beans can be optimized automatically by the container for the target data stores at deployment time.

The key to the CMP 2.0 entity bean portability is the separation of the entity bean class and its persistence representation and the delegation of the persistence management to the container at runtime. This is accomplished in CMP 2.0 entity beans with the help of the following elements:

- virtual fields declared by the developer in the CMP 2.0 entity bean class
- abstract persistence schema declarations in the deployment descriptor specified by the bean developer
- the persistent data access layer in the container provided by the vendor

To help clarify the infrastructure behind CMP 2.0, Figure 10-1 illustrates the functions of each of these elements. The vendor-provided deployment tool generates the implementation class for these abstract accessor methods at deployment time.

Abstract Accessor Methods

In the CMP entity bean class, the bean developer must declare abstract methods for container-managed persistent (CMP) fields and container-managed relationship (CMR) fields. The CMP-fields and CMR-fields are also referred to as *virtual fields* because they aren't explicitly declared in the bean class (like the persistent fields in BMP entity beans). Instead, they are used as arguments in the abstract accessor methods. The following are two sets of accessor methods from the sample application, `ScheduleEJB.java`:

```
//accessor methods for cmp fields
public abstract String getScheduleID();
public abstract void setScheduleID(String scheduleID);
//accessor methods for cmr fields
public abstract Collection getRosters();
public abstract void setRosters (Collection rosters);
```

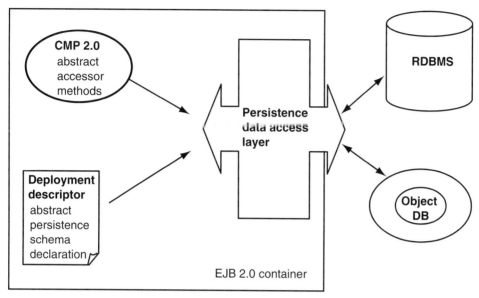

Figure 10-1 Elements of the CMP 2.0 entity bean

The CMP accessor methods `getScheduleID()` and `setScheduleID(String scheduleID)` are declared `abstract`—notice the CMP virtual field `scheduleID`. The CMR accessor methods, `getRosters()` and `setRosters(Collection rosters)`, are also declared `abstract`. The CMR virtual field is `rosters`; note that the return type is `Collection`.

CMP fields can be Java primitive types (`int`, `long`, `short`, `float`, `double`, `boolean`, `char`, and `byte`) or serializable Java objects. CMR fields can be Java primitive types, Java serializable objects, or local interfaces of related entity beans. Rules on how to write accessor methods are discussed later in this chapter.

Abstract Persistence Schema

The *abstract persistence schema* is defined in the deployment descriptor. It represents a logical persistence view and does not specify the implementation mechanism. Every CMP 2.0 entity bean is associated with an abstract persistence schema and must have a unique schema name. An abstract persistence schema can have any arbitrary name, but it's good practice to give it the EJB's name with which it's associated. (This book uses the bean name without the postfix `EJB`.) Abstract persistence schema can have two types of fields: container-managed persistent fields and container-managed relationship fields.

Container-Managed Persistent Fields

Container-managed persistent fields (cmp-fields) are fields that map directly to the database. For every persistent virtual field declared in the CMP 2.0 entity bean class, there must be a corresponding CMP field element in the deployment descriptor. These persistent fields must be either Java primitive types or a Java class that implements the `java.io.Serializable` interface.

These virtual persistent fields must correspond to the `<cmp-field>` element described in the abstract persistence schema of the deployment descriptor. The following code snippet shows the abstract accessor methods of `CourseEJB class`:

```
//accessor methods for cmp fields
public abstract String getCourseID(); // primary Key
public abstract void setCourseID(String courseID);
public abstract String getTitle();
public abstract void setTitle(String title);

public abstract double getPrice();
public abstract void setPrice(double price);
```

The following XML elements show the mapping of the abstract accessor methods of the `CourseEJB` entity bean in the deployment descriptor. The persistent-type is `Container`; the CMP version is 2.x; and the abstract-schema-name is `Course`, which maps to the associated `CourseEJB` bean. Also, note that for every virtual field from the abstract accessor methods, there's a corresponding CMP field in the deployment descriptor. The `<cmp-field>` element has two subelements: an optional `<description>` element and the mandatory `<field-name>` element. For every abstract accessor method such as `getTitle()` and `setTitle()` that declares a virtual field in the CMP 2.0 entity bean class, there's a matching CMP field such as `title` enclosed by the `<field-name>` element within the `<cmp-field>` element in the deployment descriptor. The CMP fields must correspond to a column name in the database table.

```
<entity>
    <display-name>CourseEJB</display-name>
    <ejb-name>CourseEJB</ejb-name>
    <local-home>j2eebootcamp.developingEJB.chapter11.course.Local-
CourseHome </local-home>
  <local>j2eebootcamp.developingEJB.chapter11.course.LocalCourse</local>
    <ejb-class>j 2eebootcamp.developingEJB.chapter11.course.Cour-
seEJB</ejb-class>
  <persistence-type>Container</persistence-type>
  <prim-key-class>java.lang.String</prim-key-class>
  <reentrant>False</reentrant>
  <cmp-version>2.x</cmp-version>
```

```
<abstract-schema-name>Course</abstract-schema-name>
<cmp-field>
  <description>no description</description>
  <field-name>price</field-name>
</cmp-field>
<cmp-field>
  <description>no description</description>
  <field-name>courseID</field-name>
</cmp-field>
<cmp-field>
  <description>no description</description>
  <field-name>title</field-name>
</cmp-field>
<primkey-field>courseID</primkey-field>
<security-identity>
  <description></description>
  <use-caller-identity></use-caller-identity>
</security-identity>
</entity>
```

Note that the virtual field `courseID` is repeated twice, first as a virtual field in `<cmp-field>` and then within the `<primkey-field>` element denoting that this is the primary key in the entity bean.

Container-Managed Relationship Fields

One of the benefits of CMP entity beans in EJB 2.0 is support for complex relationships between CMP 2.0 entity beans with local interfaces. *Container-managed relationship fields* (CMR field) are fields that specify the relationships among the interrelated CMP 2.0 entity beans. An entity bean accesses other related entity beans by means of CMR fields. For every abstract relationship accessor method declared in the CMP 2.0 entity bean class, there must be a corresponding CMR virtual relationship field enclosed by a `<cmr-field-name>` element within the `<cmr-field>` element in the deployment descriptor. This field type must be the abstract schema type of the entity bean denoted by the `<ejb-name>` element enclosed by the `<ejb-relationship-role>` element, as shown later in the code fragment.

The following relationships are supported in CMP (2.0) entity beans:

- *One-to-one relationships*—simple relationships; for example, between a schedule and a location, as only one specific class schedule can be offered at one location.
- *One-to-many*—for example, a class schedule might contain many students.
- *Many-to-many*—for example, a location can offer many different classes; a class can be offered at different locations.

These relationships are illustrated in Figure 10-2. The EJBlocalObject represents a single side of a relationship, while the `java.util.Collection` and `java.util.Set` represent many sides of a relationship.

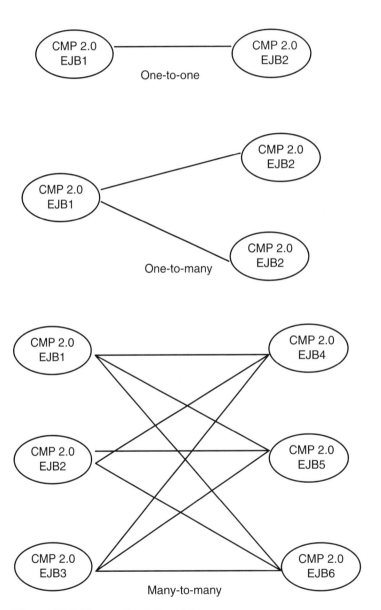

Figure 10-2 Types of relationships

These relationships can be either *unidirectional* or *bidirectional*. In a unidirectional relationship, one can traverse in only one direction, while in a bidirectional relationship, traversing in both directions is feasible. For example, in the unidirectional relationship, the caller can reference the callee, but the callee cannot reference the caller. In a bidirectional relationship, both the caller and the callee can reference each other. A bean developer typically uses unidirectional relationships to restrict the visibility of a relationship

Container-managed relationships are defined in terms of the local interfaces of the related beans. The relationship can exist only among the entity beans within the same local relationship scope, as defined by the relationship element in the deployment descriptor. An entity bean with remote interfaces can have only unidirectional relationships from itself to other entity beans. The lack of local interfaces prevents other entity beans from having a relationship with the entity bean with the remote interface.

The bean developer uses CMP 2.0 relationships in the following ways:

- to access objects and associated collections of objects
- to navigate among associated objects using EJB QL
- to automatically delete dependent objects (also known as cascade-delete)

The following set of abstract relationship accessor methods in the CMP 2.0 entity bean class deal with virtual fields and return a collection:

```
public abstract Collection getAddresses();
public abstract void setAddresses (Collection addresses);
```

Relationships are described in the deployment descriptor with corresponding CMR field as shown in the code that follows. Each relationship consists of a pair of entity beans having two roles. The role source has a relationship with another source target; there are five different elements that define the roles. Note that the `<ejb-relationship-role-name>` element and name `StudentEJB-AddressEJB` indicate that the relationship is between two `StudentEJB` and `AddressEJB` entity beans. There are no naming rules, but a common convention is to use the bean name separated by a hyphen (as shown) or to spell out the relationship (for example, `StudentEJB-has-AddressEJB`).

The multiplicity value is one but can also be many. The `<relationship-role-source>` element declares `StudentEJB` as the EJB name included by `<ejb-name>` element. The CMR field element encloses two elements (`<cmr-field-name>`) that map to the virtual relationship field in the bean class. The CMR field `addresses` enables the `StudentEJB` entity to access and manipulate the `AddressEJB` entity.

The return type should be a collection of similar objects specified by the `<cmr-field-type>` element.

```
<relationships>
    <ejb-relation>
        <ejb-relation-name></ejb-relation-name>
        <ejb-relationship-role>
            <ejb-relationship-role-name>StudentEJB-AddressEJB</ejb-relationship-role-name>
            <multiplicity>One</multiplicity>
            <relationship-role-source>
                <ejb-name>CustomerBean</ejb-name>
            </relationship-role-source>
            <cmr-field>
                <cmr-field-name>addresses</cmr-field-name>
                <cmr-field-type>java.util.Collection</cmr-field-type>
            </cmr-field>
        </ejb-relationship-role>
```

As discussed, the accessor methods map to the CMP fields and CMR fields in the deployment descriptor. The CMP fields and CMR fields know how to access the underlying data store using the EJB Query Language (QL). EJB QL is an SQL-like language that generates query statements based on the container-managed fields and relationship fields specified by the developer. It's saved in the deployment descriptor.

Persistence Data Access Layer

At deployment time, the deployment tool reads the abstract persistence schema in the deployment descriptor file and generates the appropriate classes to handle the persistence management. This enables the vendor to optimize the translation of EJB QL to the proprietary native SQL or OQL implementation. For example, the Oracle EJB container optimizes the EJB QL query and translates it into Oracle's native SQL implementation. This implementation is optimized for Oracle resulting in far better performance; in addition, the CMP entity bean code is immune to future changes to the native libraries. The deployer only needs to redeploy the beans as the deployment tool takes care of the changes in the native library. At runtime, the CMP entity bean instance delegates the persistence management task to the persistence data access layer implemented in the container.

The deployment tool automatically generates the SQL or OQL query based on the EJB QL statement from the deployment descriptor as discussed in the following section.

EJB Query Language

The EJB 1.1 specification did not specify the standard mechanism for declaring the behavior of the custom finder methods. This resulted in vendors developing proprietary solutions making the CMP entity bean not portable. The EJB 2.0 architects spent considerable effort to specify an EJB QL that defines a standard way to specify the behavior of the finder and select methods. All J2EE 1.3-certified application server vendors are required to implement EJB 2.0 specifications, thus guaranteeing portability.

EJB QL is a declarative query language specially created for use with abstract persistent schemas. It enables bean developers to specify the behavior of the custom finder and ejbSelect methods in CMP 2.0 entity beans. EJB QL is based on a subset of SQL-92 and, in many ways, is similar to the SQL common to relational databases. The biggest advantage of using EJB QL queries is portability—this is achieved due to the following:

- The EJB QL queries are defined in terms of the abstract persistence schema of entity beans and not in terms of the underlying database schema.
- During deployment, the EJB QL queries are converted to data access code optimized by the container for the target database.

At runtime, the EJB QL queries are executed in the native language of the target-underlying database. For example, when using Oracle 8i, the EJB QL queries are converted to Oracle's native language format; in the case of object databases such as Poet, however, the EJB QL queries are converted to Poet's native language format.

One benefit of EJB QL is that bean developers can now focus on the interactions and relationships between CMP 2.0 entities at the object level without having to have an intimate knowledge of the physical schema of underlying database tables. This advantage makes CMP 2.0 entity beans highly portable. Another benefit of EJB QL is its similarity to SQL—developers already having an understanding of SQL can understand EJB QL queries.

The deployment descriptor segment that follows shows the CMP 2.0 entity bean, `StudentEJB`, and the abstract persistence schema, `Student`. It declares the CMP field `StudentID`, which is also the primary key for the `StudentEJB` entity bean. Note the local reference to `AddressEJB` as specified by the `<ejb-local-ref>` element. The bean developer is responsible for specifying the query statement for the `findByLastName(String  lastName)` method declared in the `StudentHome` interface using the EJB QL in the deployment descriptor. This is

shown enclosed by the <query> element that encloses <method-name>
findByLastName along with the <method-param> element. The
findbyLastName element maps to the <ejb-ql> query **SELECT DISTINCT
OBJECT(c) FROM Student c WHERE c.lastName= ?1**. Notice that the EJB
QL query statement enclosed by the <ejb-ql> element applies to
findByLastName, specified by the <query-method> element, both enclosed
by the <query> element of the abstract persistence schema Student. The
findByLastName(String lastName) method declared in the home
interfaces maps to the findByLastname specified by the <method-name>, and
the lastName argument maps to the field specified by the <method-params>
element, both enclosed by the <query-method> element of the deployment
descriptor. We'll discuss the EJB QL query syntax shortly. It's the bean
developer's responsibility to specify the EJB QL query with the deployment tool;
when deployed, the query is converted to the appropriate underlying query
language.

```
<entity>
  <display-name>StudentEJB</display-name>
  <ejb-name>StudentEJB</ejb-name>
  <local-home>LocalStudentHome</local-home>
  <local>LocalStudent</local>
  <ejb-class>StudentEJB</ejb-class>
  <persistence-type>Container</persistence-type>
  <prim-key-class>java.lang.String</prim-key-class>
  <reentrant>False</reentrant>
  <cmp-version>2.x</cmp-version>
  <abstract-schema-name>Student</abstract-schema-name>
  <cmp-field>
    <field-name>lastName</field-name>
  </cmp-field>
  <cmp-field>
    <field-name>firstName</field-name>
  </cmp-field>
  <cmp-field>
    <field-name>StudentID</field-name>
  </cmp-field>
  <primkey-field>StudentID</primkey-field>
  <ejb-local-ref>
    <ejb-ref-name>ejb/AddressRef</ejb-ref-name>
    <ejb-ref-type>Entity</ejb-ref-type>
    <local-home>LocalAddressHome</local-home>
    <local>LocalAddress</local>
    <ejb-link>AddressEJB</ejb-link>
  </ejb-local-ref>
```

```
<query>
  <description></description>
  <query-method>
    <method-name>findByLastName</method-name>
    <method-params>
      <method-param>java.lang.String</method-param>
    </method-params>
  </query-method>
  <ejb-ql>SELECT DISTINCT OBJECT(c) FROM Student c WHERE c.last-
Name= ?1</ejb-ql>
  </query>
</entity>
```

EJB QL Query Syntax

Now, let's look at the EJB QL query syntax in detail before reviewing how to use EJB QL to describe the finder and select methods. An EJB QL query can consist of three clauses:

- SELECT clause
- FROM clause
- WHERE clause (optional)

In the following sections, we'll discuss the details and restriction of these EJB QL clauses and how to use them to declare finder and select methods for your CMP entity beans. A simple EJB QL query may only consist of SELECT and FROM clauses, with the WHERE clause being optional. Note that the EJB QL keywords are case-insensitive; for the sake of readability, however, we'll use upper case.

SELECT Clause

In an EJB QL query, the SELECT clause is used to specify the return results of a query and to traverse relationships. Let us look at the syntax:

```
select_clause ::=
SELECT [DISTINCT] {single_valued_path_expression | OBJECT
(identification_variables) }
```

The SELECT clause contains a single range variable that ranges over an entity bean abstract schema or a single valued path expression as specified by the relationship. The container maps the types returned by the query to the appropriate Java types that are returned by the finder and ejbSelect methods with which the query is associated.

The `DISTINCT` keyword is used to remove duplicate values from the query result. If the `SELECT` clause contains standalone identification variables, it must be qualified by the `OBJECT` keyword; if the `SELECT` clause uses a path expression, however, then it cannot use the `OBJECT` operator. An example of a select clause with path expression follows—note that it does not use the `OBJECT` keyword.

```
SELECT m.city FROM Student AS s, IN(s.address) m
```

The query statement says to select the city associated with the student's address.

Another example of a `SELECT` clause with an identification variable follows (note the use of the `OBJECT` keyword). The query returns a list of students as represented in the abstract persistence schema, student.

```
SELECT OBJECT(s) FROM Student AS s, Course AS c
```

In this query, two variables have been defined in the FROM clause: s and c. The `SELECT` clause enables the developer to indicate that the s variable is of interest—not the c variable.

In the following example, we're interested in the name of the student as specified by the relationship—a name log that represents a relationship between `Schedule` and `Student` object. In this case, the select is traversing the `Student` object which is related to `Schedule` object as indicated by `s.Student` and returns the last names of the students.

```
SELECT log.lastName FROM Schedule AS s, IN (s.Student) log
```

Another note, the EJB QL evaluates from left to right, enabling the declaration of Schedule `AS s`. It's available to the right for `IN (s.Students)`. The word "AS" is optional and is used only for readability. Also note that identifier variables can be more than a single character (as illustrated with `log`).

A query result can be either a CMP field or a single CMR field. The important word is *single* CMR field—the `SELECT` clause can handle only a single CMR field except in certain conditions, which we'll discuss later. This is illustrated in the following example:

```
SELECT s.firstName FROM Student s
```

This query returns the first name of all students. The `SELECT` clause uses the s.firstName path to retrieve the names of the students.

To get around the restriction of **SELECT** having to return a single CMR field rather than a collection, use the `IN` option with the `FROM` clause as follows:

```
SELECT OBJECT(stud) FROM Schedule AS s, IN (s.Students) stud
```

The query returns an individual element of the collection to the SELECT method. The result of the SELECT clause can contain duplicates, as with the above query.

This query lists a student name multiple times if the student is registered for multiple classes. However, if a program requires a list of students registered for any of the classes but doesn't want duplicate names, there are two choices. Use either the DISTINCT qualifier with the SELECT clause of the EJB QL query, or declare the return type to be java.util.Set rather than java.util.Collection for the finder, ejbSelect, and accessor methods.

The following query illustrates the navigability of the SELECT clause traversing multiple paths using the dot notation.

```
SELECT s.student.address.city FROM Schedule s
```

Here the city name is traversed and received from the AddressEJB instance related to the StudentEJB instance, which in turn is related to the ScheduleEJB instance. When traversing the dot notation, the navigability is possible only across CMR and CMP field termination points. Navigating across a collection-based relationship isn't possible.

FROM Clause and Navigation Declaration

In EJB QL, the FROM clause is used to restrict the domain of a query and to specify what entity beans one is interested in. The domain of the query may be constrained by the path expression. The FROM clause can contain multiple identification variable declarations separated by commas, as shown in this example:

```
from_clause ::= FROM identification_variable_declaration [, identi-
fication-variables_declaration]*
```

An *identifier* is a character sequence of unlimited length. An *identifier character* is any character for which the method Character.isJavaIdentifierPart returns true. An *identification variable* is a valid identifier declared in the FROM clause of an EJB QL query. Identification variables are case-insensitive and may be declared using the special operators IN and AS and can only be declared in the FROM clause. An identification variable must not be a reserved identifier such as SELECT, FROM, WHERE, DISTINCT, OBJECT, NULL, TRUE, FALSE, AND, OR, BETWEEN, LIKE, IN AS, UNKNOWN, EMPTY, MEMBER, OF, and IS or the abstract-schema name or ejb-name. For example:

```
SELECT OBJECT(sched) FROM Schedule AS sched, Student AS stud
```

The query in the FROM clause declares that we're interested in the Schedule and Student relationship, although the query isn't referencing Student in the

SELECT clause. This query returns all schedules that have registered students. Look at the FROM clause once again:

```
SELECT OBJECT(stud) FROM Schedule AS sched, IN (sched.Student) AS
stud
```

Here, `Schedule AS sched` declares a variable sched that represents any schedule entity bean, `ScheduleEJB`. The `IN (sched.Student) AS stud` declares a variable stud that represents any student linked to the schedule bean.

WHERE Clause

In EJB QL, the WHERE is used to narrow the scope of the SELECT clause and thus limit the list of the selected elements. Although the WHERE clause is optional in EJB QL, it does provide a set of conditional operator options to narrow the SELECT results. Common options available with the WHERE clause are discussed next.

The WHERE clause consists of the conditional expression used to restrict the result of the query.

```
where clause ::= WHERE conditional_expression
```

Literals

Literals, a string enclosed by single quotes, can be used to narrow a SELECT result. Literals can also be a Java integer, floating point, or Boolean type—these don't need to be enclosed within single quotes like string literals. For example:

```
SELECT OBJECT(s) FROM Schedule AS s WHERE s.title = 'J2EE Boot
Camp'
```

We're using the literal `'J2EE Boot Camp'` to match the title of the Schedule and narrow the search.

Input Parameters

Use the input parameters option to pass arguments from the client to the EJB QL query statement. The input parameter uses a ? prefix followed by an integer number (starting from 1) to specify the argument location to map to the EJB QL query statement. The following is an example of a home interface with a finder method with three arguments: city, state, and country, respectively.

```
public Collection findByCity(String city, String state, String
country);
```

The EJB QL statement in the deployment descriptor would use the input parameters as follows:

```
<ejb-ql>
    SELECT OBJECT(s) FROM Student AS s
    WHERE s.address.city = ?1 AND s.address.state = ?2 AND
    s.address.country = ?3
</ejb-ql>
```

Arithmetic Operators

Use unary (+, -), multiplication (*) and division (/), and addition and subtraction operators similarly to how they would be used in an SQL query. For example, to list the courses priced greater than $1000 after applying a discount of 10%, enter the following:

```
SELECT OBJECT( s ) FROM Schedule AS s
    WHERE   (s.cost * .90 ) > 1000.00
```

Logical Operators

Logical operators consist of NOT, OR, and AND; they function like their counterparts in SQL. Logical operators must evaluate to boolean expressions; each of the operands must evaluate to true or false.

Comparison Operators

Comparison operators like =, >, >=, < , <=, and <> are familiar; note that the symbol <> means *not equal to* because EJB QL does not use != to mean *not equal to*. The >, >=, <, and <= operators can only be used with numeric values, while = and <> may be used with EJB Object references, String and Boolean. An example narrowing search results to classes costing between $1000 and $2,500 would look like the following:

```
SELECT OBJECT(s) FROM Schedule s WHERE s.cost   >= 1000.00 AND
s.cost <= 2500.00
```

IN Operators

Don't confuse this IN conditional operator with the IN operator used in the FROM clause. This IN operator can only be used with operands that evaluate to a string value and for testing whether a literal string exists in a list of literal string values. For example, the following query would return all classes offered in the states of California or New York:

```
SELECT OBJECT ( l ) FROM Location l WHERE l.state IN ('CA', 'NY')
```

BETWEEN Operators

This operator is used to specify a range of values. Use it to list classes priced between $1000 and $2500.

```
SELECT OBJECT( s ) FROM Schedule s WHERE s.cost BETWEEN 1000.00 AND
2500.00
```

LIKE Operators

This is a flexible operator that enables you to match a string pattern. Use "%" (percent) to specify any sequence of characters or "_" (underscore) to specify a single character. "\" (escape) can be used with "%" and "_" to pass them to the LIKE operator as a character, as represented in the following examples:

- LIKE 'EJB-%' matches any course ID string starting with 'EJB-' but not those beginning with 'EJB_'.

- LIKE '_JB' matches any three character strings with any first character as long as the second and third characters are "JB".

- LIKE '_JB' matches only to the '_JB' string.

MEMBER Operators

Member operators are useful for determining whether an EJB object is a member of a specific collection-based relationship. The OF in MEMBER OF is optional. The example that follows states to list all schedules that have students registered.

```
SELECT OBJECT( s ) FROM Schedule AS s, Student AS t
    WHERE t MEMBER OF s.students
```

IS NULL Operators

This IS NULL comparison operator is used to test whether a path expression is null as follows:

```
SELECT OBJECT ( s ) FROM Schedule s WHERE s.student IS NULL
```

IS EMPTY Operators

The IS EMPTY operator is used to test whether a collection-based relationship is empty as follows:

```
SELECT OBJECT( s ) FROM Schedule s WHERE s.students IS EMPTY
```

Functional Expressions

Functional expressions include the following:

- CONCAT("Hi", "Sue") returns "HiSue"
- SUBSTRING("JavaBeans", 5, 5) returns "Beans"
- LOCATE("JavaBeans", "Beans") returns 5 the position
- LENGTH("JavaBeans") returns 9
- ABS(number) returns absolute value of the number, which could be int, float, or double
- SQRT(double) returns the square root of a double

The EJB QL query must be enclosed in <![CDATA [SELECT ....]]> when queries contain characters such as "<" and ">"(also used by XML) to avoid confusing the XML parser. This should be automatically handled by the vendor-provided deployment tool. For example:

```
<ejb-ql> <![CDATA[SELECT OBJECT(s) FROM Schedule AS s WHERE
s.enrolled > 10] ] >
</ejb-ql>
```

Finder Methods

EJB QL statements are used to describe the behavior of custom finder and ejbSelect methods related to CMP and CMR fields. EJB clients use finder methods to locate and obtain either an EJBObject or EJBLocalObject that references a specific entity bean instance. Every entity bean's home interface is required to declare a findByPrimaryKey(..) method that must return either a component interface or throw a FinderException. There can be other custom finder methods declared in the entity bean's home interface, which may return a single-object or multiobjects. These methods must use java.util.Collection or java.util.Set to return the multiobjects.

For every finder method (except findByPrimaryKey()) declared in the home interface of the CMP 2.0 entity bean, there must be a matching query declaration in the bean's deployment descriptor. Note that the bean developer must not implement a matching finder method in the CMP entity bean class. Fortunately, the vendor-provided tool creates the finder method in the deployment descriptor, leaving developers to define the EJB QL query. However, there's one exception to this rule: the container implements the findByPrimaryKey() method automatically.

The return type for finder methods can only be the `EJBObject` or `EJBLocalObject` type or a collection of either type. How does the container know which to return? In the case of finder methods, the container can look at the definition of the bean's home interface. For example, if a remote interface, the container returns `EJBObject`; if a local interface, it returns `EJBLocalObject`. Alternatively, use the `<method-intf>` element in the deployment descriptor to be specific.

Note that when a `findByFirstName` finder method is declared in the CMP 2.0 entity bean's home interface as shown below, the bean developer has to specify the EJB QL query with the deployment tool, which is saved in the deployment descriptor:

```
public Collection findByFirstName (String firstName)
    throws FinderException;
```

Notice the mapping of the `findByFirstName` method name and the argument to `?1` in the EJB QL query statement specified in the deployment descriptor:

```
<query>
    <description></description>
    <query-method>
      <method-name>findByFirstName</method-name>
      <method-params>
        <method-param>java.lang.String</method-param>
      </method-params>
    </query-method>
    <ejb-ql>SELECT DISTINCT OBJECT(c) FROM Customer AS c WHERE
c.firstName = ?1</ejb-ql>
</query>
```

At deployment, the deployment tool automatically translates the above EJB QL query to the SQL query statement

```
SELECT DISTINCT "s" "studentID" FROM "StudentEJBTable" "s" WHERE
("s" "firstName" = ?)
```

in the case of a relational database.

`ejbSelect` Methods

Unlike the finder methods, available since EJB 1.0, `ejbSelect` methods are new additions in EJB 2.0. The select methods are similar to finder methods but are more versatile. Unlike finder methods, the select methods are private and not exposed to clients. The select methods can only be used internally in the bean class and are usually invoked by business methods. The select methods must be declared as `abstract` in the bean class, similarly to the accessor methods. The select methods can query across all entity beans declared in the same deployment descriptor and aren't restricted to the context of any specific entity bean. With regard to return type, the select methods can return a single or a collection of `EJBObject` or `EJBLocalObjects` and, in addition, can also return CMP fields. In fact, select methods can return any type of EJB object and aren't restricted to the type of bean in which they're declared.

Because the return type can be local objects, remote objects, or a collection, how does the select method know which to return? Because the `ejbSelect` methods are private and cannot be declared in the interfaces, the container cannot automatically determine the return type. A developer can use the `<result-type-mapping>` element to explicitly declare the return type `local` or `remote` in the deployment descriptor. If a developer doesn't explicitly declare the result type using the `<result-type-mapping>` element, the container defaults the return type to local.

The following example shows the abstract `ejbSelectAllSchedules()` method defined in the CMP 2.0 entity bean class:

```
public abstract Collection ejbSelectAllSchedules() throws FinderEx-
ception;
```

In the corresponding EJB QL query statement shown next, note that `ejbSelectAllSchedules` and the result-type-mapping are set to remote and the query statement. The query statement returns a unique collection of all schedules.

```
<query>
    <description></description>
    <query-method>
      <method-name>ejbSelectAllSchedules</method-name>
      <method-params />
    </query-method>
    <result-type-mapping>Remote</result-type-mapping>
    <ejb-ql>SELECT DISTINCT OBJECT (s) FROM Schedules AS s</ejb-ql>
</query>
```

At deployment time, the deployment tool automatically translates the foregoing EJB QL query into the SQL query

```
SELECT "s" "scheduleID" FROM "ScheduleEJBTable" "s"
```

for a relational database.

Differences Between Finder and `ejbSelect` Methods

Although finder and ejbSelect methods can perform similar tasks, they have subtle differences. The finder and `ejbSelect` methods are pool methods—they are executed while the bean instance is in the pool state. At the end of the execution of these methods, the bean instance is still in the pool state. The `ejbSelect` methods are private methods available in CMP 2.0 entity beans only. They are meant to be accessed by business methods within the bean class and cannot be invoked by clients. The finder methods are exposed to clients and are available in both BMP and CMP entity beans. The `ejbSelect` can be invoked during pool state and/or in ready state while finder methods can only be invoked in the pool state.

The finder methods can return only `EJBObject` or `EJBLocalObject` object types, while `ejbSelect` (in addition to local and remote component types) can also return a CMP field type.

Issues with EJB QL

Although the EJB QL has helped improve the performance, portability, and flexibility in CMP 2.0 entity beans, there remain several issues with the current version of EJB QL, such as

- *No support for the ORDER BY clause*—The `ORDER BY` clause enables developers to request an ordered list in a query. Most query languages support this useful feature.
- *No support for Date*—The EJB QL language provides no native support for the `java.util.Date class`, which is a major issue. Developers cannot use comparison operators such as =, >, <=, and so on with Date CMP fields.
- *Supports limited functional expressions*—Developers familiar with SQL will be disappointed with the limited support for functional expressions. Expressions such as `MAX()`, `MIN()`, `SUM()`, and `UPPER()` aren't supported.

CMP Entity Bean Callback Methods

A CMP 2.0 entity bean class can have ejbSelect methods in addition to the BMP entity bean callback methods discussed in the last chapter. These methods are classified into four categories:

- bean instance life cycle management methods
- persistent data synchronization methods
- pool methods
- business methods

Bean Instance Life Cycle Management Methods

Methods in this category consist of `ejbCreate()`, `ejbPostCreate()`, `ejbActivate()`, `ejbPassivate()`, and `ejbRemove()`. In the case of CMP 2.0

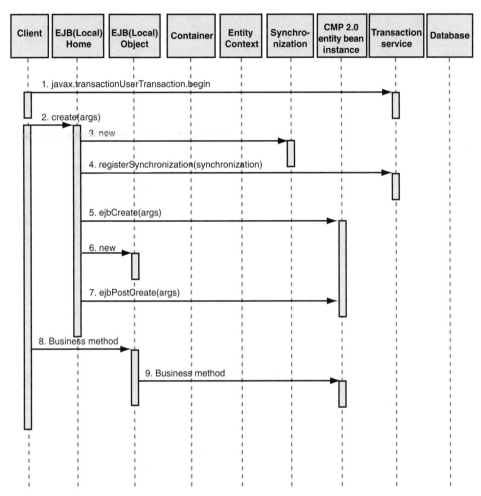

Figure 10-3 Sequence diagram of the creation of CMP 2.0 entity bean instances

entity beans, the bean developer is only required to implement the `ejbCreate()` and `ejbPostCreate()` methods. Note that the implementations must not consist of any code that directly access the underlying database. The data access task is delegated to the accessor methods, which are implemented by the container. The sequence diagram in Figure 10-3 shows object interaction in the process of creating CMP 2.0 entity beans.

The `ejbPassivate()`, `ejbActivate()` and `ejbRemove()` methods must be left empty—the container and deployment tools generate the necessary code.

There are two methods, setEntityContext() and unsetEntityContext(), that a bean developer uses to pass a reference to the EntityContext interface. The bean developer must set and unset the entity context.

Persistent Data Synchronization Methods

Because the container is responsible for synchronization, the ejbLoad() and ejbStore() methods must be left empty. The sequence diagram shows the interaction of objects during the ejbLoad(), ejbStore(), ejbPassivate(), and ejbActivate() methods. Notice that the ejbStore() and ejbPassivate() methods are called by the container when necessary to manage the resources. If the bean instance is in passivated state, and a business method is invoked by a client, the EJBObject invokes the ejbActivate() and ejbLoad() method before the business is executed. Figure 10-4 illustrates how these methods interact.

Pool Methods

Pool methods consist of ejbFinder, ejbHome and ejbSelect methods. The CMP 2.0 entity beans can have one or more finder methods declared in the home interface. In the case of CMP 2.0, the bean developer declares finder methods in the home interface but does not have to implement a matching ejbFinder method in the bean class. The bean developer uses the deployment tool to specify custom finder methods in the abstract persistence schema.

With entity beans, the developer specifies the mandatory findByPrimaryKey() methods in the home interface. The container automatically implements this method so the developer does not have to specify the EJB QL query. Other custom finder methods declared in the home interface must have corresponding EJB QL elements associated with them. The bean developer must specify the EJB QL query statement for each custom finder method. The return value, in case of a single-object finder method such as findByPrimaryKey(), is EJBObject or EJBLocalObject, or must throw finderException. Multiobject finder methods such as findAllUsers() must return a Collection of entity objects or an empty Collection. In either case, the container is responsible for the implementation of the logic.

There can be zero or more ejbHome methods in the bean class. The bean developer is required to implement the logic for the home methods in the bean class.

The ejbSelect methods are applicable to CMP 2.0 entity beans only; these methods can either be accessed while the bean instance is in the pool or ready state. There can also be one or more abstract ejbSelect methods declared in the

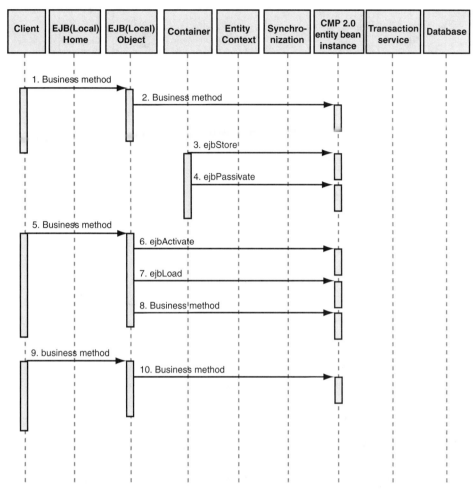

Figure 10-4 Passivation, activation, and business method invocation in
the CMP 2.0 entity bean instance

bean class. The `ejbSelect` methods apply to the entity bean class and are similar
to finder methods. For each `ejbSelect` methods declared in the bean class, the
bean developer must specify EJB QL query in the deployment descriptor.

Business Methods

There can be zero or more business methods that the bean developer must implement
in the entity bean class. The method should consist of only business logic; any data
access task is delegated to the accessor methods and `ejbSelect` methods.

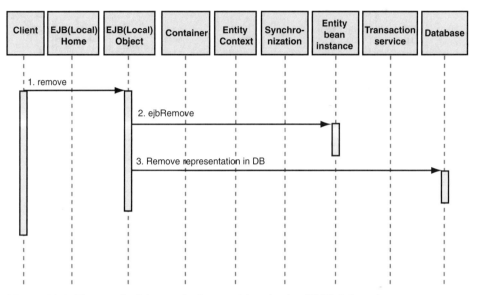

Figure 10-5 Removal of the entity bean object in the CMP 2.0 entity bean instance

A client can invoke the `remove` method on the interface, and the `EJBObject` or `EJBLocalObject` (depending on whether it's a local or a remote interface) invokes `ejbRemove()` method in the bean instance and removes the entity representation from the database as shown in Figure 10-5.

Note: The object interaction sequence diagrams for finder, `setEntityContext()`, and `unsetEntityContext()` methods are identical in CMP 2.0 and BMP entity beans so they won't be repeated. We'll look at the transaction sequence diagram for both types of entity beans in Chapter 14.

Rules for Writing CMP 2.0 Entity Bean Classes

Bean developers must adhere to the following rules to implement a CMP 2.0 entity bean class:

- The developer must directly or indirectly implement the javax.ejb.EntityBean interface.
- The CMP 2.0 entity bean class must be defined as `public` and must be `abstract`.
- The developer must define a `public` constructor that takes no argument.
- The developer must not define the `finalize()` method.

- For every `create<METHOD>()` method declared in the home interface, the developer must implement the matching `ejbCreate<METHOD>()` and `ejbPostCreate<METHOD>()` methods.

- For every business method declared in the component interface, a matching business method must be implemented in the bean class.

- For every home method declared in the home interface, `ejbHome` methods must be implemented in the bean class.

- The developer must not implement finder methods—the container automatically implements finder methods.

- The developer must declare `ejbSelect<METHOD>()` as an `abstract` method.

- The bean developer must specify the abstract accessor methods for the CMP and CMR virtual fields in the bean class and must also specify the abstract persistence schema for the CMP 2.0 entity beans in the deployment descriptor.

- The developer can implement other methods in addition to the methods required by the EJB 2.0 specification. The entity bean class may have superclasses and/or superinterfaces and can inherit business and required methods from them.

- The methods must throw the following exceptions:

  - `java.lang.IllegalArgumentException`—must be thrown when the argument to a set method in a relationship is an instance of the wrong relationship type.

  - `java.lang.IllegalStateException`—must be thrown when a method of Collection API is used to access a collection-valued CMR field within a transaction context other than one in which the CMR field was initially materialized.

  - `java.lang.IllegalStateException`—must be thrown when an iterator is used to access a collection valued CMR field with a transaction context other than the transaction context in which the iterator was initially obtained.

Rules for Writing Abstract Accessor Methods

In CMP 2.0 entity beans, accessor methods are used to declare virtual CMP and CMR fields and relationships. Here are rules for writing accessor methods:

- The bean provider must define the CMP 2.0 entity bean class as an `abstract` class.

- The CMP fields and CMR fields must not be defined in the entity bean class.

- The CMP fields and CMR fields must be specified in the deployment descriptor using the CMP field and CMR field elements respectively. These fields must be valid Java identifiers and must begin with a lower case letter. The bean provider must define abstract accessor methods for CMP fields and CMR fields. The accessor method must adhere to the JavaBean naming convention and use the `get` and `set` prefixes followed by the name of the CMP or CMR field specified in the deployment descriptor. The first character of the field name must be capitalized.

- These accessor methods must be `public`, must be `abstract`, and must bear the name of the CMP fields or CMR fields specified in the deployment descriptor. The first letter of the method name must be upper case and must have the prefix `get` or `set` (such as `getStatus()` for `<cmp-field>status</cmp-field>`) defined in the deployment descriptor.

- The accessor methods for CMR fields must be defined in terms of the local interface of the related entity beans.

- The accessor method for CMR fields for one-to-many or many-to-many relationships must use either `java.util.Collection` or `java.util.Set` for the return type to include `EJBObject` or `EJBLocalObject` interfaces.

- The CMR fields can be either an entity bean's local interface for a single object return type or a collection of local interfaces for a multiobject return type, but they can never be of the CMP fields type. So, in short, CMR fields are local interfaces by default. The local interface types of entity beans and of related entity beans must not be exposed through remote interfaces of entity beans.

- The accessor methods must expose neither the CMR fields nor the collection of CMR fields that represent the local interface via the remote interface of the entity beans.

- Once the primary key for an entity bean has been set, the bean provider must not attempt to change it by using a set accessor method on the primary key CMP field. Set accessor method for primary keys must not be exposed.

- The CMP fields are restricted to Java primitive and Java serializable types.

Rules for Writing Dependent Value Classes

Dependent value class is another name for helper class. The dependent value class can be a legacy class to be used internally with a CMP 2.0 entity bean, and it may be a class exposed through the remote or local interface of the entity bean. Here are the requirements for implementing dependent value classes:

- They must be defined as `public` and must not be `abstract`.
- They must be serializable.
- They can be the value of the CMP field but cannot be the value of the CMR field.
- The `get` accessor method for the CMP field that corresponds to a dependent value class returns a copy of the dependent value class instance. The assignment of a dependent class value to a CMP field of a set access method causes the value to be copied to the target CMP field.

The rules for writing the `ejbCreate`, `ejbPostCreate`, and `ejbHome` methods are no different from those discussed for BMP entity beans. The return value for `ejbCreate` can be set to null to allow the CMP 2.0 entity beans to be subclassed as BMP entity beans in the future.

Rules for Writing `ejbSelect` Methods

These `ejbSelect` methods apply to the bean class as opposed to the bean instance and are commonly invoked by business methods in the bean class. These methods can be invoked either in pool or ready state. There can be one or more `ejbSelect` methods declared in the CMP entity bean class and must adhere to the following rules:

- The select methods must be declared as `public` and `abstract`.
- The select methods are private query methods—they are like finder methods but differ in that the select methods aren't exposed to the clients and can only be used internally by the bean class.
- The select methods are only available for container-managed entity beans and are used within the context of the abstract persistence schema.
- The naming convention for select methods requires an `ejbSelect` prefix, as in the example `ejbSelectAllStudents()`.
- `ejbselect` methods can return a single CMR field or a collection of CMR fields. In addition, they can also return CMP fields. Note that select methods can return any type of EJB object and aren't restricted to the type of bean in which they are declared.
- Select methods must throw `javax.ejb.FinderException`, in addition to any arbitrary application specific exceptions.
- Unlike the finder methods, the select methods must be declared as `abstract` methods in the CMP entity bean class similar to other accessor methods.

- The select methods can query across all entity beans declared in the same deployment descriptor and aren't restricted to the context of any specific entity bean.
- Select methods may be invoked from the `ejbHome` methods, or any business method, or even from the `ejbLoad` and `ejbStore` methods of the entity bean class.

Responsibilities in CMP Entity Bean Development

There are three key players in the development of CMP entity beans: the bean developer, the deployment tool, and the bean deployer.

The Bean Developer

In the case of CMP 2.0 entity beans, the bean developer is responsible for declaring the accessor methods and specifying the abstract persistence schema as well as for implementing the business methods. The bean developer specifies the abstract persistence schema discussed earlier using the deployment tool provided by the EJB container provider. The deployment tool enables the bean provider to create the abstract persistence schema based on the developer specifying various persistent fields and relationship fields with the deployment tool. This results in the deployment descriptor having the logical map of the abstract persistence schema in addition to the standard information necessary for the container.

Implementing the abstract persistent schemas consists of the following steps:

1. Specify the persistent and relationship fields in the deployment descriptor.
2. Declare the abstract getter and setter methods in the bean class.
3. Write the EJB QL query for custom finder and select methods.
4. Specify the relationships between interrelated entity beans.

The Deployment Tool

The deployment tool provided by the container provider plays a central role in the development of the CMP entity beans. The deployment tool creates an XML-based deployment descriptor file containing the abstract persistence schema based on the information provided by the bean developer. Vendor-provided deployment GUI tools simplify this task—developers could use a text editor and create a deployment descriptor at considerable effort.

At deployment time, the deployment tool generates the classes necessary to implement the persistence for the bean instance. The persistence data access layer at runtime does the actual translation and manages the persistence. At runtime, the container and deployment tool function as follows:

- The container transfers data between an entity instance and the underlying data source when the entity bean's methods are executed. Because all data access is done through accessor methods, the container may optimize the data access by using eager and lazy loading and storing schemes.
- The deployment tool creates the classes, which implement the creation, removal, and lookup of the entity object in the underlying database.
- The deployment tool is responsible for generating the concrete entity bean class and persistence classes for providing the implementation of the get and set accessor methods for the abstract persistence schema.
- The container must manage the mapping between primary keys and `EJBLocalObject` or `EJBObject`.
- The container manages the mapping between the logical and physical relationship at runtime and manages the referential integrity of the relationship as specified in the deployment descriptor file.

The deployment descriptor only describes the logical relationship among entity beans. At deployment time, the EJB container and the deployment tool read the abstract schema and generate concrete classes. At runtime, the container, along with the data access layer and the concrete classes, implements and manages persistence. The container and the deployment tool generate the necessary concrete implementation of the entity bean class.

The Bean Deployer

At deployment time, the deployer is responsible for taking the logical relationships described in the deployment descriptor and mapping them to the physical relationships specific to the underlying resources (such as the database) using the vendor-provided deployment tool. The deployer also uses the vendor-provided deployment tool/container to generate the necessary concrete implementation of an entity bean class and other classes as well as the interfaces to implement the persistence management.

At runtime, the bean instance uses these classes to delegate calls from accessor methods of the entity bean to the persistent data access layer of the container.

The biggest advantage of CMP architecture is that the entity bean can be logically independent of the data source in which the entity is stored. The tool can generate classes for relational databases or object databases at deployment time.

Comparing BMP and CMP Entity Beans

There are several major differences between the CMP entity beans and BMP entity beans. The CMP entity bean class must be defined as `abstract`. At deployment time, the abstract entity bean class is subclassed by the deployment tool and creates a concrete entity bean class along with other supporting persistence classes that are required to manage the entity persistence by the container. The BMP entity bean must not be declared `abstract`. The CMP 2.0 entity bean class does not declare persistent fields but instead uses abstract accessor methods to declare virtual fields. These virtual fields must map to the CMP field and CMR fields in the deployment descriptor. In the case of BMP entity beans, the persistent fields must be explicitly declared in the bean class.

The bean developer must specify the abstract persistence schema for each CMP entity bean class in the deployment descriptor. This is then used by the deployment tool to generate the support classes to manage persistence by the container at runtime. In the case of BMP entity beans, the bean developer must write the necessary data access logic to manage persistence.

The CMP entity beans support the EJB Query Language, which enables bean developers to write standard portable query logic. Using BMP entity beans, bean developers choose SQL if the target is a relational database or OQL if the target is an object database. Note that the SQL and OQL may not be 100 percent portable across different vendor implementations.

CMP entity beans have an additional private global method, ejbSelect(), for internal use only. The ejbSelect methods apply to the CMP entity bean class type instead of the entity bean instance. The BMP entity beans don't support ejbSelect methods.

Some advantages of CMP over BMP include

- *Reduced coding*—With CMP 2.0 entity beans, developers can implement complex logic while writing less code.
- *Higher portability*—Because the container handles the persistence logic, the CMP 2.0 entity beans are highly portable and optimized.
- *Faster time to market*—Less coding results in faster time to market.

The Primary Key for CMP 2.0 Entity Beans

The bean developer must specify a primary key class in the deployment descriptor. The primary key type must be a legal Value Type in RMI-IIOP, and the class must provide a suitable implementation of the `hashCode()` and equals(Object other) methods. There are two ways to specify a primary key class in CMP 2.0. The primary key that maps to a single field in the entity bean class, and the <primkey-field> element are used to specify the primary key in the deployment descriptor. The primary key mapping to multiple fields in the entity bean class must be declared public and must have a public constructor with no parameters. All fields in the primary key class must be declared public; the names of the fields in the primary key class must be a subset of the names of the container-managed fields.

With CMP 2.0 entity beans, the bean developer may not know the primary key used by the customer's database system or may choose to not specify the primary key class or primary key field—this gives the deployer the flexibility to select the primary key field at deployment time. In this case, the bean developer must declare the type of argument of the findByPrimaryKey method to be java.lang.Object. This should be reflected in the deployment descriptor with the primary key class type set to java.lang.Object as well.

Summary

In this chapter, we discussed container-managed persistent (CMP) fields and container-managed persistent relationship (CMR) fields and how they relate to abstract accessor methods in the CMP 2.0 entity bean class. We also discussed how CMP and CMR fields map to the abstract persistence schema in the deployment descriptor. The EJB QL provides a standard query statement in CMP 2.0, and the bean maps to the query statement in the deployment descriptor. We outlined the rules on writing the CMP 2.0 entity bean class, accessor methods, and finder and ejbSelect methods. We concluded with a discussion on differences between CMP and BMP entity beans and the relative advantages of CMP entity beans.

DEVELOPING CMP 2.0 ENTITY BEANS

Topics in This Chapter

- Characteristics of CMP 2.0 Entity Beans
- Advantages of CMP Entity Beans over BMP Entity Beans
- CMP 2.0 Entity Bean Sample Application

Chapter 11

The CMP 2.0 entity bean represents a major upgrade from CMP 1.1 entity beans. In the previous chapter, we discussed the new features in CMP 2.0 entity beans, namely, abstract methods, abstract persistent schema, the EJB QL, and the respective responsibilities of bean developers, application assemblers, and deployers. To get a better understanding of how CMP 2.0 entity beans work in the real world, let's apply that knowledge to implement a CMP 2.0 entity bean in this chapter.

This chapter discusses how to implement CMP 2.0 entity beans by reviewing

- the characteristics of CMP 2.0 entity beans
- when to use CMP 2.0 entity beans instead of BMP entity beans
- a step-by-step guide to implementing, packaging, and deploying CMP 2.0 entity beans

Characteristics of CMP 2.0 Entity Beans

CMP 2.0 entity beans have the following significant characteristics:

- CMP 2.0 entity beans support rich relationships between CMP 2.0 entity bean instances. Inter-entity bean relationship is characterized by its *cardinality*. CMP 2.0 entity beans support three types of cardinality: one-to-one, one-to-many, and many-to-many. This extensive cardinality enables developers to model complex business relationships in applications.

- CMP 2.0 supports an abstract persistence schema that separates the client view of persistence from the implementation. The consequence is that developers can implement business logic based on an object model, without having to deal with the intricacies of the relational database model. During deployment, the abstract persistence schema model is mapped to the existing operational model. CMP 2.0 entity beans support EJB QL, a language for querying entity attributes and relationships between objects. At deployment time, the deployment tool converts EJB QL query statements to the query language of the underlying data source. CMP 2.0 entity beans use abstract methods to access container-managed fields and container-managed relationship fields.

- CMP 2.0 entity beans provide two new optional `ejbHome` and `ejbSelect` methods to perform global operations, thus providing developers with added flexibility to implement complex business logic.

- Bean developers don't have to implement `finder` and `ejbSelect` methods; the deployment tool is responsible for generating the implementation classes during deployment.

- The container is responsible for automatically providing the inter-entity relationship referential integrity checks as well as implementing *cascade delete*. In CMP 2.0 relationships, cascade delete enables the container to delete dependent entity objects automatically when a primary entity object is deleted, all the while ensuring referential integrity in the relationship.

- CMP 2.0 beans must be declared an `abstract` class. During deployment, the vendor-provided deployment tool is responsible for subclassing the `abstract` bean class and generating concrete classes to support the container-managed persistence.

Advantages of CMP Entity Beans over BMP Entity Beans

Factors that influence a developer's decision to use CMP entity beans as opposed to BMP entity beans include the availability of in-house expertise and the extent of a developer's experience. There are several additional reasons to consider CMP over BMP:

- *Time to market*—With CMP entity beans, the developers write only the business logic and defer the persistence and relationship management logic to the deployment tool and the container, with the result that their applications contain fewer lines of code and take less time to develop.

With BMP entity beans, on the other hand, the developer is responsible for writing the persistence and relationship management logic in addition to the business logic.

- *Portability*—With BMP entity beans, the developer may write optimized SQL query statements and logic to manage persistence for a specific relational database. The hard-coded optimized SQL query statements and the logic may not be portable to other relational databases. With CMP entity beans, the developer uses the abstract persistence schema to specify the CMP and CMR fields in the deployment descriptor. The vendor-provided deployment tool then generates the appropriate classes at deployment time, thus ensuring a high degree of portability regardless of the type of data source.

- *Flexibility*—With BMP entity beans, the developer must write the appropriate query statements to manage persistence based on the target data source. For example, the developer must write SQL statements for the relational database and OQL statements for the object database. As a result, third-party EJB providers must code and provide two sets of data access objects. The end users then must use the right combination of data access logic and query language for the query statements according to the target database. This adds unnecessary code management tasks for the user and the seller of BMP entity bean components. With CMP entity beans, on the other hand, the developer uses the abstract persistent schema to declare the CMP and CMR fields and then specifies the query using the EJB QL in the deployment descriptor. The deployment tool provides the flexibility to generate the SQL query for a relational database or the OQL query for an object database.

- *Improved performance*—To enable high performance with BMP entity beans, bean developers (the business domain experts) must also become database experts, as they must write optimized code for a particular vendor's database. Obviously, database expertise is usually the domain of database administrators, not of bean developers. A higher level of data access code optimization also leads to reduced portability of the bean class. With CMP entity beans, the vendor-provided tool can read the deployment descriptor and potentially generate highly optimized code for the target data source. The degree of code optimization (and, therefore, of real-world CMP entity bean performance) will vary among the container providers. Optimization is a matter of simply converting EJB QL into native API calls of the particular target data source during deployment. Bean developers don't have to learn any vendor-specific APIs to improve performance in CMP entity beans.

- *Referential integrity*—CMP entity beans inherit the rich relationship semantics, referential integrity, cardinality, relationship management, and cascading delete that the EJB 2.0 container provides automatically. With BMP entity beans, on the other hand, the bean developer must provide referential integrity checks and relationship management when implementing inter-entity relationships—and that's no trivial task.

- *Ease of maintenance*—With BMP entity beans, there's more code to maintain—data access code in addition to business logic code results in software code maintenance challenges. CMP entity beans have only business logic code, as the deployment tools generate complicated data access and management code automatically during deployment.

Clearly, CMP entity beans have overwhelming advantages over BMP entity beans. They do have some drawbacks, however:

- *Debug difficulty*—Because the data access and management classes are generated by the vendor's tool (meaning that the bean developers don't have access to the source code), some bugs are harder to debug in CMP entity beans. Also, CMP entity bean implementation automatically inherits any bugs inherent in the persistence class generated by the deployment tool.

- *Reduced developer control*—The developer has complete control of the data access logic when using BMP entity beans and, consequently, more control over the entity bean's persistence management. In some instances—such as when there's a requirement to use vendor-specific, optimized query features like automatic primary key generators—the benefit of better data access control may be critical.

- *Higher learning curve*—Because most developers are already familiar with writing SQL queries, it's easier to learn how to implement BMP entity beans. The CMP 2.0 abstract programming model is relatively more complex, and there's a sharp learning curve initially. To implement CMP 2.0 entity beans, the bean developer must understand the abstract persistence schema model and abstract CMP and CMR methods.

CMP 2.0 Entity Bean Sample Application

The CMP 2.0 entity bean application that we describe in this chapter allows students to create their user IDs, add one or more addresses, and register for classes. It also allows the student to list the addresses and classes for which they are currently registered. The application consists of several JSP clients that invoke create and search methods on three CMP 2.0 entity beans: `StudentEJB`, `AddressEJB`, and `RosterEJB`.

Let's examine the relationships among these three EJBs. A student can have zero or more addresses; as such, the student-address relationship is one-to-many and is a unidirectional relationship, navigating from student to address. When the student account is deleted, the address must also be deleted, requiring the use of a cascade delete option. The relationship between the student and the roster can be many-to-many (for example, a student can enroll in many classes, and a class can have many students); but, for simplicity, the relationship between student and roster is specified as one-to-many. There is no directional relationship between the address and the roster except via the student.

StudentEJB, AddressEJB, and RosterEJB are implemented as CMP 2.0 entity beans with local interfaces. The home and component interfaces of these EJBs are described and implemented in this chapter.

Steps necessary to implement CMP 2.0 entity beans are similar to the steps for implementing BMP entity beans; however, although coding for CMP entity beans is simpler, deployment is more complicated. The tasks involved in the development and deployment of the sample application include, in sequence:

1.   Implement the CMP 2.0 address entity bean (AddressEJB).
2.   Implement the CMP 2.0 roster entity bean (RosterEJB).
3.   Implement the CMP 2.0 student entity bean (StudentEJB).
4.   Implement several JSP clients to test the CMP 2.0 entity beans.
5.   Package the CMP 2.0 entity beans as EJB components.
6.   Package the JSP as a Web component.
7.   Deploy the CMP 2.0 entity bean sample application.
8.   Test the sample application.

We'll conclude with a discussion of the deployment descriptor, which results from steps followed during the packaging of an application.

Step 1: Implementing the CMP 2.0 Address Entity Bean

First, implement the local interfaces—LocalAddress, LocalAddressHome, and the AddressEJB entity bean classes. The AddressEJB bean is used to create and manage address-related information.

Implementing the Local Home Interface: `LocalAddressHome.java`

The `LocalAddressHome` interface declares two methods: `create()` and the mandatory `findByPrimaryKey()`. Notice that both methods return the LocalAddress interface and must not throw RemoteExceptions, as shown in the following example:

```
public interface LocalAddressHome extends EJBLocalHome
    {
    public LocalAddress create (String customerID, String
addressID, String street, String city, String zip, String state)
    throws CreateException;
public LocalAddress findByPrimaryKey(String addressID)
    throws FinderException;
    }
```

Implementing the Local Component Interface: `LocalAddress.java`

The LocalAddress interface declares basic getter methods to retrieve the CMP address fields from the bean class:

```
public interface LocalAddress extends EJBLocalObject
{
    public String getAddressID();
    public String getStreet();
    public String getCity();
    public String getZip();
    public String getState();
}
```

Implementing the CMP 2.0 Entity Bean Class: `AddressEJB.com`

The CMP 2.0 entity bean class must be declared `abstract`; it extends the `EntityBean` interface. Notice that the abstract methods access the container-managed persistent fields such as `addressID`, `street`, `city`, `zip code`, and `state`:

```
public abstract class AddressEJB implements EntityBean
    {
    private EntityContext context;
    //access methods for cmp fields

    public abstract String getAddressID();      //primary key
    public abstract void setAddressID(String id);

    public abstract String getStreet();
    public abstract void setStreet(String street);
```

```
public abstract String getCity();
public abstract void setCity(String city);

public abstract String getZip();
public abstract void setZip(String zip);

public abstract String getState();
public abstract void setState(String state);
```

The `ejbCreate()` method uses the abstract setter methods to set the persistent fields. Please refer to Chapter 9 for a detailed discussion and rules on writing `ejbCreate()` and `ejbPostCreate()` methods. The container automatically saves the fields in the database table. The `ejbCreate()` method returns a `String` primary key, as shown here:

```
public String ejbCreate (String sid,String id,String street,String
city,String zip,String state)
    throws CreateException {

    setAddressID(id);
    setStreet(street);
    setCity(city);
    setZip(zip);
    setState(state);

    return null;//explanation at the end of the chapter
}
```

Look at the `ejbPostCreate()` method; it looks up the student object and adds the roster object to the student list. This allows the `StudentEJB` instance to access `AddressEJB`.

```
public void ejbPostCreate (String sid,String id,String
street,String city,String zip,String state)
    throws CreateException {
    try {
        Context ic = new InitialContext();
        LocalStudentHome home = (LocalStudentHome)
            ic.lookup("java:comp/env/ejb/StudentRef");
        LocalStudent student = home.findByPrimaryKey(sid);
        student.addAddress((LocalAddress)context.getEJBLocalOb-
ject());
    } catch (Exception ex) {
        context.setRollbackOnly();
        ex.printStackTrace();
    }
}
```

Compiling `LocalAddressHome.java`, `LocalAddress.java`, and `AddressEJB.java`

In you windows terminal, change directory to APPHOME\chapter11\cmp and run `compileAddress.bat` to generate the `LocalAddressHome.class`, `LocalAddress.class`, and `AddressEJB.class` in your directory.

Step 2: Implementing the CMP 2.0 Roster Entity Bean

The Roster entity bean, `RosterEJB`, creates a roster of students. It has a local home interface (`LocalRosterHome`) and a local component interface (`LocalRoster`).

Implementing the Local Home Interface: `LocalRosterHome.com`

`LocalRosterHome` declares the `create()`, `findByPrimaryKey()`, and additional finder methods. The `findByScheduleID()` method returns a collection based on the schedule ID; the `findByStudentID()` method returns a collection based on the student ID argument.

```
public interface LocalRosterHome extends EJBLocalHome
{
    public LocalRoster create(String rosterID, String scheduleID,
String studentID) throws CreateException;
    public LocalRoster findByPrimaryKey(String rosterID) throws
FinderException;

      public Collection findByScheduleID(String scheduleID) throws
FinderException;
    public Collection findByStudentID(String studentID) throws Fin-
derException;
}
```

Implementing the Local Component Interface: `LocalRoster.java`

The `LocalRoster` component declares three plain getter business methods that return persistent fields as shown next.

```
public interface LocalRoster extends EJBLocalObject
{
    public String fetchRosterID();
    public String fetchStudentID();
    public String fetchScheduleID();
}
```

Implementing the CMP 2.0 Entity Bean Class: `RosterEJB.com`

The code snippet that follows illustrates an abstract `Roster` entity bean class with several abstract `accessor` methods for CMP fields. Note that the business method, `fetchRosterID()`, depends on the abstract method `getRosterID()` to retrieve the CMP fields from the underlying database.

```
public abstract class RosterEJB implements EntityBean
{

    //accessor methods for cmp fields
    public abstract String getRosterID();
    public abstract void setRosterID(String rosterID);

    public abstract String getScheduleID();
    public abstract void setScheduleID(String scheduleID);

    public abstract String getStudentID();
    public abstract void setStudentID(String studentID);

    //business methods
    public String fetchRosterID ()
    {
        return getRosterID();
    }

    public String fetchStudentID()
    {
        return getStudentID();
    }

    public String fetchScheduleID()
    {
        return getScheduleID();
    }
```

The `ejbCreate()` method is shown next. It calls no data access calls but rather uses the setter methods to set the persistent fields.

```
public String ejbCreate (String rosterID, String scheduleID, String
studentID)
    throws CreateException {
    System.out.println("RsoterEJB.ejbCreate...");
    setRosterID(rosterID);
    setScheduleID(scheduleID);
    setStudentID(studentID);

    return null;
}
```

The `ejbPostCreate()` method performs the JNDI lookup for the `Student` bean reference. It then uses the component interface to add the instance to the student instance object so it can be accessed by the student bean instance.

```
public void ejbPostCreate (String rosterID, String scheduleID,
String studentID) throws CreateException {
    System.out.println("RosterEJB ejbPostCreate...rosterID = "+ros-
terID);
    try {
        Context ic = new InitialContext();
        LocalStudentHome home = (LocalStudentHome)
            ic.lookup("java:comp/env/ejb/StudentRef");
        LocalStudent student = home.findByPrimaryKey(sid);
        student.addRoster((LocalRoster)context.getEJBLocalObject());
    } catch (Exception ex) {
        context.setRollbackOnly();
        ex.printStackTrace();
    }
}
```

Compiling `LocalRosterHome.java`, `LocalRoster.java`, and `RosterEJB.java`

If you are not already in the APPHOME\chapter11\cmp directory, change to this directory and run the `compileRoster.bat` batch file to compile the Roster bean class. The batch file generates `LocalRosterHome.class`, `LocalRoster.class`, and `RosterEJB.class`.

Step 3: Implementing the CMP 2.0 Student Entity Bean

The student entity bean provides the logic to create a student entity. It accesses the address bean and roster bean instance to look up the address entity assigned to the student and the classes for which the student is registered.

Implementing the Local Home Interface: `LocalStudentHome.com`

The local home interface declares the `create()` method and several finder methods. The `create()` method creates the student entity; the finder methods allow clients to query by primary key, student's first name, and last name.

```
public interface LocalStudentHome extends EJBLocalHome
{
    public LocalStudent create (String StudentID, String firstName,
String lastName) throws CreateException;
    public Collection findByLastName (String lastName)
```

```
        throws FinderException;
    public Collection findByFirstName (String firstName)
        throws FinderException;
    public LocalStudent findByPrimaryKey (String StudentID)
        throws FinderException;
}
```

Implementing the Local Component Interface: `LocalStudent.java`

The local component interface declares the getter methods. In addition, several business methods [including `getAddressList()` and `getRosterList()`] return a collection of `LocalAddress` and `LocalRoster` objects to the client. The client uses `getAddressList()` and `getRosterList()` to retrieve multiple addresses and the classes for which the student is registered. The `addAddress()` and `addRoster()` methods add local components to an existing collection.

```
public interface LocalStudent extends EJBLocalObject
{
    public String getStudentID();
    public String getFirstName();
    public String getLastName();
    public ArrayList getAddressList();
    public ArrayList getRosterList();
    public void addAddress(LocalAddress address);
    public void addRoster(LocalRoster roster);
}
```

Implementing the CMP 2.0 Entity Bean Class: `StudentEJB.com`

The student entity bean class uses abstract methods to declare several CMP fields, including `studentID`, `firstName`, and `lastName`. The unidirectional, one-to-many relationship between the student bean and address bean is represented by the CMR field addresses defined by the `getAddresses()` and `setAddresses()` abstract methods. Similarly, the rosters represent the unidirectional one-to-many relationships between student and roster beans.

```
public abstract class StudentEJB implements EntityBean {

    //access methods for cmp fields
    public abstract String getStudentID();        //primary key
    public abstract void setStudentID(String id);

    public abstract String getFirstName();
    public abstract void setFirstName(String firstName);

    public abstract String getLastName();
```

```
public abstract void setLastName(String lastName);
```

The StudentEJB class declares two CMR fields to define its one-to-many relationships with the AddressEJB and RosterEJB bean classes. The getAddresses() and getRosters() abstract methods return collections of local component objects of the respective bean type. The setAddresses() and setRosters() abstract methods take collection arguments of the local components of the respective bean type, as shown in the code fragment that follows.

```
//abstract cmr field methods for address entity bean
public abstract Collection getAddresses();
public abstract void setAddresses (Collection addresses);

//abstract cmr field methods for roster entity bean
public abstract Collection getRosters();
public abstract void setRosters(Collection rosters);
```

The business method getAddressList() calls the CMR abstract method getAddresses(), which returns a collection. The getAddressList() method then extracts the local component interface LocalAdress, creates an array list using the Iterator, and returns it to the client. The client can then invoke business methods on individual local components. The addAddress() method is used by the client to add a local component interface, LocalAddress, to the collection of LocalAddress objects. The getRosterList() and addRoster() methods (not shown here) mirror the same functionality for the roster bean. When a client invokes getAddressList(), it receives a list of LocalAddress interfaces and uses it to invoke business methods.

```
//business methods
public ArrayList getAddressList() {
    ArrayList list = new ArrayList();
    Iterator c = getAddresses().iterator();
    while (c.hasNext()) {
        list.add((LocalAddress)c.next());
    }
    return list;
}
public void addAddress (LocalAddress address) {
    getAddresses().add(address);
}
```

The ejbCreate() and ejbPostCreate() methods in the StudentEJB class are fairly simple. The ejbCreate() method invokes the abstract methods to set the id, firstName, and lastName abstract persistent fields. The ejbPostCreate() method is left empty.

```
public String ejbCreate (String id, String firstName, String lastName)
    throws CreateException {
    System.out.println(" -- StudentEJB - ejbCreate...");
    setStudentID(id);
    setFirstName(firstName);
    setLastName(lastName);

    return id;
}

public void ejbPostCreate (String id, String firstName, String lastName)
    throws CreateException {
    System.out.println("StudentEJB -ejbPostCreate(" +
            id + ", " + firstName + ", " + lastName + ")...");
}
```

Compiling `LocalStudentHome.java`, `LocalStudent.java`, and `StudentEJB.java`

If you are not already in the APPHOME\chapter11\cmp directory, change to this directory and run the `compileStudent.bat` file to compile the Student bean class. The batch file creates `LocalStudentHome.class`, `LocalStudent.class`, and `StudentEJB.class`.

Step 4: Implementing JSP Clients to Test CMP 2.0 Entity Beans

To test the entity bean application, use JSP clients. For each entity bean, there are two JSPs—one to create the data and the other to search for it. We've written six JSP files: `createAddress.jsp` and `searchAddress.jsp` for `AddressEJB`, `createRoster.jsp` and `searchRoster.jsp` for `RosterEJB`, and `createStudent.jsp` and `searchStudent.jsp` for `StudentEJB`. Because JSP and clients' implementation aren't the focus of this book, we'll look at just one JSP client, `SearchStudent.jsp`, and briefly explain its logic.

The input form is embedded in the JSP file, as shown next. Embedding the form allows three search options—student ID, last name, or first name.

```
Search for a Student:
<p>
    <form method="get" action="/cmp3/searchStudent.jsp">
    Search by
    <select name="searchCriteria">
      <option value="studentID" selected>Student ID
      <option value="lastName">Last Name
      <option value="firstName">First Name
```

```
    </select>
    <input type="text" name="searchText" size="25">
    <p>
    <input type="submit" value="Search">
    </form>
```

Depending on the search criteria, `SearchStudent.jsp` performs a JNDI lookup for a student home object and then calls finder methods, two of which return a collection. It next goes through the array list; then, using the student and roster component interface, it extracts the classes in which the students are enrolled and the students' addresses.

```
InitialContext ic = new InitialContext();
Object obj = ic.lookup("java:comp/env/ejb/StudentRef");
LocalStudentHome home = (LocalStudentHome) obj;

Collection Students = new ArrayList();
if ("studentID".equals(criteria)) {
    try {
    LocalStudent student = home.findByPrimaryKey(text);
    Students.add(student);
  } catch (ObjectNotFoundException ex) {}
}
else if ("lastName".equals(criteria)) {
    Students = home.findByLastName(text);
}
else if ("firstName".equals(criteria)) {
    Students = home.findByFirstName(text);
}
```

The following code fragment extracts the `LocalStudent` interface, invokes business methods, and displays the addresses and classes in an html table as follows:

```
<% for (int i = 0; i < Students.size(); i++) {
    LocalStudent stud = (LocalStudent)((ArrayList)Students).get(i);
    String sid = (String) stud.getPrimaryKey();
    ArrayList rosterList = stud.getRosterList();
%>
<b> <%=stud.getFirstName()%>  <%=stud.getLastName()%> </b> is reg-
istered in
<%=stud.getRosterList().size()%> classes listed below: <p>

<table border=2>
<tr><th>Roster ID</th> <th>Schedule ID</th></tr>
<%
    for (int j=0; j < rosterList.size(); j++)
    {
```

```
                    LocalRoster rost = (LocalRoster) rosterList.get(j);
%>
<tr>
<td> <%=rost.fetchRosterID()%> </td>
<td> <%=rost.fetchScheduleID()%> </td>
</tr>
<%
        }
%>
</table>
<p>
 and has
<%=stud.getAddressList().size()%> addresses<p>
<table border=3>
<tr><th>Street</th><th>city</th><th>State</th></tr>
<%   ArrayList list = stud.getAddressList();
     for (int k=0; k< list.size(); k++)
     {
         LocalAddress addr = (LocalAddress)list.get(k);
%>
<tr>
<td><%=addr.getStreet()%></td>
<td><%=addr.getCity()%></td>
<td><%=addr.getState()%></td>
</tr>
<%
      }
%>
</table>
<%
```

Step 5: Packaging the CMP 2.0 Entity Beans as an ejb-jar File

To package the sample application, we first need to create the application archive file that will hold the ejb-jar and Web war files. Let's first create the application archive file CMP20App.ear.

1.   Create an ear file that will include the EJB jar and Web war files. Start the Sun J2SDKEE1.3 RI and the deployment tool. Using the deployment tool, select File | New | Application. When a new application window pops up, click the Browse button to go to the APPHOME\chapter11 subdirectory. Enter the name of the ear file (**CMP20App.ear**) as shown in Figure 11-1. Click New Application and then OK to create this file.

2.   Package the EJB component by creating one ejb-jar file, then package all three EJBs into one jar file.

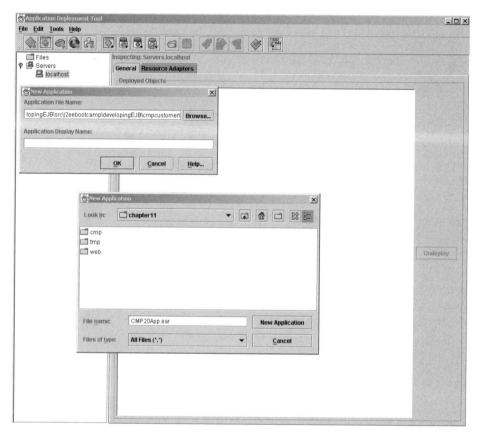

Figure 11-1 Creating an enterprise application archive file

3.   Select File | New | Enterprise Bean. When the Enterprise Bean Wizard pops
      up, click Next. In the Wizard window, ensure that the Create New Jar radio
      button is selected and displays CMP20App. If not, use the pull-down menu
      to select it.

4.   In the JAR Display Name area, enter **CMP20JAR** and click Edit to bring up
      the Edit Contents window. Using the pull-down menu, select the
      APPHOME\chapter11 directory and note the subdirectories (including cmp
      and Web). Select the cmp directory icon; it will expand and display the con-
      tents of the directory. To add classes to the jar file, select
      `AddressEJB.class`, `LocalAddressHome.class`, and `LocalAd-`
      `dress.class`. Click the Add button, as shown in Figure 11-2, and then
      click OK. The Edit Content window will close. Click Next.

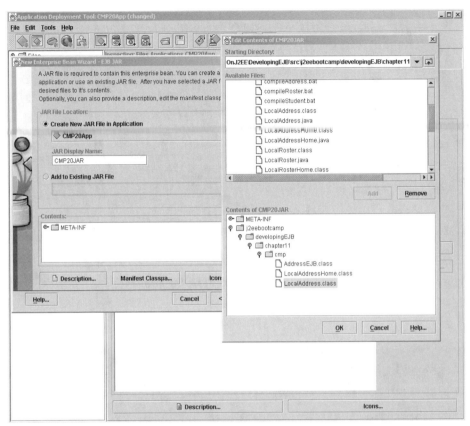

Figure 11-2 Creating an Enterprise JavaBean archive file—CMP20JAR

5. In the Wizard window, enter the general information regarding the
    `AddressEJB`. First click the radio button to specify that this is an entity
    bean; then, using the pull-down menu under Enterprise Bean Class, select
    `AddressEJB.class`. Use the default `AddressEJB` for the Enterprise Bean
    Class Name. Under the Local Interfaces, select `LocalAddressHome` and
    `LocalAddress` for the local home and local interface (see Figure 11-3).
    Click Next.

6. Now, specify the CMP fields, abstract persistence schema, and the primary key.
    In the Wizard, select the Container Managed Persistence (2.0) radio button. In
    the Fields To Be Persisted box, select all the fields. In the Abstract Schema Name
    area, enter **Address**; specify that primary key as a Java String type under the
    Primary Key Class text box by entering **java.lang.String**. Under Primary Key
    Field Name, use the pull-down menu to select `addressID` as the primary key
    field name (see Figure 11-4). Click the Next button twice.

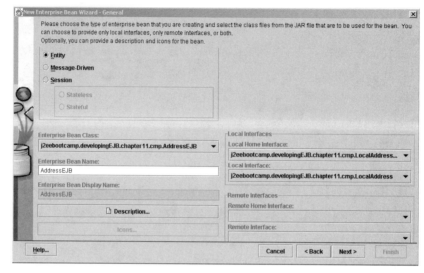

Figure 11-3 Adding the AddressEJB bean to the CMP20JAR

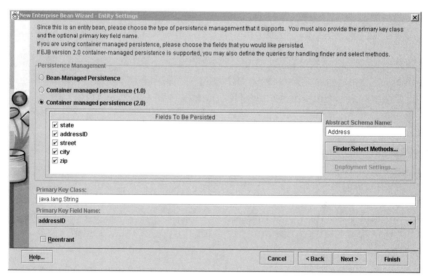

Figure 11-4 Specifying CMP fields in the abstract persistence schema

7. The `AddressEJB` bean references `StudentEJB` in the code—at runtime, `AddressEJB` needs to locate the `StudentEJB` instance. Under the Coded Name column, enter **ejb/StudentRef**; under Type and Interfaces, select Entity and Local, respectively. Under the Home Interface and Local/Remote Interface column, enter the full path of the **LocalStudentHome** and **Local-Student** interfaces. Under Enterprise Bean Name, enter **StudentEJB**. In this case, don't specify the full path name (see Figure 11-5). Click Finish.

8. The parameters for `AddressEJB` are specified; now, we'll repeat the same process for `RosterEJB` and `StudentEJB`.

9. To add the `RosterEJB` bean to the existing CMP20JAR file, select it. Then, using the deployment tool, select File | New | Enterprise Bean. Click Next in the Wizard and verify that Add to the Existing Jar File is selected and that CMP20JAR is displayed. Click the Edit button. When the Edit Content window appears, go to the CMP subdirectory under chapter11. Add `Local-RosterHome.class`, `LocalRoster.class`, and `RosterEJB.class` to the jar file by clicking the Add button for each (see Figure 11-6). Click OK and then Next.

10. In the Wizard, select Entity as the Enterprise Bean Class, and select RosterEJB from the pull-down menu. Select `LocalRosterHome` and `Local-Roster` under the Local Interfaces section as home and local interfaces (see Figure 11-7). Click Next.

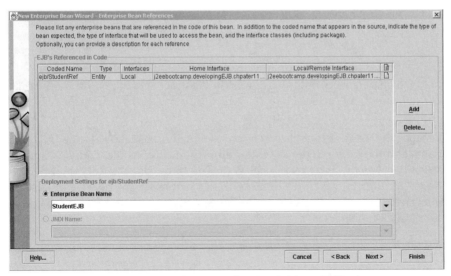

Figure 11-5 Specifying EJB references for the AddressEJB class

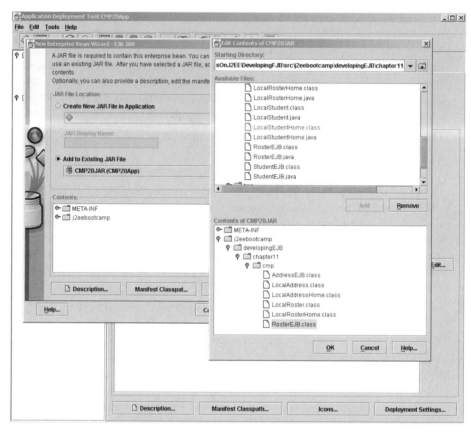

Figure 11-6 Adding the RosterEJB bean to the CMP20JAR file

11.   In the Wizard, select Container Managed Persistence (2.0). Select all the
      fields to be persisted, enter **Roster** as the Abstract Schema Name, and from
      the pull-down menu, select `java.lang.String` as the primary key class
      and `rosterID` as the primary key field (see Figure 11-8). Click Next twice.

12.   Because the `RosterEJB` class references `StudentEJB`, specify the JNDI
      name and the local references. Enter **ejb/StudentRef** as the Coded Name;
      select Local as the Type and Local as the Interface. Use the fully qualified
      `LocalStudentHome` and `LocalStudent` names for the home and local
      interfaces. Enter **StudentEJB** as the Enterprise Bean Class name (see Figure
      11-9). Click Finish.

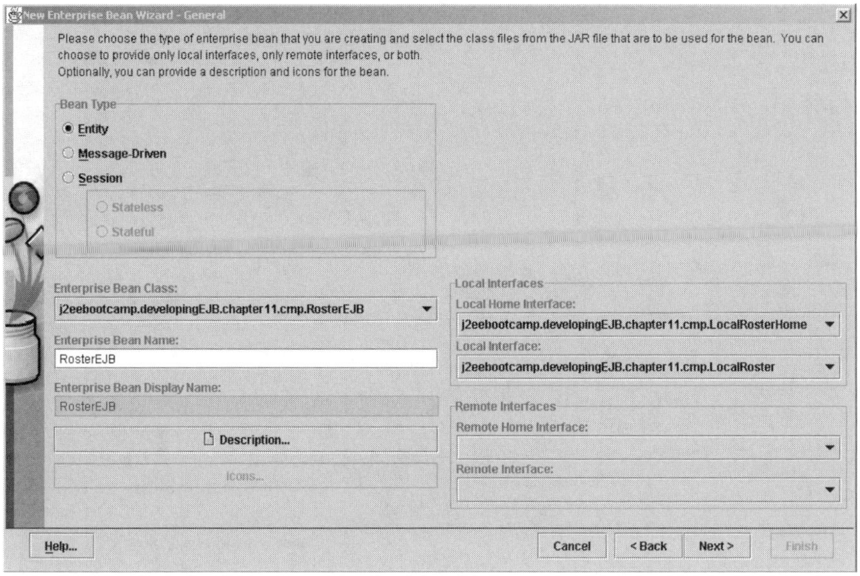

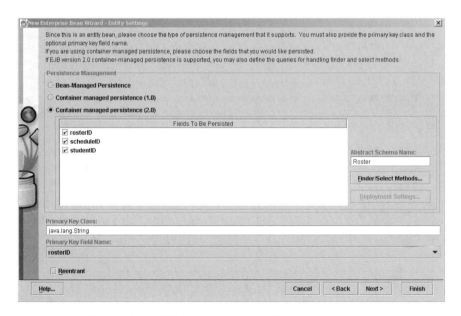

Figure 11-7 Specifying the RosterEJB bean class and local interfaces

Figure 11-8 Specifying CMP 2.0 type and CMP fields in the abstract
persistence schema

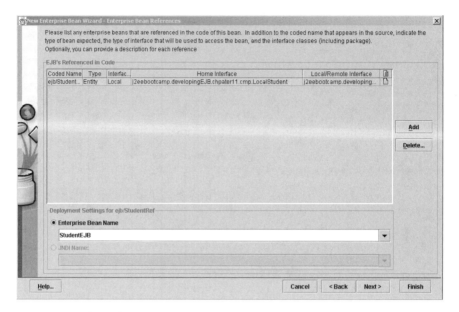

Figure 11-9 Specifying EJB references

13. Add the `StudentEJB` bean to the jar file. Using the deployment tool, select File | New | Enterprise Bean. When the Wizard pops up, click Next and then Edit. When the Edit Content window pops up, go to the APPHOME\chapter11 \cmp directory and add `LocalStudentHome.class`, `Local-Student.class`, and `StudentEJB.class` to the CMP20JAR file by clicking the Add button. Click OK and then Next (see Figure 11-10).

14. Select Entity. Using the pull-down menu, select `StudentEJB`, `LocalStudentHome`, and `LocalStudent` as the Bean Class types and Local Home and Local Interface respectively (see Figure 11-11). Click Next.

15. In the Wizard, select the Container Managed Persistence (2.0) radio button; select `studentID`, `firstName`, and `lastName` as the fields to be persisted. Enter **Student** as the abstract schema name; enter **java.lang.String** as the primary key class; and enter **studentID** as the primary field (see Figure 11-12).

16. Because the `LocalStudentHome` interface declares two finder methods, specify the EJB QL query. Select Finder/Select Methods and enter the **SELECT DISTINCT OBJECT(s) FROM Student AS s WHERE s.firstName = ?1** statement for the `findByFirstName` finder method.

17. Repeat the same for the EJB QL statement. Change the **s.firstName** to **s.last-Name** (see Figure 11-13). Click OK in the Finder/Select Method window.

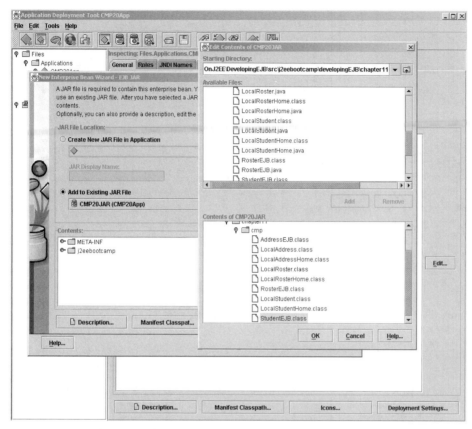

Figure 11-10 Adding the StudentEJB bean to the CMP20JAR file

18. Because the `StudentEJB` code doesn't reference any objects, there's no need to specify a JNDI lookup. Click Finish to package all three EJBs into one jar file.

19. Now, specify the relationships between the EJBs and generate the SQL statements. Select the CMP20JAR icon and select the Relationships tab. Click Add to display the Add Relationship window, in which you use the pull-down menu to specify the relationship between the `StudentEJB` and the `AddressEJB` (a one-to-many relationship). Under Multiplicity, select One to Many. Click the Description button. In the window that pops up, enter **Student-has-many-Address**. Click Apply, and then click OK.

20. Specify the relationship between these two beans. Under Enterprise Bean A, use the pull-down menu to select `StudentEJB` as the Enterprise Bean Name, addresses for Field Referencing Bean B, and the java.uti.Collection as

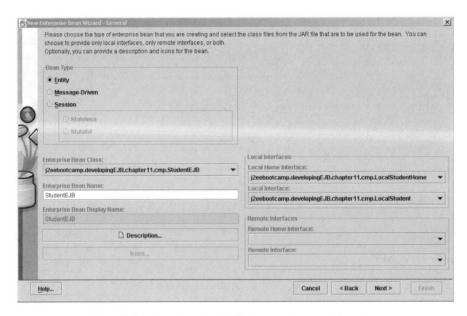

Figure 11-11 Specifying the StudentEJB bean class and local interfaces

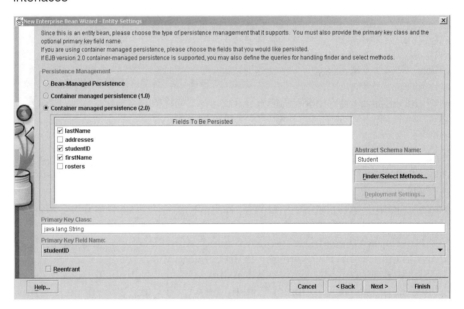

Figure 11-12 Specifying CMP fields in the abstract persistence schema

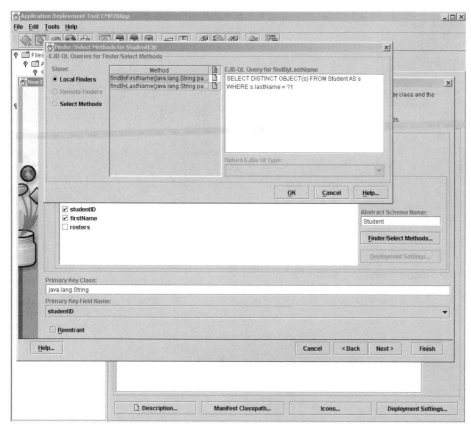

Figure 11-13 Specifying the EJB QL query statement

the Field Type (see Figure 11-14). Remember, there are two CMR abstract methods declared in the `StudentEJB` class that returned a collection. The address field corresponds to that CMR abstract method. Under Enterprise Bean Name B, use the pull-down menu and select `AddressEJB` as the Enterprise Bean Name. Because this relationship is unidirectional, use the "Field Referencing Bean B" pull-down menu to select CMR field "addresses" and leave its corresponding field to none for Enterprise Bean B. The `AddressEJB` entity is dependent on `StudentEJB` entity, and it must be deleted if the `StudentEJB` entity is deleted. To enable cascade delete, check the "Delete When Bean A is Deleted" option."

21. Next, specify the relationship between the `StudentEJB` and the `Ros-terEJB`. `StudentEJB` has a one-to-many relationship with `RosterEJB`; `StudentEJB` references `RosterEJB` with the CMR field rosters specified by the CMR abstract method, which returns a collection. This is specified in the relationship window (see Figure 11-15).

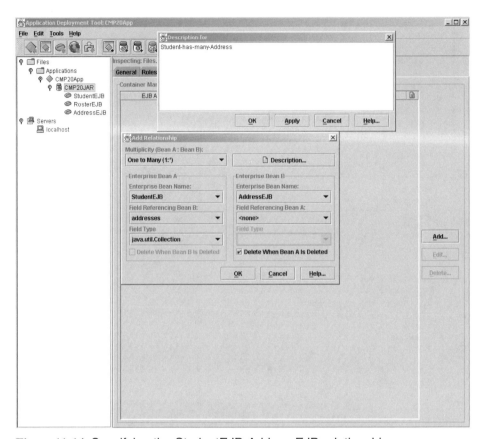

Figure 11-14 Specifying the StudentEJB-AddressEJB relationship

22. Now, generate the SQL statement. Select the StudentEJB icon, select the Entity tab, and then select Deployment Settings to display the Deployment Settings window. Provide the database setting information and then click the Database Setting button to display another Database Setting window. Enter **jdbc/Cloudscape** under Database JNDI Name; enter **j2ee** as the user name and password; and then click OK (see Figure 11-16).

23. Next, click the Create Table on Deploy and Delete Table on Undeploy buttons; then, select Generate Default SQL. If the EJB QL query was correct, the SQL Generation Complete window pops up. On the deploytool window terminal, the generated SQL statement for both finder methods should appear. Click OK, then click the OK button in the deploytool window.

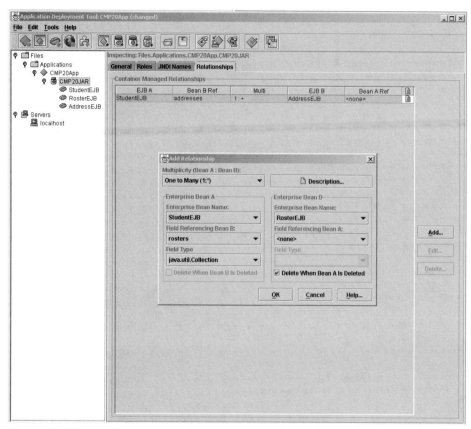

Figure 11-15 Specifying the student-to-roster relationship

24. The `LocalRosterHome` interface also declared two finder methods—
`findByScheduleID` and `findByStudentID`. Specify the EJB QL for these
finder methods. (This could have been done when packaging RosterEJB, but
we deferred this step to show how it can also be done later.) Select
Finder/Select Methods to display the EJB QL window. Select the `findBy-`
`ScheduleID(..)` method; then, in the EJB-QL Query for `FindBySched-`
`uleID` window, enter **SELECT DISTINCT OBJECTR FROM Roster AS r**
WHERE r.scheduleID = ?1.

25. Select the `findByStudentID(...)` method under Method. Enter the query
statement from the previous step, but change **r.studentID** to **r.scheduleID**
(see Figure 11-17). Click OK; then select Deployment Setting. When the
Deployment Setting window appears, check Create Table on Deploy and
Delete on Undeploy. Then select Generate Default SQL to generate the SQL

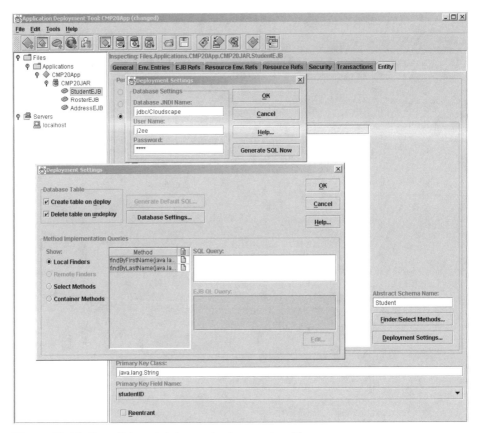

Figure 11-16 Specifying database deployment settings

statement for the finder methods. If the EJB QL was entered correctly, the SQL Generation Complete window should pop up. Click OK, and the window will disappear. Then click OK in the Deployment Setting window.

26. Select the AddressEJB icon and then the Entity tab. Select Deployment Setting to display the Deployment Setting window. Because the LocalAddressHome interface didn't declare any finder methods, don't specify any EJB QL query. Check both Create Table on Deploy and Delete Table on Undeploy; then, select Generate Default SQL. The SQL Generation Complete confirmation window should pop up. Click OK and then OK again in the Deployment Setting window.

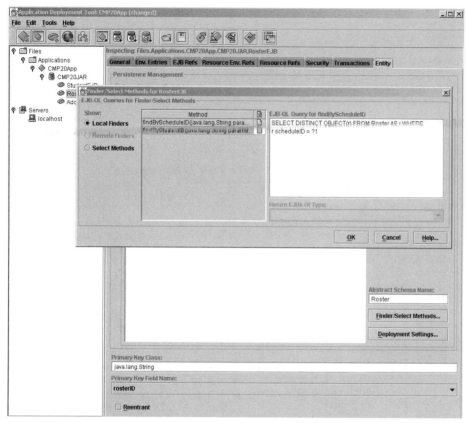

Figure 11-17 Specifying EJB QL and generating an SQL statement

Step 6: Packaging the JSP As a Web Component

We've just completed the packaging of the EJB component. Now, let's package the Web components, consisting of JSP pages, into the CMP20WAR file.

1. First, package the JSP clients for AddressEJB. In the deployment tool, select the File | New | Web component, which brings up a Web Component Wizard. Click Next. In the Wizard, select the Create New WAR File in Application button to display CMP20App. In the WAR Display Name area, enter **CMP20WAR** and then click Edit. The Edit Content window will pop up. Go to the APPHOME\chapter11\web directory, and add `index.html` and `createStudent.jsp` to the WAR file (see Figure 11-18). Click OK, and then click Next.

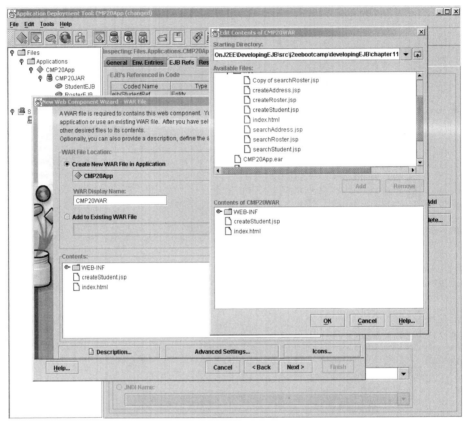

Figure 11-18 Creating a `createStudent.jsp` for CMP20WAR

2.   Next, select the JSP radio button to indicate the type of Web component, and select Next from the pull-down menu. Select `createStudent.jsp` as the JSP Filename; take all the default values (see Figure 11-19). Click Next twice.

3.   Now, specify the component alias name. Click Add and enter **createStudent.jsp** as shown in Figure 11-20. Click Next four times.

4.   Because the `createStudent.jsp` client references `StudentEJB`, specify EJB references. Click Add and then enter **ejb/StudentRef** as the Coded Name. Use the pull-down menu to select Entity as the Type and local as the Interface. Enter **LocalStudentHome** and **LocalStudent** as the Home and Local/Remote Interfaces using the full path name (for example, **j2eebootcamp.developingEJB.chapter11.cmp**). Then, as the Enterprise Bean Name, enter **StudentEJB** (see Figure 11-21). Click Finish.

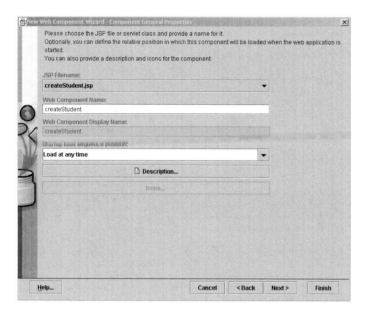

Figure 11-19 Specifying the `createStudent.jsp` type for the Web component

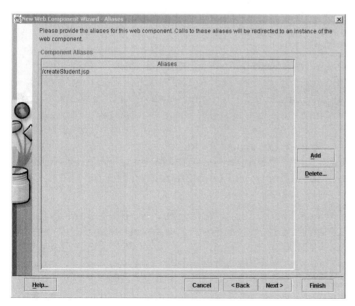

Figure 11-20 Specifying the JSP alias name

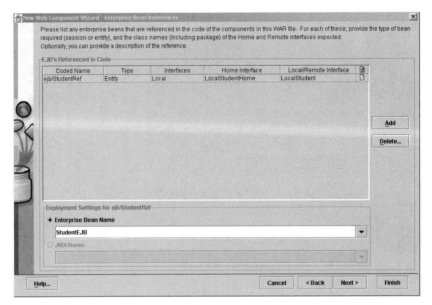

Figure 11-21 Specifying EJB references to StudentEJB

5. Now, create the `searchStudent` component. Select the File | New | Web component, and click Next. To package all the JSP files into one war file, select Add to Existing WAR File and use the pull-down menu to select CMP20WAR. Click Edit.

6. In the Edit Content window, go to the APPHOME\chapter11\cmp directory and add `searchStudent.jsp` (see Figure 11-22). Click OK; then Next, then JSP and Next again. Under JSP Filename, select `searchStudent.jsp`. Accept the default values (see Figure 11-19—note that the name should say `searchStudent`). Click Next twice; click Add and enter **searchStudent.jsp** (see Figure 11-20—note that the name should say `searchStudent.jsp`). Click Next four times. In the EJB reference window, enter **ejb/StudentRef**, **Entity**, **Local**, **LocalStudentHome**, and **LocalStudent** (see Figure 11-21). Click Finish.

7. The steps necessary to package `createAddress.jsp` is the same as the steps we used to package `searchStudent.jsp`. To package the `createAdddress.jsp` file, follow the sequence of steps we outlined for packaging the `searchStudent.jsp` file. Now add `createAddress.jsp` (see Figure 11-18) to the CMP20WAR file; specify it as a JSP component, and specify the JSP filename (see Figure 11-19). Use `createAddress.jsp` as the alias (see Figure 11-20). Then, use `ejb/AddressRef`, `entity`, `local`, `LocalAddressHome`, `LocalAddress`, and `AddressHome` in the EJB reference (see Figure 11-21) and click Finish.

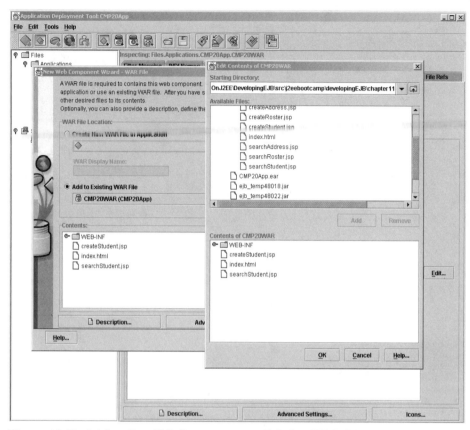

Figure 11-22 Adding the JSP Component to Existing WAR File –
CMP20WAR

8. Repeat the same sequence of steps to package `searchAddress.jsp`,
    except in this case, replace `createAddress.jsp` with `searchAd-`
    `dress.jsp` and use the EJB references (`ejb/AddressRef`, entity,
    `local`, `LocalAddressHome`, `LocalAddress`, and `AdddressEJB`) as in
    the previous steps. Click Finish.

9. Repeat the same series of steps to package `createRoster` and
    `searchRoster`. Replace the `searchAddress.jsp` with
    `searchRoster.jsp` and specify `ejb/RosterRef`, entity, `local`,
    `LocalRosterHome`, `LocalRoster`, and `RosterEJB` in the EJB reference
    window. Repeat the steps for `searchRoster.jsp`.

10. After you package both the EJB and JSP components, all six JSP components
    should be included under the CMP20WAR icon, and three entity beans
    should be included under the CMP20JAR icon. Select the CMP20App icon

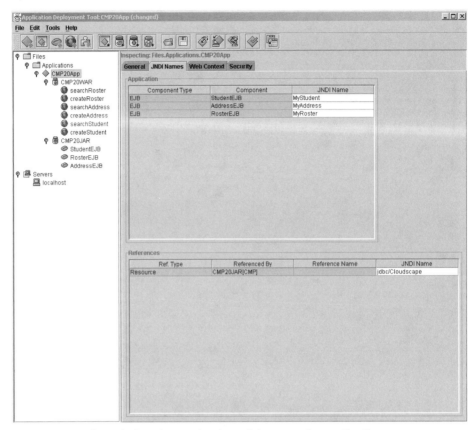

Figure 11-23 Completing the packaging of the sample application

and then select the JNDI Name tab. Enter **MyStudent**, **MyAddress**, and **MyRoster** under the JNDI Name column (see Figure 11-23).

Step 7: Deploying the CMP 2.0 Entity Bean Sample Application

We're ready to deploy the sample application, now that we've packaged the EJB and Web components into a deployable CMP20App.ear file.

1.   Select the CMP20App icon and select Tools | Deploy to bring up the Deploy window. Select CMP20App under Object to Deploy; enter **localhost** under Target Server; and check Save Object Before Deploying (see Figure 11-24). Click Next.

2.   Verify that the JNDI names are correctly set, as shown in Figure 11-25. Click Next.

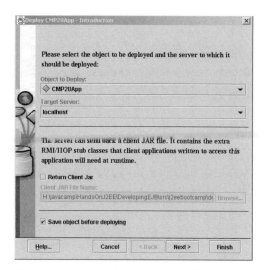

Figure 11-24 Deploying the application

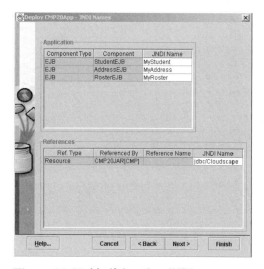

Figure 11-25 Verifying the JNDI names

3.   Under the ContextRoot column in the pop-up window, enter **/cmp3** and then click Finish. The Deployment Progress window message appears. If deployment is successful, the message changes to Deployment of CMP20App is Complete. Click OK. (See the Appendix to this book for a description of possible common errors and how to fix them.)

Step 8: Testing the Sample Application

Now you're ready to test the CMP 20 sample application by creating a student account and several addresses, enrolling the student in some courses, then searching for the student and listing the addresses and courses for which that student is registered.

1.   Open a browser and enter **http://localhost:8000/cmp3**, as shown in Figure 11-26.

2.   Create a student account. Select the Create New Student link, and the form in Figure 11-27 will appear. Click Submit to create the student account.

Figure 11-26 Sample application start page

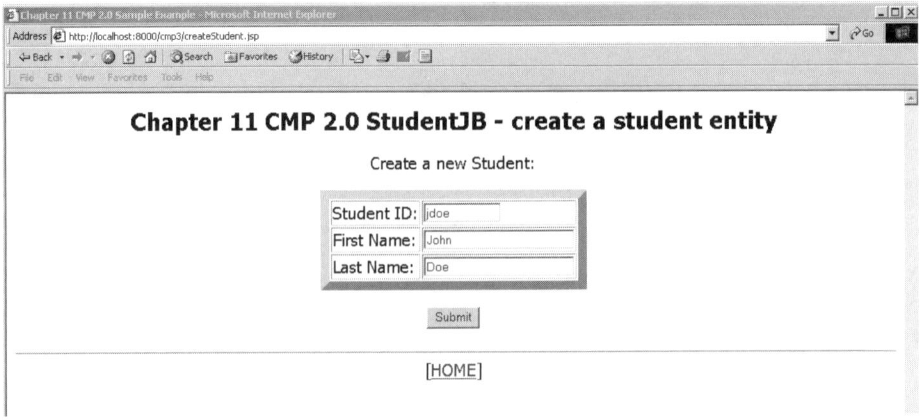

Figure 11-27 Creating a student entity

3. Create two addresses for the student, John Doe. Select the Create New Address link, and in the address create form, fill out the fields with **jdoe** as the customer ID, **100** as the address ID, **1 Market Street** as the street address, **San Francisco** for the city name, **CA** for state, and **93456** as the zip code (see Figure 11-28). Click Submit to create the address.

4. Add another address with the data **jdoe, 101, 99 Lake View Ave., Lake Tahoe, CA, 95324** for customer ID, address ID, address, city, state, and zip, respectively. Select the HOME link to return to the start page.

5. Register the student, John Doe, in couple of J2EE, EJB, and Java classes. Select Create New Roster, and then enter **1001** as the roster ID, **J2EE101** as the schedule ID, and **jdoe** as the student ID (see Figure 11-29). Register for the EJB and Java classes—enter **1002, EJB-101, jdoe** and **1003, Java-200, jdoe**.

6. Search for student jdoe, then list all his associated addresses and the classes for which he is currently registered. Select the Search For Student link and enter **jdoe**. The results are shown in Figure 11-30.

A Discussion of the Deployment Descriptor

Let's choose one EJB, `StudentEJB`, and look at the pertinent elements from the deployment descriptor file (ejb-jar.xml) that will help to elucidate the key aspects of the abstract persistent schema and the abstract persistent methods of CMP 2.0

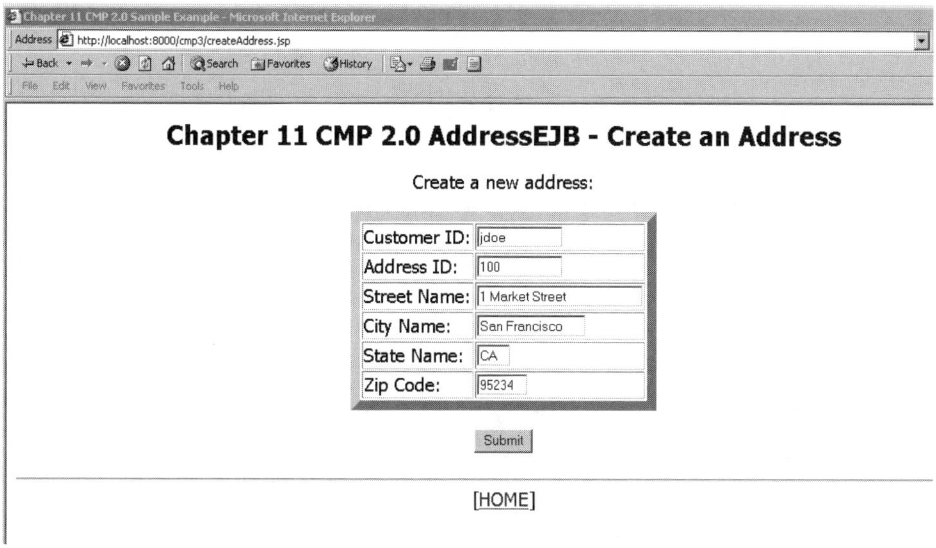

Chapter 11 CMP 2.0 AddressEJB - Create an Address

Create a new address:

Customer ID:	jdoe
Address ID:	100
Street Name:	1 Market Street
City Name:	San Francisco
State Name:	CA
Zip Code:	95234

Submit

[HOME]

Figure 11-28 Creating addresses

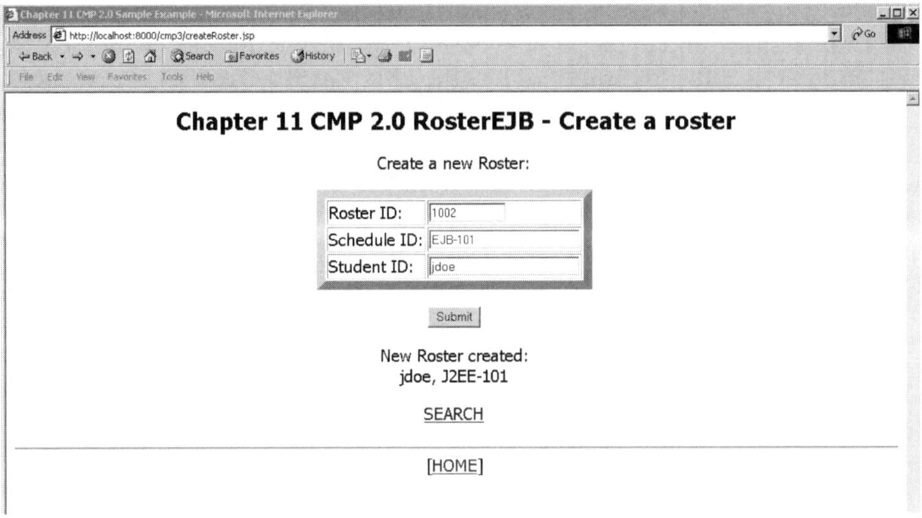

Figure 11-29 Registering a student in several classes

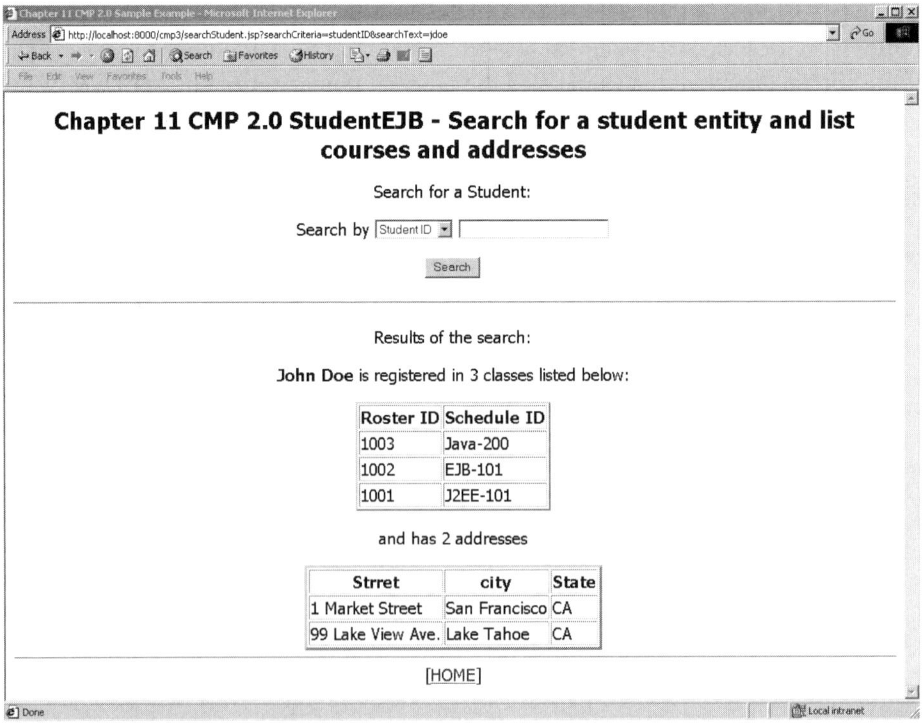

Figure 11-30 Result of search

entity beans. First, we'll review the structural information of `StudentEJB` that's familiar to us, namely, the `<local-home>`, `<local>`, and `<ejb-class>` elements specify the `LocalStudentHome` and `LocalStudent` interfaces and the `StudentEJB` bean class. The `<persistent-type>` element specifies that the persistence is managed by the container, and the `<cmp-version>` element specifies that `StudentEJB` implements EJB 2.0 persistence. The primary key class is of type `java.lang.String`, as indicated by the `<prim-key-class>` element, and `StudentEJB` does not support callbacks, as specified by the `<reentrant>` element.

```
.............. .
<enterprise-beans>
    <entity>
        <display-name>StudentEJB</display-name>
        <ejb-name>StudentEJB</ejb-name>
        <local-home>
j2eebootcamp.developingEJB.chapter11.cmp.LocalStudentHome
</local-home>
    <local>j2eebootcamp.developingEJB.chapter11.cmp.LocalStudent</local>
        <ejb-class>
        j2eebootcamp.developingEJB.chapter11.cmp.StudentEJB</ejb-
class>
        <persistence-type>Container</persistence-type>
        <prim-key-class>java.lang.String</prim-key-class>
        <reentrant>False</reentrant>
        <cmp-version>2.x</cmp-version>
```

Now, let's look at the abstract persistent schema. In the `StudentEJB` class, we declared several CMP abstract methods, such as `set/getStudentID()`, `set/getFirstName()`, and `set/getLastName()`. During the deployment of `StudentEJB`, we specified `Student` as the name of the abstract persistent schema and the EJB QL for finder methods. All of that information is saved in the deployment descriptor file, as shown in the code fragment that follows. Notice that the `<abstract-schema-name>` element specifies `Student` as the name of the schema, followed by the `<cmp-field>` element that encloses the optional `<description>` and mandatory `<field-name>` elements. The `StudentID` from the `getStudentID()` abstract method maps to the `<field-name>studentID</field-name>`, but notice that the first letter of `StudentID` must be lowercase. This rule applies to both the CMP and the CMR fields. The `<primaryKey-field>` element is used to specify the primary key for the entity bean.

```
<abstract-schema-name>Student</abstract-schema-name>
<cmp-field>
    <description>no description</description>
    <field-name>studentID</field-name>
```

```
</cmp-field>
<cmp-field>
    <description>no description</description>
    <field-name>lastName</field-name>
</cmp-field>
<cmp-field>
    <description>no description</description>
    <field-name>firstName</field-name>
</cmp-field>
<primkey-field>studentID</primkey-field>
<security-identity>
    <description></description>
    <use-caller-identity></use-caller-identity>
</security-identity>
```

Notice that we declared three finder methods in the `LocalStudentHome` interface but didn't have to implement them in the `StudentEJB` bean class. In CMP 2.0, the container is responsible for implementing the finder methods, so the finder method is mapped in the deployment descriptor with the `<query>` element. The `<query>` element encloses several elements—the `<query-method>` element that includes the method name as enclosed by `<method-name>`, and the argument-type, enclosed by the `<method-param>` element. If there were more than one argument, there would be a matching number of `<method-param>` elements. The finder method, `findByFirstName`, is mapped to the EJB QL query statement by the `<ejb-ql>` element that encloses the EJB QL statement specified during the deployment. With the exception of the `findByPrimaryKey()` method, for every other finder method declared in the home interface, the container will define `<query>` elements in the deployment descriptor.

```
<query>
    <description></description>
    <query-method>
    <method-name>findByFirstName</method-name>
        <method-params>
        <method-param>java.lang.String</method-param>
        </method-params>
    </query-method>
    <ejb-ql>SELECT DISTINCT OBJECT(s) FROM Student  AS s WHERE
s.firstName = ?1</ejb-ql>
</query>
<query>
    <description></description>
    <query-method>
        <method-name>findByLastName</method-name>
        <method-params>
```

```
        <method-param>java.lang.String</method-param>
        </method-params>
    </query-method>
    <ejb-ql>SELECT DISTINCT OBJECT(s) FROM Student  AS s WHERE
s.lastName = ?1</ejb-ql>
</query>
</entity>
```

The relationship information is enclosed within the `<relationship>` element. During the deployment phase, we specified that the `StudentEJB` and `AddressEJB` bean instances had a one-to-many relationship; this is specified in the deployment descriptor by the `<multiplicity>` element of `One` for `StudentEJB` and of `Many` for `AddressEJB`. The `StudentEJB` bean class declared two `CMR abstract` methods, and the `getAddresses ()` abstract method returned `java.util.Collection`. During deployment, we specified that `StudentEJB` has a one-to-many relationship with `AddressEJB` and that `StudentEJB` references `AddressEJB` with `CMR fields` addresses, which is a type of collection as shown in Figure 11-14. The `<cmr-field>` element uses two subelements to specify the `CMR field`; the `<cmr-field-name>` element specifies the `CMR field` and `addresses`; and the `<cmr-field-type>` element specifies the `Collection` type, as shown in the following code fragment. The `<cascade-delete>` element reflects your selection of the Delete When Bean A is Deleted option during deployment. Also notice that because `AddressEJB` declares no CMR abstract methods, there are no `<cmr-field>` elements declared in the `AddressEJB` section of the deployment descriptor.

```
<relationships>
.............. . .
<ejb-relation>
    <ejb-relation-name>Student-has-many-Addresses</ejb-relation-name>
    <ejb-relationship-role>
        <ejb-relationship-role-name>StudentEJB</ejb-relationship-
role-name>
    <multiplicity>One</multiplicity>
    <relationship-role-source>
        <ejb-name>StudentEJB</ejb-name>
        </relationship-role-source>
        <cmr-field>
        <cmr-field-name>addresses</cmr-field-name>
        <cmr-field-type>java.util.Collection</cmr-field-type>
        </cmr-field>
    </ejb-relationship-role>
    <ejb-relationship-role>
        <ejb-relationship-role-name>AddressEJB</ejb-relationship-
role-name>
```

```
        <multiplicity>Many</multiplicity>
        <cascade-delete />
        <relationship-role-source>
          <ejb-name>AddressEJB</ejb-name>
        </relationship-role-source>
    </ejb-relationship-role>
    </ejb-relation>
...........
    </relationships>
```

Why return null in ejbCreate() method?

In EJB 1.0, the `EJBCreate()` method in CMP entity beans declared the returned type `void` but in EJB 1.1 this method was changed to return primary key types with an actual return value of `null`. This change was made to facilitate using BMP entity beans to extend CMP entity beans. In essence, EJB 1.1 enabled vendors to support container-managed persistence by extending CMP entity beans with BMP entity beans. This solution worked in EJB 1.1, but was not applicable to the complexity of CMP 2.0 entity beans. Nevertheless, it provides backward compatibility and enables subclassing of bean managed persistence. In general, avoid it in EJB 2.0 unless backward compatibility is one of your concerns.

Summary

In this chapter we discussed the chief characteristics of CMP 2.0 entity beans, such as their ability to form complex relationships between entity beans, enforcement of their referential integrity, and support for the abstract persistence schema and the standard EJB Query Language. We also discussed reasons why CMP 2.0 entity beans are preferred over BMP entity beans, including enhanced portability, flexibility with persistence implementation, better performance, and reduced time-to-market. We spent the major portion of the chapter discussing the implementation of the `StudentEJB`, `RosterEJB`, and `AddressEJB` CMP 2.0 entity beans, and we showed how to deploy and run the sample application. We'll examine the Java Message Service (JMS) in the next chapter.

JAVA MESSAGE SERVICE

Chapter 12

Introduced in the Enterprise JavaBean 2.0 specification, the message-driven bean is a type of Enterprise JavaBean that uses asynchronous communication. Message-driven beans are based on the Java Message Service (JMS) architecture and require an understanding of JMS prior to writing message-driven bean applications. This chapter focuses on Java Message Services, beginning with a brief review of messaging concepts. Specifically, this chapter provides

- an introduction to JMS
- a review of the JMS architecture and messaging domain
- the JMS programming API
- JMS and its relation to EJBs

Broadly speaking, *messaging* is the exchange of information between two separate and independent entities distributed over a network such as a local area network (LAN), a wide area network (WAN), or a wireless network. Messaging entities can be either humans or applications. E-mail is an example of a messaging system that allows human-to-human exchange of messages, while the messaging middleware enables two or more client applications to communicate by sending and receiving messages in a distributed environment without any human intervention.

With messaging middleware, clients use the peer-to-peer communication model, according to which clients can either produce or consume messages. There's no distinction between consumer and producer. In fact, a client may be a producer, a consumer, or both simultaneously. Producer clients produce messages; consumer clients consume the messages as shown in Figure 12-1.

Messaging Oriented Middleware (MOM) messaging systems have been around since the 1970s (including IBM's MQSeries, Microsoft's MSMQ, and Tibco's Rendezvous), and businesses have used them extensively, from exchanging messages between incompatible systems to managing B2B (business-to-business) exchanges processes with global partners.

Introduction to Java Message Service

JMS, like JDBC and JNDI, isn't a product, but rather a Java specification for messaging middleware from Sun and its partners. JMS defines an enterprise messaging Java API that makes it easy to write business applications that can

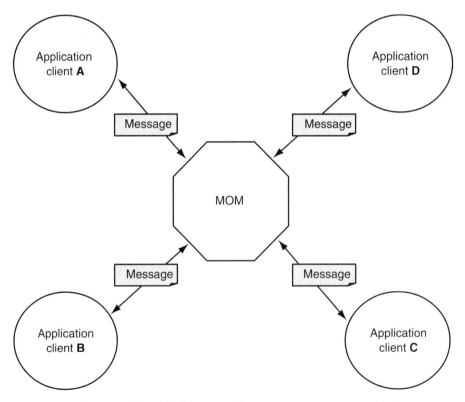

Figure 12-1 A messaging middleware with peer-to-peer communication

exchange business data and events asynchronously and reliably in a vendor-agnostic manner. The messaging server vendors provide the service provider interface that supports the standard JMS API (see Figure 12-2). Full JMS support is mandated by the J2EE 1.3 specification and is implemented by several enterprise messaging products from different vendors.

The JMS specification was written by Sun Microsystems and its partners, many who already had proprietary messaging middleware, resulting in the combination of "best of the breed" features from existing proprietary messaging middleware. One objective of JMS is to minimize the learning curve for writing messaging applications and to maximize the portability of messaging applications. As a result, JMS applications are easier to write and highly portable and support both the P2P and pub/sub messaging models.

Prior to JMS, programmers had to go through a steep learning curve to learn the complex proprietary APIs of the specific messaging server—this made writing messaging applications difficult and resulted in minimal portability. Additionally,

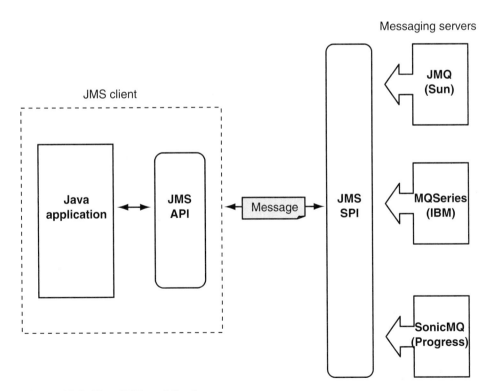

Figure 12-2 The JMS architecture

messaging servers from different vendors weren't interoperable in most cases, and businesses weren't happy with vendor lock-in and high cost of the product and support. Adoption of JMS in businesses is being driven by the following:

- *Wide industry support*—Because it's easy to implement the JMS specification in existing messaging servers, JMS is the first enterprise messaging API that has garnered wide industry support and, as a result, has become the messaging standard.

- *Standard messaging API*—By defining standard messaging concepts and conventions supported across different vendor messaging systems, JMS has simplified client application development and addressed portability issues.

- *Interoperability*—JMS leverages the existing messaging systems and is widely supported in many messaging products. For example, a client application using MQSeries as the JMS provider can communicate with another client application using the Rendezvous JMS provider. JMS clients can interoperate fully with non-JMS clients, an important consideration for businesses having proprietary applications.

- *Message-driven beans*—EJB 2.0 supports JMS-based message-driven beans, which enable developers to write scalable asynchronous EJB applications.

- *Simple API*—Application developers only have to learn the JMS API and can then write portable messaging enterprise applications easily and quickly.

JMS Architecture

JMS applications are portable across different JMS providers because the JMS architecture abstracts provider-specific proprietary information and is used by the application only at runtime. There are four elements to JMS architecture: JMS clients, the JMS provider, administered objects, and JMS messages. These elements are illustrated in Figure 12-3.

JMS Clients

JMS clients are applications that encapsulate business logic. JMS clients are written in Java and use the JMS API to send and receive messages. JMS clients can also communicate with non-JMS clients, or Java or non-Java client applications using the native client API instead of the JMS API to send and receive messages. We'll discuss how to write JMS clients later in JMS programming model section.

JMS Provider

The JMS provider is the message server that a vendor provides to implement the JMS SPI in addition to other messaging services and functionality necessary in an

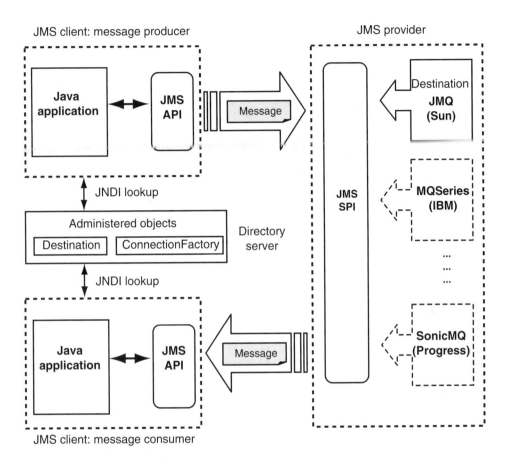

Figure 12-3 JMS architecture: producer, consumer, provider, message, and administrative objects

enterprise messaging system. The messaging server provides the necessary infrastructure services to deliver the JMS messages from one JMS client to another JMS client. These services include message routing and providing message persistence. Some of the popular messaging servers in the market today are MQSeries (IBM), JMQ (Sun), FioranoMQ (Fiorano), and SonicMQ (Progress).

Administered Objects

The JMS specification allows JMS providers to differ significantly in their underlying messaging technology and on how they are installed and administered. Therefore, for the JMS clients to be portable they must be isolated from the proprietary aspect of the JMS provider. This is accomplished by defining

JMS *administered objects*. Administered objects encapsulate provider-specific configuration information and are created and customized by the provider's administrator using the provider's tool and later used by clients. Think of administered objects as preconfigured JMS objects created by an administrator that clients use for providing messaging services. There are two kinds of administered objects: `destination` objects and `ConnectionFactory` objects. The `destination` object is the object a client uses to specify the destination of a message it's sending and the source of messages it receives; in other words, think of `destination` as a virtual address. The `ConnectionFactory` object is the object a client uses to create a connection with the JMS provider. `Destination` and `ConnectionFactory` objects are placed by an administrator in a JNDI namespace, such as an LDAP directory. The clients use a standard JNDI lookup method to locate these administered objects in a distributed environment, as shown in Figure 12-3.

JMS Messages

JMS messages, self-contained autonomous entities, are used to exchange information between JMS clients. A message can consist of data and/or logic exchanged between clients. A JMS message is created by a producer client and consumed by a JMS consumer client. A message consists of three parts: headers, properties, and payload. The header and property information is used by a messaging server for routing, filtering, and delivering the payload. The payload is the content of the message. This is very similar to a postal letter, which consists of an envelope that has a recipient's address and return address and may have optional special delivery information as well as an enclosed letter. JMS messages are composed of a header, properties, and the message body.

Message Header

The header section of a message consists of standard information necessary for a JMS provider to identify, route, manage, and deliver the message from a producer to a consumer client. There are two types of JMS headers: those that are automatically assigned by the JMS provider and others that a developer can assign. Table 12.1 briefly describes the header fields and what sets them.

The headers (`JMSCorrelationID`, `JMSReplyTo`, and `JMSType`) are assigned by the developer, while the rest are automatically assigned by the provider. There are setter and getter methods associated with these headers (documented in the Message interface), which enable these header fields to be manipulated by the application.

Message Properties

Message properties are extensions to the standard message headers that provide additional customizable fields. The properties information enables clients to add information that may be used by the provider for filtering messages. For example, using the message selector to send a message to only username called "johnsmith" would be done in the following way:

```
message.setStringProperty("johnsmith", username
```

The value of a property can be `String`, `boolean`, `byte`, `double`, `int`, `long`, or `float`.

Table 12-1 JMS Header Fields

Field	Brief Description	Send By
JMSDestination	Contains the destination to which a message is being sent. Depending on the messaging model, it could either be a `Queue` or a `Topic`. This information is used for routing messages.	`send()` or `publish()` method
JMDDeliveryMode	Contains the delivery mode. There are two types: persistent or nonpersistent. In a persistent mode, a message is guaranteed to be delivered once and only once, while in nonpersistent mode, a message may be delivered at-most-once or not at all.	`send()` or `publish()` method
JMSExpiration	Sets the length of the time during which a message is valid. The expiration time is set in milliseconds by the producer. If the expiration time is set to 0 (default), i.e., the message never expires.	`send()` or `publish()` method
JMSPriority	Message servers use the priority field to order message delivery to consumers; higher-priority messages are delivered earlier than lower-priority messages. There are ten priority levels, 0 being the lowest and 9 being the highest.	`send()` or `publish()` method
JMSMessageID	Uniquely identifies a message sent by a provider. The uniqueness isn't universally guaranteed and isn't required by JMS specification. This JMSMessageID must be a `String` value and must start with the prefix `ID:`	`send()` or `publish()` method
JMSTimeStamp	Contains the approximate time in milliseconds when a send operation was invoked on the connection, which may not be the time the message was actually transmitted to the queue.	`send()` or `publish()` method

Table 12-1 JMS Header Fields (continued)

Field	Brief Description	Send By
JMSCorrelationID	Used for associating a message with some previous message or application-specific ID and is commonly used to tag a message as a follow-up to a previous message. Frequently, although it's not required, the JMSCorrelationID field contains the JMSMessageID.	Client
JMSReplyTo	Contains the destination to where the consumer client should reply. When a producer sends a message with JMSReplyTo field set, it's expecting a response from the consumer client.	Client
JMSType	Used for identifying message structure and type of payload and not the type of message (TextMessage, MapMessage, etc.) being sent. This is an optional field.	Client
JMSRedelivered	This field indicates whether the message was delivered to the consumer client.	Provider

There are three basic categories of message properties:

- *Application-specific properties*—These are defined by the bean developers to suit the needs of their applications.

- *JMS-defined properties*—These are set by the JMS provider; you can consider them extensions to header fields, but they're optional, and a given JMS provider might support some or none of these fields.

- *Provider-specific properties*—Proprietary to the JMS provider, these properties allow the vendor to provide special features that only their client can use. These fields must have a JMS_<vendorName> prefix. Using these fields affects the portability of an application.

JMS messages can be filtered by using SQL syntax in the JMS message selector. The message selector is a java.lang.String that contains an expression having syntax based on the SQL-92 conditional expression syntax. When a message consumer registers with the destination, it can specify the filtering criteria by setting the message selector logic. The JMS provider is responsible for filtering the messages to the consumers. For example, if a message consumer were only interested in receiving messages containing the phrases "hot deal" and "Sony Laptop," the filtering message would look like the following:

```
TopicSubscriber subs =
session.createSubscriber("Hot Deal", "brand=Sony Laptop", false);
```

Or, if an e-commerce site wants to send out a special message to its best customers who spent, say, $1000 last year and live in the states of California and Washington, the message might look like this:

```
String selector = "Total > 1000.00 AND State IN ('CA', 'WA')";
TopicSubscriber subscriber = session.createSubscriber(topic,
selector, false);
```

Note that the message selector can filter only on fields in the header and properties.

Message Body

The *payload*, or message body, contains the content of the message—the data being exchanged between JMS clients. The message body supports five different message types to address the most common data types and to provide compatibility with existing messaging formats. The message is the superinterface for the message types (listed with brief descriptions in Table 12.2). The simplest type of message is the `javax.jms.Message`, which serves as a superinterface for other message types. The message type of message contains only JMS headers and properties and no payload. It's used mainly in event notification. An event notification is a simple warning or notice of an event or occurrence. The content of the message body is immutable, meaning it cannot be changed once it's created, thus requiring the content to be deleted and recreated if necessary.

Table 12-2 Message Types

Message Type	Payload Description
Message	Superinterface for other message types; carries no payload. Used mainly for event notification.
TextMessage	Payload is plain text, i.e., `java.lang.String`. Useful for exchanging simple text messages or complex data using XML.
MapMessage	Payload is name/value pair where values can be Java primitives and their wrapper class and Strings.
ObjectMessage	Message body consists of serializable Java objects.
StreamMessage	Payload consists of stream of primitive Java types, which are read from the same order they were written using the file stream metaphor.
ByteMessage	Body consists of an array of primitive bytes intended for binary data and commonly used for exchanging data in an application native format.

Messaging Domain Models

JMS supports two types of *messaging models* (also referred to as domain models) that are common in the messaging world: Point-to-Point (P2P) and Publish/Subscribe (pub/sub). Not all messaging middleware supports both models, and the JMS 1.02 specification doesn't require the JMS provider to support both models. Regardless of the messaging model, JMS clients exchange messages by sending or retrieving messages to and from a virtual address termed the "destination." JMS providers are responsible for destination services.

Point-to-Point Model

The P2P messaging model consists of message senders, receivers, queues, and the messages. A JMS client that generates messages is called the sender; a JMS client that consumes messages is called the receiver. In the P2P model, a sender sends a message to a destination called the queue; a receiver retrieves the message from the same queue, as shown in Figure 12-4.

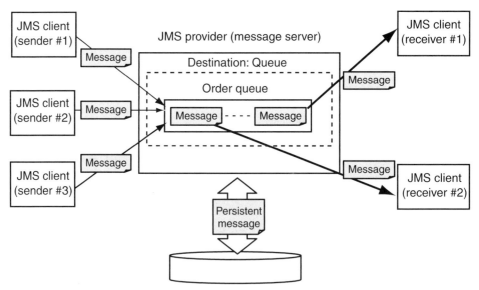

Figure 12-4 A message sent to a queue being consumed by only one receiver

Figure 12-4 illustrates the P2P messaging model with three senders sending messages to a destination queue called `OrderQueue` and the two receivers each retrieving their own message. The P2P messaging model is applicable in cases where messages should be acted upon only once. For example, a company may have its distribution warehouse in a state different from its headquarters. When customers order products, the application sends the order messages to a JMS client at the remote warehouse where the order is processed and shipped.

The P2P domain model has several significant characteristics:

- The P2P model is referred to as supporting either one-to-one or many-to-one relationships. If you look at the sender-receiver relationship where many JMS senders can send messages to a particular JMS Queue destination, the message can only be consumed by a single receiver. On the other hand, if you look at the message-receiver relationship, there can only be one receiver per message, resulting in a one-to-one relationship. The P2P model can be characterized as supporting a many-to-one relationship between senders and a single receiver.

- Each message can have only one receiver. Therefore, multiple senders can send messages to a queue and multiple receivers can access the queue, but only one receiver can consume a message from that queue.

- Once a message is consumed by a receiver, it's removed from the queue. Thus, in the P2P model, messages are guaranteed to be delivered to a receiver once and only once.

- Messages are ordered. For example, a queue delivers messages to consumers in the order in which they were placed by the provider.

- Senders and receivers can be added dynamically at runtime, thus allowing the system to grow or shrink with the demand.

Publish and Subscribe Model

The pub/sub model consists of message publishers, subscribers, and topics. A message producer is called a *publisher*; a message consumer is called a *subscriber*. The destination where a publisher sends messages and the subscribers retrieve the messages is called the *topic*. The pub/sub model is based on the concept of nodes in a content hierarchy, where a publisher publishes messages to a destination and the messages are broadcast to all registered subscribers.

The pub/sub model supports many-to-many or one-to-many relationships. When considering a publisher-subscriber relationship, there can be many publishers sending messages to many subscribers, resulting in a many-to-many relationship. On the other hand, when considering a message-subscriber relationship, a message sent by a publisher is distributed to all registered subscribers resulting in a one-to-many relationship. The pub/sub model can be characterized as supporting a many-to-many relationship between senders and receivers.

Note that every client that subscribes to a topic receives its own copy of the messages published to that topic. Messages are pushed to the registered subscribers without having to request them. Also, publisher and subscribers can be dynamically added at runtime, and a message delivery in pub/sub is once or not at all. Figure 12-5 is an illustration of the pub/sub messaging model in which many publishers are publishing messages to a destination topic, StockQuoteTopic. Each of these messages is distributed to many subscribers. The pub/sub model is applicable when one wants to broadcast a message to many clients simultaneously. For example, a financial website can publish the latest stock quotes to a topic; clients that have subscribed to a specific topic can automatically receive the latest stock price information.

Message Delivery

JMS message consumers, whether P2P or pub/sub, can choose to have messages delivered to them asynchronously by having the JMS provider *push* messages, or they may receive the messages synchronously by connecting to the JMS provider

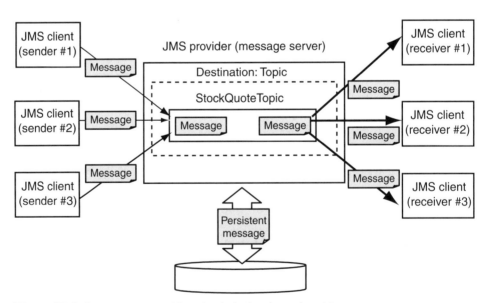

Figure 12-5 A message sent to a topic being broadcast to one or more registered subscribers

and receiving, or *pulling*, the messages from the destination. Pull delivery requires the JMS consumer to either stay connected to the JMS provider and poll the destination for messages or connect to the JMS provider and retrieve messages from the destination per regularly scheduled intervals. Note that pulling the destination for messages adds extra overhead to the system. Push delivery is simpler as the JMS provider automatically delivers messages to registered JMS consumers. Developers incorporate the pull or the push delivery mechanism based on the business logic requirements. Note that the communication between the producer client and the JMS provider is synchronous—a message producer (JMS client producer) connects to the JMS provider, sends messages, and receives acknowledgment from the provider to complete message delivery. In contrast, message consumers can either receive messages synchronously as they arrive at the destination (if the pull option is used) or asynchronously if the push option is used in the client code. Regardless of the options used, message delivery from producer to consumer can only be asynchronous. Figure 12-6 illustrates the push/pull model where a message producer client sends messages to a destination.

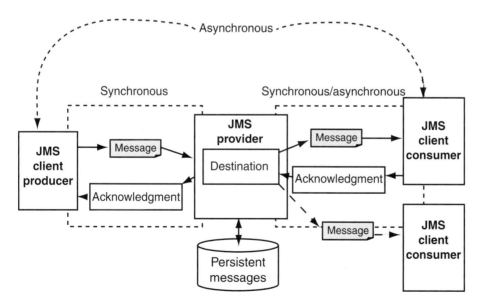

Figure 12-6 JMS architecture with interaction among clients, provider, and messages

Guaranteed Message Delivery

JMS messages can be marked as either persistent or nonpersistent. In both cases, a JMS provider will attempt to deliver the message to the consumer until the JMS consumer either receives the message and acknowledges it, or until the message expires. The difference between a persistent and a nonpersistent message is significant, yet subtle. If a message is marked as persistent, the JMS provider saves the message on the disk before acknowledging to the message producer and uses a store-and-forward mechanism. Delivery is attempted until the JMS message consumer receives the message and acknowledges it, or until the message expires. Even if the provider crashes before the message is delivered to the consumer, the provider will attempt to resend the message after the provider is rebooted. With nonpersistent messaging, the JMS provider doesn't save the message to disk before sending an acknowledgment to the message producer. For this reason, if the JMS provider were to experience a system crash before delivery of the message, the nonpersistent message would be lost.

In a pub/sub model, a subscriber can either be *durable* or *nondurable*. Messages are delivered to nondurable subscribers only if they're connected to the provider. With durable subscribers, the provider is responsible for storing the messages and will deliver unexpired messages when durable subscribers connect later. A message can be marked persistent and durable or nonpersistent and durable—there's a subtle but important difference. In the case of a nonpersistent and durable message, the provider attempts to deliver the message, and if the subscriber isn't active, then the provider will store the message for future delivery attempts. If the provider crashes before it's able to store the message, then the message is lost and will never be delivered. This won't happen with the persistent and durable message because when the message is received from the publisher it's already saved on disk and will attempt to deliver the durable message on reboot. Making a message durable and/or persistent has consequences for processing and system resources. For example, confirmation of purchased messages could be marked persistent and durable because that message cannot afford to be lost. However, stock price update broadcast messages every few minutes could be nonpersistent and nondurable, because most people (except for day traders) can afford to lose a message or two without adversely affecting their net worth.

Loose Coupling and Asynchronous Communication

In the JMS messaging architecture, the JMS clients can produce or consume messages or do both. The JMS provider is responsible for routing and delivery of messages. The JMS clients are loosely coupled and asynchronous; neither JMS client needs to be aware of the other, nor must they be running simultaneously for messages to be exchanged. JMS clients don't communicate directly but via the destination service provided by the JMS provider. Producers send messages to a destination, where they are held until consumers retrieve messages or the messages expire.

Even though the communications between JMS clients are asynchronous, the communication between producers and a JMS provider are synchronous, and the communication between consumers and a JMS provider are synchronous or asynchronous. When JMS clients send or receive messages from JMS provider destinations, they go through a receive-acknowledge handshake. Refer back to Figure 12-6 for an illustration.

Loose coupling and asynchronous communication in a JMS application give enterprise applications flexibility when implementing business workflow processes. Let's look at an e-commerce application example. During checkout, after the shopping cart component sends a persistent and durable message to a JMS provider `OrderQueue` destination, the component can continue servicing other customers and not worry about what happens next. An optimized order processing application retrieves the message from the `OrderQueue` destination and processes it. Per the application business logic that requires minimizing shipping costs, reduced delivery time, and maximum profit, the application forwards this durable message to the `NYWarehouseQueue` destination nearest the customer's shipping address. The shipping application then retrieves the message from the `NYWareHouseQueue`, extracts the necessary information, and mails the product, as well as automatically sending an e-mail with a tracking order number to the customer. As the JMS application is loosely coupled and relies on asynchronous communication, the shopping cart application is unaware of the optimized order processing application. As a result, if the shipping application and order processing go down for a while, the persistent and durable message is still delivered. When the two failed applications resume operating, the order can be completed and the products shipped.

The JMS Programming Model

Building a JMS application requires understanding of the following six building blocks:

- administered objects
- connection
- session

- message producer
- message consumer
- message

The JMS APIs are available under `java.jms.*`. We would have to import the following JMS packages to implement the example: `TopicConnectionFactory, QueueConnectionFactory, Topic, Queue, QueReceiver, Session`, and `TextMessage`.

Before a JMS producer can send messages, it must first create a session and then a connection. To create a connection, the JMS client must figure out the mechanism for creating a connection and find a destination for the message. This function is enabled using administered objects. Administered objects consist of ConnectionFactory and destination objects. The JNDI is used to locate and download these administered objects. A ConnectionFactory object encapsulates a set of vendor-specific messaging server configuration parameters defined by the administrator during deployment. JMS clients use the ConnectionFactory object to create a connection to the JMS provider. A code snippet showing the use of JNDI and the connection factory object follows:

```
.........
Context cntx = new InitialContext(env);
//in the case of Queue messaging model
QueueConnectionFactory queConnFactory = (QueueConnectionFactory)
cntx.lookup("java:comp/env/jms/QueueConnectionFactory");

...........
//in the case of Topic messaging model
TopicConnectionFactory facConnFactory = (TopicConnectionFactory)
cntx.lookup("java:comp/env/jms/TopicConnectionFactory");
...................
```

A `destination` object encapsulates vendor-proprietary destination information that message producers and consumers must use to send messages. JNDI is also used to locate and download destination objects. It's also used to locate and download destination objects from `java:comp/env/jms`, which is a commonly used JMS root context for administered objects. A destination is called a *queue* in the P2P messaging model and a *topic* in the pub/sub model, as illustrated here:

```
............
Topic hotDealTopic = (Topic)
cntx.lookup("java:comp/env/jms/HotDeal");
Queue supportQue = (Queue)
cntx.lookup("java:comp/env/jms/TechSupport");
............
```

Administered objects are created by an administrator and made available for clients to use during execution—both support concurrent access. Administered objects encapsulate the JMS provider-specific logic and hides it from the JMS client code, thus enhancing application portability. Administered objects are created and configured by an administrator using a vendor-provided deployment tool at deployment time. Connection objects encapsulate proprietary logic to establish connection to the JMS provider. Connection objects use the user name and password authentication to open a connection to the JMS provider daemon for a queue and topic destination and must close the connection when done in the following way:

```
QueueConnection queConnection = queConnFactory.createQueueConnec-
tion(username, password)
TopicConnection topicConnection = topicConnFactory.createTopicCon-
nection(username, password)
```

The session object is a factory for producing and consuming messages and is single threaded and transactional as shown here:

```
QueueSession queSession = queConnection.createQueueSession(false,
Session.AUTO_ACKNOWLEDGE)TopicSession
topicSession = topicConnection.createTopicSession(false,
AUTO_ACKNOWLEDGE)
```

The message producer (`MessageProducer`) object is created by a session object and is used by producer clients to send messages to a destination. It's a superinterface for both the `TopicPublisher` and `QueueSender` objects. With P2P, use the `send()` method of the QueueSender interface to send messages to a destination and use the `publish()` method of the `TopicPublisher` interface for the pub/sub model. For example, let's assume we want to connect to a queue destination called "HotNews" and a topic destination called "HotBargains" that was preconfigured by the administrator. First, look up the destinations and then create the sender and publisher objects as follows:

```
Queue hotNews = (Queue) jndi.lookup("java:comp/env/jms/HotNews")
Topic hotBargains = (Topic) jndi.lookup("java:comp/emv/jms/HotBargains")
QueueSender queSender = queSession.createSender(hotNews);
queSender.send(msgHotDeal)
TopicPublisher topicPublisher = topicSession.createPublisher(hotBar-
gains)
topicPublisher.publish(msgHotBargains)
```

The message consumer (`MessageConsumer`) object is also created by a session object and is used by consumer clients to receive messages from a destination. A `MessageConsumer` is a superinterface to both the `QueueReceiver` and `TopicSubscriber` interfaces. There are several variations for creating a message consumer client. A message consumer client can be created with a message selector, which enables developers to selectively filter messages the client will receive based on the selector SQL syntax. Developers also can select between synchronous and asynchronous communication modes when creating the consumer client. When selecting synchronous mode, the pull method is being selected and the `receive()` method is used to get messages. If the synchronous or push mode is preferred, the MessageListener interface is implemented and the JMS provider uses the `onMessage()` method to deliver messages. The `start()` method in `QueueConnection` and `TopicConnection` objects must be invoked before messages can arrive as illustrated here:

```
QueueReceiver queReceiver = queSession.createQueueReceiver("HotNews");
queConection.start();
Message msg = queReceiver.receive()
```

Or, asynchronous mode requires more work. First, developers must define a QueueListener class that implements the MessageListener interface and then registers the queue listener as follows:

```
QueueListener queListener = new QueueListener();
queReceiver.setMessageListener(queListener);
```

Message objects are created by the JMS producer and can be any one of five format types discussed earlier. Refer back to Table 12.2 for the different types of JMS message formats. Table 12.3 summarizes these objects, which are the building blocks for JMS applications (for both the P2P and pub/sub messaging models). Notice the symmetry of the object names and semantics.

Table 12-3 JMS API and Message Types

Object	Point-to-Point Messages	Publish/Subscribe Messages	Comment
Destination	Queue, TemporaryQueue	Topic, TemporaryTopic	Administered object
Connection-Factory	QueueConnection Factory	TopicConnection Factory	Administered object
Connection	QueueConnection	TopicConnection	
Session	QueueSession	TopicSession	

Table 12-3 JMS API and Message Types (continued)

Object	Point-to-Point Messages	Publish/Subscribe Messages	Comment
MessageProducer	QueueSender	TopicPublisher	
MessageConsumer	QueueReceiver	TopicSubscriber	
Message	TextMessage, MapMessage, ByteMessage, StreamMessage, ObjectMessage	TextMessage, MapMessage, ByteMessage, StreamMessage, ObjectMessage	Message types are common to both models

JMS Integration with EJBs

In the EJB 1.1 specification, the JMS API was required, but the implementation of JMS SPI was optional. In the EJB 2.0 specification, the JMS must be fully implemented. The EJB 2.0 specification also introduced message-driven beans, which are used to model stateless JMS consumers. Message-driven beans enable developers to write asynchronous EJB applications. We'll leave the discussion of message-driven beans to the next chapter. JMS applications help solve the following business issues:

- *Integration of disparate systems in a heterogeneous environment*—A JMS provider can facilitate the exchange of business data among incompatible systems by enabling XML message exchanges. An ERP system that isn't able to directly interface with a legacy system can use JMS provider and appropriate message format to translate information from the ERP to the legacy system and vice-versa.

- *Business information exchange*—It's common in businesses to exchange price, discount, and/or supply information. This is usually done via fax, telephone, or e-mail, functions all prone to human error. Businesses can use JMS to exchange information directly between applications and avoid human error.

- *Automation of business functions*—Businesses can use B2B JMS trading applications to buy and sell goods, thus saving time and money. For example, an inventory management application can automatically request the supplier application to replenish the inventory as well as create the necessary purchase order.

Summary

JMS applications have the following benefits:

- The loose coupling nature of JMS applications gives developers the flexibility to implement business logic in a distributed environment.
- Asynchronous communication enables the application to be deployed in a more scalable and fault-tolerant fashion than synchronous EJBs.
- Portability is a big advantage for JMS applications, as JMS applications aren't tied to one vendor-proprietary API.
- Guaranteed message delivery provided by the P2P model is inherent, relieving a developer of this coding responsibility.
- Broadcast message delivery provided by the pub/sub model is another feature automatically provided by the JMS.

The goal of the JMS specification is to provide a common set of Java APIs to enable programmers to write messaging applications easily. JMS 1.02 addresses the common message and delivery API for messaging but doesn't address the underlying complicated services that can be implemented in different ways. The JMS 1.02 specification lets JMS providers implement these services as they see fit, and it's abstracted from programmers. However, the current version of JMS specification doesn't address load balancing and fault tolerance, error notification, security, administration, wire protocol, or message type repository. These issues are generally handled by the JMS provider vendor or handled by the J2EE 1.3 compliant application server framework.

DEVELOPING MESSAGE-DRIVEN BEANS

Chapter 13

This chapter focuses on message-driven beans (MDBs), the newest addition to Enterprise JavaBeans. Specifically, this chapter discusses

- the characteristics of MDBs
- the elements of MDBs
- `MessageDrivenBean` interface
- the life cycle of MDBs
- comparing MDBs with session and entity beans
- how to write, package, deploy, and test MDB applications
- deployment descriptors

MDBs, introduced in the EJB 2.0 specification, are the newest type of Enterprise JavaBean and are designed to consume JMS messages. While session and entity beans depend on RMI-IIOP to communicate synchronously with each other, MDBs depend on asynchronous communication for exchanging JMS messages.

One of the drawbacks of synchronous communication is that the client making a method invocation on a remote instance is blocked until the remote bean instance responds. A client making RMI-IIOP method invocations expects the remote instance to be available, ready to execute the method, or guaranteed to be made available by the EJB container. If the client doesn't receive a response from the remote object within a reasonable amount of time (usually a few seconds), the client making the request throws a remote exception. In addition, there are higher resource requirements and more network traffic associated with synchronous communication, but the vast majority of interactive business applications depend on it nonetheless.

There are business applications that don't require synchronous communication and, in fact, may be better suited for asynchronous communication. Asynchronous communication is ideal for the optimized order fulfillment example we discussed in the previous chapter, and for inventory management in a B2B environment. In the B2B scenario, based on business agreements, the application at the product distributor site could automatically generate and send a message asynchronously to the supplier's application to replenish the inventory whien it reaches a certain level. The supplier's application would automatically acknowledge the message, inform manufacturing of the quantity and type of product to produce, and ship the product to the distributor.

Characteristics of MDBs

An MDB is implemented as an asynchronous JMS message consumer within the EJB framework. Similar to session and entity bean instances, MDBs implement business logic and execute within an EJB container. MDBs have the following characteristics:

- They don't have local or remote home and component interfaces.
- MDBs use lightweight, self-contained JMS messages to communicate asynchronously.
- Messages can be persistent or nonpersistent, and MDBs can provide guaranteed message delivery.
- Because MDBs are stateless, they can be pooled for efficiency and scalability.
- MDBs have a single `onMessage(msg)` business method that's invoked by the container when messages arrive. Message type is checked on arrival.
- MDB supports both P2P and pub/sub messaging models.
- MDBs can be durable or nondurable subscribers. In a pub/sub messaging domain, when a message arrives and the nondurable subscriber isn't active, the message may not be delivered, but in the case of a durable subscriber, the message is stored and forwarded when the durable subscriber is activated later.
- Even if transaction context cannot be shared between a JMS client and an MDB, MDB supports both programmatic and declarative transaction demarcation.
- MDBs cannot throw any exceptions to the message sender.

Elements of MDBs

Developers of MDBs must provide the following elements:

- a message-driven implementation class
- a JMS message type
- a deployment descriptor

MessageDrivenBean Interface

An MDB class must implement the `javax.ejb.MessageDrivenBean` and `javax.jms.MessageListener` interfaces. A `MessageListener` interface defines one method, `onMessage(Message message)`; this method is automatically invoked by the container when messages arrive at the destination. MDBs use the `onMessage` method to consume messages. See the code example below that follows.

```
public interface javax.jms.MessageListener
{
    public void onMessage(Message message);
}
```

The bean developer is responsible for implementing the `ejbCreate()` method for the MDB. This method should be used to initialize variables and resources, such as a connection to the database. As part of the MDB instantiation, the container first invokes the `newInstance()` method followed by the `setMessageDrivenContext()` method, which passes a message-driven context to the bean instance (see Figure 3-1). The message-driven context provides the container with access to the runtime context—this is valid throughout the life span of the bean instance. The container must execute the `ejbCreate()` method before the bean instance is transitioned to the ready pool and can consume any messages, as shown in the following example:

```
public interface javax.ejb.MessageDrivenBean extends EnterpriseBean
{
    public void ejbRemove() throws EJBException;
    public void setMessageDrivenContext(MessageDrivenContext mctx)
throws EJBException;
}
```

The `ejbRemove()` method is invoked by the container before the container removes the MDB instance from the pool. This method should contain logic to initialize and release any resources allocated in the `ejbCreate()` method. At the end of the `ejbRemove()` method execution, the MDB instance is transitioned from memory to the `does not exist` state.

JMS Message Type

The bean developer must specify the JMS message types and the content of the message within the application. The message producer must create a message from one of the six types—`Message`, `TextMessage`, `MapMessage`, `ObjectMessage`, `StreamMessage`, and `ByteMessage`. Upon receipt of the message, the message consumer must be able to understand the JMS message format, extract the contents of the message, and apply the business logic.

The Life Cycle of MDBs

Because MDB instances are stateless, their life cycles are simple and have two states: `does not exist` and `ready`. Figure 13-1 illustrates the life cycle of an MDB.

An MDB instance begins its life when the container invokes three methods: `newInstance()`, `setMessageDrivenContext(mdx)`, and `ejbCreate()`. Figure 13-2 illustrates this sequence. After invoking the `ejbCreate()` method,

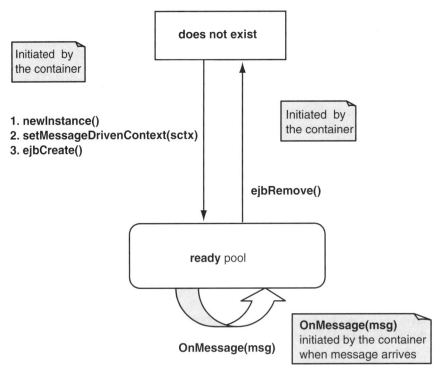

Figure 13-1 Life cycle of a message-driven bean instance

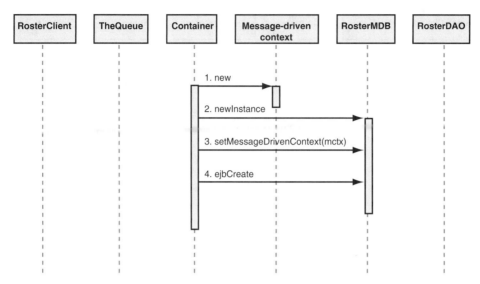

Figure 13-2 Sequence diagram of a message-driven bean initialization

the MDB instance is in the ready pool, waiting to consume incoming messages. Because MDBs are stateless, all instances of MDBs in the pool are identical; the container selects an MDB instance to process a message and then return back to the pool.

The container can remove the instance of an MDB by invoking the `ejbRemove()` method, moving the MDB instance to the `does not exist` state. (See Figure 13-3 for an illustration.) When a message arrives, the container assigns the message to an MDB instance from the ready pool, and it processes the messages by executing the `onMessage(msg)` method. After the message is processed, the MDB instance is returned to the ready pool. The pooling of message-driven bean instances enables the container to provide speed and scalability.

Comparing MDBs with Session and Entity Beans

Let's compare and contrast message-driven beans with session and entity beans. Unlike the session and entity beans, MDBs use asynchronous communication, and there are other differences as well:

- MDBs interact using lightweight JMS messages, making them fast and reliable because they consume fewer resources than the session and entity beans that depend on heavyweight RMI-IIOP and synchronous communication.

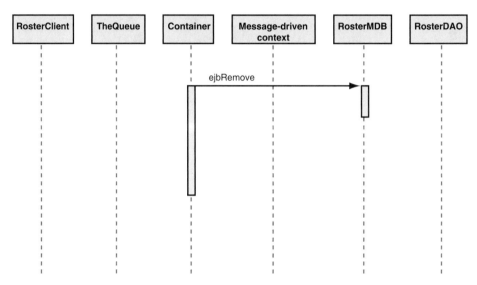

Figure 13-3 Sequence diagram of a message-driven bean removal

- The message sender and receiver don't have to be available simultaneously. If the target message receiver is down, the message is stored and forwarded later when the target server comes up. With session and entity beans, the client cannot invoke the business logic if theEJB instance is not available.

- MDBs support loosely coupled one-to-one and one-to-many delivery of messages, thus providing a more flexible solution for distributed communication. Session and entity beans are restricted to one-to-one interaction—only one client can make an RMI-IIOP invocation to one component at a time.

- Due to the asynchronous nature of MDBs, the client cannot propagate the transaction and security contexts to the MDB instance and thus cannot control the transaction and security behaviors of the MDB instances. This is in contrast to session and entity beans, where the client can indeed propagate and control the transaction and security contexts. Please refer to the matrix in Table 13-1 that compares various aspects of MDBs with session and entity beans.

An MDB developer provides the MDB implementation class and is also responsible for

- defining a JMS message type
- creating a deployment descriptor file
- providing optional helper classes

Table 13-1 Comparing Message-Driven Beans with Session and Entity Beans

Feature	MDB	SLSB	SFSB	BMP	CMP
State type	Stateless	Stateless	Stateful	N/A	N/A
Instance pooling	Yes	Yes	No	Yes	Yes
Transaction	Transaction aware	Transaction aware	Transaction aware	Transactional	Transactional
Local and remote interfaces	No	Yes	Yes	Yes	Yes
Type of communication	Asynchro-nous	Synchro-nous	Synchro-nous	Synchronous	Synchronous
Communication method	JMS messages	RMI-IIOP	RMI-IIOP	RMI-IIOP	RMI-IIOP
Business method	onMessage()	zero or more	zero or more	zero or more	zero or more

Rules for Writing the MDB Class and Its Methods

Let's look at the rules for how to implement the MDB class and the
`ejbCreate()`, `onMessage()`, and `ejbRemove()` methods.

MDB Class

A bean developer must follow the several important requirements when writing
an MDB. The MDB class must directly or indirectly implement both the
`javax.ejb.MessageDrivenBean` and `javax.jms.MessageListener`
interfaces. The class must be defined as `public` and must not be `final` or
`abstract`.

The MDB class must have a public constructor that takes no arguments and must
not define the `finalize()` method. The class must implement the `ejbCreate()`
method and `onMessage()` and is allowed to include other methods that are
internally invoked by the `onMessage()` methods, in addition to methods
required by the EJB specification.

The MDB class can have superclasses and/or superinterfaces. When this occurs,
the `ejbCreate()` method and methods of `MessageDrivenBean` and
`MessageListener` interfaces may be defined in the MDB class or any of its
superclasses.

ejbCreate Method

The MDB class must define only one `ejbCreate()` method, which must be named `ejbCreate()`. It must be declared as `public` and must not be declared as `final` or `static`. The return type must be void and must not have any arguments. The throw clause must not define any application exceptions.

onMessage Method

When a message arrives, the container picks an MDB instance from the pool, invokes `onMessage(msg)`, and passes the JMS message an argument. Let's look at the rules on how to write an `onMessage` method in an MDB.

The MDB class must define one `onMessage()` method, which must be declared as `public`. It cannot be declared `final` or `static`. The return argument must be void and must have a single argument of the type `javax.jms.Message`. The throw clause may not define any application exceptions.

ejbRemove Method

The container calls the `ejbRemove()` method to remove an MDB instance from the container. Let's look at rules for writing the `ejbRemove()` method. The MDB class must define one remove method, which must be named `ejbRemove()`. It must be declared as `public`. The method must not be declared as `final` or `static`. The return type must be void and it must have no argument. The throw clause must not define any application exceptions.

MDB EJB Sample Application: RosterMDB

The `RosterMDB` application consists of four parts: an MDB, which consumes messages and publishes messages; a JMS servlet client, which produces messages; a JMS message subscriber; and two types of messages that are exchanged among them. In the following example, an HTML form is used to submit student and schedule information to the JMS servlet. The servlet extracts the information from the form, creates a message and sends it to a destination. Upon receiving the message, the MDB extracts the fields from the message and inserts them into a database. After that, the MDB selects the `studentID` field for all the students who have registered for that `ScheduleID`, creates a text message with the `studentID` list, and then publishes it to a topic destination. The JMS subscriber receives the persistent messages when it's activated. Figure 13-4 illustrates this interaction.

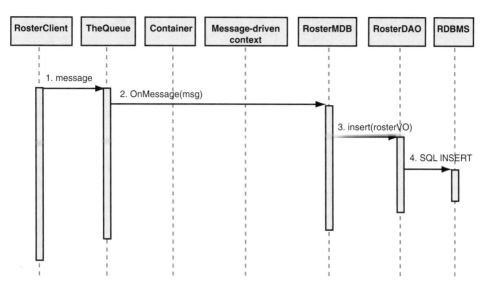

Figure 13-4 A message-driven bean consuming messages

The client application, MessageSender, creates a JMS message type, ObjectMessage, and then embeds the RosterVO object in the message body and sends it to the Queue destination. When the JMS message arrives, the container selects a RosterMDB instance, executes the onMessage() method, and bypasses the ObjectMessage as an argument to the method. The RosterMDB executes the logic to extract and insert the content of the message to the database using the RosterDAO helper class. The MDB then retrieves the current list of students who are registered for a particular class and publishes persistent messages. Another JMS client program, DurableSubscriber (a JMS subscriber), retrieves messages published by RosterMDB to the topic destination and, with the help of the MessageHandler class, prints them out.

We'll use the following steps to implement the RosterMDB application:

1. Define and implement a message object—RosterVO.
2. Implement the MDB class—RosterMDB.
3. Implement the helper class—RosterDAO and RosterDAOException.
4. Compile the RosterMDB, RosterVO, and RosterDAO.
5. Implement a servlet JMS message sender client—MessageSender.
6. Implement JMS message subscriber client—DurableSubscriber and MessageHandler.

7. Compile JMS clients—`MessageSender`, `DurableSubscriber`, and `MessageHandler`.

8. Package the EJB component into the `RosterJAR` file.

9. Package the Web component into the `RosterWAR` file.

10. Package the client into the `client jar` file.

11. Package the `ejb-jar`, `client-jar`, and war files into the `RosterApp.ear` file.

12. Deploy the `RosterApp.ear` file.

13. Test the application.

Step 1: Defining and Implementing a Message

In this example, we'll send a schedule, a student identification, and registration date using the JMS message (`ObjectMessage`) type to encapsulate our information. The example objective is to create an object, `RosterVO`, to hold the information; to encapsulate it as an `ObjectMessage` message; and, finally, to send it from a servlet to a message consumer. The roster value object class, `RosterVO`, is serializable and consists of three fields,—schedule, student identification, and date—as well as the corresponding getter methods.

```
public class RosterVO implements Serializable
{
....private String scheduleID;
    private String studentID;
    private Date theDateStamp;

    public RosterVO(String schedID, String studID, Date aDate)
    {
        scheduleID = schedID;
        studentID = studID;
        theDateStamp = aDate;
    }

    public String getScheduleID()
    {
        return this.scheduleID;
    }

    public String getStudentID()
    {
        return this.studentID;
    }

    public Date getTheDate()
    {
```

```
            return this.theDateStamp;
        }

} //;-) end of RosterVO
```

Step 2: Implementing the MDB Class

There are two parts to this class. The first part of `RosterMDB` receives the message from the queue destination, extracts the schedule, student, and registration date information from the message, and inserts this data into the database table, `roster`. The roster table is used to track the student class registration. The second part of `RosterMDB` uses the `scheduleID` from the previous message to retrieve all the `studentID` values from the roster table and then publish the list as a persistent message to a topic destination.

The `RosterMDB` class must implement the `javax.ejb.MessageDrivenBean` and `java.jms.MessageListener` interfaces. The empty constructor, `RosterMDB()`, along with the required `setMessageDrivenContext(mdct)` is used by the container to pass the bean context reference to the bean instance.

```
public class RosterMDB implements MessageDrivenBean, MessageListener
{
```

The `ejbCreate()` method is invoked by the container. At its completion, the `RosterMDB` instance has transitioned to the `ready pool` state. To create this queue, use the JNDI lookup method to get the initial context reference. Use this context reference to retrieve the Queue Connection factory, `java:comp/env/jms/TheQueFactory`, and the queue destination, `java:comp/env/jms/TheQue`. Then create the Queue connection, `createQueueConnection()`, to enable queue messages acceptance.

```
public void ejbCreate()
{
    System.out.println(" -- In RosterMDB - ejbCreate() -- ");

    Context jndictx = null;
    QueueConnectionFactory queConnFactory = null;
    TopicConnectionFactory topicConnFactory = null;

    try {
        jndictx = new InitialContext();
        //For P2P access administrative objects
        queConnFactory = (QueueConnectionFactory)
  jndictx.lookup("java:comp/env/jms/TheQueFactory");
        queue = (Queue) jndictx.lookup("java:comp/env/jms/TheQue");
        queConnection = queConnFactory.createQueueConnection();
```

We also must appropriate administrative objects for the pub/sub messaging model, as shown below. Using the JNDI lookup, retrieve the factory and the destination object and then create the connection and the session objects, as in the following example:

```
try {
//For Pub/sub access administrative objects
    topicConnFactory = (TopicConnectionFactory)
jndictx.lookup("java:comp/env/jms/TheTopicFactory");
    topic = (Topic) jndictx.lookup("java:comp/env/jms/TheTopic");
    topicConnection = topicConnFactory.createTopicConnection();
    topicSession = topicConnection.createTopicSession(false, Ses-
sion.AUTO_ACKNOWLEDGE);

} catch (NamingException ne) {
    ne.printStackTrace();
} catch ( JMSException je) {
    je.printStackTrace();
} catch (Exception e) {
    e.printStackTrace();
}


}
```

Unlike session and entity beans, MDBs don't have local and remote interfaces. When messages arrive, the container automatically invokes the onMessage(msg) method in the bean instance and passes the message as a parameter. Verify whether the received message is of the ObjectMessage type using the instance of the objMsg.getObject() method. Then, use the getter methods to extract and write out scheduleID, studentID, and the date.

```
public void onMessage(Message inMessage)
{
    System.out.println(" -- In RosterMDB - onMessage() -- \n\n");
    RosterVO rosterVO = null;

    try {
        if( inMessage instanceof ObjectMessage)
        {
            ObjectMessage objMsg = (ObjectMessage) inMessage;
            msgID = objMsg.getJMSMessageID();
            rosterVO = (RosterVO) objMsg.getObject();

        } else {
        // insert into database
        // throws Exception
    rosterDAO = new RosterDAO();
```

```
rosterDAO.insert(rosterVO);
//create a message to publish
callPublisher(rosterVO.getScheduleID());
} catch (MessageFormatException me)
```

Using the `RosterDAO` helper class, invoke `insert()`, an insert method, to insert the retrieved data into a roster table in the database. (This is discussed further in Step 3 below.) The `ejbRemove()` method is called by the container before the container ejects the bean instance from memory.

The second part of `RosterMDB`, the `callPublisher()` method, retrieves the `studentID` list with the help of the `getStudentList()` method, creates a session to connect to the topic destination, and then adds the student list and the previous message's correlation ID to the message "TextMessage message type" and then publishes it. Notice that the `publish()` method takes `TextMessage` as an argument, sets the delivery mode to `persistent`, sends it with default priority and a value of zero to indicate that the message has no expiration date.

```
public void callPublisher(String scheduleID)
{
  try {
    if (rosterDAO == null) rosterDAO = new RosterDAO();
    String textList = rosterDAO.selectStudents(schedID);
    publisher = topicSession.createPublisher(topic);
    TextMessage textMessage = topicSession.createTextMessage();
     textMessage.setText("Publishing Search Results :"+textList);
     textMessage.setJMSCorrelationID(msgID);

    publisher.publish(textMessage,
        javax.jms.DeliveryMode.PERSISTENT,
        javax.jms.Message.DEFAULT_PRIORITY,0
        );
  } catch (MessageFormatException me) {
      me.printStackTrace();
      ...............................
}
```

Step 3: Implementing the Helper Class

We've separated the database access logic from `RosterMDB` and separated it in the `RosterDAO` class. JNDI lookup is used to access the datasource in the constructor of the `RosterDAO`. The `RosterDAO` methods `getConnection()`, `closeConnection()`, `closeResultSet()`, and `closeStatement()` are used to manipulate the connection to the data source.

After extracting the `RosterVO` object from the message, `RosterMDB` then invokes the `insert()` method on `RosterDAO`, which inserts the `scheduleID`, `studentID`, and `date` in the database table, `roster`. `RosterDAO` uses the Prepared Statement feature of the JDBC API to create the SQL statement; use `executeUpdate()` to run the SQL statement.

Let's look at the code fragment showing the implementation of the JNDI lookup and the `insert()` and `selectStudents()` methods in the `RosterDAO` helper class:

```
//JNDI lookup for datasource
            InitialContext ictx = new InitialContext();
            dataSource = (DataSource)
 ictx.lookup("java:comp/env/jdbc/JCampDS");
            System.out.println("RosterDAO jcampDataSource lookup OK!");

        } catch (NamingException ne) {
          throw new  RosterDAOException("NamingException while

public void insert(RosterVO rosterVO) throws RosterDAOException
    {

    System.out.println("RosterDAO   - insert() ");
    PreparedStatement pstmt = null;

    Connection conn = this.getConnection();

    try
    {
//do the actual insert into the roster table.
        pstmt = conn.prepareStatement("Insert into roster(Sched-
uleID, StudentID, theDate) values(?,?,?)");

        pstmt.setString(1, rosterVO.getScheduleID());
        pstmt.setString(2, rosterVO.getStudentID());
        System.out.println("after setting scheduleID and stu-
dentID****\n");

        pstmt.setDate(3, rosterVO.getTheDate());

          System.out.println(" RosterDAO  prepared statment OK");

          pstmt.executeUpdate();
          System.out.println(" RosterDAO roster inserted");

        } catch(SQLException se) {
            throw new RosterDAOException(" Query exception
"+se.getMessage());
```

```
    } finally {
        closeStatement (pstmt);
        closeConnection(conn);
    }
  System.out.println("RosterDAO  - insert done");


}
```

The selectStudent() method executes the SQL select and retrieves the studentID and returns it to the RosterMDB. Notice that the query statement (selectStatement) consists of SELECT, which selects from the roster table all studentID values that contain the scheduleID value passed as an argument. The method then creates a String studentIDList (which consists of studentID values retrieved from the roster table) and returns the list to the MDB instance.

```
public String selectStudents(String schedID) throws RosterDAOException
  {
    String studentIDList = "List: ";
    PreparedStatement pstmt = null;
    Connection conn = this.getConnection();
    try {
        String selectStatement = "SELECT studentID FROM roster WHERE
ScheduleID= ?";
        pstmt = conn.prepareStatement(selectStatement);

        pstmt.setString(1, schedID);
        ResultSet rset = pstmt.executeQuery();
        while(rset.next())
          {
            studentIDList = studentIDList +", "+rset.getString("stu-
dentID");
          }
        pstmt.close();
        conn.close();
    } catch(SQLException se) {
            throw new RosterDAOException(" SQL exception while
attempting to open connection ="+se.getMessage());
          }

    return studentIDList;
  }
```

Step 4: Compiling RosterMDB, RosterVO, and RosterDAO

Now, we're ready to compile the MDB application, so change directory to APPHOME \chapter13\roster and run **compileMDB** to compile and generate the following classes: RosterMDB.class, RosterDAO.class, and RosterDAOException.class. Next, change directory to APPHOME\chapter 13\common and execute **compile.bat,** which compiles and generates the `RosterVO.class` file. Before we can package the MDB application, we need to implement the clients.

Step 5: Writing the Servlet JMS Client `MessageSender`

The `MessageSender` is a JMS servlet client—its job is to process an HTML form request, create the `RosterVO` value object, encapsulate the `RosterVO` in a JMS `ObjectMessage`, and then send the `RosterVO` to a queue destination.

The following code snippet shows the JNDI lookup for the `TheQueFactory` and `TheQue` in the `init()` method. Then, the queue connection and the queue session are created. These are the same administrative objects in this application—all cooperating JMS clients—used to send and receive messages. Recall that the `RosterMDB` also used JNDI lookup to retrieve and use the same `java:comp/env/jms/TheQueFactory` and `java:comp/env/jms/TheQue` to create the queue connection and session to read the messages. The `MessageSender` depends on the very same administrative objects to create the necessary objects to send messages to the queue.

```
public void init()
{
    QueueConnectionFactory queConnFactory = null;
//look up jndi context
    try {
    jndictx = new InitialContext();

    queConnFactory = (QueueConnectionFactory)
jndictx.lookup("java:comp/env/jms/TheQueFactory");
        que = (Queue) jndictx.lookup("java:comp/env/jms/TheQue");
```

The `queConnection` is created, followed by the creation of `queSession`, which is nontransactional but supports auto-acknowledgment, as shown in the code fragment that follows.

```
//setup for P2P - get the Queue destination and sesssion setup
        queConnection = queConnFactory.createQueueConnection();
        queSession = queConnection.createQueueSession(false,
    Session.AUTO_ACKNOWLEDGE);
        } catch (NamingException ne) {
```

The `doPost()` method extracts the `ScheduleID` and `StudentID` value from the request object and then creates a current date. The fields are then used to create a `RosterVO` value object. The `sendMessage()` method is then invoked.

The sendMessage() method creates a QueueSender object. Next, it creates an ObjectMessage object. Finally, it takes the RosterVO, wraps it within this object message format, and sends it to the queue destination.

```
public void doPost(HttpServletRequest req, HttpServletResponse resp)
{
    System.out.println("*********** RosterClient ***********\n");
//extract the schedule and student id from the form
    String schedID = req.getParameter("ScheduleID");
    String studentID = req.getParameter("StudentID");
//convert java.util.Date to java.sql.Date
    Calendar currentTime = Calendar.getInstance();
    java.sql.Date now = new java.sql.Date((currentTime.get-
Time()).getTime());

rosterVO = new RosterVO(schedID, studentID, now);

    boolean flag = sendMessage(rosterVO);
        if (flag)
           System.out.println("Message Sent!");
        else
           System.out.println("Message Not Sent!");

}

public boolean sendMessage(RosterVO obj)
{
    QueueSender queSender = null;

  try {
//create the sender object
    queSender = queSession.createSender(que);
//create a ObjectMessage type
    ObjectMessage objMessage = queSession.createObjectMessage();
//encapsulate the rosterVO in ObjectMessage
    objMessage.setObject(obj);
//now send the ObjectMessage to the destination.
    queSender.send(objMessage);
  } catch (JMSException je) {
    System.out.println(" Error in sending message:
"+je.toString());
    return false;
  }

//send message
    return true;
}
```

Step 6: Implementing the JMS Client `DurableSubscriber`

The `DurableSubscriber` is a Java program that implements durable JMS subscriber client logic. It connects to the topic destination, retrieves messages, and prints them out. The program consists of three sections—the first section completes the setup to the administrative objects and creates the connection and session objects in the constructor as in the following code snippet:

```
try {
    jndictx = new InitialContext();
//setup for pub/sub - get the Topic destination and session setup
    topicConnFactory = (TopicConnectionFactory)
jndictx.lookup("java:comp/env/jms/TheTopicFactory");
    topicConnection = topicConnFactory.createTopicConnection();
    topicConnection.setClientID("DurableSubscriber");
    topicSession = topicConnection.createTopicSession(false, Ses-
sion.AUTO_ACKNOWLEDGE);
    topic = (Topic) jndictx.lookup("java:comp/env/jms/TheTopic");

} catch (NamingException ne) {
```

The durable subscriber in the pub/sub model must set the client ID, `setClientID(DurableSubscriber)`, in order for the JMS provider to track the subscribers who have retrieved the messages.

The second section consists of the `subscribeToTopic()` method, which creates the JMS durable subscriber client by passing the topic destination and the string description as arguments and watches for messages arriving at the `Topic` destination. The third section directs the message listener and directs message events to the `MessageHandler` object, which prints the message retrieved from the destination to the terminal.

```
public void subscribeToTopic ()
{
    try {
        TopicSubscriber topicSubscriber = topicSession.create-
DurableSubscriber(topic, "student list");
        topicSubscriber.setMessageListener(new MessageHandler());
        topicConnection.start();
    } catch (JMSException je) {
```

The `MessageHandler` is a simple Java program that implements the `MessageListener` interface and the logic for the `onMessage()` method. The `onMessage()` method extracts the content of the text message and its JMS correlation ID field from the message and is used for tracking messages.

```
public class MessageHandler implements MessageListener
{
    public static void main(String argv[])
    {
        MessageHandler mh = new MessageHandler();
    }
    public void onMessage(Message message)
    {
     try {
        TextMessage textMessage = (TextMessage) message;
        String text = textMessage.getText();
        System.out.println(" Received by Subscriber\n"+text+"\n ===
after message "+message.getJMSCorrelationID());
        } catch(Exception e) {
        System.out.println("Error receiving message from Topic
"+e.getMessage());
        }
    } //onMessage()
} //Message Handler
```

Step 7: Compiling JMS Clients

Before we can package the MDB sample application, we need to compile both the
MessageSender and DurableSubscriber clients. To compile the servlet
client, change directory to APPHOME\chapter13\web\servlet and then run
compile.bat, which compiles and generates the MessageSender.class file.

Next, go to the APPHOME\chapter13\client subdirectory and run **compile.bat**,
which compiles and generates DurableSubscriber.class and
MessageHandler.class.

The Message.htm is a simple HTML form page that is used to send
scheduleID and studentID values for testing purposes.

Step 8: Packaging the EJB Component

Before we can run and deploy our MDB sample application, we must first
package the respective application classfiles into client, ejb, and Web components.

1.   First, create an enterprise archive file to hold the client jar, ejb-jar,
     and war files. Start the j2sdkee application and the deployment tool as dis-
     cussed in the Appendix.

2.   When the deployment tool GUI comes up, select File | New | Application. A
     new application window pops up, showing Application File Name and
     Application Display Name. Use the Browse button to set the location of the

destination directory. For this example, select APPHOME\chapter13. For the file name, enter **RosterApp.ear**, as shown in Figure 13-5. Click OK. A RosterApp file is now created under the Files in the left area of the deployment GUI. Two ear deployment descriptors, `application.xml` and `sun-j2ee-ri.xml`, along with a `MANIFEST.MF` file, are found in the right section of the GUI.

3.   Using the deployment tool, click File | New | Enterprise Bean to open the New Enterprise Bean Wizard. Click Next.

4.   Click Create New EJB File in Application (this is the default). Under EJB Display Name, enter **RosterJAR**.

5.   Click Edit. An Edit Content of `RosterJAR` window appears. Use the top half of this window to browse the directory tree structure. The bottom half of the window shows all the files currently added to the `RosterJAR` file.

6.   Click the `APPHOME\chapter13\roster` directory and highlight the `Roster-DAO.class`, `RosterDAOException.class`, and `RosterMDB.class`, adding them individually. The files should display on the bottom half of the window.

7.   Change the directory to `APPHOME\chapter13\common` and add `Ros-terVO.class`. Figure 13-6 shows the classes added to the `RosterJAR` file.

8.   Click OK. The pop-up window closes, and the added class files are shown on the content section of the Wizard (see Figure 13-7). Click Next.

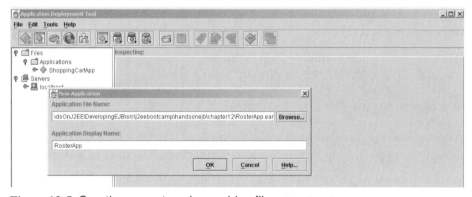

Figure 13-5 Creating an enterprise archive file—`RosterApp.ear`

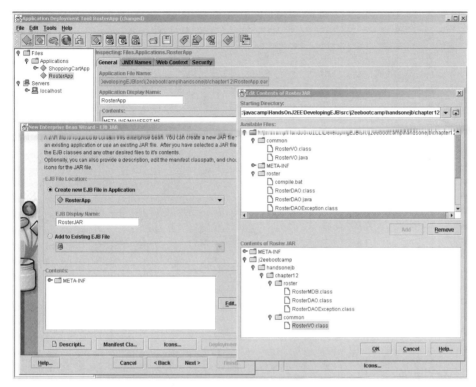

Figure 13-6 Packaging Roster bean into the RosterJAR file

9.   Select Message-Driven under the Bean Type option. Using the Enterprise Bean Class pull-down menu, select `RosterMDB.class`. Enter **RosterEJB** as the Enterprise Bean Name. The Enterprise Bean Display Name should display `RosterEJB` as shown in Figure 13-8. Click Next, as the MDB doesn't have any local or remote interfaces.

10.   Under Transaction Management, select Container Managed. This will show the `onMessage(arg)` method and the default transaction attribute as Required. Leave as is and click Next.

11.   Next, select the destination type, the destination queue name, and the connection factory name. Click Queue. Using the pull-down menu, select MyQue under Destination and MyQueFactory under Connection Factory. The destination, MyQue, and the connection factory, MyQueFactory, were previously created using the Tool | Server Configuration and then selecting the JMS option to add both MyQue and MyQueFactory, as shown in Figure 13-9. (These administrative objects were precreated by the administrator and are discussed in the Appendix.)

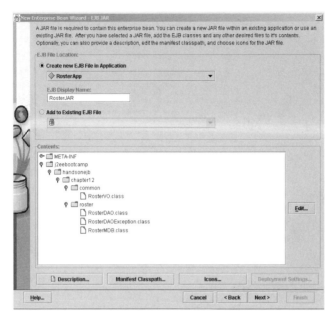

Figure 13-7 Contents of RosterJAR file

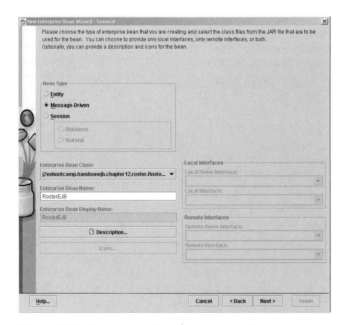

Figure 13-8 Specifying the bean type and class

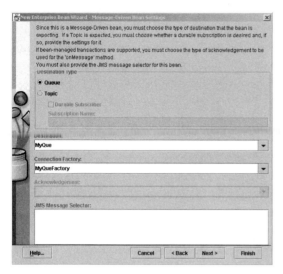

Figure 13-9 Specifying the destination type, destination queue, and connection factory

12. Click Next twice, as we are not setting any Environment Entries Reference in the code and there are no references to EJBs in the code.

13. Use the tool to map the resource referenced in the code to resource factories. In the `ejb-jar` file, map the data source, the destination, and the queue factory. Under Coded Name, enter **jdbc/JCampDS**; select Type from the pull-down menu, and enter **javax.sql.DataSource**. Under Authentication, select Container and check the Sharable option. Under Deployment Setting, set the JNDI Name and enter **jdbc/Cloudscape**. Enter **j2ee** as both the user name and password, as shown in Figure 13-10, and click Next.

14. Now, map the queue connection factory and topic connection factory. Under Coded Name, enter **jms/TheQueFactory**. Under Type, select `javax.jms.QueueConnectionFactory` from the pull-down menu. Set the Authentication to Container and check the Sharable option. Under JNDI Name enter **MyQueFactory**. Use **j2ee** as both user name and password, and then enter **jms/TheTopicFactory** as the Coded Name. Select `javax.jmx.TopicConnectionFactory` from the pull-down menu and enter **MyTopicFactory** as the JNDI name, with **j2ee** as the user name and password (as shown in Figure 13-11).

    The coded names, jdbc/JCampDS, jms/TheTopicFactory, and jms/TheQue-Factory, are the names the JNDI lookup uses to find objects in code. During deployment, these virtual names are mapped to real objects such as jdbc/Cloudscape, MyTopicFactory, and MyQueFactory, which are defined

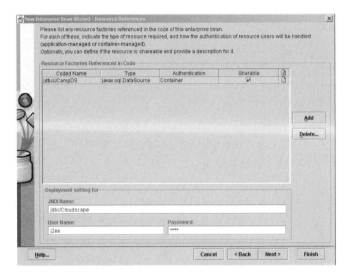

Figure 13-10 Specifying the data source

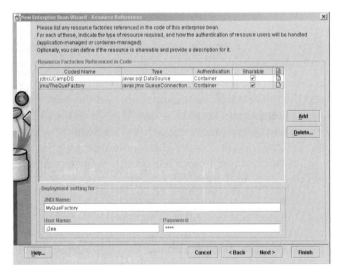

Figure 13-11 Specifying resource factories references and JNDI name

in the target application environment. At runtime, the application is able to access the actual data source object and the QueueConnectionFactory defined in the deployment environment.

15.   Click Next. Click Add and, under Coded Name, enter **jms/TheQue**. For Type, select `javax.jms.Queue` from the pull-down menu and enter

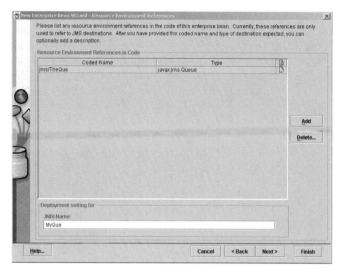

Figure 13-12 Specifying resource environment references

jms/TheTopic. Select `javax.jms.Topic` from the pull-down menu. Under the JNDI name, enter **MyQue** for jms/TheQue and **MyTopic** for jms/TheTopic, as shown in Figure 13-12. Click Next. As there are no security options being set, click Next again. Click Finish to complete the `ejb-jar` file packaging.

The deployment tool should display a `RosterJAR` under the `RosterApp` on the left-hand side of the GUI. The Content section to the right should display the `ejb-jar-ic.jar` file as shown in Figure 13-13.

Creating the Deployment Descriptor

The wizard has collected the input and created a deployment descriptor for the `ejb-jar` file for the `RosterMDB EJB` application. Notice the destination type, the factory, and the resource references such as the JCampDS, TheQueFactory, TheTopicFactory, TheQue, TheTopic, and the `onMessage()` business method are specified in the deployment descriptor.

```
<ejb-jar>
    <display-name>RosterJAR</display-name>
    <enterprise-beans>
    <message-driven>
```

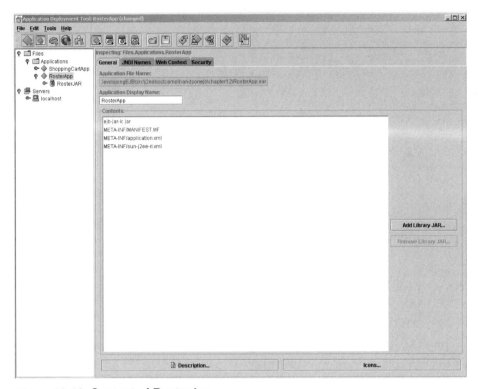

Figure 13-13 Content of RosterApp

```
<display-name>RosterEJB</display-name>
      <ejb-name>RosterEJB</ejb-name>
      <ejb-class>j2eebootcamp.developingEJB.chapter13.roster.Ros-
terMDB</ejb-class>
      <transaction-type>Container</transaction-type>
   <message-driven-destination>
    <destination-type>javax.jms.Queue</destination-type>
   </message-driven-destination>
   <security-identity>
     <description></description>
       <run-as>
         <description></description>
         <role-name></role-name>
       </run-as>
   </security-identity>
   <resource-ref>
     <res-ref-name>jdbc/JCampDS</res-ref-name>
     <res-type>javax.sql.DataSource</res-type>
```

```
      <res-auth>Container</res-auth>
      <res-sharing-scope>Sharable</res-sharing-scope>
    </resource-ref>
    <resource-ref>
      <res-ref-name>jms/TheQueFactory</res-ref-name>
      <res-type>javax.jms.QueueConnectionFactory</res-type>
      <res-auth>Container</res-auth>
      <res-sharing-scope>Sharable</res-sharing-scope>
    </resource-ref>
    <resource-ref>
      <res-ref-name>jms/TheTopicFactory</res-ref-name>
      <res-type>javax.jms.TopicConnectionFactory</res-type>
      <res-auth>Container</res-auth>
      <res-sharing-scope>Sharable</res-sharing-scope>
    </resource-ref>
    <resource-env-ref>
      <resource-env-ref-name>jms/TheQue</resource-env-ref-name>
      <resource-env-ref-type>javax.jms.Queue</resource-env-ref-type>
    </resource-env-ref>
    <resource-env-ref>
      <resource-env-ref-name>jms/TheTopic</resource-env-ref-name>
      <resource-env-ref-type>javax.jms.Topic</resource-env-ref-type>
    </resource-env-ref>
  </message-driven>
</enterprise-beans>
<assembly-descriptor>
  <container-transaction>
    <method>
      <ejb-name>RosterEJB</ejb-name>
      <method-intf>Bean</method-intf>
      <method-name>onMessage</method-name>
      <method-params>
        <method-param>javax.jms.Message</method-param>
      </method-params>
    </method>
    <trans-attribute>Required</trans-attribute>
  </container-transaction>
</assembly-descriptor>
</ejb-jar>
```

Step 9: Packaging the Web Component

Now, we're ready to package the servlet, JSP, and HTML files as Web components for the MDB application.

1. Using the deployment GUI, click File | New | Web Component to open a New Web Component Wizard. Click Next.

2. Select Create New WAR File in Application. Ensure that `RosterApp` is selected in the pull-down menu. Under WAR Display Name, enter **Roster-WAR**. Click Edit. An Edit Content of RosterWAR window appears. Use the top part of this window to navigate to APPHOME\chapter13\web\servlet, and highlight the `MessageSender.class`. Click Add. The Content of Ros-terWAR window should display the added class. Go up a directory and add the `Message.htm` file. Now go back to APPHOME\chapter13\common and add `RosterVO.class` to the `RosterWAR` file. This is shown in Figure 13-14. Click OK.

3. Click Next. The Web component type is servlet. Select Servlet, and then click Next again.

4. Use the pull-down menu to select `MessageSender` as the Servlet Class. `MessageSender` should automatically appear as the Web Component

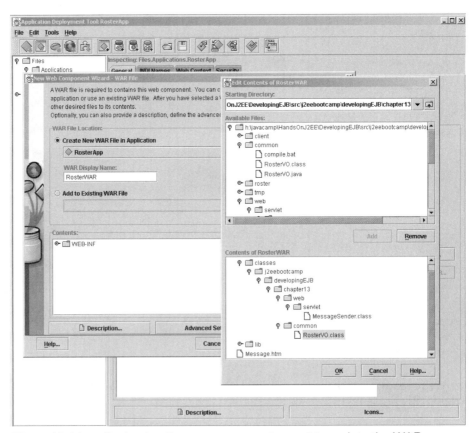

Figure 13-14 Packaging the `MessageSender.Client` into the WAR file

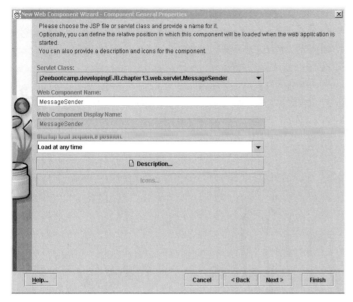

Figure 13-15 Specifying the client name and type

Name. Leave the startup load sequence position to the default load at any time, as shown in Figure 13-15.

5. Click Next twice, as there are no initialization parameters being set. Click Add and enter **RosterAlias**. The alias is useful because it enables the developer to give a virtual name and map it to the actual Web component on the server. Click Next until Resource References appears.

6. Click Add. Under Coded Name, enter **jms/TheQueFactory**. Under the Type pull-down menu, select `javax.jms.QueueConnectionFactory`. Under Authentication, select Container. Check the Sharable option. Under the JNDI Name, enter **MyQueFactory** with **j2ee** for both the user name and password. See Figure 13-16 for an example.

7. Click Next. Enter **jms/TheQue** under Coded Name and take the default value, `javax.jms.Queue` as the Type, and for JNDI name enter **MyQue**, as shown in Figure 13-17.

8. Click Add on the Welcome Files area. Using the pull-down menu, select the `Message.htm` file as illustrated in Figure 13-18. Click Next twice.

9. Click Finish. Note the `RosterWAR` file under the `RosterApp` on the left-hand side of the deployment GUI as well as the JNDI Names and references (as shown in Figure 13-19).

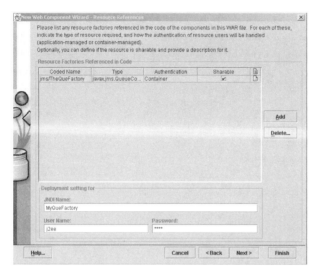

Figure 13-16 Specifying the resource factory reference and JNDI name

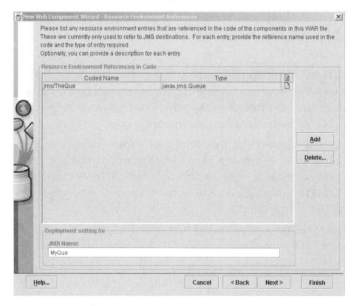

Figure 13-17 Specifying the queue destination and JNDI name

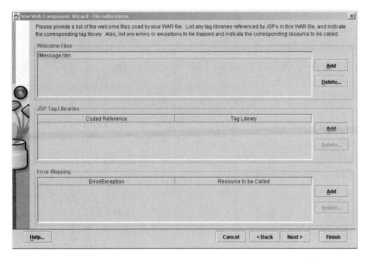

Figure 13-18 Specifying the default home page

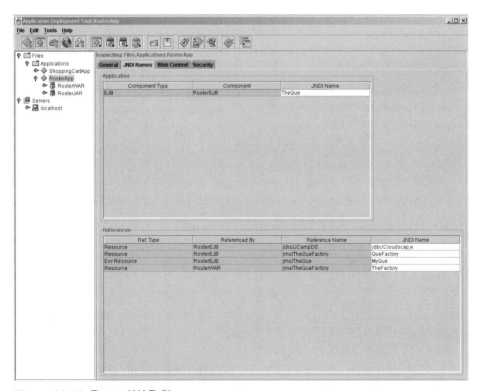

Figure 13-19 RosterWAR file

Deployment Descriptor for the Web Component

The deployment tool has recorded the inputs and created a deployment descriptor file (web.xml) for the Web component (as listed below).

```
<web-app>
    <display-name>RosterWAR</display-name>
    <servlet>
    <servlet-name>MessageSender</servlet-name>
    <display-name>MessageSender</display-name>
    <servlet-class>j2eebootcamp.developingEJB.chapter13.web.serv-
let.MessageSender</servlet-class>
    </servlet>
    <servlet-mapping>
    <servlet-name>MessageSender</servlet-name>
    <url-pattern>/RosterAlias</url-pattern>
    </servlet-mapping>
    <session-config>
    <session-timeout>30</session-timeout>
    </session-config>
    <welcome-file-list>
   <welcome-file>Message.htm</welcome-file>
    </welcome-file-list>
    <resource-env-ref>
    <resource-env-ref-name>jms/TheQue</resource-env-ref-name>
    <resource-env-ref-type>javax.jms.Queue</resource-env-ref-type>
    </resource-env-ref>
    <resource-ref>
    <res-ref-name>jms/TheQueFactory</res-ref-name>
    <res-type>javax.jms.QueueConnectionFactory</res-type>
    <res-auth>Container</res-auth>
    </resource-ref>
</web-app>
```

Step 10: Packaging the Client into a Jar File

Next, we need to package `DurableSubscriber` and `MessageHandler` as a client jar file.

1. On the deployment tool, select File | New | Application Client, and click Next. Then click the Edit button that appears. Select the client icon and then add `DurableSubscriber.class` and `MessageHandler.class` as shown in Figure 13-20.

2. Click OK and then click Next. Use the pull-down menu to select Durable-Subscriber under the Main class heading. The display name should also show `DurableSubscriber` as shown in Figure 13-21.

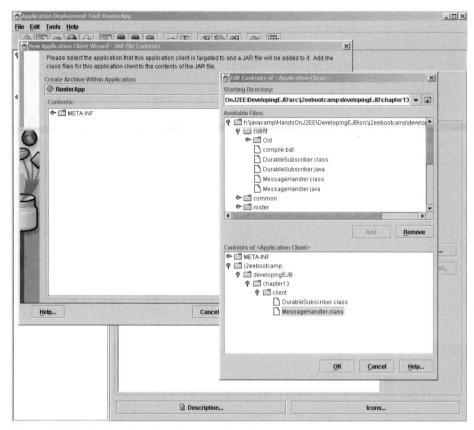

Figure 13-20 Packaging the client application

3. Click Next several times until the Resource Factory window appears. Click the Add button and enter **jms/TheTopicFactory** under Coded Name. Select the `javax.jms.TopicConnectionFactory` under Type; then select Sharable. For JNDI name, enter **MyTopicFactory** with **j2ee** as the user name and password, as shown in Figure 13-22.

4. Click Next, and then click the Add button. Enter **jms/TheTopic** under Coded Name and select `javax.jmx.Topic` from the Type pull-down menu. As the JNDI name, enter **MyTopic** and click Next, which displays the deployment descriptor. Then click Finish, and you're done with packaging the Roster application.

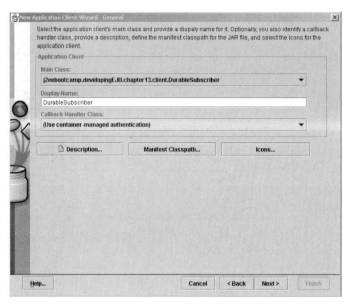

Figure 13-21 Specifying the client's class and display name

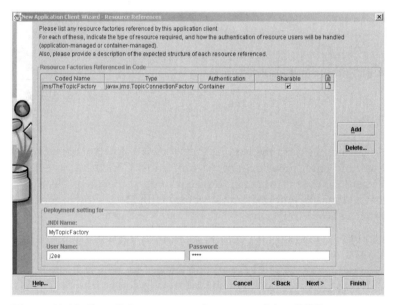

Figure 13-22 Specifying resource factory and the JNDI name

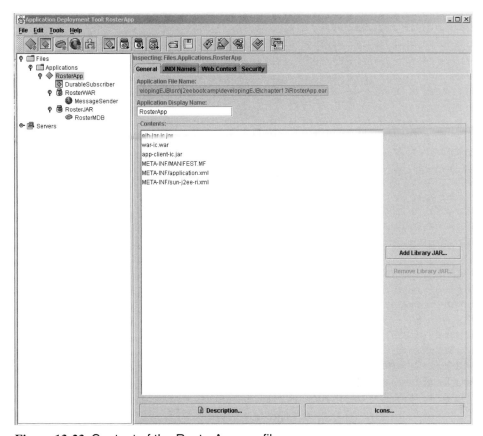

Figure 13-23 Content of the RosterApp.ear file—
`DurableSubscriber`, `RosterWAR`, and `RosterJAR`

5.   Select the General tab on the right-hand side of the GUI to see `ejb-jar-ic.jar`, `app-client-ic.jar`, and `war-ic.war` as well as `sun-j2ee-ri.xml`, `application.xml`, and `MANIFEST.MF` under the `META-INF` directory in the Content section of the GUI. This is shown in Figure 13-23.

The client-jar deployment descriptor is shown next.

```
<application-client>
    <display-name>DurableSubscriber</display-name>
    <resource-ref>
    <res-ref-name>jms/TheTopicFactory</res-ref-name>
    <res-type>javax.jms.TopicConnectionFactory</res-type>
    <res-auth>Container</res-auth>
    <res-sharing-scope>Sharable</res-sharing-scope>
```

```
      </resource-ref>
      <resource-env-ref>
      <resource-env-ref-name>jms/TheTopic</resource-env-ref-name>
      <resource-env-ref-type>javax.jms.Topic</resource-env-ref-type>
      </resource-env-ref>
  </application-client>
```

Step 11: Deploying the Application

To deploy the `RosterApp.ear` file, do the following:

1. Select Tools | Deploy and the Deploy RosterApp window appears. Under Object to Deploy, `RosterApp` should display. If not, use the pull-down menu to select it. Under Target Server, select the local host. Check Save Object before deploying. Then click Next. (See Figure 13-24.)

2. Verify the JNDI naming setup and change if needed. (See Figure 13-25.)

3. Click Next. Set the ContextRoot to /RosterContextRoot as shown in Figure 13-26.

4. Click Next twice and then click Finish. The deployment tool starts the deployment process. See Figure 13-27.

Step 12: Testing the Application

Test the Roster application by opening a browser and entering the URL **http://localhost:8000/RosterContextRoot.** This brings up the `Message.htm` file as shown in Figure 13-28. Use it to submit a schedule and student user name

Figure 13-24 Specifying the application and host for deployment

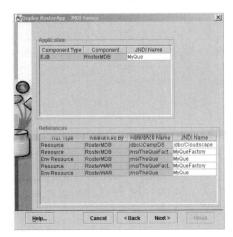

Figure 13-25 Verifying the JNDI name setting

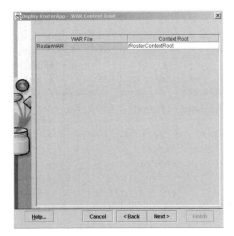

Figure 13-26 Specifying the Web context root for the application

identification. The `RosterMDB` accepts the message, writes the content of the user input to the window terminal, and then inserts the schedule and student identification along with a date into a roster database table.

Figure 13-28 depicts the `Message.htm` page with the user input `ScheduleID` set to EJB-300 and `StudentID` set to `pvt@javacamp.com` before the form is submitted.

Figure 13-27 shows the output from a `RosterMDB` to the Windows terminal. Keep the `ScheduleID` set to EJB-300 and change the `StudentID` to a different e-mail

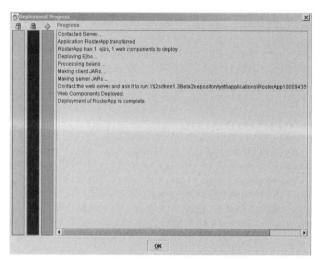

Figure 13-27 Successful deployment

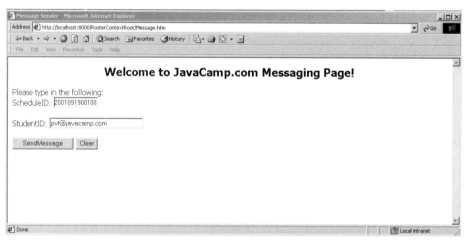

Figure 13-28 HTML form to send message to the MDB

address and submit the form several times (for example, submit another form with `studentID` set to tom@sun.com). According to the design, the `RosterMDB` should be publishing a list of students who have registered for EJB-300 as a persistent message. Now, we'll execute `DurableSubscriber` and see whether we can retrieve any of those messages.

Change the directory to APPHOME\chapter13 and run the client application as follows:

```
APPHOME\chapter13\runclient -client RosterApp.ear -name Durable-
Subscriber GetMessage -textauth
```

and then click Enter. You'll be asked to enter user name and password—enter **j2ee** for both, and the subscriber client retrieves the messages and displays them on the terminal as shown in Figure 13-29. Notice that the list in the message gets longer as new users are being added to the roster.

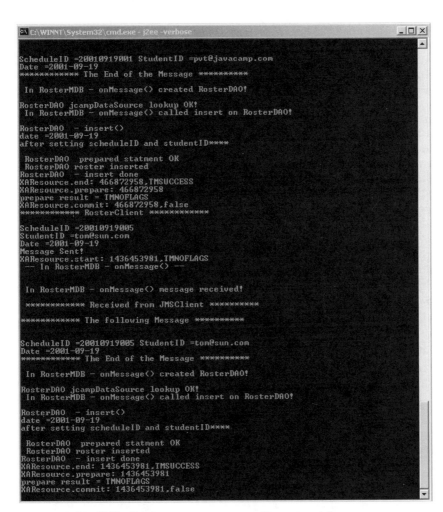

Figure 13-29 JMS client `DurableSubscriber` receiving messages

RosterApp Deployment Descriptors

There are several deployment descriptors created in the process of deploying the Roster application: the `RosterApp.ear` with all the deployment descriptors and the class file that make up the `ejb-jar` and `war` files.

The `RosterApp.ear` package contained three deployment descriptors—standard J2EE, `application.xml`, and vendor-specific `sun-j2ee-ri.xml`. The `application.xml` descriptor contains information about the content of the `RosterApp.ear` file, including the ejb-jar component, the Web component, and the root context for the application to be used during deployment.

```
<application>
    <display-name>RosterApp</display-name>
    <description>Application description</description>
    <module>
    <web>
      <web-uri>war-ic.war</web-uri>
      <context-root>/RosterContextRoot</context-root>
    </web>
    </module>
    <module>
    <java>app-client-ic.jar</java>
    </module>
    <module>
    <ejb>ejb-jar-ic.jar</ejb>
    </module>
</application>
```

The `sun-j2ee-ri.xml` deployment descriptor file consists of information targeted to a specific vendor's application server—our example is specific to Sun's Reference Implementation Server. In general, this deployment descriptor deals with the high-level reference to JNDI name mapping for both Web and EJB components. Applicable lines are highlighted in the code fragment that follows. All information was derived during the deployment process. Also note that this file has no component-specific information, but most assembly-specific information is handled differently by different application servers.

```
<?xml version="1.0" encoding="UTF-8"?>
<!DOCTYPE j2ee-ri-specific-information PUBLIC '-//Sun Microsystems
Inc.//DTD J2EE Reference Implementation 1.3//EN' 'http://local-
host:8000/sun-j2ee-ri_1_3.dtd'>

<j2ee-ri-specific-information>
    <server-name></server-name>
    <rolemapping />
```

```
<web>
<module-name>war-ic.war</module-name>
<context-root>/RosterContextRoot</context-root>
<resource-ref>
   <res-ref-name>jms/TheQueFactory</res-ref-name>
   <jndi-name>MyQueFactory</jndi-name>
   <default-resource-principal>
     <name>j2ee</name>
     <password>j2ee</password>
   </default-resource-principal>
</resource-ref>
<resource-env-ref>
   <resource-env-ref-name>jms/TheQue</resource-env-ref-name>
   <jndi-name>MyQue</jndi-name>
</resource-env-ref>
</web>
<enterprise-beans>
<module-name>ejb-jar-ic.jar</module-name>
<unique-id>0</unique-id>
<ejb>
   <ejb-name>RosterMDB</ejb-name>
   <jndi-name>MyQue</jndi-name>
   <ior-security-config>
     <transport-config>
       <integrity>supported</integrity>
       <confidentiality>supported</confidentiality>
       <establish-trust-in-target>supported</establish-trust-in-
target>
       <establish-trust-in-client>supported</establish-trust-in-
client>
     </transport-config>
     <as-context>
       <auth-method>username_password</auth-method>
       <realm>default</realm>
       <required>true</required>
     </as-context>
     <sas-context>
       <caller-propagation>supported</caller-propagation>
     </sas-context>
   </ior-security-config>
   <principal>
     <name></name>
   </principal>
   <resource-ref>
     <res-ref-name>jdbc/JCampDS</res-ref-name>
     <jndi-name>jdbc/Cloudscape</jndi-name>
     <default-resource-principal>
       <name>j2ee</name>
```

```
            <password>j2ee</password>
          </default-resource-principal>
        </resource-ref>
        <resource-ref>
          <res-ref-name>jms/TheQueFactory</res-ref-name>
          <jndi-name>MyQueFactory</jndi-name>
        </resource-ref>
        <resource-env-ref>
          <resource-env-ref-name>jms/TheQue</resource-env-ref-name>
          <jndi-name>MyQue</jndi-name>
        </resource-env-ref>
        <gen-classes />
        <mdb-connection-factory>MyQueFactory</mdb-connection-factory>
      </ejb>
    </enterprise-beans>
  </j2ee-ri-specific-information>
```

The `ejb-ic.jar` file had one deployment descriptor file: `ejb-jar.xml`. This deployment descriptor is specific to the EJB component; it maps names to a specific class and defines the EJB type, as we discussed previously.

The `war-ic.war` file contained one deployment descriptor—`web.xml`. This deployment descriptor is read by the Web container at runtime and contains information on the Web component, which we looked at earlier during the application packaging process.

Summary

In this chapter we discussed how message-driven beans provide an option to implement business logic that doesn't require synchronous communication. MDBs are stateless, can be pooled, and provide a fast, reliable guaranteed messaging solution. MDBs support both P2P and the pub/sub messaging model. Our example implemented both these messaging models. We also discussed the rules and requirements for writing `ejbCreate()`, `onMessage()`, and `ejbRemove()` methods and the MDB class.

ADVANCED TOPICS

TRANSACTIONS

Topics in This Chapter

Chapter 14

In Part 2 of this book, we purposely deferred discussing transaction and focused on fundamentals of understanding and implementing stateless and stateful session beans, bean-managed and container-managed persistent entity beans, and message-driven beans. In Part 3, we explore more advanced topics. This chapter covers topics dealing with transactions, including:

- an introduction to transactions and their benefits
- the transaction model
- the ACID properties of transactions
- the six transaction attributes
- programmatic versus declarative transactions
- transactional behaviors of stateful, BMP, and CMP entity beans
- issues in initiating transactions
- bean-managed versus container-managed transaction demarcation
- isolation levels
- the roles played by each party involved in developing and implementing transactions

An Introduction to Transactions and Their Benefits

Before discussing the value proposition of transactions, let's first examine the mechanics of an enterprise application, specifically, a Web application that allows users to register for Java training courses. This scenario involves a user searching for his or her desired Java courses, registering for the courses, and attending the training courses.

The registration process consists of the following logic:

- check course availability
- register for course and make payment
- registration confirmation

Transaction Methods and Pseudocodes

Assuming that this logic is encapsulated in three different beans, let's determine the methods and pseudocodes representing the subtasks these methods would encapsulate.

ScheduleBean

```
checkAvailability(ShoppingList classList)
{
    Verify the availability of the classes.
}
```

RegistrationBean

```
registerForClass(Schedule schedule)
{
    Reserve a seat in the class.
    Adjust the availability of "open seats" in the class.
}

sendConfirmation(ShoppingList classList, Student student)
{
    Update the accounting application with the registration
    information.
    E-mail registration information to the student.
}
```

```
PaymentBean

  makePayment(Card cc)
  {
      Verify the credit card.
      Calculate tax and add to total.
      Debit the total amount from the student's bank account.
      Credit the total amount to the company's account.
  }
```

```
Client

  scheduleBean.checkAvailability(list);
  registrationBean.registerForClass(schedule);
  paymentBean.makePayment(cc#);
  registrationBean.sendConfirmation();
```

The Impact of Failures

Let's take a scenario in which a student is attempting to register for a Java course using a client and the "Update the accounting application with the registration information" logic in the sendConfirmation() method of the RegistrationBean. It fails due to an accounting software crash on a remote machine. The previous subtasks, such as debiting the credit card company's account, would have to be undone, the student's bank account would need to be credited, the student would have to removed from the class roster, and the number of open seats for this class would have to be readjusted. The logic to handle failure has to be implemented for the application.

One possible implementation for managing such a failure is to wrap the methods in each line in the client application, within the try-catch block, and by writing the appropriate logic to handle all possible failures. This would consist of many nested try-catch blocks with logic to handle all sorts of errors. Implementing error handling with try and catch would not only prove to be an arduous programming task, but the lines of code would also increase significantly, as would the debugging effort. Our example registration logic is fairly simple—consider the complexity of real-world business applications.

Furthermore, error handling is just one issue. In a distributed, multiuser environment, data consistency and isolation also have to be considered. Application developers must consider:

- How can the developer easily group interdependent subtasks executed in different beans into one task so that if one of the subtasks were to fail, the entire task would be forced to fail?

- How can the developer provide a consistent user view of the data and avoid data corruption while it's being accessed and updated by different users?

- How can the developer isolate the actions of one user from others who are all using the same application and modifying the shared data?

- How can the developer guarantee that the results of business operations are saved permanently and available in the future?

Transactions are the solution and are an integral part of EJB architecture. Transaction functionality frees developers from having to handle failure recovery and multiuser programming issues, thus simplifying programming business logic.

Transactions allow developers to take a series of business subtasks in an application and combine them into one large atomic task. At runtime, the EJB container executes the business subtasks serially and ensures that each of these subtasks are either successfully completed (in which case the result of the task is saved) or a failure. A failure in any of the subtasks results in the failure of the task, and the results of all the participating subtasks must then be rolled back and undone. In the previous example, transaction functionality enables the `checkAvail-ability()`, `registerForClass()`, `makePayments()`, and `sendConfirmation()` methods in four different EJBs to be grouped as one atomic task, or one transaction. As such, either all the methods in the transaction are completed successfully and the transaction is successful (the results of the methods are saved), or if one method fails, the transaction fails and is rolled back (the results of previous methods are undone) in the bean instance. See Figure 14-1.

Types of Transactions

There are four types of transactions: nested, flat, chained, and sagas. This section focuses on nested and flat transactions.

A *nested transaction* can have one or more level of transactions, as shown in Figure 14-2, where the circle represents the transaction. The nested transaction model can have one or more child transactions and can share data and handle partial aborts. It has a parent/child relationship with nested transactions enabling parent transactions to manage multiple child transactions. Note that the failure of one child transaction doesn't necessarily result in the entire transaction being aborted. Nested transactions map well to many real-world situations such as planning an airplane trip from San Francisco to Kathmandu, where the parent transaction

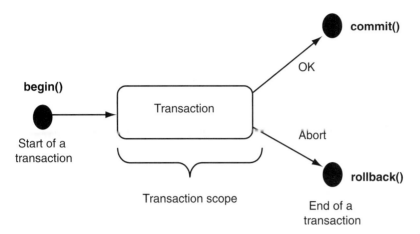

Figure 14-1 The fundamentals of a transaction

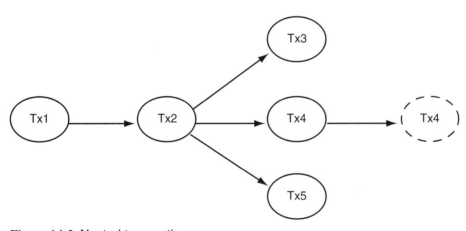

Figure 14-2 Nested transaction

controls multiple child transactions such as find the best air-fare and route from San Francisco to Tokyo. Another child transaction could consist of multiple child transactions to figure out all the possible routes from Tokyo to Kathmandu. Nested transactions aren't required by the EJB 2.0 specification but may be supported in the future.

Flat transactions are simple. Flat transactions support only a single transaction; nested child transactions aren't supported. If a new transaction needs to start, the previous transaction is suspended and waits until the new transaction completes

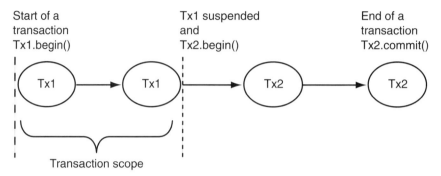

Start of a
transaction
Tx1.begin()

Tx1 suspended
and
Tx2.begin()

End of a
transaction
Tx2.commit()

Transaction scope

Figure 14-3 Flat transaction

before continuing. Data associated with a successful flat transaction is saved in a persistent store; if it fails, the updated data is rolled back. Figure 14-3 illustrates a flat transaction. Flat transactions are simpler, easier to implement, and are supported by the EJB 2.0 container provider.

Benefits of Transactions

Implementing low-level transactional features into business logic is an extremely complicated and difficult task best left to transaction gurus and the EJB container. However, EJB's support for transactions enable developers to focus efforts on implementing complex business logic rather than writing code to handle concurrency, consistency, and durability of the business data.

EJBs enable developers to delegate the task of handling transactions to the EJB container. Developers can implement EJB transactions programmatically or declaratively. The declarative implementation enables assemblers and/or deployers to modify the EJB transactional features.

Participants in a Transaction

A transaction can involve a number of participants:

- *Transactional objects*—These are the main participants: the business objects in a transaction. These objects interact among themselves and usually play the role of requestor or responder objects. These roles are interchangeable. Figure 14-4 shows EJB1 as a responder to a client and a requestor to EJB2.
  - *Requestor*—A transactional object in a requestor role makes requests to other transactional or nontransactional objects. A requestor can be a fat client, a Web component, or an EJB that invokes business methods. A

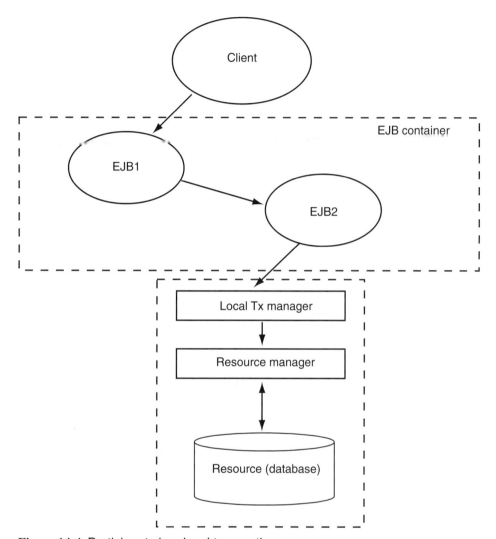

Figure 14-4 Participants in a local transaction

requestor can also be a responder for another requestor. The requestor object is labeled "client" and "EJB1" in Figure 14-4.

- *Responder*—A transactional object in a responder role executes the business logic on behalf of the requestor. A responder usually consists of the server and an EJB component that is executing the business method on behalf of the client. The responder can be a requestor to other transactional objects as shown via EJB1 and EJB2 in Figure 14-4.

- *Resource*—A resource is a type of permanent data store that the transactional objects can read from and write to. In most cases, it's usually a relational database, but it can also be a JMS connection or an ERP system. In this chapter, the term "resource" represents the database. Transactional components don't access resources directly but rather delegate that task via the EJB container to the local transaction manager and resource manager.

- *Resource manager*—A resource manager is an interface that interacts with resources. The resource manager sits between the local transaction manager and the resources (such as the native database implementation) and translates the request from the container to the resources. The resource managers are resource type and vendor specific. For example, a resource manager from Oracle is specific to the Oracle database, as the resource manager for DB2 is specific to DB2. The communication protocol between resource managers and their resources are usually proprietary.

- *Local transaction manager*—The local transaction manager sits between the resource manager and the EJB container. Like the resource manager, the local transaction manager is also vendor and resource-manager specific and can only manage transactions limited to a single database type. For example, a local transaction manager for an Oracle database can manage transactions only for Oracle but not for Sybase. Local transaction managers use the XA communication protocol to communicate with the distributed transaction manager. The X/Open's XA communication protocol is the industry standard widely supported by most vendors.

- *Distributed transaction manager*—A distributed transaction manager's task is to coordinate transactions across the listed local transaction managers and to perform two-phase commits in a distributed transaction. The distributed transaction manager can be part of the EJB server; with some EJB servers, however, different transaction servers/managers can be plugged in. The EJB container delegates the task of performing the two-phase commit to the distributed transaction manager. It uses the X/Open multivendor-supported XA protocol to coordinate and interact with local transaction managers. With local transactions the container can bypass the distributed transaction manager and use its local optimized data layer to communicate with the resource manager via the local transaction manager as shown in Figure 14-4. Unlike the local transaction managers, the distributed transaction managers can coordinate transactions involving different databases such as Oracle, Sybase, and DB2 via their respective local transaction managers.

The Transaction Model

There are two transaction models: local and distributed. The model used is based on participation of the resource managers.

Local Transactions

The *local transaction model* is simple and fast. Participants include a local transaction manager, a resource manager that handles one or more resources, and one or more transactional objects. The distributed transaction manager isn't included. All interaction between the transaction objects, such as the EJB component with the database, must be made via the local transaction manager to the resource manager. The resource manager manages interactions with the database. See Figure 14-4.

Distributed Transactions

The *distributed model* is complex and involves two-phase commits. Participants include the transaction objects, local transaction managers, resource managers, resources, and the distributed transaction manager. The distributed transaction manager is the coordinator of the two-phase commit and makes the final decision as to whether the transaction is to be committed or rolled back. Distributed transactions are shown in Figure 14-5, which illustrates a distributed transaction manager coordinating the transaction between two local transaction managers using the standard XA protocol. The local transaction managers in turn communicate with the databases using the resource managers.

Figure 14-5 is a simple configuration of a distributed transaction with a distributed transaction manager in an EJB server coordinating two local transaction managers. In a complex configuration, there can be several EJB servers with multiple local transaction managers participating in a single transaction, being coordinated by a single distributed transaction manager.

Two-Phase Commit

Distributed transactions must support a *two-phase commit*; transaction managers rely on a two-phase commit to coordinate the transaction. A two-phase commit is often abbreviated as TPC or 2PC (see Figure 14-6 for an illustration).

In **phase one** (the ready to commit phase), using the XA protocol, the distributed transaction manager sends the **1. prepare to commit updates** command (as shown in Figure 14-6) to all the local transaction managers participating in the transaction. Each local transaction manager is responsible for writing the details of the data operation to the transaction log, creating a local transaction, and notifying their respective resource managers of the operation. The resource manager completes the processing steps short of committing the changes to its resource(s) and then returns a status to the local transaction manager. If the status

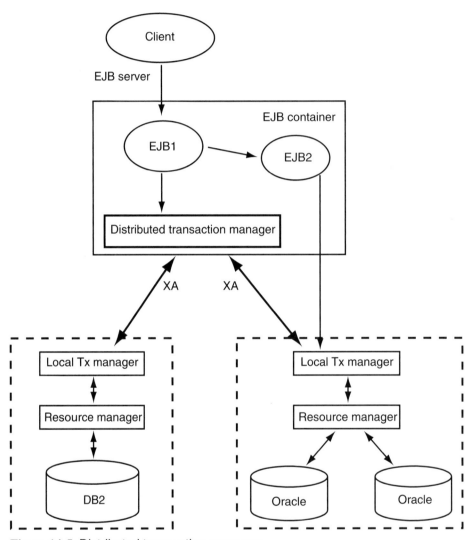

Figure 14-5 Distributed transaction manager

is a success, then the local transaction manager responds to the distributed transaction manager with a **2a. ready to commit** vote. If even one local transaction manager encounters an error and is unable to respond back with a **2a.ready to commit** vote but instead responds with a **2b commit error**, the distributed transaction manager aborts the entire transaction. Only if all the participating local transaction managers respond with **2a. ready to commit**, will the distributed transaction manager enter phase two.

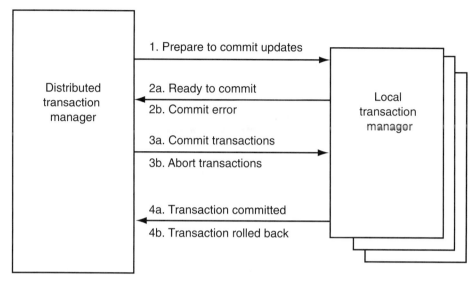

Figure 14-6 Two-phase commit

In **phase two** (the commit phase), if the prepare phase was successful (that is, if a unanimous vote to commit occurred), then the distributed transaction manager issues the **3a. commit transactions** command to all the participating local transaction managers. Each of the local transaction managers then send a commit command to their respective resource managers, which attempts to commit the updates performed in the prepare phase and responds back to the local transaction manager with either a success or a failure command. The local transaction managers respond with **4a. transaction committed** if they successfully commit the updates and the results of the transaction are saved. If any local transaction manager reports back with a failure, then the distributed transaction managers issue a **3b. abort transaction** command to all the local transaction managers. They respond with **4b. transaction rolled back** after issuing a rollback command to all the participating resource managers and roll back the entire transaction. The distributed transaction manager only commits the transaction and ensures that the changes are saved in the persistent store if all the participating transaction managers report back with successful commits.

TPC in distributed transaction is resource-intensive, requires locking/unlocking of distributed resources across multiple servers, and generates high network traffic, thus having a negative performance impact on your application.

Note that most of the complicated, low-level transaction tasks in TPC are transparent to the bean developers.

ACID Properties of a Transaction

Implementing transactions in the EJB platform requires an understanding of the Java Transaction API (JTA) and the Java Transaction Service (JTS). Bean developers are only concerned with JTA, which is used to implement transactions programmatically. JTA is one of the Java technologies required by the J2EE 1.3 and EJB 2.0 specifications and is the preferred way to control transactions programmatically.

The EJB container provider implements JTS. JTS is the Java implementation of CORBA Transaction Service (OTS) 1.1 for a distributed transaction model. The EJB container depends on JTS and IIOP to provide transaction interoperability with other application servers.

To further understand transaction and to appreciate its benefit to bean developers, let's take a look at the basic properties of a transaction known by the acronym ACID (atomicity, consistency, isolation, and durability). ACID is a way to identify the benefits of transactions:

- *Atomicity*—This characteristic gives the bean developer the ability to "group" several methods in different enterprise beans into a single transaction. As such, either all of the methods in the transaction are successful and it commits, or, if one of the methods fails, the transaction is rolled back to its original state. In the Java course registration example, the bean developer can group the `checkAvailability()`, `registerForClass()`, `makePayment()`, and `sendConfirmation()` methods as one transaction. Then, if any of the methods in the transaction fail, the entire transaction is rolled back. If all of the methods are successful, the transaction is committed.

- *Consistency*—Consistency refers to the integrity of the data in the persistent resource, regardless of the outcome of the transaction. Transactions must leave the data in a consistent and predictable state. In the Java course registration example, a student shouldn't be able to register for a class that doesn't exist nor be able to register if the class is full. When the student has successfully registered for a class, he or she should be able to verify registration even if the system crashes.

- *Isolation*—This characteristic deals with concurrency issues. It ensures the isolation of one transaction's results, keeping these results from adversely affecting another transaction when both are accessing shared data. The EJB container and the transaction manager rely on the resource manager and the underlying resource to implement the resource-specific synchronization protocol to implement the isolation mechanism, such as a different type of row and record-level locking in a relational database.

- *Durability*—This characteristic guarantees that any change to the data that has been committed in a transaction is permanently stored in the resource and can be retrieved in the future. This characteristic depends on atomicity and isolation.

Every transaction is required to have the ACID properties. How do developers ensure that transactions are atomic, consistent, isolated, and durable? Let's discuss transaction attributes and how they help answer that question next.

Transaction Attributes

Every EJB method must have a transaction attribute associated with it. These transaction attributes enable the bean developer or the application assembler to set the scope of a transaction enabling the atomicity, which can span multiple transactional objects across different EJB containers.

The six types of transaction attributes allow the developer or assembler to control the scope of a transaction. To understand how transaction attribute settings affect a transaction, let's look at a simple example (shown in Figure 14.7) with three transaction participants. The client invokes bizMethod() on the EJB component, which in turn updates the database via the resource manager (RM). Transaction attribute settings are specified for the bizMethod() in EJB. Transactions Tx1 and Tx2 denote two transactions and their scope within the context of this example. Figure 14-7 summarizes the transaction attributes and depicts participating objects for the sake of clarity. We'll refer to the objects in Figure 14.7 as we discuss the various transaction attributes and their implications, next.

NotSupported

Use this attribute to ensure that the method won't execute in a container-generated transaction. If a method is called within the context of an existing transaction, the transaction is suspended before the method is invoked. Figure 14-7 illustrates the two scenarios of setting the NotSupported transaction attribute on bizMethod():

- If the client isn't in a transaction and calls bizMethod() on an EJB instance, the bizMethod() method executes normally without a transaction and invokes the resource manager without a transaction.

- However, if the client is in transaction Tx1 and invokes bizMethod(), the EJB instance suspends Tx1 while bizMethod() is being executed.

Transaction attributes	Client's transaction	Transaction associated with business method	Transaction associated with resource manager
Client	EJB bizMethod()	Resource manager	
NotSupported	None	None	None
	Tx1	None	None
Required	None	Tx2	Tx2
	Tx1	Tx1	Tx1
Supports	None	None	None
	Tx1	Tx1	Tx1
RequiresNew	None	Tx2	Tx2
	Tx1	Tx2	Tx2
Mandatory	None	Error	Not applicable
	Tx1	Tx1	Tx1
Never	None	None	None
	Tx1	Error	Not applicable

Figure 14-7 Implication of the Transaction Attribute Setting on Transactional Objects

The suspended transaction context of Tx1 isn't propagated to the resource manager when EJB invokes the resource manager. After the `bizMethod()` is returned, the client continues with the transaction Tx1.

Use the `NotSupported` attribute when the EJB needs to interact with resource managers that don't support transaction and in such case, set attributes to NotSupported for all methods in your bean.

Required

Use this attribute as the default transaction attribute, as it works with most transactions. The `Required` attribute indicates that the method must always execute within a transaction. If `methodA()` without a transaction context calls `methodB()` with a `Required` transaction attribute, then the container starts a new transaction for methodB(). If the transactional `methodA()` calls `methodB()`, then an existing transaction is propagated, for example.

- If the client in an existing transaction (Tx1) invokes `bizMethod()` in EJB, then the transaction Tx1 is propagated to the EJB, which in turn propagates the Tx1 context to the resource manager when EJB calls the resource manager.

- If the calling client isn't in a transaction and invokes `bizMethod()`, the container automatically starts a new transaction, Tx2, and delegates a method call to `bizMethod()` in the EJB within the Tx2. The EJB propagates the transaction context Tx2 to the resource manager. The container executes a `commit()` or `rollback()` before the `bizMethod()` returns the result back to the client.

Use the `Required` attribute whenever you want to ensure the operation will be executed within a transaction. By default, all the transaction attributes in your entity beans' methods should be set to `Required`. This guarantees that your methods will always be in a transaction. In most application servers this is the default setting.

Supports

Use this attribute with caution. If a method has the `Supports` attribute, then the method supports and propagates the caller's existing transaction, but if the caller has no transaction context, then the method executes without a transaction. Here are two possible scenarios if the `bizMethod()` transaction attribute is set to `Supports`:

- If the client without a transaction context calls `bizMethod()` on the bean instance, it delegates the request to `bizMethod()`. There's no transaction context to propagate.

- If the client is in transaction Tx1, on the other hand, the container invokes `bizMethod()` and propagates Tx1 to the resource manager.

This attribute can avoid the overhead of suspending and resuming preexisting transactions, but because of its nondeterministic transaction support, it should be used with caution. Unless in special circumstances, you should avoid the `Supports` attribute because you can't predict the outcome of the business logic.

RequiresNew

With this attribute, regardless of whether the client is or isn't in an existing transaction, the container starts a new transaction. Use this attribute to always run your method in a new transaction. Let's look at two possible scenarios:

- In the case of the client without a transaction, the container starts transaction Tx2 before delegating a request to `bizMethod()`; it propagates the transaction context Tx2 to the resource managers. It executes `commit()` or `rollback()` before returning the results of `bizMethod()` to the client.

- If the client was already in a transaction (say, Tx1), the container suspends transaction Tx1 and starts a new transaction (Tx2) and then delegates a request to `bizMethod()`. The container propagates Tx2 to the resource manager; the Tx2 either commits or rolls back before returning to the client. After transaction Tx2 ends, it resumes with the suspended transaction Tx1.

Use the `RequiresNew` attribute if your method must execute in a separate, new transaction regardless of previous caller's transactional status.

Mandatory

Use this attribute if `bizMethod()` can only be called within a client's existing transaction context. This is the opposite of the `never` attribute. Let's look at the scenarios of setting the `bizMethod()` attribute to `Mandatory`:

- If the client without a transaction invokes `bizMethod()` on the EJB instance, the container throws the `javax.transaction.Transaction-RequiredException` to remote clients and `javax.transaction.Trans-actionRequiredLocalException` to local clients.
- If the client is in transaction Tx1, the container delegates the request to `bizMethod()` within the Tx1 context and propagates transaction context Tx1 to the resource manager.

Use the `Mandatory` attribute if you want to force clients to always call a method within a transaction context.

Never

Use this attribute if the method should never run with a client's transaction context. This attribute is the opposite of the `Mandatory` attribute. Let's look at two scenarios with `bizMethod()` attribute set to `Never`:

- If a client in transaction Tx1 invokes `bizMethod()`, the container throws `java.rmi.RemoteException` for remote clients and `javax.ejb.EJBException` for local clients.
- If the client isn't in a transaction, the bean instance delegates the request to `bizMethod()`; there's no transaction context by this bean to propagate.

Use this attribute if you want to ensure that a method can never be invoked within a transaction. Note the difference between `NotSupported` and `Never` attributes: When a caller with a transaction context calls a method with `Never` attribute, the method throws an exception, but when the caller calls a method with `NotSupported` attribute, the method simply suspends the caller's transaction until the method returns. For example, you should use the `Never` attribute if your EJB method will be accessing a legacy resource that doesn't support transaction and thus should never be allowed to invoke in a transaction.

Implementing Transactions Programmatically or Declaratively

The scope of a transaction boundary is marked when the transaction's begin or end boundary either commits or rolls back. Marking the start and end boundaries of a transaction is referred to as *demarcation*. Demarcation marks the scope of the transaction. In the EJB architecture, transaction demarcation can be implemented in one of two ways:

- *Programmatically or bean-managed*—When the transaction demarcation is managed programmatically or is bean-managed, the bean developer is responsible for implementing the code that initiates the `begin()` and `commit()` or `rollback()` methods of the `javax.transaction.User-Transaction` interface.

- *Declaratively or container-managed*—When the transaction demarcation is managed declaratively or container-managed, the container is responsible for initiating the `begin()` and `commit()` or `rollback()` methods based on the attributes specified for the methods in the deployment descriptor.

Note that we use the terms programmatically and bean-managed interchangeably in this chapter and that the phrase *bean-demarcated transaction* implies Web and EJB components, whereas *programmatically demarcated transaction* is more general and includes Java clients in addition to Web and EJB components. The declarative and container-demarcated transactions apply to EJB components only (refer to Table 14-1). Regardless of whether the transaction demarcation is bean-managed or container-managed, the burden of implementing complicated low-level transaction management tasks (such as implementing and coordinating local and distributed TPC and transaction context propagation) falls on the EJB container/server and resource manager providers. In the case of bean-managed transaction demarcation, the bean developer is responsible for implementing the code that manages the invocation of `begin()` and `commit()` or `rollback()`

methods programmatically in applications. In container-managed demarcation, the assembler or the deployer must specify the transaction attributes declaratively.

Table 14-1 Transaction Demarcation Support with EJB

Bean Type	Bean-Demarcated TX	Container-Demarcated TX
Session beans	Yes	Yes
Message-Driven beans	Yes	Yes
Entity beans	Never	Always

Demarcating a Transaction Programmatically

Stand-alone Java clients, session beans, and message-driven beans support programmatic transaction demarcation. The bean developer is responsible for writing the code to start and end transactions in addition to implementing the business logic. The EJB container and servers perform the low-level transaction management.

Bean developers have three options for implementing transaction demarcation programmatically:

- Java Transaction API (JTA)
- JDBC API
- JMS API

Java Transaction API

JTA provides the most flexibility when implementing transaction demarcation programmatically; it's also the preferred option.

The **javax.transaction.UserTransaction** *Interface* To demarcate transactions programmatically in JTA, the bean developer needs to understand one of the most useful JTA interfaces, the javax.transaction.User-Transaction interface, which contains several methods:

```
javax.transaction.UserTransaction {
    public void begin() throws
    NotSupportedException, SystemException;
    public void commit() throws RollbackException,
    HeuristicMixedException, HeuristicRollbackException,
    SystemException, java.lang.SecurityException,
```

```
      java.lang.IllegalException;
      public void rollback() throws SystemException,
      java.lang.SecurityException, java.lang.IllegalException;
      public void setRollbackOnly() throws SystemException,
      java.lang.IllegalException;
      public void getStatus() throws SystemException;
      public void setTransactionTimeOut(int seconds) throws
      SystemException;
   }
```

Let's briefly discuss these useful methods in the `UserTransaction` interface.

begin *method*

```
      public void begin() throws NotSupportedException, SystemException
```

This method is used to initiate a new transaction and associates it with the current thread. Use begin() to start the transaction, which demarcates the start of the transaction. If the thread is already associated with an existing transaction, the transaction manager throws NotSupportedException because nested transactions aren't currently supported. For any other errors, it throws SystemException.

commit *method*

```
      public void commit() throws RollbackException,
         HeuristicMixedException, HeuristicRollbackException,
         java.lang.SecurityException, java.lang.IllegalStateException,
         SystemException
```

When the commit() method is executed, the transaction is completed and the thread is no longer associated with the transaction indicating that another transaction can safely begin. Invoke this method to end the transaction. If the commit is unsuccessful (perhaps due to a problem with the Resource), an exception is thrown.

- RollbackException—This exception is thrown to indicate that the transaction has been rolled back by the resource manager.
- HeuristicMixedException—This exception is thrown to indicate that a heuristic decision was made by the resource manager; some relevant updates have been committed while others have been rolled back.
- HeuristicRollbackException—This exception is thrown to indicate that a heuristic decision was made and relevant updates have been rolled back.

- `SecurityException`—This exception indicates that there is a security violation and the thread isn't allowed to commit the transaction.

- `IllegalStateException`—This exception is thrown if the current thread isn't associated with a transaction.

- `SystemException`—This is thrown if any unexpected error is encountered.

rollback() method

```
public void rollback() throws java.lang.IllegalStateException,
    java.lang.SecurityException, SystemException
```

The current transaction can be called back and the updates undone by calling the `rollback()` method. This method can only be called after a transaction has begun and when the method completes and is no longer associated with any transaction. If the thread lacks the security credentials to execute the `rollback()` method, it throws a `SecurityException`.

If the current thread isn't associated with a transaction, it throws `IllegalState-Exception`. For any unexpected errors, it throws `SystemException`.

setRollbackOnly method

```
public void setRollbackOnly() throws java.lang.IllegalStateExcep-
tion,
    SystemException
```

Calling the `setRollbackOnly()` method marks the current transaction for roll back even if the transaction succeeds. Attempts to invoke this method when the thread isn't associated with the transaction results in `IllegalStateException` being thrown.

SetTransactionTimeout method

```
public void setTransactionTimeout(int seconds) throws SystemEx-
ception
```

This method enables the programmer to override the default timeout value of the transaction. Use this method to set the time-out before beginning the transaction. By default, the transaction takes the default transaction time-out specified by the EJB Server.

getStatus method

```
public int getStatus() throws SystemException
```

This method is used to obtain the current status of the transaction and returns one of the status messages on the next page.

- **STATUS_ACTIVE**—Indicates that the transaction is associated with the UserTransaction object. It also indicates that the transaction has begun prior to a transaction manager starting a two-phase commit.

- **STATUS_MARKED_ROLLBACK**—Indicates that the transaction is associated with the UserTransaction object and has been marked for rollback.

- **STATUS_PREPARED**—Indicates that the transaction is associated with the UserTransaction object and that the first phase of the two-phase commit process has been completed and is waiting for the transaction manager to respond.

- **STATUS_COMMITTING**—Indicates that the transaction is associated with the UserTransaction object and is in the process of committing the changes, perhaps waiting for a response from one or more resources before being fully committed.

- **STATUS_COMMITTED**—Indicates that the transaction is associated with the UserTransaction object and that the transaction has successfully committed.

- **STATUS_ROLLING_BACK**—Indicates that the transaction is associated with the UserTransaction object and that the transaction has decided to roll back and is in the process of rolling back.

- **STATUS_ROLLEDBACK**—Indicates that the transaction is associated with the UserTransaction object and that the transaction has been identified as rolled back.

- **STATUS_UNKNOWN**—Indicates that the transaction is associated with the UserTransaction object and that the transaction status cannot be determined. This is a transient condition; a subsequent invocation results in another status.

- **STATUS_NO_TRANSACTION**—Indicates that the transaction isn't associated with the UserTransaction object. This could result due to the completion of the current transaction or to a transaction never having been created.

- **STATUS_PREPARING**—Indicates that the transaction is associated with the UserTransaction object and that the transaction is in the process of preparing (the transaction manager is executing the first phase of the TPC).

How are UserTransaction interfaces accessed and associated with the bean instance? The getUserTransaction() method in the EJBContext interface returns the javax.transaction.UserTransaction interface. The SessionContext, EntityContext and MessageDrivenContext interfaces all extend EJBContext and thus the UserTransaction interface is readily available in EJB instances. Let's examine EJBContext interface next.

The **java.ejb.EJBContext** *Superinterface* The EJBContext
superinterface is extended by the EntityContext, SessionContext, and
MessageDriven-Context interfaces, making it available in all EJB instances.
EJBContext provides access to the container-provided runtime context of an
enterprise bean instance. Let's take a look at each of the methods pertaining to
transaction for this interface.

public javax.transaction.UserTransaction getUserTransaction()

throws java.lang.IllegalStateException

This method returns the java.transaction.UserTransaction interface,
whose begin() method is used to demarcate the transaction boundary
programmatically. It's only applicable to session beans and message-driven beans
with bean-managed transaction demarcation. Attempts to call it from container-
managed transaction demarcated beans result in
java.lang.IllegalStateException being thrown.

public void setRollbackOnly()

throws java.lang.IllegalStateException

This method is used to force the transaction to rollback and is only applicable for
beans with container-managed transaction.

public boolean getRollbackOnly()

throws java.lang.IllegalStateException

This method returns a boolean and is useful for testing if the current transaction is
marked for rollback. Call this method to verify the current transaction before
proceeding with long complex calculations that could prove to be pointless.

Restrictions with the Bean-Managed Transaction in EJB There are certain
restrictions related to transaction when you use the Java Transaction API.
These include:

- *EJBContext restriction*—The EJB with bean-managed transaction
  demarcation must not use the getRollbackOnly() and
  setRollbackOnly() methods of the EJBContext interface but instead
  use the corresponding methods from the JTA, JMS and JDBC API. For
  example, the JTA provides the rollback() and setRollbackOnly()
  methods to perform the same functionality.

- *Not allowed to use javax.ejb.SessionSynchronization Interface*—With bean-managed transaction demarcation, stateful session beans are not allowed to implement SessionSynchronization interface.

The following simple code snippet illustrates the use of JTA to control transactions. The steps include using the `getUserTransaction()` method of the context object to retrieve the context to the bean instance; using the transaction context to demarcate the `utx.begin();` executing a business method, `changeAddress()`, and then executing the `utx.commit()` method to complete the transaction. If the transaction fails, it throws `EJBException`, which forces a rollback of the transaction.

```
.........................  . .
utx = (UserTransaction) context.getUserTransaction();
.........................
try {
    utx.begin();
     student.updateAddress(address);
     utx.commit();
    } catch (RemoteException re) {
        throw new EJBException(" address change failed!");
    }
```

Java Database Connectivity (JDBC) API

Bean developers may also use the JDBC API to manage transactions when working with relational databases. Although restricted only to relational database resources, it offers flexibility with setting up isolation levels other than transaction demarcation.

The bean developer is required to use the JDBC API, namely the methods in the `java.sql.Connection` interface. When using this interface, developers are directly interacting with the resource manager—this provides a high level of flexibility to set the transaction attribute and isolation level as well as the ability to control transaction demarcation. The connection interface and the isolation levels and methods pertaining to transactions in this interface are below. Note that the connection interface lacks the `begin()` method— it's not required because when the connection to the database is opened, the transaction is started. The transaction is completed by calling `commit()` and making the changes durable or undoing the changes by calling the `rollback()` method.

- `public void commit()  throws SQLException`—Call `commit()` to make the changes to the database durable.

- public void rollback() throws SQLException—Call rollback() to abandon the changes to the database since the last commit.

The following code fragment gives an example of how to use JDBC API for controlling transaction with a relational database. Note that the auto commit option is turned off so that the code has control of when to commit the transaction in the try and catch blocks. If the ps.executeUpdate() method is successful, the transaction is commited [connection.commit()], but if executeUpdate() fails, the transaction is rolled back [connection rollback()] in the catch block.

```
............... . .
    InitialContext ictx = new InitialContext();
    DataSource ds = (DataSource)
ictx.lookup("java:comp/env/jdbc/JcampDS");
    Connection connection = ds.getConnection();

    //turn off auto commit it can be controlled programmatically.
    connection.setAutoComit(false);
.........

    try {
    String sqlString  = "UPDATE AddressTable SET
     Street = ? , city = ?, zip = ?, state = ?, country = ?
        WHERE studentID = ?";
            PreparedStatement ps = connection.prepareStatement(query);
             ps = setString(1, street);
             ps = setString(2, city);
             ps = setString(3, zip);
             ps = setString(4, state);
             ps = setString(5, country);
             ps = setString(6, studentID);

// transaction begins
  ps.executeUpdate()
  ps.close();

// end the transaction
    connection.commit();
 } catch (Exception e) {
 try {
 // rollback the transaction
 connection.rollback();
  throw new EJBException(" TX failed "+e.getMessage());
  } catch (SQLException sqe) {
    throw new EJBException("TX rolled back"+sqe.getMesage());
  }
}
.........................
```

When using the JDBC API, remember that the transaction is controlled by the transaction manager of the RDBMS and not JTS. Since transaction with database can be demarcated using the JTA or the JDBC API, the question is when should developers use the JDBC API to manage transactions as opposed to JTA? Consider using the JDBC transaction if you need to use session beans as a façade (we'll discuss EJB design patterns in chapter 16) to the PL/SQL or other legacy applications. Also, use the JDBC transaction if finer control of various aspects of the transaction (such as the isolation level) is needed and the target resource is a relational database.

JMS API: `javax.jms.Session` Interface

Bean developers needing to programmatically control transactions in message-driven beans or JMS clients can use JTA or JMS APIs. Remember that JMS supports an asynchronous messaging environment, so there are two separate transactions. One is between the message producer and the message provider, which guarantees that the message will be delivered to the message server. The second is between the message server and the message consumer, where the message is guaranteed to be delivered. The transaction applies to each of these operations. Attempts to use request/response messaging between the message producer and a message consumer in one transaction isn't supported.

When using the JMS API, use the transaction features of the `javax.jms.Session` interface to handle the transaction. Although the following example uses the point-to-point messaging model, the concept applies to the publish/subscribe mode as well. The JMS API has two methods that deal with the transaction as follows:

- `public void commit()  throws JMSException`—This method commits all the messages in the current transaction and releases the lock. It can throw `TransactionRolledBackException` if the commit fails as well as `JMSException` and `IllegalStateException`.
- `public void rollback()  throws JMSException`—This method rolls back any messages in the current transaction and releases the lock.

Note that there are no `begin()` methods; rather, there are only `commit()` and `rollback()` methods. This means that the first step to demarcating a transactional message is to initialize the Session Object, `qSession`, and the transaction is complete when `qSession.commit()` is executed.

```
............
    Context ctx = new InitialContext();

    queueConnectionFactory qConnFactory = (QueueConnectionFactory)
ctx.lookup("java:comp/env/jms/MyQueFactory");
    Queue que = (Queue) ctx.lookup("java:comp/env/jms/MyQue");
    qConn = qConnFactory.createQueueConnection();

    //begin the transaction.
   qSession = qConn.createQueueSession(true, Ses-
sion.AUTO_ACKNOWLEDGE);
  qSender = queueSession.createSender(que);


............
    message = qSession.createTextMessage();
    message.setText("Testing JMS transaction features~");

  qSender.send(message);
    ....................... .
    //commit the transaction.
    q.Session.commit();
............
```

When to Use the JTA, JDBC, or JMS API

JTA transaction is versatile and can be used with clients, session, and message-driven beans, but the JDBC transaction is only applicable for database access. In addition, the JMS transaction applies to only JMS clients and message-driven beans. The following section discusses the various options that enable a bean developer to demarcate transactions programmatically. Note that one cardinal rule of programmatically demarcating transactions is that transaction methods from these APIs cannot mix and match. Therefore, when implementing enterprise beans with bean-managed transaction demarcations, use *either* JTA, JDBC, or JMS transaction-related methods. Don't use the `begin()` method from JTA's `javax.transaction.UserTransaction` interface and then attempt to use the `commit()` method from the JDC's `java.sql.Connection` interface or the `rollback()` method from the JMS's `java.jms.Session` interface.

Among the options discussed with bean demarcated transaction, JTA provides the most flexibility and highest portability as it doesn't depend on relational databases (as does the JDBC API) nor does it require any message infrastructure (as does the JMS API.) The JDBC and the JMS APIs are very specific and only applicable to their respective resources. On the other hand, the JDBC API does allow finer control over the transaction attributes and isolation that JTA cannot provide. The JMS provides transaction control between the message producer and the message server, or between the message server and the message consumer.

Rules for Implementing Bean-Managed Transactions with EJBs

A bean developer should keep a few basic rules in mind when implementing bean-managed transactions. Here's a brief discussion of these rules

- Only session beans and message-driven beans support bean-managed demarcation.
- The EJB instance that initiates the transaction must complete the transaction before stating a new transaction, because only flat transactions are supported by the current EJB 2.0 specification.
- If the bean developer uses the `javax.transaction.UserTransaction` interface to manage transactions explicitly in a bean-managed transaction, then all updates to the resource manager must be enclosed between the `begin()` and `commit()` methods. While the bean instance is in a JTA transaction, it's illegal to invoke the `commit()` or `rollback()` methods from the `java.sql.Connection` or the `javax.jms.Session` interface.
- In a stateful session bean instance, a transaction can span multiple business methods, and a transaction can be initiated in one business method and committed or rolled back in a different business method. This rule is also applicable to stand-alone Java programs using the `UserTransaction` interface. It's recommended, however, that transactions begin and end in the same business method for the sake of simplified coding and ease of maintenance.
- In stateless bean instances, the transaction must begin and end within the same method because of its stateless nature.
- In the case of message-driven beans, a transaction must start and end in the `onMessage()` method.
- For stateless and message-driven beans (which are also stateless), the transaction must begin and complete before the business method returns. If the bean developer begins the transaction but fails to `commit()` or `rollback()`, the container does the following during execution of the bean instance:
  - It logs the transaction as an application error.
  - It forces a rollback on the transaction.
  - It discards the instance of the SLSB or MDB.

- And, in the case of stateless session beans, the container throws the `javax.rmi.RemoteException` to the remote client or the `javax.ejb.Exception` for a local client. Message-driven beans don't have interfaces, so there's no need to throw an exception.

Demarcating Transactions Declaratively

Container-managed transaction demarcation is the preferred way to implement transactions in EJBs, mainly because it provides flexibility. With container-managed transaction demarcation, the transaction attributes for the business methods are specified in the deployment descriptor to mark the transaction scope. At runtime, the EJB container demarcates the transaction scope by calling the appropriate `begin()` and `commit()` or `rollback()` methods based on the transaction attributes specified in the deployment descriptor.

A bean deployer or an application assembler may use the vendor-provided deployment tool to specify the transaction attributes of the EJB in the deployment descriptor. Transaction attributes also can be manually specified by using a text editor to write a deployment descriptor, although this is a tedious process.

Whereas session and message-driven beans support both bean-managed and container-managed transaction demarcation, entity beans support only container-managed transaction demarcation. In a container-managed transaction demarcation, methods in EJBs must not use any transaction methods such as `commit()`, `rollback()`, or so forth from JTA, JDBC, or JMS APIs we discussed previously. The EJBs in the container-managed transaction demarcation can use the `setRollbackOnly()` and `getRollbackOnly()` methods of the `javax.ejb.EJBContext` object to force a transaction to rollback or to test whether the current transaction has been marked for rollback.

A deployment descriptor consists of two types of information—structural information and assembly information. A bean developer, in addition to other structural information, may explicitly specify whether the transaction demarcation in the case of the session and MDB beans is bean managed or container managed by specifying the `<transaction-type>` element to `bean` or `container`. The structural information is enclosed by the `<enterprise-bean>` and `</enterprise-bean>` elements of the deployment descriptor of a session bean. Note that the `<transaction-type>` element encloses `Bean` to indicate to the container that this instance uses bean-managed transaction demarcation.

```
<ejb-jar>
  <display-name>CartJAR</display-name>
```

```
<enterprise-beans>
    <session>
        <display-name>ShoppingCartEJB</display-name>
        <ejb-name>ShoppingCartEJB</ejb-name>
<home>j2eebootcamp.developingEJB.chapter7.shop.ShoppingCartHome</home>
<remote>j2eebootcamp.developingEJB.chapter7.shop.ShoppingCart</remote>
        <ejb-class> j2eebootcamp.developingEJB.chapter7.shop.Shop-
pingCartEJB</ejb-class>
        <session-type>Stateful</session-type>
        <transaction-type>Bean</transaction-type>
        <security-identity>
        <description></description>
        <use-caller-identity></use-caller-identity>
        </security-identity>
    </session>
</enterprise-beans>
<assembly-descriptor>
............................................ . .
    </assembly-description>
</ejb-jar>
```

Entity beans support only container-managed transaction demarcation, so the `<transaction-type>` element isn't applicable. In the case of entity beans, then, the question isn't who manages the transaction but whether the persistence is container managed (CMP) or bean managed (BMP) as specified by the `<persistence-type>` element encloses Container to indicate it is CMP and `<cmp-version>` element encloses 2.x to indicate it is CMP 2.0 entity bean. The next example makes this clearer.

```
<entity>
    <display-name>AddressEJB</display-name>
    <ejb-name>AddressEJB</ejb-name>
    <local-home>chapter10.student.LocalAddressHome</local-home>
    <local>chapter10.student.LocalAddress</local>
    <ejb-class>chapter10.student.AddressBean</ejb-class>
    <persistence-type>Container</persistence-type>
    <prim-key-class>java.lang.String</prim-key-class>
    <reentrant>False</reentrant>
    <cmp-version>2.x</cmp-version>
    <abstract-schema-name>Address</abstract-schema-name>
```

Let's review how transaction attributes are specified in the assembly section (enclosed by `<assembly-descriptor>` and `</assembly-descriptor>` elements) of the deployment descriptor. You can tell that the name of the EJB is StudentEJB as specified by the `<ejb-name>` element, and that findAllStudents is the method from the home interface (indicated by the `<method-intf>` element) that has no parameters (indicated by empty element

<method-params>). The transaction attribute for findAllStudents()
method is set to Required as specified by the <trans-attribute> element.
And the transaction is container managed as indicated by <container-
transaction> element.

```
     <ejb-jar>
      <enterprise-bean>
      <entity>
     ............... .
      </enterprise-bean>
   <assembly-descriptor>
   <container-transaction>
        <method>
          <ejb-name>StudentEJB</ejb-name>
          <method-intf>Home</method-intf>
          <method-name>findAllStudents</method-name>
          <method-params />
        </method>
        <trans-attribute>Required</trans-attribute>
     </container-transaction>
    <container-transaction>
    ............... . .
    </container-transaction>
   ...............
       </assembly-descriptor>
   </ejb-jar>
```

The Stateful Session Bean with the SessionSynchronization Interface

In chapter 7, we noted that session beans aren't inherently transactional, like the
entity beans, but are transaction aware, and earlier in this chapter we discussed
how to implement session bean transaction programmatically. Now let's discuss
how to implement container-managed transaction demarcation with session
beans. By implementing the javax.ejb.SessionSynchronization interface
in a session bean, developers are essentially inheriting the transactional callback
methods afterBegin(), beforeCompletion(), and afterCompletion(),
which the container invokes automatically. Only stateful session beans can
implement the SessionSynchronization interface to support container-
managed transaction demarcation.

Figure 14-8 illustrates the life cycle of a stateful session bean with transactions:
business methods with transaction attributes execute within a transaction.

The process of instantiating a transactional stateful session bean instance is the
same as for a regular stateful session bean, as we discussed in chapter 7. The
newInstance(), setSessionContext(), and ejbCreate methods are

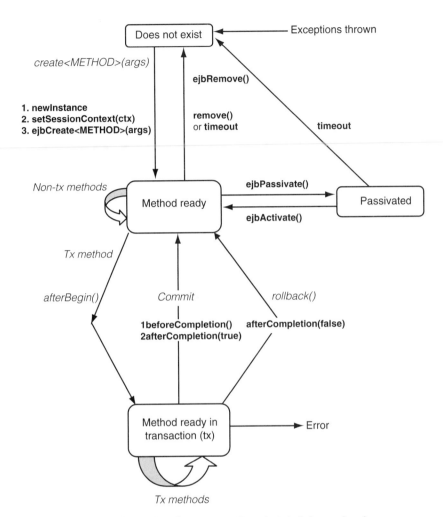

Figure 14-8 The life cycle of a transactional stateful session bean

invoked by the EJB container when a client invokes the create method on its home interface and transitions to the method-ready state. Note, however, that when a client calls a transactional business method, the container calls the `afterBegin()` method prior to calling the business method. This is followed by the `before-Completion()` and the `afterCompletion()` callback methods before the transaction returns.

A bean developer can use these transactional callback methods to perform data caching. After the completion of the business method (but prior to committing the changes), the `beforeCompletion()` method is called by the container. The bean instance should take this opportunity to write any cache data to the database. The container invokes the `beforeCompletion()` method to make the bean instance force the transaction to rollback by invoking `EJBContext.setRollbackOnly()` method if the update to the database failed.

The container calls `afterCompletion()` to indicate that the transaction is completed with a boolean status. A status of `true` indicates that the transaction was a success and committed; a status of `false` indicates that the transaction failed and was rolled back.

The following code snippet shows an `updateAddress()` business method with one task—to update an address. In the example, the address is set to the original address if the update to the new address fails. We'll use the callback methods and synchronize the data cache. The order of method calls in this transaction is as follows: `afterBegin()`, `updateAddress()`, `beforeCompletion()`, and `afterCompletion()`. Use the `afterBegin()` method—this method marks the beginning of the transaction to save the original address as `oldAddress` and then checks the result of the `afterCompletion()` method. If the transaction is successful, the status (txStatus) returns `true`. If the transaction fails, txStatus is `false` and then resets the address to the original value, `oldAddress`.

```
public class StudentBean implements SessionBean, SessionSynchronization
{

.....
    Address address; //Value object.
    Address oldAddress;
.....
    SessionContext ctx;

    void afterBegin()
    {
        oldAddress = selectAddress(id);
    }

    public void updateAddress(Address newAddress)
    {
        try {
        boolean flag = addressDAO.update(id, newAddress);
        if (!flag) {
            ctx.setRollbackOnly();
            throw new AddressUpdateException();
            }
        } catch (Exception e) {
.............. . .
```

```
}

public void beforeCompletion()
{
}

public void afterCompletion(Boolean txStatus)
{
    if (txStatus == false)
        address = oldAddress;
}
```

Although stateful session beans with the SessionSynchronization interface are transactional, note that the newInstance(), setSessionContext(), ejbCreate(), ejbRemove(), ejbActivate(), ejbPassivate(), and afterCompletion() methods are called with unspecified transaction contexts.

Note that session beans with bean-managed transaction demarcation aren't allowed to implement the SessionSynchronization interface as the bean is in control of the begin(), commit(), and rollback() methods in the UserTransaction interface to manage transactions.

Transaction Attributes As They Apply to EJB Methods

In the case of container-managed transaction demarcation, transaction attributes are specified for methods of a session bean's or entity bean's home and component interfaces or for the onMessage() method of MDB. At runtime, the container uses these attributes to manage transaction for the EJB instances. Not all transaction attributes discussed are applicable to all bean-managed and container-managed EJBs. Rules for specifying transactional attributes in EJBs include:

- *Entity beans*—The transaction attributes must be specified for entity bean methods defined in a bean's component and home interfaces and its superinterfaces that it inherits directly or indirectly. The transaction attributes must not be specified for the getEJBLocalHome(), getHandle(), isIdentical(), and getPrimaryKey() methods in the entity bean's component interface nor for the getEJBMetaData and getHomeHandle methods in the component interface.

- *CMP 2.0 entity beans*—In addition (for CMP 2.0 entity beans only) the Required, RequiredNew, or Mandatory transaction attributes should be used for business methods defined in the bean's component interface and in all its direct and indirect superinterfaces.

- *Message-driven beans*—In MDB, the transaction attributes can only be specified for the onMessage() method; only Required and Not

Supported transaction attributes are applicable. Because the message-driven beans don't have interfaces, interface-related attributes make little sense.

- *Session beans*—The transaction attributes must be specified for methods defined in the session bean's component interface and its superinterfaces that it inherits directly or indirectly, except for methods of the EJBObject and EJBLocalObject interfaces. In other words, transaction attributes must be specified for all business methods, but the transaction attributes must not be specified for the methods in the session bean's home interface. Only Required, RequiredNew, and Mandatory attributes are applicable to methods of stateful session beans that implement the javax.ejb.SessionSyncrhonization interface.

Only the EJB methods having a transaction context available can enable bean instance access to resource managers.

Forcing Transaction Rollback

There are cases when a bean developer may want to force a transaction to roll back in a container-managed transaction demarcation. For example, after a transaction is started, an early check of data may indicate that the result could be erroneous in CPU-intensive calculations. Since throwing an application exception does not force a transaction to rollback, the developer has two options to abort a transaction:

- System Exception—If the method throws a System Exception, such as EJBException, then the container performs the rollback.
- Invoke setRollbackOnly()—Another option is to force the transaction to roll back by calling the setRollbackOnly() method from the EJBContext interface.

EJBs with bean-managed transaction demarcation cannot call setRollback() methods from the EJBContext to force a rollback, because a developer can use the corresponding rollback() method of JTA, JDBC, or JMS APIs.

When the transaction fails, the container does the following:

- throws a RemoteException or EJBException
- logs the exception error to a log file
- rolls back the transaction
- discards the EJB instance

Note that a bean with container-managed transaction demarcation cannot use

- transaction-related methods such as commit, rollback, and the `setAutoCommit` of the `java.sql.Connection()` interface

- transaction-related methods such as commit and rollback from the JMS API

- any methods from the `javax.transaction.UserTransaction` interface

This restriction makes sense because container-managed and bean-managed transaction demarcation cannot be mixed in the same bean instance. You should choose either bean-managed or container-managed, but not both.

Transaction Behavior of SFSB, BMP, and CMP Entity Beans

Next, we'll look at the object interaction diagram of the transaction behavior of the start and commit protocol of the stateful session bean and the BMP and CMP 2.0 entity beans. Let's look at the various objects participating in a transaction. The client invokes a transactional business method on the bean instance with the help of the `EJBObject` (or `EJBLocalObject`). The transaction service object, along with the synchronization object, are responsible to coordinate the interactions between the bean instance, database and the `EJBObject`. Now let's look at unique behavior of each of the bean instances in a transaction.

The Stateful Session Bean

Figure 14-9 shows the object interaction diagram (OID) of a transactional business method in a stateful session bean. The JTA interface, `javax.transaction.UserTransaction`, must be implemented for the stateful session bean to be transactional. The transaction begins when `UserTransaction.begin()` is invoked by a client.

When the transaction business method is invoked within a transaction by a client, the stateful session bean (if it is in a passivated state) is activated. Then the `EJBObject` creates a new instance of `SessionSynchronization` object and passes it an argument to the `registerSynchronization(..)` to register with the transaction service object. The `EJBObject` then calls the `afterBegin()` method in the bean instance, which triggers the instance to read data from the database. The database registers with the transaction service object, and the business method is executed in the bean instance. The next time the client invokes, the business method is executed directly because the data is synchronized and the objects have already registered with the transaction service object, which controls the transaction.

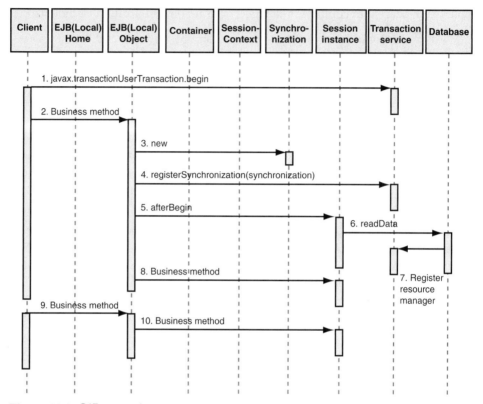

Figure 14-9 OID—starting a transaction in a stateful session bean

Figure 14-10 shows the `UserTransaction.commit()` issued by the client to the transaction service object. It invokes the `beforeCompletion()` method on the synchronization object, which invokes the `beforeCompletion()` method on the bean instance. The session bean instance writes the updates to the database, and the transaction service coordinates the prepare and commit and then informs the synchronization object of the status of commit, which in turn invokes the `afterCompletion()` method in the bean instance. If the `afterCompletion()` returns `true`, the transaction was successful and the results saved; but if it return `false`, then the transaction is rolled back.

The CMP 2.0 Entity Bean

In the case of CMP 2.0 entity beans, the transaction starts with `UserTransaction.begin()` being invoked by the client. The client invokes a business method on the `EJBObject`, which creates a `Synchronization` object and then registers with the Transaction Service object. There are three possible

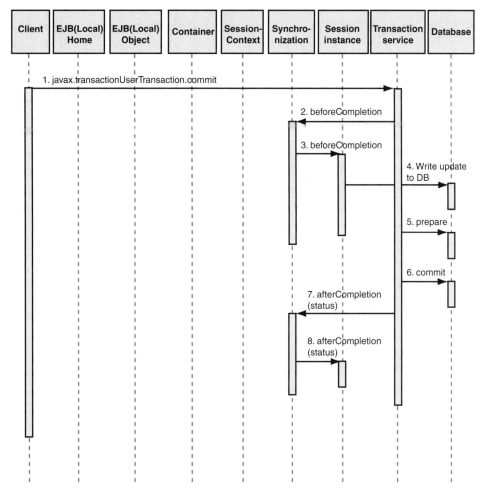

Figure 14-10 OID—commiting a transaction in a stateful session bean

scenarios, depending on the commit option; they are described below. Figure 14-11 shows the start of a transaction business of CMP 2.0 entity bean and the three commit options.

The EJB 2.0 specification gives the container the flexibility to select a commit strategy to associate entity object identity with the bean instance. An EJB container provider may select one of the three commit strategies, which we'll call Option A, Option B, and Option C.

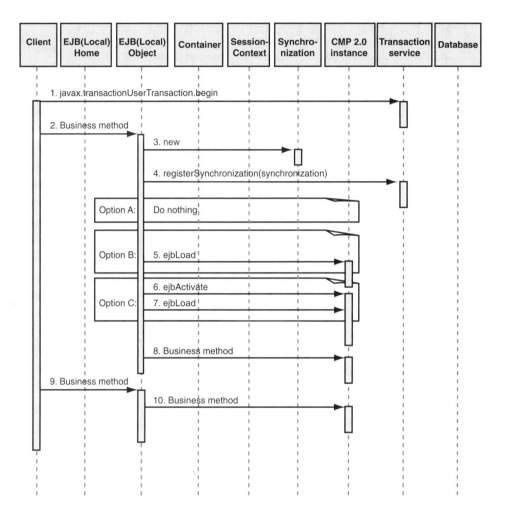

Figure 14-11 OID—starting a transaction in a CMP 2.0 entity bean

Option A

With this strategy, the container caches a CMP 2.0 entity bean instance in a `ready` state between transactions and the container guarantees that the instance has an exclusive access to the state of the object in the persistent storage. Consequently, the container doesn't have to synchronize the instance state with the persistent storage at the beginning of the transaction. If the container implemented Option A, then after the `registerSyncrhonization()` method is invoked, it is followed by the business method invocation. This has best performance among the three options but is nontrivial for vendors to implement.

Option B

With this strategy, the container caches a CMP 2.0 entity bean instance in a `ready` state between transactions, but the container doesn't guarantee that the instance has exclusive access to the state of the object in the persistent storage. Consequently, the container has to synchronize the instance state with the persistent storage at the beginning of each transaction by calling `ejbLoad()` call method. If the Option B strategy was selected by the container, then the `ejbLoad()` is invoked between the `registerSynchronization()` and business methods.

Option C

With this commit strategy, the container does not cache the CMP 2.0 entity bean instance in a `ready` state between each transaction. In fact, the container releases the bean instance back to the pool at the end of the transaction. Consequently, the container has to select an instance from the pool, invoke `ejbActivate()` followed by `ejbLoad()` at the beginning of each transaction to synchronize the instance state with the persistent storage before the business method is executed. This is the least efficient commit strategy and also the slowest, but it is the simplest for vendors to implement.

In the case of a commit in the CMP 2.0 entity beans, when the `UserTransaction.commit()` method is invoked, it registers with the transaction service, as shown in Figure 14-12. The transaction service invokes `beforeCompletion()` method on the synchronization object, which invokes the callback method `ejbLoad()` on the bean instance and then updates the entity state in the database. The transaction service executes the prepare and commit and returns `afterCompletion()` method with a status to the synchronization object. Depending on the vendor's implementation strategy, one of the three things can happen. In the case of Option A, the data is marked `not registered`. For Option B, the data is marked `invalid state`. For Option C, the callback method `ejbPassivate()` is invoked to save the instance of the data before the instance is released to the pool.

The BMP Entity Bean

Let's now look at the start of a transaction in a BMP entity bean as shown in Figure 14-13. The transaction starts when `UserTransaction.begin()` is invoked by the container and registers with the transaction service. Depending on the container's commit strategy, there are three scenarios. With Option A, the data is automatically synchronized so the `EJBObject` creates a new synchronization

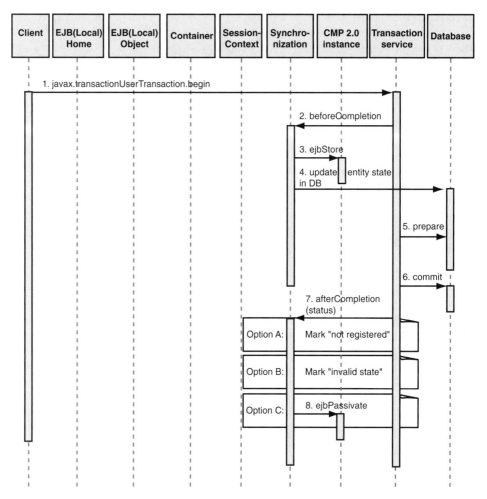

Figure 14-12 OID—committing a transaction in a CMP 2.0 entity bean

object and then invokes the `registerSynchronization()` method to register with the transaction service object and then executes the business method. With Option B, the bean instance is in ready pool, so the `EJBObject` first invokes a callback method, `ejbLoad()`, on the bean instance to synchronize the data. The bean instance then reads the data from the database, and the database registers with the transaction service. With Option C, the bean instance is in the pooled state, so the `EJBObject` calls `ejbActivate()` followed by `ejbLoad()` on a bean instance. Then the `EJBObject` creates a synchronization object followed by `registerSynchronization()` to register with the transaction service before invoking the business method in the bean instance.

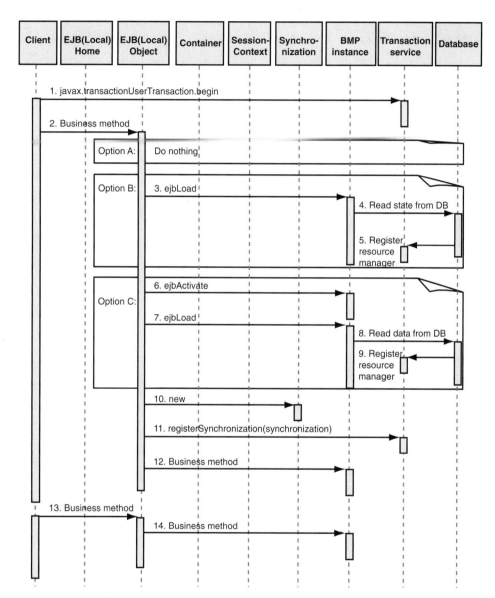

Figure 14-13 OID—starting a transaction in a BMP entity bean

Notice the object interaction's difference between the start of a transaction in CMP 2.0 and BMP entity beans—the creation of the synchronization object and the registering with the transaction service precedes any of the commit options in the BMP entity bean and instance interaction with the database compared to CMP 2.0 entity beans.

The object interaction diagram for the commit in BMP is the same as in the commit in CMP, so it isn't shown here.

Initiating a Transaction

A transaction can be initiated by a client, an EJB component, or an EJB container.

- *Non-EJB client-initiated*—In this case, client refers to Java or non Java stand-alone application clients or non EJB components that initiate transactions. The bean developer must programmatically implement the code to manage the transaction.

- *Non-EJB client-initiated*—In the case of EJB with the bean-managed transaction demarcation, the bean developer must implement the `javax.transaction.UserTransaction` interface and write the necessary code to manage the transaction programmatically.

- *Container-initiated*—In the container-initiated transaction (also known as container-managed transaction demarcation), the EJB container is responsible for initiating the transaction specified in the deployment descriptor for the EJBs. The application assembler and/or deployer may have to specify the transaction attributes in the deployment descriptor but doesn't write any code to handle the transaction.

Note that only session beans and message-driven beans support both bean-managed and container-managed transaction demarcation. Entity beans support only container-managed transaction demarcation and non-EJB clients can only support programmatic transaction demarcation.

Client-Initiated Transactions

The client can be a Web component, a stand-alone Java or CORBA application, and/or another EJB component initiating the transaction. A JMS client can use the JMS API or JTA to demarcate transactions. A client interacting with a relational database can use the JDBC API or JTA to demarcate transactions. However, if the client is interacting with different types of synchronous EJB components and initiating transactions, JTA is the only option for demarcating transactions. Client initiated transactions do not apply to MDBs because MDBs do not have interfaces.

In the J2EE environment, a client must obtain the UserTransaction object using the JNDI lookup method before it can demarcate a transaction on the remote EJB components. Figure 14-14 and the following code snippet depict a client starting a transaction and invoking methods on two EJB components.

```
.....   Context ctx = new InitialContext();
//jndi lookup - transaction context.
```

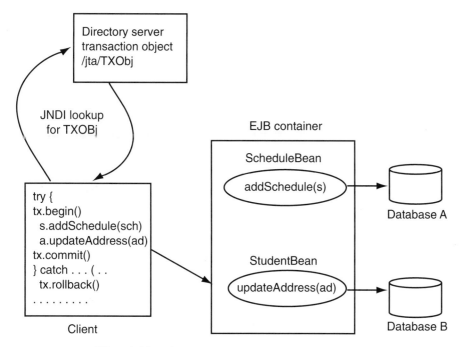

Figure 14-14 Client-initiated transaction

```
UserTransaction utx = (UserTransaction)
        ctx.lookup("java:comp/jta/UserTransaction");
................. .
try {
    tx.begin();
//business method
    s.addSchedule(id);

    a.updateAddress(address);

    tx.commit();
} catch (Exception ......)
    handle exceptions and abort....
    tx.rollback();

}
```

If an error is encountered during a client-initiated transaction propagated to an EJB, javax.transaction.TransactionRolledbackException is thrown to the client.

Unspecified Transaction Context

Not all methods in a bean instance must execute with a transaction context. In fact, a method can run explicitly without a transaction context. The EJB specification allows for that flexibility, defined as the method executing in "an unspecified transaction context." The EJB specification doesn't specify how the container should manage the execution of such a method, leaving that up to the container provider.

If a method accessing a resource manager (and running in an unspecified transaction context) fails in the middle of execution, the resource manager can be left in an unknown state, possibly resulting in unpredictable application behavior. The following methods execute in an unspecified transaction context:

- Session beans with container-managed transaction demarcation
    - `ejbCreate` and `ejbRemove` methods
    - `ejbPassivate()` and `ejbActivate()` methods
- Message-driven beans with container-managed transaction demarcation
    - `ejbCreate` and `ejbRemove` methods

A bean developer can also explicitly execute methods of container-managed transaction-demarcated EJBs in an unspecified transaction context in cases where the legacy system does not support transaction by setting the transaction attributes to one of the following:

- `NotSupported`
- `Never`
- `Supports` (when a client without a transaction context calls the method)

Bean-Managed versus Container-Managed Transaction Demarcation

Should a developer use bean-managed or container-managed transaction demarcation? Before we can answer that question, let's look at the advantages and disadvantages of each.

Advantages of bean-managed transaction demarcation include

- *Finer control of the transaction scope*—A developer can start and end multiple transactions programmatically within a business method.
- *Greater flexibility*—A developer has the option to use the JDBC, JMS, or JTA transactional methods to control the transaction.

- *Direct control of transactional features*—Bean-managed demarcation implies the ability to set the transaction timeout and isolation level and to find out the status of a transaction.

Disadvantages of bean-managed transaction demarcation include

- *Coding intensive*—Bean-managed demarcation requires extra coding.
- *Steeper learning curve*—Although the APIs are simple, developers need to learn how to use the various transaction methods.
- *Restricted portability*—The use of bean-managed demarcation restricts the portability of the component, as the transaction demarcation is hard-coded.
- *Debugging complexity*—With the use of bean-managed demarcation comes the increased likelihood of nasty transactional bugs that are difficult to debug.

On the other hand, container-managed transaction demarcation also has its advantages, such as

- *Flexibility*—The transaction scope of an application is easily modifiable at deployment time by changing the transaction attributes in the deployment descriptor with a tool.
- *Portability*—Because the transaction demarcations aren't hard-coded, they can be changed to suit a customer's transaction requirements during deployment.
- *Fewer bugs*—The code to handle transaction demarcation in the bean class doesn't have to be written which means fewer bugs.
- *Reduced time to market*—The time to market is reduced because the developer leaves the transaction management to the container.
- *Shallower learning curve*—Developers don't have to learn new vendor proprietary transaction APIs.

Disadvantages of container-managed transaction demarcation include

- *Coarser transactions*—Transaction attributes can only be applied at the method level, so a fine-grained line level transaction is not possible with a CMP transaction. One way around this is to make the methods that perform a fine-grained logic transaction very specific.
- *Difficulty of enforcing transaction boundaries*—In the case of a bean-managed transaction, a bean developer enforces the transaction boundaries. In some cases, this may be desirable as customers without source code access cannot change them. With a container-managed transaction, the assembler and the deployer can change the transaction attributes and thus the transaction boundaries.

Generally, unless your application requires low-level access to the transaction and has special needs to control transaction programmatically, avoid bean-managed transaction demarcation. Because of its portability, flexibility, and faster time-to-market advantages container-managed transaction demarcation should be used whenever possible.

The transaction attributes solve only the transaction scope issues such as atomicity and the durability of the ACID properties. Transaction does not solve the issues with concurrency and consistency in an enterprise application but isolation property does so let's discuss isolation next.

Isolation Levels

In a multitasking, multiuser environment running EJB applications the operation of one EJB object in a transaction must be isolated from adversely affecting the operation of other EJB objects in transaction. This property of a transaction is called the *isolation* characteristic and solves concurrency issues. For example, how are multiple users allowed access to a common data set, and how do they receive a consistent view of their data while being prevented from adversely affecting another user? Transaction isolation is achieved by controlling access to data and depends on data locking and request serialization mechanism. Transaction can enforce read locks or write locks on the data. *Read locks* on data are nonexclusive locks so multiple transactions can read the data simultaneously, while *write locks* are exclusive locks that allow a single transaction at a time to update the data. In a concurrent environment with multiple transactions, serialization enforces sequential access to the data by a transaction at a time. Consequently, transaction isolation levels control the type of access to the data.

Transactions without isolation characteristics suffer from three basic concurrency issues: dirty reads, repeatable reads, and phantom reads. The following section uses an example with two transactions, Tx1 and Tx2 without any isolation, to highlight concurrency issues and discusses how isolation can solve concurrency problems.

Dirty Reads

In an example where two objects with two different transactions are interacting, the second transaction, Tx2, reads the changed but uncommitted data from the first transaction Tx1. Before the commit, the first transaction, Tx1, encounters an exception, conducts a rollback and undoes the changes. The second transaction has effectively read an invalid data, thus it's a *dirty read*. To understand dirty reads, imagine two bean instances, the supplier bean and consumer bean, in action as in Table 14.2. The supplier bean instance's job is to maintain the widget inventory to a daily total of 500. Each time the consumer bean instance consumes the widgets, it's automatically replenished by the supplier bean instance.

Table 14-2 Dirty Reads

Time	ConsumerBean	Total	SupplierBean	Total
T0		500		500
T0		500		500
T1	`Tx1.begin()`	500		
T2	`update(total - 200)`	300	.... Tx2.begin()	
T3	.....		`select(total ....)`	300
T4	} catch (Exception e) {		AddToTotal = 200	
T5	`Tx1.rollback()`	**500**	newTotal = total + addToTotal	500
T6	....		`update(newTotal)`	**700**
	.....		.....	

At time T1, the consumer instance begins a transaction (Tx1) and at time T2
removes 200 widgets from the inventory to fulfill an order from a client leaving
the total to 300 widgets. At time T2, the SupplierBean starts a transaction (Tx2)
and finds the inventory has 300 widgets at T3. It will then add 200 to the total at
T5. Before the SupplierBean updates the total, the ConsumerBean finds an
error in the client's order and decides to roll back the transaction. The total is set
back to 500. When the SupplierBean adds 200 to the total, the inventory total is
700 widgets.

Unrepeatable Reads

Take two different transactions—while Tx1 is updating fields in a row of a table in
a database, transaction Tx2 is reading the same row of the same table. Every read
is different resulting in *unrepeatable reads*. For this example, refer to Table 14.3. A
PriceFinder bean instance at T2 reads the price of a book with the title
"EJB101" and retrieves a price of $39.99. At T3, the PriceManager instance is
updating the price of the book to $29.99. If the PriceFinder instance repeats the
same read at T5, it would display the updated price of $29.99, thus generating an
unrepeatable read.

Phantom Reads

Phantom reads occur when new rows appear and old rows disappear. For example,
say Tx1 does a select with certain search criteria. Right after the search is
completed, the second transaction, Tx2, inserts or deletes rows of data that match

the Tx1 search criteria. Tx1 repeats the same search and is unable to see all the new rows while the old rows have disappeared.

Table 14-3 Unrepeatable Reads

Time	PriceFinderBean	Price	PriceManagerBean	Price
T0				
T0			`update("EJB101"` `Price=$39.99 …)`	39.99
T1				
T2	`select( Price where` `title="EJB101" …)`	39.99	….	
T3	…..		`update("EJB101"` `Price=$29.99 …)`	29.99
T4				
T5	`select( Price where` `title="EJB101" …)`	29.99		
T6	….			
	…..		…..	

For a phantom read example, refer to Table 14.4. A `BookFinderBean` instance at T2 selects rows of books with search criteria "EJB," while the `BookInventoryBean` instance at T3 and T4 inserts a new book titled "EJB500" and deletes a row containing "EJB101." A subsequent select query by `BookFinderBean` at T5 searching for the parameter "EJB" would find "EJB500," but the row with "EJB101" wouldn't be found resulting in a phantom read.

Setting Isolation Levels

Isolation levels are resource-manager specific. For this reason, the EJB specification doesn't define an API for managing isolation levels. In most cases, isolation levels are resource-manager specific and are set by the database administrator. In a distributed scenario (where the bean instances are accessing different resource managers), each resource manager can have different isolation levels associated with it.

Table 14-4 Illustration of Phantom Reads

Time	BookFinderBean	Titles	BookInventoryBean	Titles
T0				500
T0				500
T1			Tx2.begin()	
T2	`select(title="EJB" …)`	"EJB101", "EJB200", "EJB300", "EJB400"	….	
T3	…..		`delete("EBJ101"`	"EJB101" deleted
T4			`insert("EJB500" …)`	"EJB500" added
T5	`select(title="EJB" …)`	"EJB200", "EJB300", "EJB400"	**"EJB500"**	
T6		….		
		…..		…..

For session beans and message-driven beans with bean-managed transaction demarcation, the bean developer can set the isolation level programmatically in the bean's method only when using the JDBC API. The developer uses the `setTransactionIsolationLevel(type)` method of the `java.sql.Connection` interface. Methods and the isolation level that can be used programmatically follow:

- public void **setTransactionIsolation**(int level)throws SQLException—This method enables the programmer to set the isolation level.

- public int **getTransactionIsolation**() throws SQLException—This method retrieves the current transaction isolation level.

- public void **setAutoCommit**(boolean autoCommit)throws SQLException—Although this isn't strictly a transactional method, autoCommit must be set to false to control the transaction programmatically.

The following Isolation levels are discussed next.

- `public static final int` **`TRANSACTION_NONE`**
- `public static final int` **`TRANSACTION_READ_UNCOMMITTED`**
- `public static final int` **`TRANSACTION_READ_COMMITTED`**
- `public static final int` **`TRANSACTION_REPEATABLE_READ`**
- `public static final int` **`TRANSACTION_SERIALIZABLE`**

To solve the concurrency issues discussed above, you should implement various locking techniques at the resource level. Most relational databases have implemented locking techniques to isolate reads and writes to the database by transactions to resolve issues with dirty reads, unrepeatable reads, and serializable phantom reads. The four isolation levels are as follows:

1. **`TRANSACTION_READ_UNCOMMITTED`**—The read uncommitted isolation level allows other transactions to read uncommitted data. As it provides no isolation, the underlying resource doesn't need to acquire data locking on shared data and thus provides the highest level of performance. This level allows dirty reads, unrepeatable reads, and phantom reads. This isn't an acceptable isolation for most business applications. The read uncommitted isolation level is most appropriate in cases where the data isn't being actively updated and in cases where users can tolerate inconsistency, such as historical data of sporting events records.

2. **`TRANSACTION_READ_COMMITTED`**—The read committed isolation level reads only committed shared data. This level does solve dirty reads, but unrepeatable reads and phantom reads are possible. This isolation level is appropriate in cases where the data isn't mission critical, such as Web sites that publish daily breaking news events.

3. **`TRANSACTION_REPEATABLE_READ`**—The repeatable read isolation level guarantees that subsequent reads will yield results identical to previous reads. This isolation level solves dirty reads and unrepeatable reads, but phantom reads are still possible. This isolation level is most appropriate for applications having repeatable reads, such as flight or train schedules.

4. **`TRANSACTION_SERIALIZABLE`**—The serializable isolation level provides the highest level of isolation. At this isolation level, the access to the shared data is serialized—the current transaction has exclusive read and update privileges. This means that it has an exclusive lock on the shared data and is completely isolated from other transactions. Note that at this setting, isolation results in the slowest performance among the four levels. This isolation level solves dirty reads, unrepeatable reads, and phantom reads. You should only use the serializable isolation level when serialized transactions are mandatory for mission-critical applications. Use it sparingly as it does impact per-

formance, especially in distributed transactions. If an isolation level is set to TRANSACTION_NONE, the underlying resource does not support transaction. Please refer to the Table 14.5 for a summary of isolation levels.

Table 14-5 Summary of Isolation Levels and Their Benefits

Isolation Levels	Dirty Reads	Unrepeatable Reads	Phantom Reads
TRANSACTION_READ_UNCOMMITTED (Fastest)	Yes	Yes	Yes
TRANSACTION_READ_COMMITTED	No	Yes	Yes
TRANSACTION_REPEATABLE_READ	No	No	Yes
TRANSACTION_SERIALIZABLE (Slowest)	No	No	No

Restriction with Isolation Levels

Isolation levels must not be changed in the middle of a transaction as this may result in undesirable behavior. Session beans and message-driven beans with bean-managed transaction demarcation using JTA and JMS API must defer the isolation level to the resource manager. The isolation is deferred to the resource manager with entity beans as well. Isolation levels are set in the resource manager by the database administrator, and the isolation attributes in the resource managers aren't accessible from the EJB. As a result, the EJB instance must work the isolation level set by the administrator. The deployer can work the administrator to set the desirable isolation level in the resource manager. Only in cases where the bean developer is programmatically managing transaction with databases can the isolation level be set within session and message-driven beans. Data access classes generated by the container at deployment time manage the isolation level for entity beans with container-managed persistence. The isolation level set by the data access class must not conflict with the isolation level set at the resource manager within a transaction; this is ensured via the vendor's tool.

The database administrator sets the isolation level on the resource manager so the bean developer, the assembler, and the deployer must work together with the database administrator and coordinate the isolation level setting to ensure optimal application performance.

Transaction Roles and Responsibilities

Now, let's specify the different roles and responsibilities for each component in transactions. Bean developers are responsible for these tasks:

- setting the transaction attributes and writing the code for bean-managed transaction demarcation
- may also use the deployment descriptor to provide a suggestion on the optimal setting of the transaction attributes for EJBs with container-managed transactions

Application assemblers are responsible for one task:

- setting the transaction attributes of EJBs with container-managed transaction demarcation in the application. The assembler may follow or ignore the hints provided by the developer regarding transaction attributes.

Deployers are responsible for one task:

- setting the transaction attributes of EJBs with container-managed transaction demarcation before deploying the application, especifically when the developer and assembler don't set the transaction attributes

And database administrators execute this task:

- setting the isolation level for the resource managers

When coding EJBs with container-managed transaction demarcation, the bean developer, assembler, deployer, and the database administrator must cooperate and coordinate application deployment to ensure that isolations are set correctly and optimally for the application.

Summary

In this chapter we started our discussion with a definition of a transaction, followed by a discussion of the types of transactions and the need for transaction in implementing business logic. We then looked at the participants in a transaction and local and distributed transactions. We also looked at ACID properties of a transaction, how to set the transaction attributes, and their implications. The difference between local and distributed transaction and the role TPC performs in complex business logic was also addressed. We discussed how to implement transaction declaratively and programmatically. We looked at three ways, using JTA, JMS API, and JDBC API, to demarcate transaction programmatically. We then focused on the transaction characteristics of EJB and the various objects that interact in a transaction. We also looked at the three types of commit options a container might implement. We examined a stateful session bean with SessionSynchronization interface and its life cycle. We then discussed the pros and cons of bean- and container-demarcated transaction and looked at isolation settings. We concluded with a look at the transactional responsibilities of bean developers, assemblers, and deployers.

ENTERPRISE JAVABEAN SECURITY

Topics in This Chapter

- Understanding the EJB Security Model
- Implementing Security Declaratively
- Implementing Security Programmatically
- Declarative versus Programmatic Security
- Implementing Resource Manager Security
- Security Applicability and Restrictions
- Security Interoperability
- Roles and Responsibilities in Implementing Security

Chapter 15

In an enterprise application, security plays a critical, central role. In Part 2 of this book, we concentrated on the development aspects of EJBs and deferred a discussion of transaction and security issues until later. We covered transaction in Chapter 14. This chapter now focuses on Enterprise JavaBean (EJB) security issues.

Understanding the EJB Security Model

In the traditional enterprise application-programming model, the developer not only writes the business logic but also implements the security logic. For example, the developer must define users and groups, associate application privileges to the groups and then to individual users, provide a mechanism for storing and accessing these users and groups efficiently, and implement the necessary logic to check for authorization at run time. Implementing such a complex security mechanism is tedious, requiring knowledge of low-level system APIs and expertise in security issues. The business logic programmer (who typically has little or no security expertise) must implement code to manage security using low-level operating system security APIs. The resulting business applications are often bloated and buggy with security holes.

The EJB security framework takes the responsibility for implementing security from the bean developers (the business logic experts) and delegates it to the

EJB container vendor, the security expert. The EJB architecture has the following security management goals:

- to remove the burden of implementing an application's security from bean developers by delegating that task to the EJB container
- to discourage hard-coding of security policies in the bean class by encouraging the application assembler and deployer to set security policies declaratively
- to allow portability of EJB applications across multiple EJB servers, regardless of the security mechanism

Roles in Implementing EJB Security

Let's take a closer look at the security goal of the EJB architecture and its implementation. One goal of the EJB component model is to encourage the development of off-the-shelf EJB components, enabling independent software vendors and resellers to sell standard EJB components and prepackaged J2EE applications. Thanks to this design, businesses can buy various EJB components from different software vendors. These vendors with expertise in implementing business logic may also develop some of their own custom EJB and Web component front ends. They assemble a complete J2EE application consisting of third-party EJB and in-house developed components.

Alternatively, a business might choose to build a custom J2EE application consisting of all in-house-developed EJB and Web components. A third option might be to buy a complete prepackaged J2EE application from a value-added reseller (VAR) and then service specific needs by customizing the application for the operating environment during deployment. The EJB market scenario is illustrated in Figure 15-1. Participants include:

- *The EJB component provider*—The EJB component provider (also referred to as the bean developer) can be an individual EJB developer or a company that specializes in EJB development. Their EJB components encapsulate discrete business logic packaged and sold as ejb-jar files. If the bean developer implements security logic in the bean class then they must specify the security requirements in the deployment descriptor. For example, a bean provider develops a shopping cart EJB component and then sells it on the Web.
- *The J2EE application provider*—Application providers are usually VARs, who take EJB components developed by various bean developers and then add Web components to create a complete J2EE application. The complete J2EE applications are packaged and sold as ear files. The

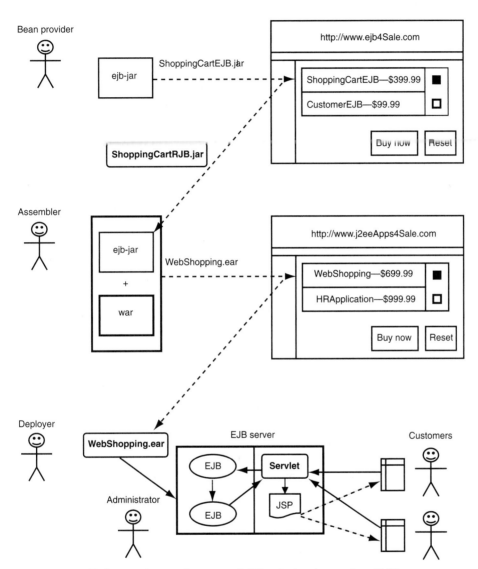

Figure 15-1 Roles, tasks, and responsibilities in implementing EJB security

application assembler creates an application with EJBs and Web components and sets the security requirements for the application. Figure 15-1 illustrates complete shopping cart application, `WebShopping.ear`.

- *The J2EE application buyers*—In the EJB marketplace, application buyers are businesses that either buy a prepackaged J2EE application (such as the WebShopping.ear from the application provider) or EJBs and web components from component providers. These businesses may also write custom components and then assemble their own applications. Once the application is developed in-house or a prepackaged application is bought, the deployer takes the J2EE application, resolves any resource- and security-related mapping issues, and deploys it on the J2EE application server. The example in Figure 15-1 shows a Web retailer buying the shopping application, `WebShopping.ear`; the deployer then deploys it to a specific environment. The system administrator is responsible for creating user accounts, groups, security realms, and so forth and ensuring that the system runs smoothly.

- *The J2EE application server or EJB container vendor*—This party provides the J2EE 1.3 certified application server on which the J2EE applications are deployed.

As you can see in Figure 15-1, the bean providers, the application provider, and the application users might be located in San Jose, London, and Tokyo, respectively, posing an interesting security implementation challenge. In such a scenario, the bean developer is unable to predict the security requirements of the J2EE application assembled by the assembler or the operating environment where the application will eventually be deployed.

The assembler probably doesn't fully know the operating environment security requirements where the application will eventually be deployed. Nor does the assembler know of any security requirements hard-coded into the bean implementation class by the bean developer, because the assembler in most cases has no access to the source code. The deployer, who is responsible for mapping the security requirements to the operating environment, must know the security requirements of the application as specified by the assembler and any hard-coded security logic that the bean developer may have implemented.

The challenge to EJB security is to convey the security requirements implemented in the bean class to the application assembler, who will use the EJB components to create a J2EE application. The assembler, in turn, must convey the security requirements of the J2EE application to the deployer, who will ensure that the environment security requirements are met when the application is deployed.

EJB 2.0 security is based on the Java 2 security model and Java Authentication and Authorization Services (JAAS) version 1.0. Because the Java 2 security and JAAS discussion is beyond the scope of this book, we'll only discuss the basic concepts of principal, authentication, and authorization before discussing EJB security. Please refer to the appendix for references for Java 2 security and JAAS topics.

Principals, Authentication, and Authorization

To understand the concepts behind EJB security, it helps to first understand the concept of a *principal*. A principal might represent an individual user, a user group, a login ID, a business, or a service. Upon successful authentication, a principal becomes associated with a business service it represents. Authentication typically involves a client verifying that the client is who he or she claims to be. Verification is performed in number of ways, such as with username and password, through digital certificates, or using smart cards. Once the client is authenticated, a principal (`java.security.Principal`) object is associated with the client. In the EJB security scenario, it is assumed that the client has already been authenticated, that the client has a principal associated, and that the principal is stored in the `javax.naming.Context` object that is created. So the principal object is implicitly propagated when the client makes requests to the EJBs in the container.

Once a client has been authenticated successfully, the EJB security model must enforce access control to protected resources and services based on permissions provided by security access policy. Authorization is the process of checking to allow or deny a client who is associated with a principal the right to execute methods of EJB components based on the security roles defined in the deployment descriptor. We'll focus on the specifics of how authorization works in the EJB security model.

Not all clients must be authenticated in order to be able to execute methods on EJBs. When a client executes in an unauthenticated mode, it has no principal object associated with it when it makes requests and executes common business logic such as a search for books or access to static html pages. It's quite common in enterprise applications to have anonymous user names such as "world" or "default," to which unauthenticated clients default.

There are two options for implementing security in EJB components: declaratively or programmatically. The preferred option is to implement the EJB security declaratively because of the comparative flexibility and portability of this approach.

Implementing Security Declaratively

In a declarative security implementation, the bean developer defers the security implementation to the assembler and the deployer. The bean developer just implements the business logic and doesn't bother with security issues.

To understand the EJB security model, you should first understand the *security view* concept, which consists of logical security roles, method permissions, and mapping of security roles to the security entities in the operational environment.

Security Roles

Security roles are a semantic grouping of permissions that a given type of abstract user of an application must possess to execute various methods in an application successfully. The security role must be defined in the context of the security view. It consists of the `<security-role>` element that encloses two subelements: an optional `<description>` element used for documentation, and the required `<role-name>` element that specifies a particular abstract role name. The bean developer and/or the assembler should use the `<description>` element to convey security information to the developer. The scope of the security roles applies to all the EJBs in the ejb-jar file. Let's look at how security roles are specified in the deployment descriptor of a sample application that declares four security roles: `Student`, `PreferredStudent`, `Instructor`, and `Manager`.

A security "role" is an abstract representation of a type of user who has been assigned certain groupings of permissions necessary to use an application successfully. Application assemblers have no knowledge of the final security environment. The security roles are meant to be logical roles, each representing a type of user who should have access rights to the application.

Each security role must be defined using the <security-role> element in the deployment descriptor and then the <role-name> element. Although it's optional to use the description element, description elements document roles and help the deployer. The scope of the security roles applies to all the enterprise beans in the ejb-jar file.

The security view is specified in the assembly section of the deployment descriptor. It consist of the `<security-role>` element that encloses two elements, an optional `<description>` element that can be used for documentation, and a `<role-name>` element that must include a role name, as shown in the code fragment that follows. In the online registration application for which code is excerpted here, there are four security roles: `Student`, `PreferredStudent`, `Instructor`, and `Manager`.

```
<assembly-descriptor>
    <security-role>
        <description>
        This role applies to all potential students who are allowed
        to register for courses on line. This role would allow the
        students to access their information.
```

```
      </description>
      <role-name>Student</role-name>
</security-role>
<security-role>
      <description>
      This role represents students who have taken one or more
      classes in the past year. This role has all the privileges of
      the regular student and some additional specialized services.
      </description>
      <role-name>PreferredStudent</role-name>
</security-role>

<security-role>
      <description>
      This role must only be assigned to instructors who will teach
      the Java courses. This role allows the instructors to update
      and add themselves to the various instructor-related records.
      </descriptor>
      <role-name>Instructor</role-name>
</security-role>

<security-role>
      <descriptor>This role should only be assigned to users who are
      able to add new courses and schedules, delete schedules, and
        directly affect schedule availability. This should be a
      restricted role.
      </descriptor>
      <role-name>Manager</role-name>
</security-role>

  </assembly-descriptor>
```

The foregoing example only specifies the potential abstract security role; permissions aren't specified. Now, let's assign method permissions to the security role.

Method Permission

Method permission declares which groups of the enterprise bean's home and component interface methods one or more security roles may execute. Method permissions are defined as binary relations from the set of security roles to the set of the methods of the EJB's home and component interfaces (including their superinterfaces). The method permission element defines method permissions; each <method permission> element can include a list of one or more security roles and a list of one or more methods. Each security role in the list is identified by the <role-name> element; each method or set of methods is defined by the method name. The <method permission> element can include an optional

<description> element. A security role or method may appear in multiple <method-permission> elements. Before we show you how to apply method permissions, let's first look at different ways to distinguish and specify methods in the deployment descriptor.

There are three ways to specify the method element with the <method permission> elements. To specify the same privileges to all the methods in the bean class, use the asterisk character (*) as the method name:

```
<method>
    <ejb-name>ScheduleEJB</ejb-name>
    <method-name>*</method-name>
</method>
```

To specify the same privilege to a method or to all the overloaded methods, use the method name:

```
<method>
    <ejb-name>StudentName</ejb-name>
    <method-name>getScheduleList</method-name>
</method>
```

Finally, to denote a specific method in cases with overloaded method names, use parameters to select the desired method:

```
<method>
    <ejb-name>StudentEJB</ejb-name>
    <method-name>getScheduleList</method-name>
    <method-params>
        <method-param>String</method-param>
    </method-params>
</method>
<method>
    <ejb-name>StudentEJB</ejb-name>
    <method-name>getScheduleList</method-name>
    <method-params>
        <method-param>String</method-param>
        <method-param>String</method-param>
    </method-params>
    <method-name>getScheduleList</method-name>
    <method-params>
        <method-param>String</method-param>
        <method-param>StartDate</method-param>
    </method-params>
</method>
```

In rare cases (for example, when the method name giveDiscount(arg) is declared as the home method in the home interface and as a regular business method in the component interface), you can distinguish between a method having both a home and component interface with exactly the same signature by using the `<method-intf>` element. If you specify this element as `Remote`, it implies that the method is in the component interface. Specifying the element as `Home` implies that the method is in the home interface:

```
<method>
<ejb-name>StudentEJB</ejb-name>
<method-intf>Home</method-intf>
<method-name>giveDiscount</method-name>
</method>
```

In the following example, notice that the student role is specified by the `<role-name>` element and is followed by the methods in the two EJBs that it is permitted to execute. The client with a `Student` or `PreferredStudent` role may execute all the methods in the `StudentEJB` instance and all the overloaded `addSchedule` methods and `deleteSchedule` methods with a single `String` argument in the `RosterEJB` instance. Now, let's apply role name and method permission in the context of an example.

```
<method-permission>
      <role-name>student</role-name>
      <role-name>PreferredStudent</role-name>
      <method>
            <ejb-name>StudentEJB</ejb-name>
            <method-name>*</method-name>
      </method>
      <method>
            <ejb-name>RosterEJB</ejb-name>
            <method-name>addSchedule</method-name>
            <method-name>deleteSchedule</method-name>
                <method-params>
                    <method-param>String</method-param>
                </method-params>
      </method>
</method-permission>
```

Now, let's look at another example of method permission. The `PreferredStudent` role has access to only two methods in the `PromotionEJB`, while the `Manager` role has access to all the methods in `StudentEJB`, `PromotionEJB`, and `ManagerEJB`.

```
<method-permission>
      <role-name>PreferredStudent</role-name>
      <method>
      <ejb-name>PromotionEJB</ejb-name>
      <method-name>getSpecialDiscount</method-name>
```

```
    <method-name>getReferralDiscount</method-name>
    </method>
</method-permission>
<method-permission>
    <role-name>Manager</role-name>
    <method>
    <ejb-name>StudentEJB</ejb-name>
    <method-name>*</method-name>
    </method>
    <method>
    <ejb-name>PromotionEJB</ejb-name>
    <method-name>*</method-name>
    </method>
    <method>
    <ejb-name>ManagerEJB</ejb-name>
    <method-name>*</method-name>
    </method>
</method-permission>
```

In the above two snippet examples from the deployment descriptor of an application, there are three different roles and three different bean classes. The application declares three security roles: Student, PreferredStudent, and Manager, each having a different level of permissions. The Student role has the basic permission; it can execute all the methods in the StudentEJB bean. The PreferredStudent role has a higher level of permission; it can execute all the methods in the StudentEJB bean plus two additional methods in the PromotionEJB bean that enable it to get special discounts that the Student role cannot obtain. The Manager role has the highest level of permission; it can run all methods in the StudentEJB, PromotionEJB, and ManagerEJB beans.

If you don't want some methods to be checked for authorization, use the <unchecked> element to mark such methods and prevent the container from checking for authorization. The code example that follows says not to check for authorization when any client executes the giveDiscount() or getPastWinners() method of the PromotionEJB bean.

```
  <method-permission>
    <unchecked></unchecked>
    <method>
    <ejb-name>PromotionEJB</ejb-name>
    <method-name>giveDiscount</method-name>
    <method-name>getPastWinners</method-name>
    </method>
  </method-permission>
```

There might be cases when you want to restrict a client from executing a list of methods from a bean class. To indicate a set of methods that should not be called, use the `<exclude-list>` element. This is sometimes necessary when creating a J2EE application with EJB components from third parties that include methods that clients don't need to access. The methods listed in the `<exclude-list>` are not callable regardless of the role, and in cases where a method is specified both in the `<exclude-list>` and in `<method-permission>`, the deployer must configure the security so that the methods in the `<exclude-list>` cannot be invoked. Use the `<exclude-list>` element to restrict these methods as follows:

```
<exclude-list>
    <description> clients should not have access to these methods
    </description>
    <method>
       <description>We don't support this promotional option at the
       moment.
       </description>
    <ejb-name>PromotionEJB</ejb-name>
    <method-name>getFourForThePriceOfThree</method-name>
    <method-name>getFifthClassFree</method-name>
    </method>
    <method>
       <description>We want to restrict students from running this
       method for security reasons.</description>
    <ejb-name>StudentEJB</ejb-name>
    <method-name>listStudentsByCompanyName</method>
    <method-name>listStudentEmailAddresses</name>
    <method-name>listStudentsHomeAddresses</student>
    </method>
</exclude-list>
```

You've now seen how EJB security can be implemented declaratively. Application assemblers use the `<security-identity>` element and `<method-permission>` elements in the deployment descriptor to specify the security requirement of the application. The application deployer is ultimately responsible for implementing the security view by first resolving any security issues and then mapping the logical security roles specified in the deployment descriptor to users or groups of users before deploying the application.

Propagation of Security Identities

To understand EJB security better, look at Figure 15-2, which illustrates a client invoking `methodX()` on EJB1 on EJB server A. EJB1 is invoking `methodY()` on EJB2 on EJB server B. Assume that the client is authorized, possesses a principal security identity, and is allowed to invoke `methodX()` on EJB1. First, what is the

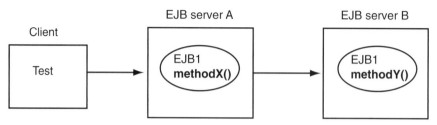

Figure 15-2 Propagating security identity

principal under which methodX() of EJB1 will execute? Second, what are the security identities associated with the threads of execution when EBJ1 invokes methodY() on EJB2 components?

The answers to the foregoing questions depend on what is specified by the <security-identify> element. The EJB methods can execute in one of the two security identities: the caller's security identity (specified by the <use-caller-identity> element) or the bean instance-specific identity (specified by the <run-as> element in the deployment descriptor.) So, in Figure 15-2, if the client's caller principal is Student and the <security-identity> element encloses the <user-caller-identity> element for methodX() in EJB1 and methodY() in EJB2, then these methods will execute with the principal identity Student of the caller, Test. In essence, the caller security identity is propagated from the client to the EJBs. But on the other hand, if the <security-identity> element with the <run-as> element specified by the <role-name> element is set to the principal Manager for methodX() in EJB1 and if the <role-name> element is set to the principal Instructor for methodY() in EJB2 as shown in Table 15-1, then the client's principal wouldn't be propagated. Instead, the methods would acquire the appropriate principal during execution.

If the <user-caller-identity> is specified, the EJB container propagates the caller's principal while executing the method on the bean. If both EJB1 and EJB2 have their security identity set to the <user-caller-identity> option and the client's security identity is Student, methodX() and methodY() execute with a Student security identity (see Table 15-1).

Table 15-1 Security Identity Propagation

Security-Identity	<user-caller-identity>	<run-as>
Client principal is student	N/A	N/A
EJB1— methodX()	Student	<role-name> Manager<role-name>
EJB2 — methodY()	Student	<role-name> Instructor</role-name>

In the following example from the deployment descriptor, ShoppingCart's <security-identity> has specified the option <use-caller-identity> with no value and, when a client invokes the ShoppingCartEJB instance, the shopping cart bean instance assumes the principal of the caller and executes in the security identity of the caller.

```
<ejb-jar>
  <display-name>CartJAR</display-name>
  <enterprise-beans>
    <session>
      <display-name>ShoppingCartEJB</display-name>
      <ejb-name>ShoppingCartEJB</ejb-name>
      <home>j2eebootcamp.developingEJB.chapter7.shop.ShoppingCart-
Home</home>
      <remote>j2eebootcamp.developingEJB.chapter7.shop.ShoppingCart
</remote>
      <ejb-class> j2eebootcamp.developingEJB.chapter7.shop.Shop-
pingCartEJB</ejb-class>
      <session-type>Stateful</session-type>
      <transaction-type>Bean</transaction-type>
      <security-identity>
        <description>Assume the identity of the calling cli-
ent.</description>
        <use-caller-identity></use-caller-identity>
      </security-identity>
    </session>
  </enterprise-beans>
  ........................ . .
```

If the <run-as-identity> option is specified, the container establishes the identity of the bean instance specified by the role name; it propagates its role-name as its security identity when it calls on other EJB components. This applies to the bean instance as a whole, which means that all the methods of the bean instance (including those in the home and component interfaces) will run in the identity specified by the <run-as> element in the deployment descriptor. Table 15-1 shows that the client has the Student security identity, whereas EJB1 and EJB2 have their security identity elements set to the <run-as> option, with role names Manager and Instructor.

Note that the security identity setting affects only the bean instance's security identity; it doesn't affect the identities of the callers to the bean instance. For this reason, methods such as getCallerInPrincipal() and isCallerInRole() are still applicable. The <uncheck> element can be used to indicate that a method should not be checked for authorization.

Let's look at another example that uses the <run-as> option; it encloses a <role-name> element that specifies a dbLogger role name and an optional description element, as shown in the next code fragment. When the RosterEJB bean is executed by a client, it runs with a dbLogger principal, and this identity must exist in the operational environment; otherwise, it will throw security exceptions.

```
<display-name>RosterEJB</display-name>
<enterprise-beans>
  <entity>
    <display-name>RosterEJB</display-name>
    <ejb-name>RosterEJB</ejb-name>
    <home>j2eebootcamp.developingEJB.chapter9.roster.RosterHome</home>
    <remote>j2eebootcamp.developingEJB.chapter9.roster.Roster</remote>
    <ejb-class> j2eebootcamp.developingEJB.chapter9.roster.Ros-
terEJB</ejb-class>
    <persistence-type>Bean</persistence-type>
    <prim-key-class>java.lang.String</prim-key-class>
    <reentrant>False</reentrant>
    <security-identity>
      <description>Use database to log with dbLogger user-
name</description>
        <run-as>
        <role-name>dbLogger</role-name>
        </run-as>
    </security-identity>
    <resource-ref>
      <res-ref-name>jdbc/JCampDS</res-ref-name>
      <res-type>javax.sql.DataSource</res-type>
      <res-auth>Container</res-auth>
      <res-sharing-scope>Shareable</res-sharing-scope>
    </resource-ref>
  </entity>
</enterprise-beans>
```

The <run-as> element identifies a logical role-name that must correspond to one of the security roles specified in the deployment descriptor. There are two cases where <run-as> security identity is useful: when you want to control access to a resource with a single user identity for security reasons, and when you have a limited database license so that assigning one user to the dbLogger role name and making all clients use that name is both economical and desirable.

The run-as security identity option is useful when a business needs to allow callers to perform certain operations on restricted resources without transferring the privileges to the caller. For example, the Online Java course registration application has two security identities: Student (without access to some fields of the administrative table) and Manager (with high-level access to the administrative database table). To allow a client with a Student security identity to update administrative database tables without giving the client the database access privilege of a manager, specify the security identity as run-as with the role name Manager for the DBA bean instance. When the client with the Student security identity invokes a method on the DBA bean instance to update the administrative table, the DBA bean instance executes with Manager security identity, which is allowed to update the restricted table. Use the <user-caller-identity> element option to propagate the security identity from the caller to the callee.

Implementing Security Programmatically

Even though declarative EJB security is preferred, there are times when it might not satisfy special security requirements. For example, the developer might need to implement a time-based system administrative task to restrict certain methods to "run on Sunday only if the caller's security identity is administrator."

Most of the difficult and low-level security implementation tasks are handled transparently by the EJB container, leaving the bean developer to perform only two security-related tasks—checking for permissions and checking for identity—programmatically using the EJBContext interface. Session, entity, and message-driven beans have their respective SessionContext, EntityContext, and MessageContext interfaces that implement the javax.ejb.EJBContext interface. The EJBContext interface encapsulates the security and transaction contexts. Let's take a closer look at the two tasks that are necessary to implement EJB security programmatically.

Checking the Identity of the Caller

Programmatically implementing EJB security consists of checking the identity of the caller and matching the identity to the role that is permitted to execute the method. To achieve that, a bean developer must use the `javax.ejb.EJBContext.getCallerPrincipal()` method from the `EJBContext` interface. This method checks whether the bean instance's caller has a particular role and returns `java.security.Principal`, which identifies the caller of the EJB instance. As we discussed earlier, a bean instance can run with an identity of the caller if the `<use-caller-identity>` option is specified, or the instance can run with a specified `<role-name>` if the `<run-as>` option is specified. So if the `getCallerPrincipal()` method is invoked in the bean instance, it returns the principal of the caller of the method in the bean instance—not the principal that corresponds to the `<run-as>` element. This is significant because we want to check the identity of the caller calling the method—not the principal of the instance, which we already know. Because the caller must always be associated with a principal, it should never turn a `null`. Use the `getName()` method of the `java.security.Principal` interface to obtain the name of the caller principal.

The `java.security.Principal` interface represents the abstract notion of principal (such as user ID or individual) and declares several methods, including:

- `boolean equals(Object another)`—useful in comparing the principal to another principal object; returns true if it matches
- `String getName()`—returns the name of the principal
- `int hashCode()`—returns a hash code associated with the principal
- `String toString()`—returns a string representation of the principal

The sample code fragment that follows shows how to use the `getCallerPrincipal()` method. As discussed earlier, the authenticated caller has a principal associated with it, which is passed implicitly during invocations. In this example, the `getCallerPrincipal()` method gets the user's login name and then uses that ID to update the address.

```
public class AddressBean implements SessionBean
{
    EJBContext ejbContext;

    public void setSessionContext(sessionContext)
    {
        ejbContext = sessionContext;
    }
```

```
...............................
    public void changeAddress(AddressVO address) {
    callerPrincipal = ejbContext.getCallerPrincipal();

    studentID = callerPrincipal.getName();
  //use the address data access object to update the
  //address of the student with studentID

    addressDAO.updateAddress(studentID, address);
  }
}
```

Checking for Permission

If a bean developer wants to check whether the caller has a particular role for permission to execute a method, the `javax.ejb.EJBContext.isCaller-InRole()` interface from the EJBContext is useful. This method can be used to test whether the caller has a given security role and returns a value of either `true` or `false`. This method allows the bean developer to code security checks using the method permission that cannot be easily defined declaratively in the deployment descriptor.

The `isCallerInRole(String roleName)` method is used in the code to test whether the current caller has been assigned to a given security role. It tests the principal that represents the caller of the EJB, not the principal that corresponds to the `run-as` security identity of the bean instance.

The following code example implements the logic that a class schedule can be canceled only if the caller has a security identity of `supervisor` and the total number of students registered is less than four.

```
If ( schedule.getStudentCount() < 4  &&
     ejbContext.isCallerInRole("supervisor") )
{
    cancelCourse(scheduleID);
} else {
    throw new NotAuthorizedSecurityException(...)
    ...............
```

It wouldn't be possible to implement such logic declaratively in the deployment descriptor.

When the EJB security is implemented programmatically, the bean developer must implement the `getCallerPrincipal()` and/or the `isCallerInRole()` method in the bean class. If the bean class references any security roles, the bean developer needs to inform the application assembler and deployer of the security roles used in the source code, which might not be available to the assembler and the deployer. The bean developer is responsible for declaring each security role referenced by the isCallerInRole() methods in the bean class using the <security-role-ref> elements in the deployment descriptor. In a sense, the bean developer declares an abstract security role name that's different from the role name an assembler might specify later during assembly phase. But it's the application assembler's responsibility to map the abstract security role to the logical role that he or she defines during the assembly phase.

The <security-role-ref> element consists of the security <role-name> element, which the Bean developer must specify, and optional description and <role-link> elements. The security role name must match the roleName parameter used in the isCallerInRole(String roleName) method. The scope of the security role reference includes the name defined by the <role-name> element and spans to the session and entity beans elements whose declarations contain the <security-role-ref> elements.

The following code example illustrates the <security-role-ref> element in the deployment descriptor with an optional description element and a required security <role-name> of supervisor. This role-name must match the argument of the isCallerContextInRole('supervisor') in the bean code as shown previously.

```
<enterprise-beans>
...........
    <entity>
        <ejb-name>AddressEJB</ejb-name>
        <ejb-class>com.j2eebootcamp.ejbbook.AddressBean</ejb-class>
        ............ .
        <security-role-ref>
          <description>
            This security role should only be assigned to select people
              allowed to add, delete and change schedules of classes.
          </description>
          <role-name>supervisor</role-name>
        </security-role-ref>
    </entity>
    ................ .
</enterprise-beans>
```

The bean developer is responsible for declaring the abstract security role name (as specified by the <role-name> element) in the <security-role-ref> element of the deployment descriptor. The role name supervisor is an arbitrary name that may not exist in the operational environment.

A bean developer can invoke the `getCallerPrincipal()` and `getCallerIn-Role()` methods only in a bean's business methods for which the container has a client security context. Attempting to invoke these methods when no security context exists results in the `java.lang.IllegalStateException` runtime exception being thrown.

Linking the Security Role Reference to Security Roles

The role name `supervisor` specified by the bean developer is just an abstract security name used in the EJB code; it must be linked to the security role specified within the J2EE application. In the J2EE application, the assembler may have specified the supervisory role as the security identity `manager`, so the developer maps the specified security role name `supervisor` used in the EJB code to a corresponding security role `manager` specified in the application by the `<role-link>` element of the `<security-role-ref>` element. The following code example illustrates the use of the `<role-link>` element that maps to the abstract role-name `supervisor` and to the application security role name `manager` enclosed by the `<security-role-ref>` element. Notice that the application security identity name `manager` specified by the `<role-link>` element must be declared in the `<role-name>` element of the `<security-role>` element of the `<assembly-description>` portion of the deployment descriptor.

```
<enterprise-beans>
..........
    <entity>
        <ejb-name>AddressEJB</ejb-name>
        <ejb-class>com.j2eebootcamp.ejbbook.AddressBean</ejb-class>
        ..............
        <security-role-ref>
            <description>
            This role should only be assigned to individuals having
the
            authority to create, delete and update class schedules.
            </description>
            <role-name>supervisor</role-name>
            <role-link>manager</role-link>
        <security-role-ref>
    </entity>
....................
<assembly-description>
    <security-role>
        <description> Has a privileges of a manager of the group.Can
        add, delete or modify schedules data </description>
    <role-name>manager</role-name>
```

```
    </security-role>
    <security-role>
        <description> registered students </description>
        <role-name>student</role-name>
    </security-role>
    ......................... . .
 </assembly-description>
 ......... .
 </enterprise-bean>
```

Even if the security role name declared by the bean developer happens to match the role name assigned by the assembler, the `<security-role-info>` element still must include the `<role-link>` element with the matching role name.

Even when the EJB security is implemented programmatically, the application assembler will still use the `<security-identity>` and `<method-permission>` elements in the deployment descriptor to define the security view to specify the security requirement of the application. The assembler may also link the security role specified by the bean developer in the EJB code to the security role specified in the application in the `<security-role-ref>` element.

Regardless of whether the EJB security is implemented declaratively or programmatically, the application deployer is responsible for implementing the security view by resolving any security issues and by mapping the logical security roles specified in the deployment descriptor before deploying the application.

Deployment

The application deployer is ultimately responsible for implementing the security policies and ensuring that they are enforced during runtime. The deployer depends on the EJB container provider's deployment tool to accomplish the tasks.

One of the deployer's tasks is to assign logical security roles specified in the security view to the principals (users) or group of principals (user groups) used for managing security in the operational environment. The assignment is on a per-application basis. If multiple independent ejb-jar files use the same security role name, each may be assigned differently.

The deployer also must specify the principal delegation for intercomponent calls by configuring the security-identity element as either `user-caller` identity or `run-as` identity. If the option selected is `run-as`, the deployer must also map the role name to a principal in the operational environment. A principal is assigned to a role; all the permissions of the role are available to the principal as long as the principal is "in" role.

If access to resources is managed by the container, the deployer must provide the necessary information (such as username and password) for the application to authenticate and access the resources. The deployer may use the security view specified in the deployment descriptor by the assembler as a hint but is free to override it. In the absence of a security view, the deployer is responsible for specifying and implementing the security policy. The security mapping is done at application deployment phase using the vendor-provided tool specific to the application server.

Declarative versus Programmatic Security

Given the choice, implementing EJB security declaratively is encouraged, as a declarative implementation provides high flexibility and portability. The EJB security should be implemented programmatically only if the security requirement cannot be fulfilled declaratively. Table 15-2 shows the relative advantages and disadvantages of both types of implementation.

Table 15-2 Comparing Declarative and Programmatic Security Implementations

Feature	Declarative Security	Programmatic Security
Flexibility	Flexible security model	Less flexible security model (security role and logic are hard coded)
Portability	Can be modified by deployer at deployment time	Security logic can be modified only by the bean developer
Security	Few security holes	Greater susceptibility to security holes
Control	Unable to implement fine-grained security control; only coarse-grained (method-level) security can be applied	Boasts fine-grained security control; can be modified by deployer
Security policy	Security policies applicable only at the method and class levels only	Security policies customizable and applicable at the code-line level

Implementing Resource Manager Security

When resource managers are accessed within an EJB class, the bean developer must use the resource manager connection factories to create connections to these resources. There are two choices when it comes to authenticating and associating a principal with the resource managers: container-initiated or application-initiated authentication. The <res-auth> element is used to indicate the authentication type.

Container-Initiated Authentication

In the case of container-initiated authentication for a resource manager, the deployer is responsible for setting up the resource manager sign-on information, such as user name and password, using the vendor-provided deployment tool. The bean developer must use the `<res-auth>Container</res-auth>` element to specify that the authentication is container initiated. The following code fragment represents a section of the `<resource-ref>` element from the deployment descriptor for a database resource with the resource reference name set to `jdbc/JCampDS`, as specified by the `<res-ref-name>` element. The `<res-type>` element specifies the type of resource—`DataSource` in this case—and the `<res-auth>` element specifies that the authentication is provided by the container. The `<res-sharing>` element specifies that the data source resource is sharable with other clients. In all our examples that access the database, we've use the container-authenticated option.

```
<resource-ref>
    <res-ref-name>jdbc/JCampDS</res-ref-name>
    <res-type>javax.sql.DataSource</res-type>
    <res-auth>Container</res-auth>
    <res-sharing-scope>Shareable</res-sharing-scope>
</resource-ref>
```

Application-Initiated Authentication

In the case of application-initiated authentication, the bean developer must provide all the sign-on and authentication information as method parameters to the resource manager connection factory method.

Security Applicability and Restrictions

The security options we have discussed so far are not equally applicable for all types of EJBs in all situations. Let's briefly discuss the applicability of security restrictions for different types of EJBs and clients.

Security Applicability by Bean Type

Table 15-3 shows the applicability of the security option to the various types of EJBs. The security identity element `<run-as>` option can be used with session, entity, and message-driven beans, but the `<user-caller-identity>` element can be used only with session and entity beans. Because message-driven beans have no interfaces and use messages to communicate with clients, the following restrictions apply:

- MDB cannot use the `<user-caller-identity>` security option because it implies that a client is invoking methods via interfaces.

- MDB cannot implement programmatic security because the `isCallerInRole()` and `getCallerPrincipal()` methods have no meaning for message-driven beans. Also, the security context cannot be propagated from clients to MDB instances.

Table 15-3 shows that although session and entity beans support both declarative and programmatic security implementation, only the `<run-as>` declarative security option is supported by message-driven beans.

Table 15-3 Applicability of Declarative and Programmatic Security Options to EJBs

Security Options	Session Beans	Entity Beans	Message-Driven Beans
`<use-caller-identity>`	Yes	Yes	No
`<run-as>`	Yes	Yes	Yes
`getCallerPrincipal()`	Yes	Yes	No
`isCallerInRole()`	Yes	Yes	No

EJB Client Security Restrictions

When a client calls an enterprise bean, its security context is propagated, and it must follow certain rules to avoid violating EJB security policies:

- A client cannot change its principal in the middle of a transactional call.

- When a client is communicating with a session bean, it must not change its principal association for the duration of the conversation.

- A transaction is associated with a single security context. In cases where requests from multiple clients arrive within a single transactional request, all requests within the same transaction must be associated with the same security context.

Security Interoperability

To support interoperability between J2EE applications, the EJB 2.0 and J2EE 1.3 specifications require that the EJB, Web, and application client containers support all the requirements of Conformance Level 0 of the Common Secure Interoperability version 2 (CSIv2) specification from the Object Management

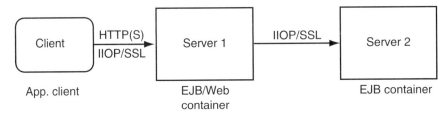

Figure 15-3 Security interoperability

Group (OMG). The EJB, Web, and client containers are required to support Secure Socket Layer (SSL 3.0) and standard Transport Layer Security (TLS 1.0) protocols as the security protocol over IIOP.

Figure 15-3 illustrates the interaction between a client and two servers (server1 and server2). In the case of a thin client communicating with a Web container (S1), the secure HTTPS protocol is used. But in the case of a rich client communicating with an EJB container (S1), IIOP/SSL is used. EJB container to EJB container communication always uses the IIOP/SSL protocol.

Roles and Responsibilities in Implementing Security

Roles and responsibilities of bean developers, assemblers, deployers, and EJB providers can be summarized as follows. The EJB 2.0 specification doesn't specify how to implement security; that task is left to the EJB container vendors. All participants depend on the vendor-provided deployment tool to configure and set up security parameters in EJB applications.

Bean Developer

When implementing declarative EJB security, bean developers can focus their attention on writing the business logic and let the assembler, deployer, administrator, and EJB container manage and implement security. If security is implemented programmatically, the bean developer is responsible for declaring all the security role names used in the EJB code by using the `<security-role-ref>` element of the deployment descriptor. The EJB architecture discourages the bean developer from implementing security mechanisms declaratively or programmatically in the EJB's business methods. Instead, the architecture delegates that responsibility to the EJB container, application assembler, and deployer. The bean developer is, however, encouraged to use the deployment descriptor to convey to the deployer security-related information regarding appropriate security policy for the EJB.

Application Assembler

The application assembler may define the security view of the J2EE application by declaring the security roles and method permissions required by the application in the deployment descriptor. In cases with programmatic security, when the bean developer has specified a `<security-role-ref>` element, the assembler must use the `<role-link>` element of the `<security-role-ref>` element to link all bean developer-specified security role references to the security role defined by the assembler using the `<role-name>` element. The security view is only a logical requirement of the application's security.

The assembler may also specify whether the bean instance will run with the caller's security identity or using its own by declaring the `<user-caller identity>` or `<run-as>` element in the `<security-identity>` element. Although the EJB specification doesn't mandate the responsibility for security to the application assembler, the assembler, who has intimate knowledge of the application, is encouraged to provide the security view of the EJB to simplify the deployer's job.

Application Deployer

Regardless of whether the security is implemented declaratively or programmatically, it is the application deployer who is ultimately responsible for implementing EJB security according to the EJB specification. The deployer is responsible for mapping the logical security view (provided by the assembler) to the operational environment, which is the deployer's domain of expertise. And it's the deployer who ensures that the security policies of the application are enforced at runtime. The deployer may ignore the security view specified by the assembler and override the security roles as appropriate. If the bean developer failed to specify the `<security-role-ref>` element or the assembler chose not to specify the security view, it is still the deployer's responsibility to find out the security view and map the security roles to the operating environment. In particular, the deployer is responsible for assigning the security domain and principal realm to an EJB application. The deployer must also assign the principals used for managing security in the operational environment to the security role defined by `<security-role>` elements of the deployment descriptor. In addition, the deployer is responsible for following the instructions from the assembler in configuring the principal delegation for intercomponent calls and configuring access to resource managers.

System Administrator

The system administrator is responsible for system administrative tasks such as creating user accounts and groups, conducting system audits, and maintaining proper maintenance of the system that runs the EJB servers. The deployer and administrator work cooperatively to create, manage, and map security identities to the ones available on the system. The administrator is responsible for the review and management of security audit trails.

EJB Container Provider

The EJB container vendor (or the application server vendor) supplies the J2EE 1.3 certified application server with EJB 2.0 support. In addition to providing the application server, the vendor also provides the deployment tools, which enable the involved parties to create, assemble, and deploy J2EE applications. The container must enforce the EJB security discussed at runtime and provide a security audit trail mechanism. The mechanism must log all `java.security.Exceptions` and denials of access to EJB servers, containers, and home and component interfaces.

Summary

In this chapter, we began with a discussion of the basic concepts behind principal, authentication, and authorization. We then looked at two ways to implement EJB security: declaratively and programmatically. In the context of declarative security, we discussed the concept of roles, their association with principals, and how these roles relate to method permissions that enable EJB containers to enforce security checks before allowing access to methods of the EJBs. We also discussed how to implement security programmatically using the `javax.ejb.isCallerInRole()` and `javax.ejb.getCallerPrincipal()` methods of the `javax.ejb.EJBContext` interface.

We also looked at the issues of EJB security restrictions, interoperability, and propagation of security context between containers, and we explored two options for authenticating access to resources. We also discussed the relative advantages and disadvantages of implementing EJB security declaratively or programmatically. We concluded with a discussion on the respective security roles of the bean developer, assembler, deployer, administrator, and EJB container provider.

EJB DESIGN PATTERNS, INTEROPERABILITY, AND PERFORMANCE

Topics in This Chapter

- Introduction to EJB Design Patterns
- Data Access Object
- Value Object
- Value Object Assembler
- Value List Handler
- Service Locator
- Session Facade
- Business Delegate
- Additional Patterns
- EJB Interoperability
- EJB Performance Issues

Chapter 16

The ability to implement business logic with EJBs is only a first step. Successfully implementing large, scalable, high-performance EJB applications requires that bean developers understand and use proven design patterns effectively in their EJB applications. In this chapter, we'll discuss

- EJB design patterns
- EJB interoperability
- EJB performance issues

Introduction to EJB Design Patterns

In their book *Design Patterns*, E. Gamma, R. Johnson, and J. Vlissides, quote architect Christopher Alexander, who defines a design pattern in this way: "Each pattern describes a problem which occurs over and over again in our environment, and then describes the core of the solution to that problem, in such a way that you can use this solution a million times over, without ever doing it the same way twice." Mr. Alexander was referring to building architecture, but the same principles apply to software design. (See the Appendix at the back of this book for a complete reference.)

Note: In the Java development field, *Design Patterns* is commonly referred to as *GoF*.

From an EJB programmer's perspective, we may consider design patterns as blueprints or template solutions that can be easily adapted to solve recurring problems in context. For example, if you have programmed for some time, you have probably observed recurring solutions to similar problems and have a collection of codes that you have reused to solve those problems. Once these solutions are catalogued and named, they become *design patterns*. The use of design patterns saves time and effort. When developers recognize certain types of problems, proven design patterns can be applied.

There are several sources of information about design patterns. The book *Design Patterns* catalogs 23 of them. The Sun Java Center (SJC) J2EE Pattern Catalog (beta version 1.0) describes seven business-tier patterns and two integration patterns, which we'll describe shortly. The ServerSide.com (http://www.theserverside.com) also serves as a repository of independent J2EE design patterns. Design patterns evolve with technology and with experience; over time, new patterns emerge, and some existing patterns lose applicability.

In this chapter, we'll discuss seven of the nine EJB design patterns catalogued by the Sun Java Center that are useful and applicable in EJB 2.0. Our discussion won't include code examples in this chapter, but we'll implement several design patterns in Chapter 18. For a thorough discussion on J2EE design patterns, including code examples, I recommend the Sun java Center Web site at http://developer.java.sun.com/developer/technicalArticles/J2EE/patterns/ and an excellent book from Sun Press/Prentice Hall titled *Core J2EE Patterns.* More information about these sources is available in the Appendix.

The modified format that we use to describe EJB design patterns in this chapter is based on the popular design pattern description format that appears in the *Design Patterns* book. It consists of the following elements:

- *Pattern name*—the name commonly used to describe the pattern name; it should succinctly convey the essence of the pattern. We use as the primary name the name designated by Sun Java Center.
- *Context*—the environment the problem addresses.
- *Problem*—the challenges described in detail.
- *Forces*—a list of motivations (causes), limitations, and rationales that have shaped the solution.
- *Solution*—describes the approaches to solve the problem. Solutions must include class and sequence diagrams to explain their structures as well as suggestions and strategies for implementing the pattern.

- *Structure*—includes a discussion of the class diagrams of the object involved in the pattern.
- *Participants and responsibilities*—a list of all the objects participating in the pattern.
- *Strategies*—ways in which the design pattern can be implemented.
- *Consequences*—also known as *rationale*; includes a discussion of tradeoffs and side effects of the solution that the developer should know about. It also can include variants of the current pattern or other patterns that might be applicable.
- *Related patterns*—a description of patterns that are similar.

EJB Design Patterns and EIS Tiers

The seven design patterns we examine in this chapter include

- Data Access Object
- Value Object
- Value Object Assembler
- Value Object List Handler
- Service Locator
- Session Facade
- Business Object Delegate

Selecting an EJB Design Pattern

Selecting an EJB design pattern is a straightforward process, due to the limited number of EJB patterns and their specific applicability. The pattern name gives a sense of the pattern's function, which is further clarified by the description of the context. The problem section should discuss situations similar to the problem being encountered, while the list in the forces section should address the real-world problem's issues. The resolution to the problem should match the solution provided by the design pattern. Finally, check the consequences of the design pattern to ensure that the tradeoffs offered by the design pattern are acceptable in your particular situation.

Let's discuss the seven EJB-related design patterns one by one.

Data Access Object

The Data Access Object pattern is related to the EIS tier.

Context

In J2EE applications, Web and EJB components need to access data stores (such as RDBMs and OODBMs) from different vendors. They must also be able to access flat files to read and write persistent data.

Problem

The EJB components (session beans, BMP entity beans, the servlet, and JSP) need to access data stores to retrieve and modify persistent data. The underlying data stores in most cases are relational databases (relational database management system or RDBMS) but can also be object-oriented databases (object-oriented database management system, or OODBMS), file system-based Indexed Sequential Access Methods (ISAMs) or just flat files. Each of these has its own proprietary APIs and features. Component developers must understand these data stores as well as vendor-specific APIs to write the logic that can access the persistent data. Standard SQL and JDBC APIs can be used if the data store is a relational database; however, non-standard SQL is used to access advanced proprietary database features.

Including the data access logic in the Web and EJB components ensures tight coupling between the components and the underlying data store. Although this results in better data access performance, it violates the EJB portability rule. The component code is dependent on a particular data store; migrating the component to a different data store requires enabling the data access logic to use a different set of APIs that renders the component not portable.

Forces

This design pattern must address several issues:

- The APIs that currently access the data store are vendor specific.
- The API and the capabilities of the data store vary depending on the type of data store.
- Web and EJB components need to access persistent data from the data store.
- The portability of the components is directly affected when specific APIs are used.
- The components should remain portable if possible; developers should provide the flexibility to replace the underlying data source without affecting the logic encapsulated by the components.

Solution

The Data Access Object (DAO) pattern abstracts and encapsulates all data-access implementations to the data store. The DAO pattern manages the connection and the data access to the data store. The DAO implements the API and the necessary logic required to work with the specific data store; implementation details are isolated from the component code and expose simple interfaces. The business components can then use the simple exposed interfaces to access the persistent data in the underlying data store.

When the underlying data store changes from an RDBMS to an OODMS, the API of the DAO must be replaced with an OODMS API. (This also applies to the implementation logic; but note that the exposed interface can remain the same, and the business component is not affected by the changes in the data store.) Using the DAO restores the portability of business components. The Data Access Object design pattern has been used in several of the sample applications in Part 2 of this book and will also be seen in the ScheduleDAO example in Chapter 18.

Structure

Figure 16-1 shows the class diagram, in which the BusinessObject uses a DAO to access the DataSource. The DAO in turn creates a ValueObject to efficiently pass the requested data to the BusinessObject.

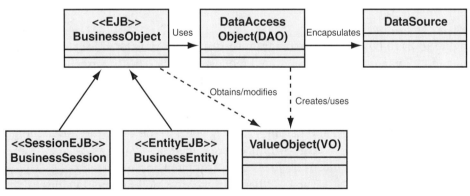

Figure 16-1 Data Access Object class diagram

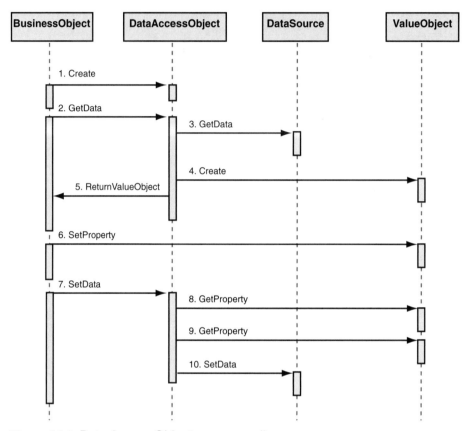

Figure 16-2 Data Access Object sequence diagram

Figure 16-2 is a DAO sequence diagram showing a BusinessObject creating a DAO and then making a coarse-grained request for data. The DAO executes the request, accesses the data source, and then creates a ValueObject. It then populates the ValueObject with the data and returns the ValueObject to the BusinessObject. The BusinessObject can then perform fine-grained access methods, such as setting and getting property fields in the ValueObject. The BusinessObject uses a coarse-grained access method—(such as SetData(arg)—with ValueObject as an argument and returns the ValueObject to the DAO. The DAO then retrieves the modified field value and saves that field in the DataSource.

Participants and Responsibilities

As Figure 16-2 shows, there are four participating objects in the DAO patterns:

- `BusinessObject` accesses the persistent data using the DAO. The `BusinessObject` can be implemented as a stateless, stateful, or BMP entity bean, or as a servlet, JSP object, or Java object that needs to access the persistent data.

- `DataAccessObject` is the pattern object that abstracts the data access implementation details from the `BusinessObject` and enables transparent access to persistent data stored in the `DataSource`. The `BusinessObject` delegates the data access operation to the `DAO`.

- `DataSource` is the persistent store (also called the data store), which can be an RDBMS, ODBMs, XML, or flat file system. To the `BusinessObject`, it doesn't matter, as the `DAO` handles the `DataSource`.

- `ValueObject` is a serializable Java object with `setter` and `getter` methods, and it's used primarily to pass data across different J2EE tiers.

Strategies

Several strategies can be helpful in implementing DAO patterns:

- *Simple Java DAO object*—This simple yet effective strategy is applicable for most situations, especially when the data source is a relational database. It's a plain Java file with the JDBC API and logic to access the relational database. This strategy lacks the ability to use different types of data sources, however. The code examples throughout this book use this strategy.

- *Factory for the DAO pattern*—This strategy provides a DAO factory object that can generate different types of DAO factory methods. Each factory supports different types of storage implementations. The strategy enables support for different relational database vendors such as Oracle, Sybase, or DB2 (RDBMS factory) or object database vendors such as ObjectStore, Versant, or Poet. `DAOFactory` is a base class from which different DAO factories—such as `RdbDAOFactory`—inherit and implement a data source-specific (Oracle or Sybase) access mechanism for different implementations. Each DAO is responsible for connecting to the appropriate data source and obtaining and providing access to the persistent data for the business object it supports (see Figure 16-3).

- *Automatic DAO code generation*—With the DAO pattern, each `BusinessObject` corresponds to a specific DAO, and each DAO corresponds to a specific type of data store. With this relationship established, developers can write a code generation utility that generates

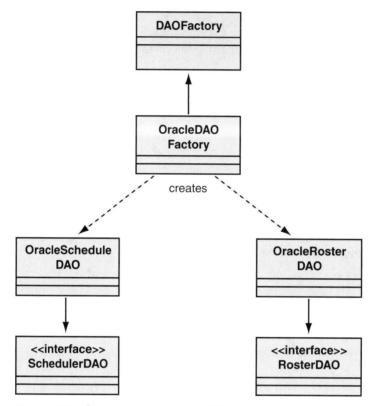

Figure 16-3 Strategy for using the DAO factory

all the DAOs required by the application. This works for simple cases, but for complicated scenarios, developers typically use sophisticated object-to-relational mapping tools.

Consequences

Using the DAO pattern has several advantages and no major negative impacts. Chief among them are:

- *Clean separation of business logic from data-access logic*—With DAO design patterns, the implementation logic can be separated from the business logic and made transparent to the component.

- *Simplified migration to different types of data source*—DAO does not enable portability completely, but it does simplify the task. By modifying the APIs and the logic in the DAO, the maintainability of both the BusinessObject and the DAO code is improved.

- *Reduced complexity for the business object*—Localizing data access logic to separate classes means that the business object isn't cluttered with data access code. This localization reduces and isolates the complexity of business objects.

- *Possible code reusability*—Depending on the design and implementation, the DAO object is reusable with similar components.

Note that because the container handles persistence management with CMP entity beans, DAOs cannot be used with CMP entity beans.

Related Patterns

The Abstract Factory design pattern provides an interface for creating dependent objects without specifying their concrete classes.

Value Object

Now, let's examine the characteristics of the Value Object pattern.

Context

Remote clients need to exchange data with the EJB.

Problems

EJBs use `get` and `set` methods in their component interfaces to enable remote clients to access bean instance attributes. A remote client may invoke one or many such methods within its logic. Remote method calls have high overhead; an increased frequency of `get` methods impacts the performance of the application.

Forces

The Value Object design pattern addresses these issues:

- *Reducing the number of remote method calls from clients to EJB components*—In J2EE applications with many components, keeping the level of remote calls low while fulfilling client's requests reduces overall network traffic.

- *Sending read-only data to the presentation tier while keeping network traffic down*—A client might require read-only data for presentation to the end user.

- *Reducing the chattiness of an application*—would reduce the network traffic by reducing the frequency of remote method calls.

- *Aggregating requests to multiple components*—In cases where clients might need data from different components and their dependent objects, clients are forced to make multiple remote calls to different components before they have the necessary data to apply their logic.

Solution

Use a `ValueObject` to encapsulate the data so it can be transferred in a single call. In the `ScheduleClient` example from Chapter 5, individual get methods are called to retrieve the attributes of a `Schedule` object from a client generating heavy network traffic. Instead of using several get methods, use the serializable value object, `ScheduleVO`, to populate the object with attributes the client is interested in. Then pass the `ScheduleVO` object in one method call. The value object, along with data, also includes accessor methods to retrieve the attributes it holds. Once the client retrieves the value object `ScheduleVO`, it can use the value object's accessor methods to access the attributes locally without any remote method overhead. The pattern thereby lessens the number of remote method calls, but each call now contains more data. This design pattern has been featured in several examples in this book—such as the `ScheduleVO` and `RosterVO` object patterns implemented in Chapter 18.

Structure

Figure 16-4 shows a `ValueObject` class diagram in which a `BusinessObject` creates a `ValueObject` and returns it to the client. As the client then has its own copy of `ValueObject`, it can access `getter` methods. Figure 16-5 shows the sequence diagram of a client interaction with the `BusinessObject` and the `ValueObject`.

Participants and Responsibilities

There are three participating objects in the Value Object design patterns, one of which has three variations:

- `Client` can be a thin client or rich client application that interacts directly with the `BusinessObject`. The client can also be a session bean in a Session Facade (a design pattern to be discussed later in this chapter), a servlet, or a JSP.

- `BusinessObject` is most likely an entity bean that creates the `ValueObject` and populates it with persistent attributes. It's then returned when a client invokes the `getData` method on its remote component interface. The `BusinessObject` can be implemented as one

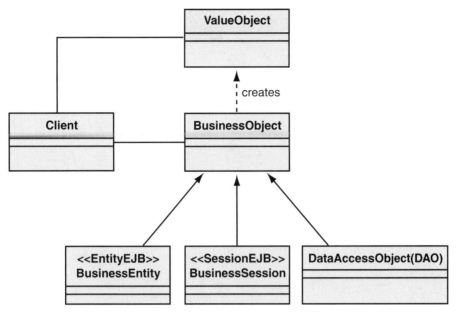

Figure 16-4 Value Object strategy class diagram

of three variations: `BusinessEntity`, `SessionEntity`, or `DataAccessObject`.

- `ValueObject` is a serializable Java class with a constructor that accepts all the attributes necessary for the creation of the `ValueObject`. If the `ValueObject` is read-only, it includes the `get` methods for all the attributes. If it's an updateable `ValueObject`, it includes `set` methods for all the attributes in addition to the get methods.

Strategies

There are several options for implementing Value Object strategies:

- *Read-only or immutable* `ValueObject`—`BusinessObjects` are responsible for creating immutable `ValueObjects` and pass data in a compact and efficient manner from a `BusinessObject` to clients. These immutable `ValueObjects` have only accessor or `get` methods for their attributes and no `set` methods. The client invokes the `getData` method to retrieve the `ValueObject` in one remote component call; it then uses the local `get` method of the `ValueObject` to access the attributes, thus reducing the number of remote calls.

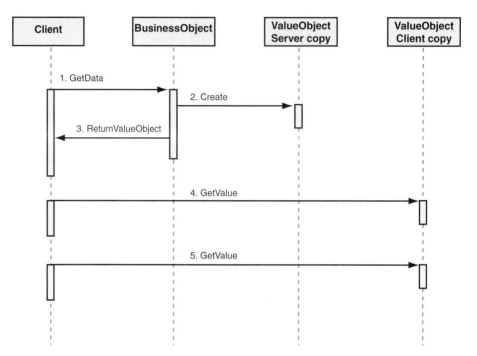

Figure 16-5 Value Object strategy sequence diagram

- *Updateable or mutable* ValueObject—Mutable ValueObject attributes can be modified by the client. Mutable ValueObjects must therefore include the setter and getter methods. The setter methods are represented by setXXX, where XXX is the name of the attribute. The Business-Object provides an update method in its remote component interface that accepts the mutable ValueObject. This enables clients to return the updated ValueObject. A client can use the local set methods to change the attributes of the ClientValueObject before invoking the update method on the component interface. Upon receiving the modified ValueObject, the BusinessObject merges the changes with its own attributes, which can lead to update propagation, synchronization, and version control issues that must be addressed.

- *Single-entity, multiple* ValueObjects—The BusinessObject exposes multiple methods (such as getDataX and getDataY). It instantiates ValueObjectX or ValueObjectY depending on the getData invoked by a client. Another variation of this strategy is to use role-based security to provide the appropriate ValueObject. The BusinessObject provides a generic getData method, but when a client invokes this method, the BusinessObject creates and returns a type of

`ValueObject` appropriate to the client's role. For example, a client with a student role called `getData` would return an immutable `ValueObject` with limited attributes. However, a client with an administrator called `getData` would return a mutable `ValueObject` with other pertinent attributes that the client could change.

- *Entity inherits from a* `ValueObject`—There's no reason why the entity bean class cannot extend the `ValueObject` class. In fact, by doing so, developers avoid code duplication—there's no need to define the same attributes and the corresponding get and set methods for the attributes in the bean class. Note that changes in `ValueObject` (such as the addition of a new attribute or removal of an existing attribute) result in adjustments to the parameters in the constructor, which requires changes in the entity bean class. This problem can be avoided if the `ValueObject` defines its clone method to clone itself. This strategy eliminates the code duplication and keeps the `ValueObject` code separate from the bean code.

- `ValueObject` *factory*—This strategy provides the most flexibility, as `ValueObject` patterns can be extended to support multiple types of `ValueObjects` for an EJB. Extension is enabled by defining different interfaces for each kind of `ValueObject` that can be returned. The `ValueObject` superclass of the EJB class must implement all of these interfaces, and a separate implementation class must be created for each defined interface. The `ValueObject` factory strategy needs a method that takes two arguments, including

  - the EJB instance for which a `ValueObject` must be created, and
  - the interface that identifies which kind of `ValueObject` must be created.

At runtime, the `ValueObject` factory strategy can instantiate an object of the correct class, set the correct attribute values, and return the created `ValueObject`.

Consequences

Using the Value Object pattern has several consequences, chiefly positive ones:

- *Reduction of network traffic*—Instead of using several multiple accessor methods to retrieve attributes on the remote component interface, a client with a single `get` method can retrieve a `ValueObject` that contains all the necessary attributes. The client can then use the local accessor methods to retrieve the attributes. This process results in fewer remote calls, which translates to reduced network traffic.

- *Simplified remote component interface and bean implementation*—Instead of declaring set and get methods for all attributes in the remote component's interface and in the corresponding implementation of the declared get and set methods for the bean class, the programmer can replace them with one get method for the ValueObject and one set method for the modified ValueObject in the component interface. The result is that only two corresponding methods need to be implemented in the bean class.

- *Fewer calls but larger data transfer per call*—With the ValueObject pattern, there are fewer calls from a client to the BusinessObject. The amount of data per call, however, is larger. Before making this tradeoff, a bean developer must take into account the production environment and the impact on the overall performance of the application.

- *Reduced code duplication*—The use of the ValueObject inheritance strategy or the ValueObject factory strategy eliminates code duplication. There is, however, an associated cost in the form of more complex implementation and negative effects on runtime performance.

- *Update propagation and stale* ValueObject—If the mutable ValueObject strategy is used, clients can modify attributes of the ValueObject locally and pass the modified ValueObject to the entity bean BusinessObject. The BusinessObject is responsible for merging the updated attributes from the modified ValueObject with its current attributes. However, there could be other clients with a copy of the ValueObject. If such is the case, the entity bean has no way of propagating the updated ValueObject to the clients when it updates the attributes. This results in clients holding a "stale" ValueObject.

- *Addition of synchronization and version control complexity*—To resolve the potential problems resulting from update propagation and stale ValueObjects, the entity bean can implement version control. Version control would require the ValueObject to have an additional last-modified time stamp or version number attribute. Any attempts by clients to update the ValueObject with a time-stamp or version number earlier than the time stamp or version number on the ValueObject in the entity bean would be rejected. The clients would be required to retrieve the latest version of the ValueObject and modify the attributes before attempting to update the ValueObject. Note that these attempts to handle synchronization of the mutable ValueObject add complexity to the existing code, and the bean developer must factor those possibilities and an acceptable solution into the design logic.

- *Effect of the transaction attribute setting on concurrent access*—When multiple clients are concurrently accessing a BusinessObject, the EJB container can enforce transaction semantics. If the transaction isolation level is set to TRANSACTION_SERIALIZED, the container allows only one client per transaction, thus ensuring maximum isolation and data integrity. In such a case, performance takes a hit, but the integrity of the ValueObject is preserved. This means that while the first client is updating the ValueObject, other clients must wait their turn. Only after the first client is done can a second client access the ValueObject. Note that an isolation level lower than serialized access can lead to compromising the integrity of the ValueObject, as higher levels allow multiple clients to modify its attributes.

Related Patterns

- Session Facade (SJC)
- Value Object Assembler (SJC)
- Factory (*GoF*)

Value Object Assembler

Following is a discussion of the characteristics of the Value Object Assembler design pattern.

Context

Application clients often need to retrieve data efficiently from different EJB components for processing or presentation purposes.

Problem

A J2EE application consists of several EJBs providing services to an application client. The client might need to make several remote method calls to various EJBs before assembling data to be displayed. This creates several potential problems:

- *High volume of network traffic*—Because the application client might have to make remote calls to the EJB components, the network traffic is directly proportional to the number of components that the client needs to access, the granularity of the methods, and the frequency of the method invocation.
- *Tight coupling between the client and the EJB components*—Because the application client must access the distributed EJB components directly, there's a tight coupling between the client and the components. This generates higher network traffic and makes the relationship brittle; for example, changes in any one of the components can cause problems with the client.

- *Complexity of the client-component relationship*—If the client needs to retrieve data from multiple EJB components to construct the data model before displaying it to an end user, this added complexity in addition to the network traffic from the remote calls to the EJB components is directly proportional to the complexity of the data model.

Forces

The Value Object Assembler design pattern must address the following issues:

- The application client must include the logic to handle the construction of the client-side data model from the data retrieved from various EJB components. The effect of this requirement adds unnecessary complexity to the client code and introduces even tighter coupling between the remote client and the EJB components.

- The number of client relationships needs to be reduced. The number of relationships a client has is dependent on the number of EJB components from which it needs to retrieve data in order to create its data model. Having a high number of relationships introduces further complexity to the client code and increases the number of remote calls. Reducing the number of relationships results in simpler client code and reduced chattiness, both of which benefit application performance.

- The clients frequently need a read-only data model for presentation purposes.

- The client updates a small subset of the data model data using fine-grained methods, which creates unnecessary network traffic.

- The enterprise application might have several different clients that require the same data model. In that case, each of the clients must have available the logic to construct the data model, with the result that code is duplicated. If the data model changes, then these clients will have to be modified.

- If the client is a rich client running on a desktop with limited resources, the data model could impact the performance of the client or run into runtime errors. Whether this occurs depends on the complexity of the data model and the logic for construction.

Solution

Use the `ValueObjectAssembler` to construct the model or submodel according to the `ValueObject` pattern to retrieve required data from various `BusinessObjects` and other objects. The `ValueObject` data model can be complex; it can consist of `ValueObjects` from multiple `BusinessObjects`.

The intention of the `ValueObjectAssembler` is to create a `ValueObject` and send the data back to the client in a single call. For simplicity purposes, the composite `ValueObject` should be read-only.

Structure

Figure 16-6 illustrates the Value Object Assembler class diagram, which consists of the `ValueObjectAssembler` that builds the composite `ValueObject` from data retrieved from the `BusinessObject`—which may be, for example, session, entity, DAO, or plain Java objects. The composite `ValueObject` is passed to the client. The sequence diagram illustration in Figure 16-7 shows the `Value-ObjectAssembler` retrieving data from various objects to create a composite `ValueObject`, which is returned to the client.

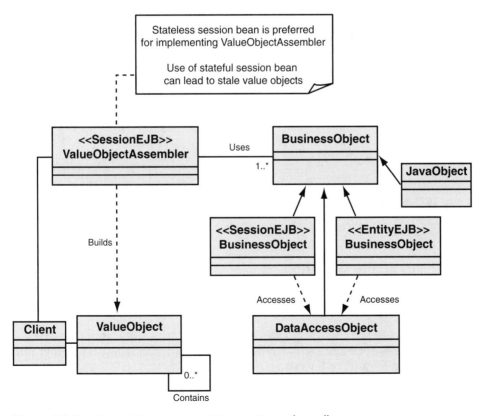

Figure 16-6 `ValueObjectAssembler` pattern class diagram

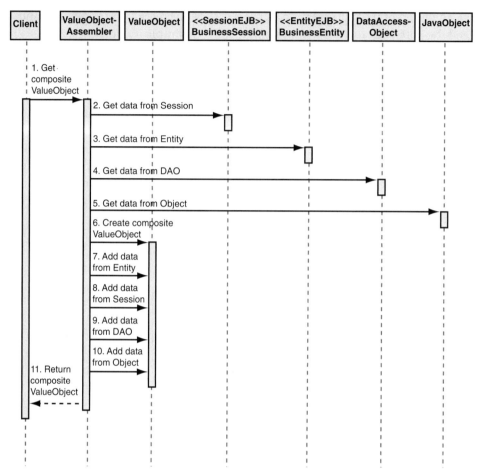

Figure 16-7 Value Object Assembler pattern sequence diagram

Participants and Responsibilities

The four main players in the Value Object Assembler design pattern are:

- Client—The client requests the composite ValueObjects from the ValueObjectAssembler. The client can be a standalone Java program, Session Facade, or Java object.

- ValueObjectAssembler—The main class for this pattern. It is responsible for constructing composite ValueObjects by assembling the required data from different BusinessObjects and returning the data to the client.

- BusinessObjects—A BusinessObject cooperates with the ValueObjectAssembler in creating the composite ValueObjects. BusinessObjects can be implemented as session and entity beans, DAOs, or Java objects.

- ValueObject—The composite ValueObject is constructed from data retrieved from various participating BusinessObjects. The ValueObjectAssembler creates the ValueObject and returns it to the requesting client.

Strategies

There are three main strategies for implementing the ValueObjectAssembler, which must always run in the business tier:

- *Implement the* ValueObjectAssembler *as a regular Java object*—In such cases, the client is usually a Session Facade, which fronts the ValueObjectAssembler and provides other business services to the remote clients. This strategy localizes the interaction between the ValueObjectAssembler and the BusinessObjects, thereby reducing remote network traffic.

- *Implement the* ValueObjectAssembler *as a session bean*—In an environment with a dynamic data model, the ValueObjectAssembler is preferably implemented as a stateless session bean because it's suited for capturing the snapshot of the data at the time a ValueObject is created. In an environment with a fairly static data model, the ValueObjectAssembler can be implemented as a stateful session bean. However, because the ValueObjectAssembler maintains state between invocation, the bean developer must write the logic to refresh the state when the data model of the BusinessObjects changes. The client can be a Session Facade or another ValueObjectAssembler.

- *Implement the* ValueObjectAssembler *to maximize reliance on* BusinessObjects—The ValueObjectAssembler depends on the participation of the BusinessObjects to create the composite ValueObject. The BusinessObjects can be implemented as session beans, entity beans, data access objects, and/or regular Java objects.

Consequences

There are both advantages and disadvantages to implementing Value Object Assembler patterns in EJB applications. Here's a summary of them:

- *Reduced network traffic*—The `ValueObjectAssembler` moves the task of assembling a composite `ValueObject` from the remote client to the business tier, thus closer to the participating `BusinessObjects`. This reduces network traffic and improves application performance.

- *Reduced coupling*—Instead of the remote client retrieving data from several `BusinessObjects` and constructing a composite `ValueObject`, it now delegates that task to the `ValueObjectAssembler`. This tight coupling with several `BusinessObjects` results in one method call to the `ValueObjectAssembler`, resulting in better performance.

- *Simplified client code and improved client performance*—The client doesn't need to worry about constructing composite `ValueObjects`. Because the client no longer has to implement the logic to retrieve and assemble data from various `BusinessObjects`, the client code is simpler and requires fewer lines. Thus the client code runs faster and network latency is reduced.

- *Issue with stale value*—Once the `ValueObjectAssembler` constructs a composite `ValueObject` and returns it to the client, the data encapsulated by the business objects can change, and there's no way for the `ValueObjectAssembler` to notify the client of changes in the data model. This results in a stale `ValueObject`.

Related Patterns

- *Session Facade (SJC)*—A Session Facade can manage a client request to the composite `ValueObjects` from the `ValueObjectAssembler`.

- *Value Object (SJC)*—The `ValueObjectAssembler` creates `ValueObjects` and returns them to a client.

- *Data Access Object (SJC)*—This pattern can supply the persistent data to the `ValueObjectAssembler`.

- *Aggregate Entity (SJC)*—An Aggregate Entity can be one of the `Business-Objects` supplying the `ValueObjectAssembler` with the data.

Value List Handler

Following is a summary of the characteristics of the Value List Handler design pattern.

Context

The client might need to retrieve a list of items from the EJB components and display them to the end user. The number of items in the list is unknown and could be large.

Problem

Problems occur when a customer initiates an interaction with a J2EE application by performing a search for a certain entity, such as for a book with the word "Java" in the title. This search returns a large list of books, and the customer might select a book from the list and then interact further with the book entity, or abandon the search and try again with a different search. From the implementation viewpoint, the search could translate to a `finder` method in an entity bean. Unfortunately, with the implementation of the `finder` method, the container is required to create an `EJBObject` instance for every matching object found in the query. With a broad query, this becomes inefficient and expensive, as it locks large amounts of container resources. In most cases, the client might need the list for read-only purposes only, and the list might be abandoned before the client has perused it thoroughly.

Forces

The Value List Handler design pattern must address these issues:

- Implementing a search with the entity bean's `finder` method results in the creation of an `EJBObject` for every item returned in the query. The client needs a more efficient solution.

- Some type of caching mechanism on the business tier enabling a client to fetch a portion of the result set and loop through the result set would increase the efficiency of the application.

- Using `finder` methods for broad searches results in high overhead associated with creation of the `EJBObject` instance.

- The `finder` methods are unsuitable for caching; the client could use some server-side caching mechanism for speed.

- The client might not be equipped to handle a large result set in a single call; implementing caching on the server-side along with the ability to navigate the result sets forward and backward by the client would increase efficiency.
- The query constructs associated with ejbFinder methods previous to the advent of EJB 2.0 were limiting and inflexible.

Solution

Instead of entity beans, use a session bean (e.g. SessionFacade) to execute the query, cache the results, and provide the result set size desired by the client. It's also important to provide the ability to scroll the result set.

Structure

Figure 16-8 shows a Value List Handler class diagram that creates a `ValueList` and returns it to the client. Figure 16-9 is the Value List Handler sequence diagram that shows the interaction between the various objects. Notice that the client makes a request to the `ValueListHandler`, which in turn makes the appropriate method calls to the `ValueList` object.

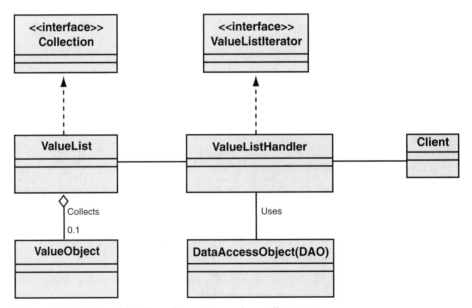

Figure 16-8 Value List Handler pattern class diagram

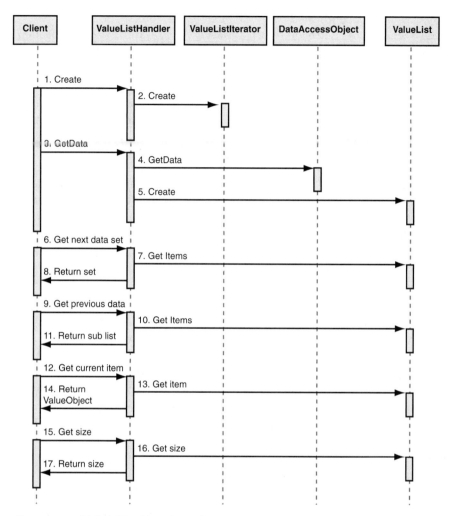

Figure 16-9 Value List Hander pattern sequence diagram

Participants and Responsibilities

There are five significant players in the Value List Handler design pattern:

- ValueListIterator—The ValueListIterator declares several useful methods, such as getSize() to get the size of the result set; getCurrentElement() to obtain the current ValueObject from the list; getPreviousElements(int size) to return a collection of

`ValueObjects` indicated by the size before the element; `getNext-Elements(int size)` to return a collection of `ValueObjects` indicated by the size after the current element in the list; and `resetIndex()` to initialize the index to the start of the list. There can be additional methods besides these basic ones, as required by the application logic.

- `ValueListHandler`—A `ValueListHandler` is modeled with a stateful session bean and implements the `ValueListIterator`. When a client makes a request, the `ValueListHandler` executes the query, creates the `ValueList`, populates it with `ValueObjects`, and caches the private list. Depending on the client request, the `ValueListHandler` creates a new collection of `ValueObjects`, serializes it, and returns it to the client. The `ValueListHandler` is responsible for the creations, manipulating the `ValueList`, and keeping track of the size of the value list and the current index.

- `DataAccessObject`—As we discussed earlier, the `DataAccessObject` provides the `ValueListHandler` with transparent access to the underlying database.

- `ValueList`—The `ValueListHandler` uses the `ValueList` to store the results of the query request to the `DataAccessObject`. The `ValueList` is created once and cached by the `ValueListHandler`. The `ValueList` is manipulated by the `ValueListHandler`. By creating the `ValueList`, the `ValueListHandler` avoids repeated expensive calls to the `DataAccessObject`. If the query fails, it creates an empty `ValueList`.

- `ValueObject`—The `ValueObject` represents an individual record returned from a query executed by the `DataAccessObject`.

Strategies

Two strategies are important to mention for this design pattern:

- *Implement* `ValueListHandler` *as a Java object*—It can then be used by any client that needs caching and listing functionality. In a non-EJB environment, one may implement a `ValueListHandler` as a Java object, and a business delegate could use it to query for a list of `ValueObjects`.

- *Implement a* `ValueListHandler` *as a stateful session bean*—In an EJB environment, the `ValueListHandler` then provides the caching and listing functionality to the client. In this scenario, the `ValueListHander` session bean provides the function of a facade or a proxy pattern.

Consequences

Implementing the Value Object Assembler design pattern generates several consequences. Among them:

- *Alternative to entity bean* `finder` *methods*—This pattern provides an efficient and elegant alternative to entity bean `finder` methods for large queries. The entity bean `finder` method is unsuited to queries that return large result sets because there's significant overhead associated with creating a collection of `EJBObject` references by the EJB container. In comparison, `ValueObjects` have relatively lower overheads. Implementing `ValueListHandler` as a stateful session bean or arbitrary Java object provides more flexibility with query logic and better performance.

- *Customized server-side caching*—In cases where a client is able to display only a subset of the query results and/or is unable to provide client-side caching, the `ValueListHandler` provides sever-side caching. The `ValueListHandler` gives the client the option to request a subset of the data, thus offloading the overhead and the task of caching on the server side.

- *Client-controlled flexible query option*—With `ValueListHandler`, the client controls when and how much data to retrieve from the server-side. This design pattern also makes it possible for the client to traverse the `ValueList` on the server side by allowing the client to scroll forward and backward on the list.

- *Reduced network traffic*—Instead of sending large query results blindly from the server to the client and incurring huge network traffic, the `ValueListHandler` enables the client to control when and what subset of the result set it needs. In most cases, the end user may abandon the search after viewing just a few lines of data, drastically reducing network traffic. On the other hand, the client makes several remote calls if the end user is interested in viewing the entire result set. The `ValueListHandler` is a far superior performance alternate to blindly sending the entire result set.

- *Deferred transaction*—With `ValueListHandler`, the entity bean transaction is deferred until the end user selects an item from the list. Only when an end user selects an item (representing an entity bean) to view details will the entity bean transaction be involved.

Related Patterns

- SessionFacade (SJC)
- Iterator (*GoF*)

Service Locator

Next, let's discuss the characteristics of the Service Locator design pattern.

Context

Clients must look up and retrieve home objects and then create EJB instance before they can access any services on the distributed object. This process involves complex interfaces, dependencies, and network overhead.

Problem

In a J2EE application, clients can request services from EJB components in the business tier. But before clients can invoke business service requests, they must first locate the synchronous bean's home object. Then, they must find and create a new bean instance using the home interface before they can execute the business logic. In the case of message-driven beans, a JMS client must locate the JMS Connection Factory to obtain the JMS Session and the destination before it can send or receive JMS messages. The clients in both cases must use the JNDI API and perform the following steps:

1. *Setup of the JNDI environment*—In a J2EE environment, this step is completed during the application installation.

2. *Provision of the initial context*—The client must then execute a new `Initial-Context()` JNDI method to create a placeholder for the component name-to-object bindings.

3. *Use of the initial context to perform look up for the desired object*

   - In the case of session and entity beans, the client uses the initial context and the bean's home object's JNDI name to retrieve the bean's home object.

   - In the case of message-driven beans, the JMS client uses the initial context to obtain one of the `Topic` or `Queue` destination objects by supplying the JNDI name for the topic or the queue. The client then uses the initial context to obtain a `TopicConnectionFactory` or `QueueConnectionFactory` by supplying the JNDI name for the topic or the queue connection factory.

4. *Accessing the bean instance*

   - In the case of synchronous beans, the client can invoke the `create` method on the home object; in addition with entity beans, the client can invoke the `finder` method, which returns a component object. Once the client has a reference to the component object, it can execute business methods.

- In the case of message-driven beans, the JMS client uses the `TopicConnectionFactory` to create the `TopicConnection`, or the `QueueConnectionFactory` to create the `QueueConnection`. The client then uses the `TopicConnection` to create a `TopicSession` and the `QueueConnection` to create a `QueueSession`. The JMS client uses the topic or the queue session to send and receive JMS messages.

The lookup and creation process just described is a common set of processes often repeated by clients in a J2EE application. The creation of a component involves vendor-specific context factory class implementations; this creates a vendor dependency in the client application, which is undesirable.

Forces

The Service Locator design pattern must address these issues:

- Clients are required to use the JNDI API to resolve the EJB names to EJB home objects mapping.
- Creation of components involves the vendor-provided context factory to create the initial context.
- The J2EE applications use the lookup and create code repeatedly in different clients, which has a negative impact on client performance.
- The frequent execution of lookup and create code also has a negative impact on performance of the EJBs.

Solution

Use of a Service Locator pattern provides the following solutions:

- It abstracts all the complexity of JNDI lookup and create processes and hides that complexity from the clients.
- It provides a caching facility to improve performance.

The Service Locator object can be reused by different clients, resulting in a single point of control that reduces code complexity in the clients and provides improved performance. Two variations of the Service Locator pattern (`ServiceLocatorEJB` and `ServiceLookUp`) are implemented in Chapter 18.

Structure

There are two sets of figures related to the Service Locator pattern: one set to illustrate the pattern for session and entity beans and the other set to illustrate the same pattern when implemented for message-driven beans. Figure 16-10 shows

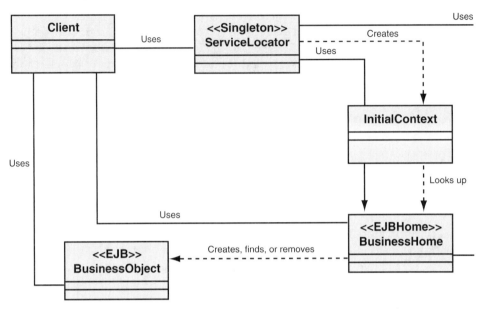

Figure 16-10 EJB Service Locator class diagram for session and entity beans

the Service Locator class diagram for session and entity beans, and Figure 16-11 shows the sequence diagram of the Service Locator pattern for these bean types. The client relies on the `ServiceLocator` to create the `InitialContext` and returns a home interface of the desired session or entity bean. Figure 16-12 shows the Service Locator class diagram for message-driven beans. Figure 16-13 shows the sequence diagram for message-driven beans.

Participants and Responsibilities

There are five significant roles in the Service Locator design pattern:

- `Client`—When a client needs to locate a `BusinessObject`, it uses `ServiceLocator` to find, create, and remove the `BusinessObject` and access the services.

- `ServiceLocator`—The `ServiceLocator` abstracts the complexity of setting up the correct initial context using the vendor-supplied values and then using naming service APIs to locate the desired object. It then creates the `BusinessObject` from clients and provides a simple interface to the client. Clients can use the simple interface to create a

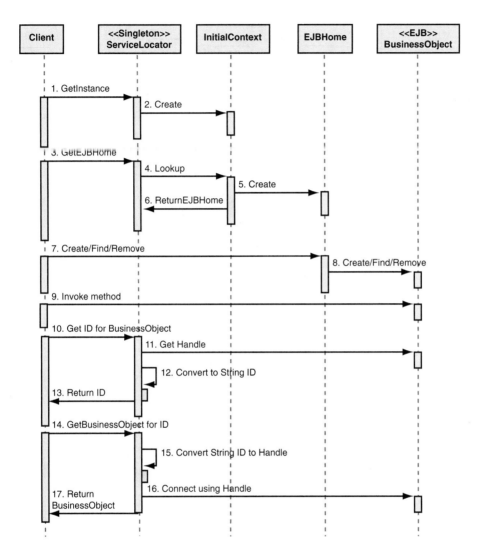

Figure 16-11 EJB Service Locator sequence diagram for session and entity beans

BusinessObject, which simplifies the client code. Other clients can reuse the ServiceLocator.

• InitialContext—The InitialContext creates the context object, which is the starting point for looking up and retrieving objects. The contexts are proprietary and provided by the vendor.

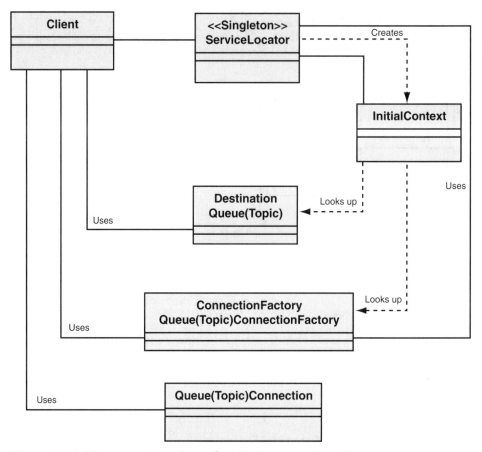

Figure 16-12 Message-driven bean Service Locator class diagram

- `ServiceFactory`—The `ServiceFactory` object provides the life cycle management for the `BusinessObject`. For the session and entity bean `BusinessObject`, the `ServiceFactory` object is the `EJBHome` object. For JMS components, the `ServiceFactory` can be the `JMSConnectionFactory` object, such as `QueueConnectionFactory` or `TopicConnectionFactory`, depending on the messaging model.

- `BusinessService`—The access to services provided by `Business-Service` is the ultimate goal of the client, who uses the `Service-Locator` to find existing business services or to create a new `Business-Service`. The client uses the `ServiceLocator` to create the `BusinessService`, which is an EJB bean instance in the case of session and entity bean applications. In the case of JMS applications, the

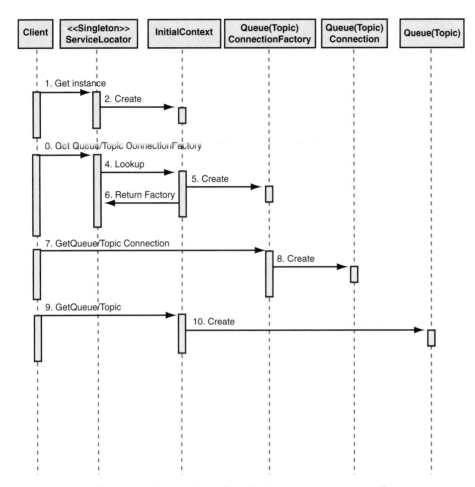

Figure 16-13 Message-driven bean Service Locator sequence diagram

BusinessService can be TopicConnection or QueueConnection, which are used by the clients to send and receive messages.

Strategies

Regardless of the strategies, the ServiceLocator caches the lookup results. As a result, when a client sends the ServiceLocator a lookup request, the ServiceLocator checks its cache. If there's a match, it returns the object, thus saving a JNDI lookup remote call to the directory server. Three specific strategies deserve mention:

- *Session and Entity EJB Service Locator* uses the `EJBHome` object in the role of the `ServiceFactory` and applies only to synchronous EJBs (session and entity beans).

- *JMS Destination Service Locator* uses the `QueueConnectionFactory` object in the role of the `ServiceFactory` in the event of `Queue` destination. The client looks up the `QueueConnectionFactory` and uses it to create `QueueConnection`. The client uses the `QueueConnection` to create `QueueSession`, which sends or receives messages. In the case of topic destination, the `TopicConnection-Factory` object is used in the role of the `ServiceFactory`. The client looks up the `TopicConnectionFactory` to create the `TopicConnection` object, and the `TopicConnection` is used to create `TopicSession`, which the client uses to publish messages.

- *Combined EJB Service Locator* combines the previous two strategies.

Consequences

Use of the Service Locator pattern offers these advantages:

- *Improved client performance*—Because clients don't need to include JNDI lookup logic, the code is simpler, tighter, and faster.

- *Lookup caching*—Because the `ServiceLocator` caches previous lookups, subsequent lookups for objects from different clients are returned faster.

- *Uniform service access for clients*—Because the `ServiceLocator` provides a simple standard `BusinessService` lookup interface, it provides uniform access from all clients. Any new addition of service to the `ServiceLocator` is transparent to clients.

Related Patterns

- Business Delegate (SJC)
- Session Facade (SJC)
- Value Object Assembler (SJC)

Session Facade

Next, let's examine the characteristics of the Session Facade design pattern.

Context

In a complex EJB application, a client is exposed to interfaces of server-side business objects that encapsulate business logic and business data in session and entity beans. The complexity of the client code is proportional to the number of server-side business objects it needs to access.

Problem

There are several problems with exposing business objects directly to clients:

- Tighter coupling between the client and the business objects increases the dependency of the client on the specific business object implementation. This results in an application being "brittle."

- Clients make fine-grained method calls on all the participating business objects, thus increasing the volume of network traffic. The volume of network traffic is proportional to the number of participating business objects.

- Because the business objects are directly exposed to clients, there is no unified strategy for accessing them, and the possibility of business object misuse increases.

- Client code becomes complex and bloated because it must perform a lookup every time it needs to access a business object.

Forces

The solution must satisfy the following requirements:

- It should provide a simpler interface from the business objects to the clients and reduce the burden of managing and executing business methods on business objects.

- It should reduce network traffic volume by reducing the number of business objects exposed to the clients.

- It should hide the underlying complexity and interaction from the clients. Clients should not be responsible for managing complex interactions between business objects and should not even be aware of the interdependencies among the business objects.

- Clients should require only coarse-grained access to the unified service layer that separates business object implementation from the business service abstraction.

- Exposing business object interfaces to clients introduces tight coupling, thus increasing brittleness and reducing flexibility. Use of this design pattern should reduce the degree of coupling between client and business object.

Solution

Use a session bean as a `SessionFacade` to encapsulate and hide the complexity of the interactions between the business objects participating in the workflow. The `SessionFacade` provides a uniform, coarse-grained access layer to the clients and is responsible for locating, creating, and executing business logic in the business objects. The `SessionFacade` also handles the interactions and relationships between the business objects.

The `SessionFacade` handles all the necessary fine-grained interactions between the business objects. This reduces network traffic and also provides a uniform access to business objects. This design pattern is implemented in two example applications—as `ScheduleManagerBean` in Chapter 17 and as `StudentFacadeEJB` in Chapter 18.

Structure

Figure 16-14 is the `SessionFacade` class diagram that shows the `SessionFacade` hiding the details of the business objects from the client. Figure 16-15 is the sequence diagram that shows the client invoking a coarse-grained method invocation and interacting with the `SessionFacade`.

Participants and Responsibilities

There are three types of participants in the Session Facade design pattern:

- `Clients` make requests to the `SessionFacade` to access business services. The client can be a Web component, a standalone Java client, a session bean, or a business delegate.
- The `SessionFacade` is implemented as a session EJB and provides a service layer that hides the complexity of relationships among the business objects from clients. The `SessionFacade` is responsible for managing the relationships between business objects and offers clients coarse-grained access to the participating business objects.
- The `BusinessObject` can be a session bean, entity bean, data access object, or plain Java object that implements business logic and provides data and business services to the `SessionFacade`. A `SessionFacade` interacts with several `BusinessObject` instances to service client requests.

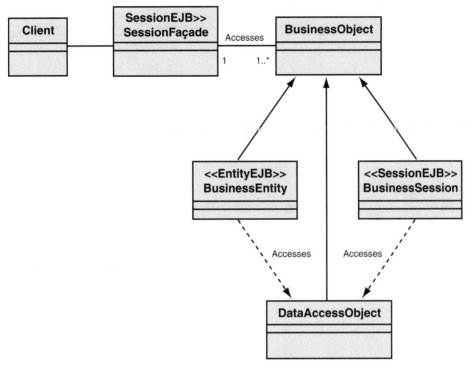

Figure 16-14 Session Facade pattern class diagram

Strategies

There are two strategies for implementing the SessionFacade design pattern. First determine whether the SessionFacade bean can be a stateless or a stateful session bean. The use case and scenarios are helpful for making this decision.

- *Implementing* `SessionFacade` *as a stateless session bean*—Implement the `SessionFacade` as stateless session bean if the use case is non-conversational. When a method completes, the use case also completes, and there's no need to save the conversational state between method calls.
- *Implementing* `SessionFacade` *as s stateful session bean*—If the use case is conversational and requires multiple method calls to complete a single use case, the need to save a conversational state to execute subsequent method calls suggests implementing the `SessionFacade` as a stateful session bean.

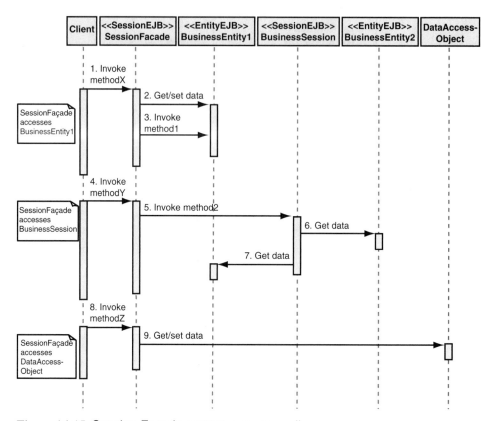

Figure 16-15 Session Facade pattern sequence diagram

There are several implementation strategies for BusinessObjects in this pattern; they can be implemented as session beans, entity beans, data access objects, or regular Java objects.

- *Implementing* BusinessObject *as a session bean*—The BusinessObject can be implemented as a session bean. The session bean may typically provide business services or in some cases provide access to business data. The SessionFacade can use the business logic encapsulated by the session BusinessObject.

- *Implementing* BusinessObject *as an entity bean*—BusinessObjects are commonly implemented as entity beans and provide fine-grained access to the SessionFacade. The SessionFacade wraps entity bean BusinessObjects and hides the complexity of entity bean interaction, providing coarse-grained access to the clients.

- *Implementing* `BusinessObject` *as* `DataAccessObject`—The `BusinessObject` can be a `DataAccessObject`, and the `SessionFacade` can directly access the business data, thus bypassing the entity beans.

- *Implementing* `BusinessObject` *as a regular Java object*—Certain non-EJB and non-`DataAccessObject` logic (such as JNDI lookup service) can be implemented as a regular Java object, which `SessionFacade` can use for JNDI lookup.

Consequences

Implementing the SessionFacade design pattern has the following conseuqences:

- *Provision of a business service layer*—`SessionFacade` provides a common service layer to the clients wishing to access business services. In a complex application, a client may access several `SessionFacades`, each providing a specific type of business service to the client.

- *Provision of a simpler and more uniform interface to the clients*—`Session-Facade` handles the complex interactions among the business objects and provides clients with simpler and more uniform access to the clients via its coarse-grained interface.

- *Reduced coupling and increased manageability*—`SessionFacade` provides a layer of abstraction and reduces the coupling between the clients and the business objects. The business objects can be modified or even replaced by newer and improved business objects without affecting the clients. Because the workflow logic is centralized by the `SessionFacade`, any changes in the workflow logic can be managed in the `SessionFacade` without impacting clients.

- *Reduced network traffic and improved performance*—With `SessionFacade`, many fine-grained access methods from the clients to many business objects is eliminated and replaced by fewer course-grained access methods to `SessionFacade`, thus reducing unnecessary network traffic. The `SessionFacade` and the business objects are closer to each other, their proximity enabling more efficient management of the interactions among the participating business objects. Reducing the network traffic and fine-grained access improves the overall performance of the application.

- *Provision of coarse-grained access to the clients*—A `SessionFacade` provides a coarse-grained abstraction of the workflow and provides coarse-grained access to the clients. Providing a single `SessionFacade` for the entire system adds unnecessary complexity and inefficiency to the `SessionFacade`. The challenge is to determine the optimal granularity of the `SessionFacade` for the application by partitioning the

application into different logical subsystems and then providing a
`SessionFacade` that's appropriate for each subsystem.

- *Elimination or reduction of remote interface and fine-grained access to the
  clients*—`SessionFacade` provides coarse-grained access to the clients
  and hides the interfaces of the business objects from the clients.

- *Centralized security management*—Because all the interaction between the
  clients and the business objects must go through the `SessionFacade`,
  it's ideal for implementing and managing coarse-grained security policies
  for the participating business objects in the workflow. The business
  components can offer fine-grained access control to the business logic.

- *Centralized transaction control*—`SessionFacade` represents the workflow
  for the use cases; it's a logical place to define, apply, and manage coarse-
  grained transaction control.

- *Additional object introducing communication delays*—Although the Session
  Facade pattern helps resolve some of the major issues already discussed,
  it does mean adding another object and another layer between the client
  and the business objects. Adding more objects introduces delay in
  communications, but the overall benefits from the use of the Session
  Facade pattern outweigh this minor drawback.

Related Patterns

- *Facade (Design Pattern)*—The `SessionFacade` is based on the Facade
  Design pattern.

- *DataAccessObject (SJC)*—One strategy for `BusinessObject` is to use the
  `SessionFacade` with `DataAccessObject` to provide a simple access
  to business data when compared with the use of entity beans.

- *ServiceLocator (SJC)*—The `SessionFacade` can make use of the
  `ServiceLocator` object to look up services such as JNDI lookup.

- *Broker (POSA1)*—The `SessionFacade` performs the role of a broker to
  decouple entity beans from their clients.

Business Delegate

Following are the characteristics of the Business Delegate design pattern.

Context

In a multitier environment, a remote client can request and receive data across
tiers. The business tier may expose the entire business service API to a client
across a network.

Problem

When a presentation tier component interacts directly with the business components in the business tier, the interaction exposes the underlying implementation details of the business service API to the presentation components. This results in tight coupling between the presentation components and the business services, thus making the presentation components vulnerable to the changes in the business services implementation.

Due to tight integration between the presentation components and the business services, the interactions can be fine-grained and chatty. This results in unnecessary network traffic, which negatively affects performance. Exposing the business service API to clients results in presentation components having to deal with networking issues as well as with the distributed characteristics of EJBs, such as performing JNDI lookup and accessing remote component interfaces.

Forces

The solution must address these issues:

- Clients on the presentation tier need to access the business service.
- As business requirements evolve, business services' APIs must change also.
- Minimizing the coupling between the clients on the presentation tier and the business services' API is desirable.
- Implementing a caching mechanism for business service information would improve the application performance.
- It's desirable to reduce the network traffic between the presentation client and the business services.

Solution

Use a Business Delegate pattern to reduce the coupling between the presentation tier client and the business services as well as to hide the underlying implementation details of the business services from the client.

The `BusinessDelegate` provides a client-side abstraction for the business services and hides the implementation details of the business services. This reduces the coupling between the presentation-tier client and the business services and shields the clients from changes in the business service APIs. Even though the clients are immune to changes in the business service APIs, the `BusinessDelegate` itself might require modification when the business service API changes. Benefits of using a `BusinessDelegate` are as follows:

- The BusinessDelegate handles the naming and lookup services transparently for the client.

- The BusinessDelegate intercepts the exceptions generated by the business services and generates appropriate application-level exceptions for easier handling by the client.

- The BusinessDelegate can perform retry or recovery operations in the event of business service failure without exposing the problem to the client (at least until it's determined that the failure is not recoverable).

- The BusinessDelegate can provide result-caching features and references to remote business services. Caching prevents unnecessary and costly round trips over the network and can significantly improve application performance.

- The BusinessDelegate can benefit from other services, such as the Lookup Service responsible for providing JNDI lookup.

- The BusinessDelegate is used with the SessionFacade and enables a one-to-one relationship between the two.

- Besides decoupling the presentation tier from the business tier, the BusinessDelegate can be used with other tiers to reduce coupling.

This design pattern is implemented in a sample application (ServiceDelegate) in Chapter 18.

Structure

Figure 16-16 shows a Client invoking a request to the BusinessDelegate. The Client uses the LookUpService to locate the appropriate BusinessService and execute the appropriate business methods. Figure 16-17 is the Business Delegate sequence diagram; the complexity of the business logic is well hidden from the client.

Participants and Responsibilities

The three key roles in the Business Delegate design pattern are:

- BusinessDelegate provides access control over the business service and provides two request options. If the request is made to the BusinessDelegate without a StringID, the BusinessDelegate requests the service from the LookupService implemented as a ServiceLocator pattern, which returns the ServiceFactory (such as EJBHome). When initialized with an ID string, the BusinessDelegate uses the ID to reconnect to the BusinessService. The BusinessDelegate hides the underlying

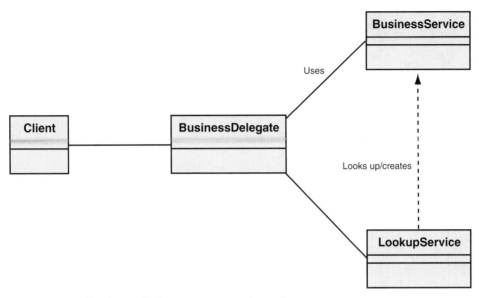

Figure 16-16 Business Delegate pattern class diagram

implementation details of BusinessService naming and lookup services from the client and prevents clients from directly making remote invocations on a BusinessService.

- LookupService encapsulates the implementation details of a BusinessService lookup. The BusinessDelegate depends on the LookupService to locate the BusinessService.

- BusinessService is an EJB component, such as a session, entity, or message-driven bean, in the business tier that provides the required services to the client.

Strategies

There are two significant implementation strategies for the Business Delegate design pattern:

- *Proxy Strategy*—With this strategy, the BusinessDelegate exposes its simpler interface to clients and provides a proxy function to the complex methods of the business services API. The BusinessDelegate may also cache any necessary data (such as references to home interfaces or remote objects) to improve performance. It may also use the services of the ServiceLocator to convert references to string IDs and vice versa.

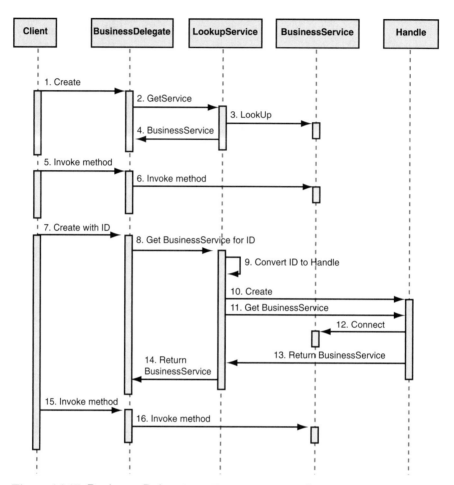

Figure 16-17 Business Delegate pattern sequence diagram

- *Adapter Strategy*—With this strategy, developers can integrate disparate systems using XML as the integration language. In such cases, the client invokes a request with XML data to an XMLAdapter object, which in turn parses the XML data and creates a BusinessDelegate to invoke requests to the BusinessService. When the result is returned by the BusinessDelegate, the Adapter creates the XML output and returns it to the client.

Consequences

Let's look at the consequences of implementing Business Delegate design patterns:

- *Simpler and more uniform interface to the presentation tier*—The `BusinessDelegate` provides a simpler and more uniform variant of the interface to clients than those provided by the underlying EJBs.

- *Reduced coupling and increased manageability*—The `BusinessDelegate` reduces the coupling between the presentation tier and the business services, hiding the business services implementation details. As a result, the presentation components are less negatively impacted by changes to the business service API. When there are changes required, they're more easily managed because they're centralized.

- *Translation of business service exceptions*—The `BusinessDelegate` intercepts network or infrastructure-related exceptions and translates them into business exceptions for the clients.

- *Failure recovery option*—The `BusinessDelegate` can implement logic to handle automatic recovery features when it encounters failures with the business services without exposing the problem to the client. Only when the recovery attempts fail does the `BusinessDelegate` inform the clients.

- *Addition of an additional layer but with improved performance*—The `BusinessDelegate` adds another layer between the client and the business services but provides many benefits such as loose coupling, better error handling, and improved performance.

Related Patterns

- *Service Locator (SJC)*
- *Proxy (GoF)*—provides a surrogate for another object to control access to that object. For example, a HomeObject is a proxy used by a client to control an EJB instance via the home interface.
- *Adapter (GoF)*—This pattern is applicable when it's necessary to convert the interface of one class into another interface that a client expects, thus making it possible for classes with incompatible interfaces to work together.

Additional Patterns

Two additional design patterns catalogued by Sun Java Center are the Composite Entity and Service Activator patterns. These patterns are not discussed in this book because they were most useful in the EJB 1.1 environment. The container-managed persistence in entity beans in EJB 2.0 solves issues with the Composite

Entity (also known as the Aggregate Entity addressed in EJB 1.1). Finally, with the introduction of message-driven beans in EJB 2.0, the Service Activator pattern is less useful.

EJB Interoperability

The EJB 2.0 interoperability goal is to enable a client in one container from one application server provider to make a successful method call to an EJB component in a different container from a different application server. Interoperability is achieved by relying on existing open standards. The client can be a Web component, an applet, a standalone Java program, or another EJB. The EJB 2.0 specification addresses only interoperability between J2EE compliant products; it doesn't address interoperability between EJB and non-J2EE components.

The interoperability between J2EE compliant components is based on the CORBA/IIOP standard that all J2EE 1.3 compliant application servers must support. CORBA clients written in Java and/or C++ are able to invoke methods on EJB 2.0 components regardless of the container provider. Note that the following discussion does not cover CORBA in depth. Read Chapter 19 of the EJB 2.0 specification and the CORBA specification at http://www.omg.org for more information.

Remote Invocation Interoperability

All EJB, Web, and application client containers must support the IIOP 1.2 protocol for remote `EJBObject` and `EJBHome` invocation, in addition to the vendor's proprietary protocol. The IIOP protocol is part of the CORBA 2.3.1 specification from OMG. Because the remote home objects are required to support the IIOP 1.2 protocol, they must explicitly apply the `javax.rmi.PortableRemote-Object.narrow()` method after JNDI lookup (to convert from a general reference type to the desired `EJBHome` reference type). J2EE containers are required to support (among other code sets) the Unicode UTF16 code set for transmission of character and string data.

Transaction Interoperability

Transaction interoperability between containers provided by different vendors is an optional feature in the EJB 2.0 specification. If transaction interoperability is supported by the vendor's container, then a distributed transaction started by a Web or EJB container must be able to propagate to a remote EJB invocation in the EJB container provided by a different vendor. The container must participate in the distributed two-phase commit protocol. The EJB container relies on the CORBA Object Transaction Service (OTS) 1.2 specification for transaction context propagation between two containers. J2EE containers must not use nested transactions.

If the container doesn't support transaction interoperability and a J2EE client expects its transaction to propagate to the EJB, the container must throw `java.rmi.RemoteException` to roll back the client's transaction. If the client container doesn't support transaction interoperability, the transaction context must be set to `null`. Setting the transaction context to `null` indicates that there's an active global client transaction but that the client isn't capable of propagating the transaction to the server. The presence of the `null` transaction context allows the EJB container to find out whether the J2EE client expects the client's global transaction to propagate to the server. Clients that use the OTS transaction context format but don't support transaction interoperability with other vendors must throw a CORBA system exception.

Naming Interoperability

All EJB containers are required to publish `EJBHome` object references using the CORBA CosNaming service. When a client invokes a JNDI lookup at runtime, the CosNaming service resolves the name mapping and returns the `EJBHome` object reference to the client.

Security Interoperability

Security interoperability requirements for EJB 2.0, Web, and application containers support Secure Socket Layer (SSL 3.0) and IETF standard Transport Layer Security (TLS 1.0) for authentication and message protection at the transport level. When using IIOP over SSL, a secure channel is established between the client and server containers at the SSL layer. Web containers are required to provide support for SSL over HTTP (HTTPS).

EJB Performance Issues

Factors affecting the performance of the EJB application include

- network bandwidth and the amount of network traffic
- the hardware and operating system platforms
- proprietary features, scalability and performance of the application servers (and their configuration)

- the knowledge and expertise of the EJB application deployer optimize the application for the specific application server
- the EJB application design and implementation

The most optimized EJB application will perform poorly if the deployer fails to set the deployment parameters optimally for the operating environment and the application server. And even if the deployer sets the deployment parameters optimally for the environment, the application performs only as well as the application server on which the application is running. The brand of application server, its configuration, and its setup affect the performance and the scalability of the application server and, thus, the performance and scalability of the EJB application. The hardware and operating system directly affect the scalability and performance of the application server and thus the EJB application performance. Finally, the most optimized EJB application running on a finely tuned application server on the most scalable hardware will falter if there's low network bandwidth and high network traffic.

In most instances, the bean developer has no control over the network bandwidth, types of hardware in use, and the brand of application server. There are two things a bean developer can and must do, however. The first is to strive to optimize the EJB implementations for performance, and the second is to provide the assembler and deployer with as much information as possible regarding the optimal settings of assembly parameters.

Here are several points to consider when implementing an EJB application:

- *Reduce remote calls*—Authors Halter and Munroe, in their book *Enterprise Java Performance* (see the Appendix to this book), illustrate a method call spectrum graph indicating that a remote call on a LAN can be approximately 600 times slower than a local bean method call. Additionally, remote calls on the same host (for example, an EJB making a remote method call on another EJB in the same container) can be approximately 300 times slower than a local bean method call. Remote EJB calls are expensive, whereas local EJB calls are quite fast. By replacing remote calls with local calls, developers automatically improve the performance of their applications. Reducing remote calls also reduces the volume of network traffic. In EJB 2.0, developers can use either remote or local interfaces. Using local interfaces avoids the RMI-IIOP overhead. Arguments are passed by reference, avoiding the marshalling and unmarshalling overhead. Note that the EJB with a local interface cannot be distributed.

- *Reduce network traffic volume*—High network traffic volume can affect the performance of an application adversely. Distributed EJB applications are generally network intensive. Reduce unnecessary network traffic by implementing a local interface.

- *Ignore the myth of using only stateless session beans for their speed and avoiding entity beans because they're slow*—Among the EJBs, stateless session beans have the best performance, and it's true that entity beans are slow. But that's not the whole story. Rather, look at the overall performance and scalability of the EJB application. Spend time on the object-oriented analysis and design phase, and then choose the appropriate EJB to model the business logic. Use stateless session beans for business logic that doesn't require management of state information; use stateful session beans for conversational business logic; and use entity beans for modeling persistent business data. Attempting to model both conversational and persistent business data logic with stateless session beans has undesirable consequences. For example, modeling conversation business logic with stateless session beans means that the bean developer must write additional logic to manage the state. Modeling persistent business data with stateless session beans also means that the bean developer must write the necessary code to manage the persistent data and synchronize with the underlying data store. In most instances, the stateless session bean implementation of conversational business logic and persistent data might not be any faster and can, in fact, introduce more bugs due to the necessity of implementing complicated logic.

- *Consider the new and improved CMP 2.0 entity beans of the EJB 2.0 specification*—It's too early to determine what the consensus will be regarding the CMP 2.0 entity bean performance in a large-scale application because only two J2EE application servers have passed J2EE 1.3 certification as of December 2001. The new abstract persistence schema model, EJB QL, and the persistence data access layer provide much more flexible solutions and, based on the technical specification, they're expected to result in better-performing CMP 2.0 entity beans. If possible, select CMP entity beans over BMP entity beans in EJB 2.0 applications.

- *Apply design patterns*—Use of the design patterns discussed throughout this chapter will improve the design and performance of the application.

- *Use transactions appropriately*—Implement transactions declaratively whenever possible, as they make EJBs more portable and flexible. Implement transactions programmatically only when the business logic requires fine-grained transaction control that cannot be met by declarative transactions. When implementing transactions programmatically, use fine-grained transactions, and minimize transaction context. Note that the transaction attributes must be set correctly to benefit from the application optimization.

- *Set the appropriate timeout and passivation timeout values for stateful session beans*—Most application servers have default session timeout and passivation timeout values; if these values aren't specified for the stateful session beans, the application server applies the default values. It's advisable to set the session timeout and passivation timeout value whenever possible, or to give hints to the deployer regarding the optimal bean values. The deployer can always ignore suggestions based on his or her expertise.

- *Manage the EJB life cycle explicitly when possible*—Even though the container handles the life cycle of EJBs, the bean developer can take steps to help the container optimize the management tasks. For example, with session beans, clients should call the `remove()` method when they're finished with the business logic.

Note that the new standard ECperf benchmark from Sun Microsystems (http://java.sun.com/j2ee/ecperf) is designed to measure the performance and scalability of J2EE application servers. It would be highly useful if all J2EE 1.3-compliant vendors publicly posted their Ecperf benchmark results as part of their J2EE 1.3 compliance procedure.

Summary

In this chapter, we discussed seven design patterns which, when applied, will help implement an improved EJB application that also performs better. The interoperability of EJB is based on the CORBA/IIOP protocol, which makes it possible for EJB components distributed in J2EE 1.3-certified application servers from different vendors to communicate with one another. The key to EJB application performance is to reduce remote calls, reduce network traffic volume, and apply design patterns. It's also important to have scalable application servers running on robust and fast hardware.

MIGRATING EJB 1.1 APPLICATIONS TO THE EJB 2.0 CONTAINER

Topics in This Chapter

- Migration Options and Approaches
- EJB 1.1 Shortcomings
- Migrating EJB 1.1 Applications to EJB 2.0

Chapter 17

This chapter focuses on issues related to migrating EJB 1.1 applications to the EJB 2.0 container. Since the majority of existing EJB applications are based on EJB 1.1, the bean developers will most likely have plenty of opportunities to migrate EJB 1.1 applications to EJB 2.0 containers. This chapter highlights this migration effort, covering topics such as

- the three migration options
- the drawbacks of EJB 1.1
- migration issues with various EJB types
- steps for migrating an EJB 1.1 application to an EJB 2.0 container

Note: If you've jumped to this chapter directly, a review of Chapters 4, 10, and 11 is recommended before you proceed with this chapter.

Migration Options and Approaches

When it comes to migrating EJB 1.1 applications to the EJB 2.0 container, there are three options, ranging from redeploying an EJB 1.1 application without any changes—which results in only minimum benefits from EJB 2.0 features—to refactoring the EJB1.1 application to take full advantage of the EJB 2.0 container framework. We'll concentrate our discussion to the latter option, refactoring the EJB 1.1 application.

Redeploying EJB 1.1 Applications to an EJB 2.0 Container

The EJB 2.0 specification mandates that EJB 2.0 container providers include support for the EJB 1.1 runtime environment. This means that existing EJB 1.1 applications will run unmodified in an EJB 2.0 container, which is convenient because migration can be done in phases without disrupting existing services. The EJB 1.1 application runs in an EJB 1.1 runtime environment of an EJB 2.0 container but cannot take advantage of most of the EJB 2.0 features.

Replacing Remote Interfaces with Local Interfaces As Applicable

Depending on the existing application, developers can replace remote interfaces with local interfaces of stateless, stateful, and bean-managed entity beans and quickly benefit from local calls. The corresponding bean implementation class doesn't have to be modified. The usual restriction of local views applies (this is discussed in detail in Chapter 4).

Redesigning Applications to Take Advantage of EJB 2.0

The EJBs with coarse-grained business logic and helper classes can be redesigned with local interfaces to handle fine-grained business logic and improve performance. However, CMP 1.1 entity beans cannot be migrated to use CMP 2.0 in an EJB 2.0 container without some major work.

EJB 1.1 Shortcomings

Although the EJB 1.1 specification improved on the EJB 1.0 specification, it still had unresolved issues, including

- lack of support for asynchronous communication
- no support for local interfaces
- no support for complex relationships between entity beans
- not addressing interoperability among EJB containers

EJB 1.1 doesn't support local interfaces for session and entity beans—only remote interfaces are supported. Consequently, every method invocation in EJB 1.1 is a potential remote method call that comes with the overhead of marshalling and unmarshalling objects and conducting security checks, transaction implementations, exception checking, and logging calls.

The EJB 1.1 specification encourages the use of EJBs to model coarse-grained business logic and to use dependent value classes to implement fine-grained business logic.

There's a slight difference in interface naming conventions between EJB 1.1 and EJB 2.0. In EJB 2.0, there are remote and local home interfaces and remote and local component interfaces. The remote home interface in EJB 2.0 corresponds to the home interface in EJB 1.1; the remote component interface in EJB 2.0 corresponds to the remote interface in EJB 1.1. To avoid confusion, this book uses the term *remote home* and *remote component interfaces* instead of home and remote interfaces (as in EJB 1.1). In EJB 1.1, Java class used with EJB was commonly referred to as helper class. In EJB 2.0, it was referred to as dependent value class. The Java class, helper class, and dependent value class are used interchangeably in this book.

Next, we'll examine what it takes to convert EJB version 1.1 session and entity beans to take advantage of EJB 2.0 container features.

Session Beans

There are no significant changes in the session beans class from EJB 1.1 to EJB 2.0, so the migration is straightforward except for the option to replace the remote interface with the local interface. The bean developer can take advantage of the local interfaces when migrating the EJB 1.1 session bean to the EJB 2.0 container, depending on the application design.

Entity Beans

Because EJB components are designed to model coarse-grained business logic, one of the biggest issues, especially with entity beans in EJB 1.1, was how to efficiently model fine-grained business logic with coarse-grained entity beans. There are two basic options; to illustrate, we'll use a purchase order example. A purchase order consists of line items, and each line item has a part number, a product description, a model number, a price, and so forth. In EJB 1.1, the bean developer would implement the order using the entity `OrderBean` class and line items with the `LineItem` dependent class. The `LineItem` dependent value class could be implemented as a simple Java class or another dependent entity beans class, as illustrated in Figure 17-1. Let's look at the issues with these two options.

Dependent Entity Beans

Implementing a dependent class as an entity bean class has several disadvantages. The biggest drawback is that entity beans are heavyweight components—they require more system resources. All the method calls in EJB 1.1

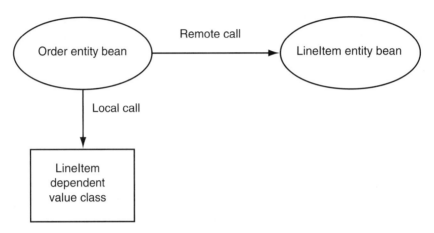

Figure 17-1 The entity bean's relationship with dependent value classes

are potential remote calls; as a result, the overhead of marshalling and unmarshalling objects, security checks, transaction implementation, exception checking, and logging calls result in poor performance. Additionally, fine-grained business methods in the `LineItem` entity bean are exposed to the `OrderBean` entity bean, which results in tight coupling. In addition, the `OrderBean`-`LineItem` relationship is managed programmatically, making an application more complicated. Benefits of using entity beans include the container taking care of data access, synchronization, and persistence management of the LineItem entity beans, as well as providing the ability to implement customized transactions and security during deployment.

Java Class

Implementing a dependent value class as a simple Java class has several drawbacks. In addition to implementing fine-grained business logic to handle line items in the dependent value class, the bean developer must also implement the logic to synchronize the state of the dependent object with the underlying data source. The code to implement state management can be complicated and prone to bugs, leading to potential data aliasing problems. Data aliasing results when there are multiple representations in memory of the same underlying data and in-memory view isn't synchronized with the underlying data in the database.

The bean developer also must implement optimization logic, such as load-on-demand and dirty checking. *Load-on-demand* indicates that data is loaded from the database only when required; *dirty checking logic* updates the database only when the in-memory data has been modified. The resulting custom optimization logic can lead to bugs and render the dependent class not portable. The advantages of using the Java class as a dependent value class to encapsulate fine-grained logic is that developers aren't exposing fine-grained methods to clients, which reduces network traffic. The LineItem dependent class is tightly integrated with the order entity bean class and the underlying data source, resulting in better performance.

Bean-Managed Persistent Entity Beans

The BMP entity beans in EJB 1.1 and EJB 2.0 are similar to one another, except for an optional home method that's new for BMP entity beans in EJB 2.0.

In simple cases, it's easy to migrate CMP 1.1 entity beans with fine-grained business logic to CMP 2.0 entity beans by replacing remote interfaces with local interfaces—this can be done without changing the entity bean class and, depending on the application logic and the container implementation, can result in immediate performance improvements. To benefit from CMP 2.0 features and capabilities, CMP 1.1 entity beans will have be refactored for implementing home methods and fine-grained business logic.

When migrating an EJB 1.1.application to an EJB 2.0 container, the bean developer can implement both coarse-grained and fine-grained business logic with entity beans without penalizing performance and network traffic or suffering the implementation headache of a dependent Java object. In the EJB 2.0 container, the bean developer can take the LineItem dependent value class with fine-grained business methods and refactor it into the entity bean with the local interface, then modify the OrderBean with coarse-grained business logic to reference the LineItemBean entity bean via its local interfaces.

With availability of the optional home methods during the migration, a bean developer should also consider whether certain business logic that applies to the entity bean class type might be better implemented as home business methods. For example, in the Online Registration application, how would a 15% discount be applied to all EJB training classes? When using EJB 2.0, you would implement a home business method, ejbHomeApplyDiscount(course_category, percentage), in the CourseEJB entity bean class.

Container-Managed Persistent Entity Beans

The most significant changes from EJB 1.1 to EJB 2.0 have been in the container-managed persistence model (CMP 2.0). For a better perspective of the changes, let's briefly compare and contrast the CMP 1.1 and CMP 2.0 models.

CMP 2.0 Entity Bean Class

In EJB 1.1, CMP entity beans are declared as `public` entity bean class, but the CMP 2.0 entity bean class must be declared `abstract`. Thus, when migrating CMP entity beans from EJB 1.1 to EJB 2.0, the CMP entity bean class must be declared `public abstract` class.

Abstract Methods

In CMP 1.1, the bean developer must declare the container-managed persistence (cmp-field) fields in the bean class and also provide getter and setter methods to access the cmp-fields. These methods may not contain any data access logic code; the cmp-fields must map to the corresponding fields of the table in the underlying database. In the case of EJB 2.0, the bean developer must declare the virtual CMP fields in the context of the abstract persistent getter and setter methods (i.e., only as arguments to the method) and must not implement these methods. The container, in turn, generates the necessary logic to access and synchronize the CMP fields automatically at deployment time in both EJB 1.1 and EJB 2.0. These CMP fields may be any Java primitive type or serializable object, including home and remote interface types.

Relationships

Unlike the CMP entity beans in EJB 2.0, the CMP entity beans in EJB 1.1 don't support one-to-one, one-to-many, and many-to-many container-managed relationships. For this reason, there's no elegant way to represent sophisticated relationships between CMP entity beans in EJB 1.1.

Abstract Persistence Schema

The notion of abstract persistence schema and the enforcement of referential integrity checks that are an integral part of EJB 2.0 don't exist in EJB 1.1; the bean developer must write logic programmatically to create relationships between entities using the remote interfaces in CMP 1.1 entity beans. This approach not only puts an unnecessary burden on the bean developer, but the complexities of the relationship are also hard to implement, especially in nontrivial applications, and they affect the quality and portability of the application.

EJB Query Language

There's no standard way to query relationships in EJB 1.1, as with EJB QL in EJB 2.0. Unlike standard EJB QL query statements in EJB 2.0, the `finder` method query statements in EJB 1.1 are vendor-specific—they may not be optimized and are certainly not portable across different application servers.

When it comes to migrating CMP 1.1 entity beans, there's no quick fix migration option as there is with stateless, stateful, and BMP entity beans. CMP 1.1 entity beans must be refactored to use the CMP 2.0 abstract persistence model. Later in the chapter, we illustrate a complete example for migrating a CMP 1.1-based application to CMP 2.0.

Life Cycle

The entity bean life cycle is the same in the EJB 1.1 and EJB 2.0 specifications; however, there are a couple of new methods in EJB 2.0. Figure 17-2 illustrates the life cycle of entity beans. Note the new methods, `ejbHome<METHOD>()` in bold and `ejbSelect<METHOD>()` in bold and italics. These two new methods in EJB 2.0 apply to the bean class. The other callback methods—`ejbActivate`, `ejbPassivate`, `ejbLoad`, `ejbStore`, `ejbRemove`, `setEntityContext`, and `unsetEntityContext`—are similar in EJB 1.1 and EJB 2.0. See Chapter 9 for a detailed discussion concerning the entity bean life cycle.

Home methods are available in both BMP and CMP entity beans in EJB 2.0, and clients can invoke them. Select methods are only available in CMP 2.0 entity beans—they are for internal use only with the CMP entity bean class and aren't exposed to clients. The select methods can be invoked either in a `pool` state or `ready` state.

The CMP entity bean class in both EJB 1.1 and EJB 2.0 must directly or indirectly implement the `javax.ebj.EntityBean interface`; it must be defined as `public`. The class cannot be defined as `final`, nor can it include the `finalize()` method. Additionally, the CMP entity bean class in EJB 2.0 must be defined as `abstract`—the CMP entity bean class cannot be defined as `abstract` in EJB 1.1.

Message-Driven Beans

Message-driven beans were first introduced in EJB 2.0, so EJB 1.1 bean developers usually used stateless session beans to implement business logic that was actually more suitable for message-driven beans. A bean developer migrating an EJB 1.1 application might want to reevaluate the business logic and the application design and determine whether some of the business logic—especially logic

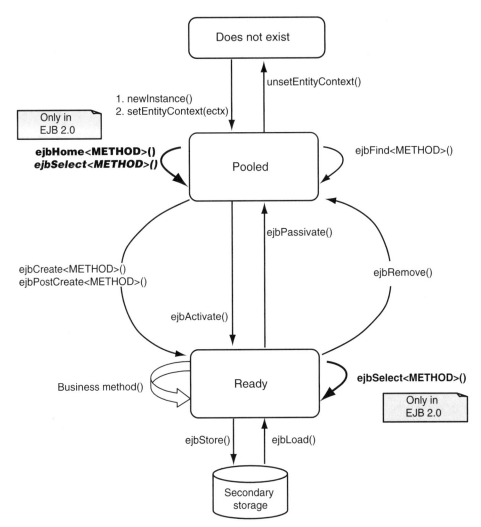

Figure 17-2 The entity bean life cycle

implemented as stateless session beans—is better suited for message-driven bean implementation.

Minimal Interoperability Among EJB Servers

One of the biggest drawbacks of EJB 1.1 was the lack of support for EJB interoperability—the deployer couldn't deploy an EJB application in a heterogeneous environment with EJB 1.1 containers from different vendors and guarantee that the EJBs could communicate.

To conform to the CORBA standard, the EJB 1.1 specification mandates the argument and reference types to be Java RMI-IIOP types. Consequently, bean developers are required to use the `narrow()` method on remote references and cast them before the references can be used. The EJB 1.1 specification doesn't define the underling protocol; as a result, each application server vendor implemented its optimized proprietary underlying protocols, resulting in a lack of network interoperability among EJB servers.

EJB 2.0 specification mandates the implementation of the CORBA IIOP 1.2 protocol (as defined by the CORBA 2.3.1 specification) as the underlying protocol for intercontainer communication by all vendors, and vendors are free to provide additional proprietary protocols, thus ensuring interoperability among EJB servers. This is an infrastructure feature that any EJB 2.0-compliant EJB container provider must implement and make available to the application when it's deployed.

Migrating EJB 1.1 Applications to EJB 2.0

Now that we've discussed some of the changes in CMP entity beans in EJB 1.1 and EJB 2.0, we'll use that knowledge in the following migration example. The goal is to illustrate how to migrate EJB 1.1-based beans to the EJB 2.0 container. We'll use a sample Schedule Manager application. First, we'll discuss the EJB 1.1 implementation, followed by the EJB 2.0 implementation of the sample application. The Schedule Manager is an EJB 1.1-based application used for creating Java training schedules. Once the schedule is created and published, students can search, register, and attend the Java training courses. This example shows a subset of the application that consists of a standalone Java client (`ScheduleClient`) and two entity beans, `ScheduleBean` and `CourseBean` (see Figure 17-3). All communication between the client and the entity beans and communication between the entity beans are potential remote calls in the EJB 1.1, which are expensive. Both entity beans are accessing their respective tables in the database and are shown to exist in one EJB container; however, because they use remote interfaces, they can be distributed in separate containers from the same vendor.

The migration goal is to convert the existing Schedule Manager application based on EJB 1.1 to an EJB 2.0-based application and, in the process, improve application performance, scalability, and portability. First, we'll analyze the EJB 1.1 application and then refactor the application to enable conformance to EJB 2.0 standards.

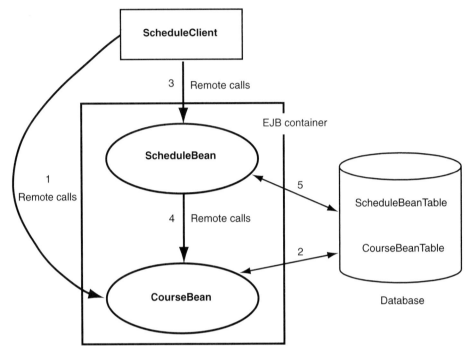

Figure 17-3 CMP 1.1 schedule manager application

EJB 1.1 Implementation

The Schedule Manager application example consists of two CMP 1.1 entity beans and a Java client. The client `ScheduleClient` invokes methods on `CourseBean` to create a course entity and on `ScheduleBean` to create class schedule. The students can then query for available class schedules. Refer to the diagram in Figure 17-4, which shows a remote call (1) from the `ScheduleClient` to the `CourseBean`. The `CourseBean`, in turn, creates a course entity and inserts it (2) into the `CourseBeanTable` of the database. (Note that in this chapter I've departed from EJB naming conventions to show you another naming convention and to distinguish the EJBs in this example from others with the same bean name.) The `ScheduleClient` then makes another remote call (3) to `ScheduleBean`, which, in turn, makes another potential remote call (4) to `CourseBean` to retrieve course-related information. It then creates a schedule entity(5) and inserts it into the `ScheduleBeanTable` of the database. Let's look at the pertinent code fragment, first looking at the `CourseBean`, followed by the `ScheduleBean`, and finally the `ScheduleClient`.

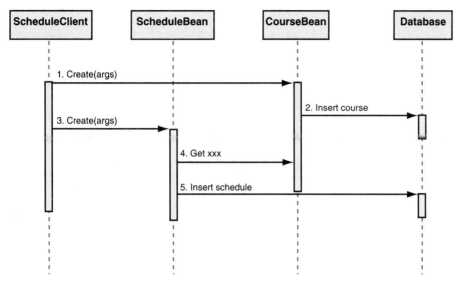

Figure 17-4 CMP 1.1 schedule manager sequence diagram

CourseBean

The `CourseBean` entity bean encapsulates the logic to handle course-related issues. In this example, it's used to create courses and provide `ScheduleBean` with information regarding a particular course. The remote home interface, `CourseHome`, extends the `EJBHome` interface and consists of the mandatory `findByPrimaryKey()` method and a `create()` method with arguments such as `courseID`, title, class format, and course description. `ScheduleClient` invokes the `create()` method to create a course entity.

```
public interface CourseHome extends EJBHome
{
    public Course findByPrimaryKey(String courseID) throws
        FinderException, RemoteException;
    public Course create(String courseID, String title, String
classFormat, String description,  String preRequisite, String text-
Book, double price, int size ) throws CreateException,
        RemoteException;
}
```

The remote component interface, `Course`, extends the `EJBObject` interface and includes several fine-grained set and get methods that are used to access the container-managed persistent fields. These methods are remote method calls from the `ScheduleBean` entity bean (resulting in high overhead).

```
public interface Course extends EJBObject
{
    public String getCourseID() throws RemoteException;
    public void setCourseID(String courseID) throws RemoteException;

    public String getTitle() throws RemoteException;
    public void setTitle(String title) throws RemoteException;

    public String getSummary() throws RemoteException;
    public void setSummary(String summary) throws RemoteException;

    public String getClassFormat() throws RemoteException;
    public void setClassFormat(String classFormat) throws RemoteException;

    public String getPreRequisites() throws RemoteException;
    public void setPreRequisites(String preRequisites) throws RemoteException;

    public String getTextBooks() throws RemoteException;
    public void setTextBooks(String textBooks) throws RemoteException;

    public double getPrice() throws RemoteException;
    public void setPrice(double price) throws RemoteException;

    public int getClassSize() throws RemoteException;
    public void setClassSize(int classSize) throws RemoteException;

}
```

The methods declared in the remote interfaces must throw `RemoteExceptions` in addition to application-related exceptions as required.

The following is a code snippet from the `CourseBean` entity bean class. The `CourseBean` class implements the `EntityBean` interface, and the corresponding `get` and `set` methods have been declared `public` as required. The `ejbCreate()` method assigns the arguments to the corresponding cmp-fields of the bean class. Notice there's no implementation data access code for `get` and `set` methods or `ejbCreate()` and `ejbPostCreate()` methods; the deployment tool and the container implement these methods and generate concrete classes. The `ejbPostCreate()` method is empty. The rest of the callback methods for the CMP entity beans—`ejbLoad()`, `ejbStore()`, and `ejbActivate()`—are left empty but not shown here.

```
public class CourseBean implements EntityBean
{
    private EntityContext context;
```

```java
//declare the cmp-fields
public String   courseID;
public String   title;
public String   classFormat;
public String   summary;
...............
.....................

// now getter and setter methods for cmp-fields

public String getCourseID()
{
    return  this.courseID;
}

public void setCourseID(String CourseID)
{
    thiscourseID = courseID;
}


public String getTitle()
{
    return  this.title;
}

public void setTitle(String title)
{
    thistitle = title;
}


public String getClassFormat()
{
    return  this.classFormat;
}

public void setClassFormat(String classFormat)
{
    thisclassFormat = classFormat;
}

public String getSummary()
{
    return  this.summary;
}
public void setSummary(String summary)
```

```
    {
         thissummary = summary;
    }
    ................................. .

         .........................................................


    public String ejbCreate(String courseID, String title, String
classFormat, String summary, String preRequisites, String text-
Books, double price, int classSize) throws CreateException
    {
         thiscourseID = courseID;
         this.title = title;
         this.classFormat = classFormat;
         this.preRequisites = preRequisites;
         this.textBooks = textBooks;
         this.price = price;
         this.classSize = classSize;
         this.summary = summary;

         return courseID;
    }

    public void ejbPostCreate(String courseID, String title, String
classFormat, String summary, String preRequisites, String text-
Books, double price, int classSize) throws CreateException
    {
    }
```

At deployment time, the container creates the necessary persistence code to
manage the persistence of the bean instance.

The `ScheduleBean` entity bean creates a course based on the client request. In
this example, it uses the primary key of the course to extract the course-related
fields from a course entity to create the schedule. Let's look at the remote interfaces
of `ScheduleBeans`, namely the `ScheduleHome` and `Schedule` interfaces.

ScheduleBean

The remote home interface, `ScheduleHome`, implements the `EJBHome` interface
and declares two methods—the mandatory `findByPrimaryKey()` and a
`create()` method with arguments necessary to create a schedule. The
`ScheduleClient` invokes the `create()` method to create the schedule entity.

```
public interface ScheduleHome extends EJBHome
{
    public Schedule findByPrimaryKey(String scheduleID) throws FinderEx-
ception, RemoteException;
```

```
    public Schedule create(String scheduleID, String courseID, String loca-
tionID, String instructorID, GregorianCalendar startDate, GregorianCalen-
dar endDate) throws CreateException, RemoteException;
}
```

The remote component interface, `Schedule`, also extends the `EJBObject`
interface and has several fine-grained methods that can be invoked by its client,
the `ScheduleManager` bean.

```
public interface Schedule extends EJBObject
{
    public ScheduleVO getTheSchedule() throws RemoteException;

    public String getCourseID() throws RemoteException;
    public void setCourseID(String courseID) throws RemoteException;

    public String getLocationID() throws RemoteException;
    public void setLocationID(String LocationID) throws RemoteException;

    public String getInstructorID() throws RemoteException;
    public void setInstructorID(String instructorID) throws RemoteException;

    public GregorianCalendar getStartDate() throws RemoteException;
    public void setStartDate(GregorianCalendar startDate) throws RemoteEx-
ception;

    public GregorianCalendar getEndDate() throws RemoteException;
    public void setEndDate(GregorianCalendar endDate) throws RemoteException;

    public int getClassSize() throws RemoteException;
    public void setClassSize(int classSize) throws RemoteException;
}
```

The following is a pertinent code snippet of the `ScheduleBean` class, which
implements `EntityBean` and declares cmp-fields and their corresponding `get`
and `set` methods.

```
public class ScheduleBean implements EntityBean
{
    private EntityContext context;
    public ScheduleVO scheduleVO;

    //declare the cmp-fields
    public String scheduleID;
    public String  courseID;
    public String  courseStatus;
    public GregorianCalendar startDate;
        ........................ . .
        ........................ .
```

```
// now getter and setter methods for cmp-fields

public void setScheduleID(String scheduleID)
{
    this.scheduleID = scheduleID;
}

public String getScheduleID()
{
    return this.scheduleID;
}

public String getCourseID()
{
    return this.courseID;
}

public void setCourseID(String CourseID)
{
    this.courseID = courseID;
}

public GregorianCalendar getStartDate()
{
    return this.startDate;
}

public void setStartDate(GregorianCalendar startDate)
{
    this.startDate = startDate;
}

public String getCourseStatus()
{
    return this.courseStatus;
}

public void setCourseStatus(String courseStatus)
{
    this.courseStatus = courseStatus;
}
```

The `ejbCreate()` method initially creates a schedule entity. But it's the `ejbPostCreate()` method that looks up and finds a bean entity represented by the primary key, `courseID`, retrieves information (such as the title and cost) from the `CourseBean`, and assigns them to the cmp-fields.

```
public String ejbCreate(String scheduleID, String courseID, String
locationID, String instructorID, GregorianCalendar startDate,
```

```
                GregorianCalendar endDate) throws CreateException
{
    this.scheduleID = scheduleID;
    this.locationID = locationID;
    this.instructorID = instructorID;
    this.startDate = startDate;
    this.endDate = endDate;
    courseStatus = "OPEN";
    currentEnrollment = 0;

    return scheduleID;
}

public void ejbPostCreate(String scheduleID, String courseID,
String locationID, String instructorID, GregorianCalendar
startDate,GregorianCalendar endDate) throws CreateException
{
    CourseHome courseHome = null;
    Course course = null;
    try
    {
        Object ref = lookUp("java:comp/env/ejb/CourseRef");
        courseHome = (CourseHome) javax.rmi.PortableRemoteOb-
ject.narrow(ref, CourseHome.class);
        course = courseHome.findByPrimaryKey(courseID);
        this.courseID = (String)course.getPrimaryKey();
        this.title = course.getTitle();
        this.classSize = course.getClassSize();
        this.title = course.getTitle();
        summary = course.getSummary();
        this.price = course.getPrice();
    } catch (Exception e) {
        System.out.println(" *** ScheduleBean - Exception in ejb-
PostCreate() "+e.getMessage() );
    }
}
```

The ScheduleBean class uses the dependent Java class, ScheduleVO, to facilitate the efficient transfer of data from the bean instance to the client.

```
public ScheduleVO getTheSchedule()
{
    scheduleVO = new ScheduleVO(this.scheduleID, this.courseID,
this.locationID, startDate, endDate, this.courseStatus,
this.title, this.cost, this.classSize, this.currentEnrollment);

    return scheduleVO;
}
```

ScheduleClient

The client is a standalone Java program that performs two functions—it first creates a course by using the `Course` entity bean and then creates a schedule using the `Schedule` bean. It uses JNDI to look up the `MyCourse` home object and then calls a `create()` method with arguments to create an entity bean instance with `EJB-101` as its primary key. It then does another JNDI look up to access the `MySchedule` home object and then creates the schedule entity.

```
public class ScheduleClient {

    public static void main(String[] args) {
    try {
        Context initctx = new InitialContext();
         Object objref1 =
initctx.lookup("java:comp/env/ejb/MyCourse");
        CourseHome courseHome = (CourseHome) javax.rmi.PortableRe-
moteObject.narrow(objref1, CourseHome.class);

        String textBook ="J2EE Boot Camp: Developing Enterprise Java-
Beans";
        String title = "Intermediate EJB";
        String summary = "This is hands-on intermediate EJB programming
class";
        double cost = 2500.00;
        int size = 15;

        Course course = courseHome.create("EJB-101", title,   "hands-
on", summary, "EJB-101", textBook, cost, size);

         Object objref2 = initctx.lookup("java:comp/env/ejb/MySched-
ule");
        ScheduleHome schedHome = (ScheduleHome) javax.rmi.PortableRe-
moteObject.narrow(objref2, ScheduleHome.class);
        GregorianCalendar startDate = new GregorianCalendar(2002, Cal-
endar.MARCH, 25);
        GregorianCalendar endDate = new GregorianCalendar(2002, Calen-
dar.MARCH, 29);

        Schedule sched = schedHome.create("2001092406", "EJB-101",
"CA-SF-001", "sam@javacamp.com", startDate, endDate);

        .....................
        ...........................
```

EJB 1.1 Deployment Descriptor

Let's look at the deployment descriptor and analyze the elements of one entity bean, ScheduleBean. The <ejb-name> element specifies the name of the entity bean class, followed by the fully qualified name of the remote home and remote interfaces and entity bean class name, identified by the <home>, <remote>, and <ejb-class> elements, respectively. The <persistence-type> element indicates that this is a CMP with string type as the <prim key class>. It's a <non-reentrant> element, which specifies false loopback calls; it's using CMP 1.1 as indicated by the value 1.x enclosed by the <cmp-version> element. All the declared, container-managed persistence fields are specified by the <cmp-field> element, which consists of the optional <description> element and the mandatory <field-name>. Notice the primary key class marked by the <primary-key> element.

```xml
<?xml version="1.0" encoding="UTF-8"?>

<!DOCTYPE ejb-jar PUBLIC '-//Sun Microsystems, Inc.//DTD Enterprise
JavaBeans 2.0//EN' 'http://java.sun.com/dtd/ejb-jar_2_0.dtd'>

<ejb-jar>
   <display-name>Ejb117JAR</display-name>
   <enterprise-beans>
      ............................................. . .
      .............................................................
      <entity>
         <display-name>ScheduleBean</display-name>
         <ejb-name>ScheduleBean</ejb-name>
      <home>j2eebootcamp.developingEJB.chapter17.schedule.Schedule-
Home </home>
         <remote>j2eebootcamp.developingEJB.chapter17.schedule.Sched-
ule </remote>
         <ejb-class> j2eebootcamp.developingEJB.chapter17.sched-
ule.ScheduleBean </ejb-class>
         <persistence-type>Container</persistence-type>
         <prim-key-class>java.lang.String</prim-key-class>
         <reentrant>False</reentrant>
         <cmp-version>1.x</cmp-version>
         <cmp-field>
           <description>no description</description>
           <field-name>scheduleID</field-name>
         </cmp-field>
         <cmp-field>
           <description>no description</description>
```

```
        <field-name>startDate</field-name>
      </cmp-field>
      <cmp-field>
        <description>no description</description>
        <field-name>locationID</field-name>
      </cmp-field>
      <cmp-field>
        <description>no description</description>
        <field-name>endDate</field-name>
      </cmp-field>
      ............................................. . .
      <cmp-field>
        <description>no description</description>
        <field-name>courseStatus</field-name>
      </cmp-field>
      <cmp-field>
        <description>no description</description>
        <field-name>summary</field-name>
        <cmp-field>
        <description>no description</description>
        <field-name>courseID</field-name>
      </cmp-field>
      <primkey-field>scheduleID</primkey-field>
      <ejb-ref>
        <ejb-ref-name>ejb/CourseRef</ejb-ref-name>
        <ejb-ref-type>Entity</ejb-ref-type>
        <home> j2eebootcamp.developingEJB.chapter17.course.Course-
Home
</home>
<remote> j2eebootcamp.devel-
opingEJB.chapter17.course.Course</remote>
        <ejb-link>CourseBean</ejb-link>
      </ejb-ref>
      <security-identity>
        <description></description>
        <use-caller-identity></use-caller-identity>
      </security-identity>
    </entity>
    ............................................. . .
</ejb-jar>
```

The ScheduleBean references CourseBean. This relationship is specified by the
<ejb-ref> element, which includes the EJB reference name <ejb-ref-name>
of the component and the EJB type <ejb-ref-type>. The corresponding home
and component interfaces are included as well, and the component is linked to it
using <ejb-link> elements.

EJB 2.0 Implementation

The new and improved Schedule Manager application with participating objects is illustrated in Figure 17-5. After refactoring, the EJB 1.1 Schedule Manager application is now a CMP 2.0-based Schedule Manager application consisting of two entity beans, a stateful session bean, and one standalone Java client. This new implementation reflects the goals of reducing both network traffic and coupling between the client and the EJBs.

The refactored CMP 2.0 entity bean classes, ScheduleBean and CourseBean, have been refactored to use the container-managed persistence fields and container-managed relationship fields of the abstract persistent schema. Their remote interfaces have been replaced with local interfaces, and the one-to-one container-managed relationship between ScheduleBean and CourseBean is defined.

Instead of entity beans directly interacting with a Java client, Schedule-ManagerClient, a session facade, EJB Design Pattern, is being used to separate the client from the entity beans. The session façade in this application helps hide the complexity and methods of local entity beans from the client, reduces the network traffic, and provides a single point of interaction for the client. (EJB design patterns are discussed in the Chapter 16). The session facade ScheduleManagerBean is implemented as a stateful session bean, which manages the creation of the course and schedule entity and hides the implementation details from the client.

The client, ScheduleManagerClient, now interacts with a single object, thus simplifying the client code. The object interaction (illustrated in Figure 17-5) and the sequence diagram (illustrated in Figure 17-6) show the Schedule-ManagerClient invoking remote calls (1) only on the ScheduleManager-Bean. The ScheduleManagerBean invokes local method calls (2) on the CourseBean, which creates a course entity and inserts it into the CourseBeanTable in the database (3). The ScheduleManagerBean then makes another local method call (4) to ScheduleBean, which in turn makes local calls (5) to the CourseBean, creates a schedule entity, and inserts it into the ScheduleBeanTable in the database (6).

Compare Figures 17-3 and 17-5 to review the results of the refactored Schedule Manager application. The migration effort goal was to reduce network traffic, increase scalability, and make the application portable. The entity beans consist of fine-grained business methods. In EJB 1.1, the calls to these methods were remote calls that created high overhead, resulting in high network traffic. By converting remote interfaces to local interfaces in EJB 2.0, overhead associated with remote

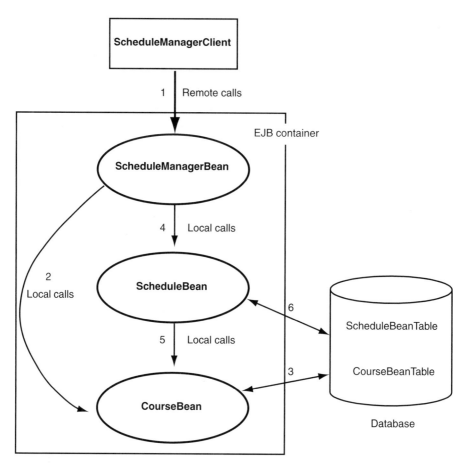

Figure 17-5 Refactored CMP 2.0 schedule manager application

calls are gone. Through use of the session facade, the `ScheduleManagerBean` hides the fine-grained methods of the entity beans from the `ScheduleManager-Client`, reducing the brittleness of the application and localizing the method calls within the EJB container (further reducing the network traffic). The single heavy line in Figure 17-4 represents remote calls; the light line represents the local calls. Note that remote calls are reduced from three to one; compare Figure 17-4 and 17-6.

The abstract persistence schema and EJB QL in CMP 2.0 enable bean developers to write vendor- and database-agnostic CMP entity beans. At deployment time, the EJB container generates database-optimized code to handle persistence. The

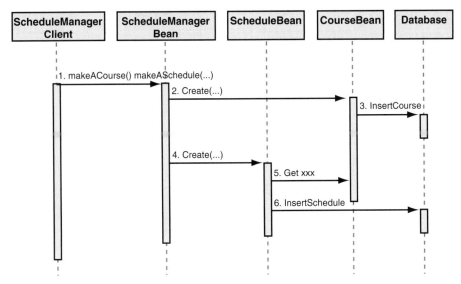

Figure 17-6 CMP 2.0 schedule manager sequence diagram

resulting migrated Schedule Manager application not only performs better but is also highly portable. See Chapters 10 and 11 for more information on abstract persistence schema.

CourseBean

The remote interface was converted to a local interface; to reflect the change, the local home interface, LocalCourseHome, has been renamed and extends EJBLocalHome. Note that RemoteException is gone—in fact, it's illegal to throw a RemoteException in local method calls. The declared methods return the corresponding LocalCourse interface. The methods have changed.

```
public interface LocalCourseHome extends EJBLocalHome
{
    public LocalCourse findByPrimaryKey(String courseID) throws
FinderException;
    public LocalCourse create(String courseID, String title, String
classFormat, String description,  String preRequisite, String text-
Book, double price, int size ) throws CreateException;
}
```

Next, look at the local component interface, LocalCourse. It extends the EJBLocalObject interface. The methods are identical, except that RemoteException is gone.

```
public interface LocalCourse extends EJBLocalObject
{
    public String getTitle() ;
    public void setTitle(String title) ;

    public String getSummary() ;
    public void setSummary(String summary) ;

    public String getClassFormat() ;
    public void setClassFormat(String classFormat) ;

    public String getPreRequisites() ;
    public void setPreRequisites(String preRequisites) ;

    public String getTextBooks() ;
    public void setTextBooks(String textBooks) ;

    public double getPrice() ;
    public void setPrice(double price) ;

    public int getClassSize() ;
    public void setClassSize(int classSize) ;
}
```

Now look at CourseBean and see the changes under CMP 2.0. Note that in the class definition, CourseBean still implements the EntityBean interface; it's declared public but has an additional modifier, abstract. CMP entity beans in EJB 2.0 must be declared abstract. Rather than declaring the public cmp-fields along with get and set methods, EJB 2.0 defines the cmp-fields as abstract set and get methods.

```
public abstract class CourseBean implements EntityBean
{
    private EntityContext context;

    public abstract String getCourseID();
    public abstract void setCourseID(String courseID);

    public abstract String getTitle();
    public abstract void setTitle(String title);

    public abstract String getClassFormat();
    public abstract void setClassFormat(String classFormat);

    public abstract String getSummary();
    public abstract void setSummary(String summary);

    public abstract String getPreRequisites();
    public abstract void setPreRequisites(String preRequisites);
```

In the `ejbCreate()` method, you should use the previously defined abstract set method to set the argument to the appropriate cmp-fields. It has an empty `ejbPostCreate()`; callback methods are also empty and now shown.

```
public String ejbCreate(String courseID, String title, String
classFormat, String summary, String preRequisites, String text-
Books, double price, int classSize) throws CreateException
{
    setCourseID(courseID);
    setTitle(title);
    setClassFormat(classFormat);
    setPreRequisites(preRequisites);
    setTextBooks(textBooks);
    setPrice(price);
    setClassSize(classSize);
    setSummary(summary);

    return courseID;

}

public void ejbPostCreate(String courseID, String title, String
classFormat, String summary, String preRequisites, String text-
Books, double price, int classSize) throws CreateException
{
}
```

ScheduleBean

There are no differences in `LocalScheduleHome` other than extending `EJBLocalHome` and `EJBLocalObject` and throwing `EJBException` rather than `RemoteException`.

```
public interface LocalScheduleHome extends EJBLocalHome
{
    public LocalSchedule findByPrimaryKey(String scheduleID) throws
FinderException, EJBException;
    public LocalSchedule create(String scheduleID, String courseID,
String locationID, String instructorID, GregorianCalendar start-
Date, GregorianCalendar endDate) throws CreateException, EJBExcep-
tion;
}
```

In addition, the `LocalSchedule` interface for the `ScheduleBean` is shown refactored for the local interface.

```
public interface LocalSchedule extends EJBLocalObject
{
```

```
    public String getLocationID() throws ScheduleException;
    public void setLocationID(String LocationID) throws ScheduleEx-
ception;

    public String getInstructorID() throws ScheduleException;
    public void setInstructorID(String instructorID) throws Schedu-
leException;

    public GregorianCalendar getStartDate() throws ScheduleExcep-
tion;
    public void setStartDate(GregorianCalendar startDate) throws
ScheduleException;

    public GregorianCalendar getEndDate() throws ScheduleException;
    public void setEndDate(GregorianCalendar endDate) throws Schedu-
leException;

    public int getClassSize() throws ScheduleException;
    public void setClassSize(int classSize) throws ScheduleExcep-
tion;
}
```

Looking at the `ScheduleBean` class next, note the replacement of the container-managed persistent fields and the `get` and `set` methods of EJB 1.1 with abstract methods for the cmp-fields.

```
public abstract class ScheduleBean implements EntityBean
{
    private EntityContext context;
    public ScheduleVO schedVO;

    public abstract void setScheduleID(String scheduleID);
    public abstract String getScheduleID();

    public abstract String getCourseID();
    public abstract void setCourseID(String courseID);

    public abstract String getLocationID();
    public abstract void setLocationID(String locationID);

    public abstract String getInstructorID();
    public abstract void setInstructorID(String instructorID);

    public abstract GregorianCalendar getStartDate();
    public abstract void setStartDate(GregorianCalendar startDate);
```

The one-to-one relationship between the `ScheduleBean` and the `CourseBean` is declared by the `ejbSelectCourse()` method, which returns a local interface, `LocalCourse`, to the `CourseBean`.

```
//container-managed relationship fields
    public abstract LocalCourse ejbSelectCourse(String courseID)
throws FinderException;
```

The ejbCreate() method uses the abstract method to specify the persistent fields in the bean instance, as shown here.

```
public String ejbCreate(String scheduleID, String courseID, String
locationID, String instructorID, GregorianCalendar startDate,Gre-
gorianCalendar endDate) throws CreateException
{
    setScheduleID(scheduleID);
    setLocationID(locationID);
    setInstructorID(instructorID);
    setStartDate(startDate);
    setEndDate(endDate);
    setCourseStatus("OPEN");
    setCurrentEnrollment(0);

    return scheduleID;
}
```

In `ejbPostCreate()`, the bean instance uses the local handle to the `CourseBean` through the `ejbSelectCourse()` method and then invokes the fine-grained business methods to retrieve course related information before completing the creation of the entity bean instance.

```
public void ejbPostCreate(String scheduleID, String courseID,
String locationID, String instructorID, GregorianCalendar start-
Date,
GregorianCalendar endDate) throws CreateException
{
    LocalCourse localCourse = null;
    try
    {
        localCourse = ejbSelectCourse(courseID);
        setCourseID(courseID);
        setTitle(localCourse.getTitle());
        setClassSize(localCourse.getClassSize());
        setSummary(localCourse.getSummary());
        setPrice(localCourse.getPrice());
    } catch (Exception e) {
        System.out.println(" *** ScheduleBean - Exception in ejb-
PostCreate() "+e.getMessage() );
```

```
    }

}
```

The method invocation necessary to create the course and schedule entity is
done by the ScheduleManagerBean on behalf of the client, Schedule-
ManagerClient.

ScheduleManagerBean

The ScheduleManagerBean hides the methods from the client, localizes
method invocations, and facilitates communication between the client and the
entity beans. It uses stateful session beans with the ScheduleManagerHome and
ScheduleManager remote interfaces. It needs to have the remote interface so
remote clients can call its methods.

The remote home interface, ScheduleManagerHome, extends EJBHome and has
a single mandatory create() method.

```
public interface ScheduleManagerHome extends EJBHome
{
    public ScheduleManager create() throws CreateException, RemoteException;
}
```

The remote component interface, ScheduleManager, extends EJBObject and
has two business methods: makeASchedule() (with arguments to create a
schedule) and getASchedule() (which retrieves a dependent value object,
ScheduleVO).

```
public interface ScheduleManager extends EJBObject
{
    public boolean makeASchedule(String scheduleID, String courseID,
    String locationID, String instructorID, GregorianCalendar startDate,
    GregorianCalendar endDate) throws RemoteException;

    public ScheduleVO getASchedule(String scheduleID) throws RemoteEx-
    ception;

    public boolean makeACourse(String courseID, String title, String
    description, String courseFormat, String preRequisites, String course-
    Books, double cost, int classSize) throws RemoteException;
}
```

Because these are remote methods, they must throw RemoteExceptions. The
following ScheduleManagerBean class code snippet is a session bean that
implements the SessionBean interface. There are three business methods:
makeACourse(), makeASchedule(), and getASchedule().

The `ScheduleBean` invokes the `makeACourse()` method to create a course entity instance. It performs two tasks: first, it finds the local home object of the `CourseBean`. Then, it invokes the `create()` method to instantiate a course entity bean. At the end of this method, an entity representing a course is created in the database.

```
public boolean makeACourse(String courseID, String title, String
description, String courseFormat, String preRequisites, String
courseBooks, double cost, int classSize)
    {
    LocalCourseHome localCourseHome = null;
        LocalCourse localCourse = null;
        try
        {
            localCourseHome = (LocalCourseHome)javax.rmi.Porta-
bleRemoteObject.narrow(lookUp("ejb/CourseRef"), LocalCourse-
Home.class);
            localCourse = localCourseHome.create(courseID, title,
description, courseFormat, preRequisites, courseBooks, cost, class-
Size);
        } catch (Exception e) {
            System.out.println(" makeACourse failed! ="+e.getMes-
sage());
            return false;
        }
        return true;
    }
```

The business method, `makeASchedule()`, performs two tasks. First, it uses the JNDI `lookUp()` method to get a handle to `ScheduleBean`'s home object. Then, it uses the home object to create an entity bean instance, `ScheduleBean`, with specific arguments. This results in the creation of a schedule entity.

```
public class ScheduleManagerBean implements SessionBean
{

    private SessionContext context;
    .............................. . .


    //business methods
    public boolean makeASchedule(String scheduleID, String
courseID, String locationID, String instructorID, GregorianCalendar
startDate, GregorianCalendar endDate)
    {
    ScheduleHome scheduleHome = null;
        Schedule scheduleComponent = null;
```

```
        try
        {
            scheduleHome = lookUp();
            scheduleComponent = scheduleHome.create(scheduleID,
courseID, locationID, instructorID, startDate, endDate);

        } catch (Exception e) {
            System.out.println(" makeASchedule failed! ="+e.getMes-
sage());
            return false;
        }
        return true;
    }
```

The ScheduleBean also includes a getASchedule(), which returns a schedule value object to ScheduleManagerClient.

```
public ScheduleVO getASchedule(String scheduleID)
{
    // lookup a schedule
    if (scheduleComponent != null) {
    try {
      ScheduleVO schedVO = schedulecomponent.getTheSchedule();
      return schedVO;
        } catch(Exception e) {
            System.out.println("getASchedule exception "+e.getMes-
sage());
        }
    } else
        return false;
}
```

Finally, a standalone Java client, ScheduleManagerClient, invokes two coarse-grained calls—makeACourse() and makeASchedule()—on ScheduleManagerBean. In contrast to the ScheduleClient implementation in EJB 1.1, only a single lookup for MyScheduleManager (representing ScheduleManagerBean's remote home object) must be made. It then instantiates the stateful session bean, ScheduleManagerBean, and invokes two remote method calls—makeACourse() and makeASchedule(). Notice that the refactored client is much simpler and calls only course-grained methods, delegating the implementation details to the ScheduleManagerBean instance. It prints out cmp-field values.

```
public class ScheduleManagerClient {

    public static void main(String[] args) {
        try {
```

```
        Context initctx = new InitialContext();
          Object objref2 =
initctx.lookup("java:comp/env/ejb/MyScheduleManager");
          ScheduleManagerHome schedMgrHome =  ScheduleManagerHome)
javax.rmi.PortableRemoteObject.narrow(objref2, ScheduleManager-
Home.class);
          ScheduleManager schedMgr = schedMgrHome.create();

      String textBook ="J2EE Boot Camp: Developing Enterprise Java-
Beans";
      String title = "Intermediate EJB";
      String summary = "This is hands-on intermediate EJB programming
class";
      double cost = 2500.00;
      int size = 15;

      System.out.println("-- Client -- before makeACourse() ---");

      // first part - create a course entity
        schedMgr.makeACourse("EJB-200", title, summary, "hands-on",
"EJB-101", textBook, cost, size);
            System.out.println(" created a course .....");

      System.out.println("-- Client -- before makeASchedule() ---");

      GregorianCalendar startDate = new GregorianCalendar(2002, Cal-
endar.MARCH, 25);
      GregorianCalendar endDate = new GregorianCalendar(2002, Calen-
dar.MARCH, 29);

      // part two - create a schedule entity
        schedMgr.makeASchedule("2001092406", "EJB-101", "CA-SF-001",
"pvt@javacamp.com", startDate, endDate);
            System.out.println(" created a schedule.....");
```

CMP 2.0 Deployment Descriptor

The CMP 2.0 deployment descriptor with the abstract persistence schema is
slightly more complex. Note that the container-managed persistent fields in EJB
2.0 are enclosed within <cmp-field> elements with optional <description>
and required <field-name> elements. The <cmp-version> with the 2.X field
indicates the use of CMP 2.0. Note that the new <abstract-schema-name>
element specifies the persistence schema name.

```
<?xml version="1.0" encoding="UTF-8"?>
```

```
<!DOCTYPE ejb-jar PUBLIC '-//Sun Microsystems, Inc.//DTD Enterprise
JavaBeans 2.0//EN' 'http://java.sun.com/dtd/ejb-jar_2_0.dtd'>

<ejb-jar>
<display-name>Ejb201JAR</display-name>
    <enterprise-beans>
    <entity>
        <display-name>ScheduleBean</display-name>
        <ejb-name>ScheduleBean</ejb-name>
        <local-home>
j2eebootcamp.developingEJB.chapter17.schedule.LocalScheduleHome
        </local-home>
        <local>
j2eebootcamp.developingEJB.chapter17.schedule.LocalSchedule
        </local>
        <ejb-class>
j2eebootcamp.developingEJB.chapter17.schedule.ScheduleBean
        </ejb-class>
        <persistence-type>Container</persistence-type>
        <prim-key-class>java.lang.String</prim-key-class>
        <reentrant>False</reentrant>
        <cmp-version>2.x</cmp-version>
        <abstract-schema-name>Schedule</abstract-schema-name>
        <cmp-field>
        <description>no description</description>
        <field-name>scheduleID</field-name>
            </cmp-field>
    <cmp-field>
        <description>no description</description>
        <field-name>startDate</field-name>
    </cmp-field>
     <cmp-field>
        <description>no description</description>
        <field-name>locationID</field-name>
    </cmp-field>
        ........................

    <cmp-field>
        <description>no description</description>
        <field-name>courseID</field-name>
    </cmp-field>
    <primkey-field>scheduleID</primkey-field>
        <security-identity>
        <description></description>
        <use-caller-identity></use-caller-identity>
        </security-identity>
    <query>
        <description></description>
```

```
        <query-method>
        <method-name>ejbSelectCourse</method-name>
        <method-params>
            <method-param>java.lang.String</method-param>
        </method-params>
        </query-method>
        <result-type-mapping>Local</result-type-mapping>
        <ejb-ql>
SELECT OBJECT(c) FROM Course AS c WHERE c.courseID = ?1
        </ejb-ql>
    </query>
    </entity>
    <session>
        <display-name>ScheduleManagerBean</display-name>
        <ejb-name>ScheduleManagerBean</ejb-name>
    <home>
j2eebootcamp.developingEJB.chapter17.schedule.ScheduleManagerHome
    </home>
    <remote>
j2eebootcamp.developingEJB.chapter17.schedule.ScheduleManager
    </remote>
    <ejb-class> j2eebootcamp.developingEJB.chapter17.sched-
ule.ScheduleManagerBean
    </ejb-class>
    <session-type>Stateful</session-type>
    <transaction-type>Bean</transaction-type>
    <ejb-local-ref>
        <ejb-ref-name>ejb/ScheduleRef</ejb-ref-name>
        <ejb-ref-type>Entity</ejb-ref-type>
        <local-home> j2eebootcamp.developingEJB.chapter17.sched-
ule.LocalScheduleHome
        </local-home>
        <local>
j2eebootcamp.developingEJB.chapter17.schedule.LocalSchedule
        </local>
        <ejb-link>ScheduleBean</ejb-link>
    </ejb-local-ref>
    <security-identity>
        <description></description>
        <use-caller-identity></use-caller-identity>
    </security-identity>
    </session>
    <entity>
    ....................
```

The abstract method, ejbSelectCourse(), which declares the one-to-one ScheduleBean-CourseBean entity relationship in ScheduleBean, is represented by the <query> element. Note that the abstract method name, ejbSelectCourse, is mapped by the <method-name> element of the <query-method>, the string argument by <method-param>, and the return type by the <return-type-mapping> element. The query statement associated with the ejbSelectCourse() method was specified with the deployment descriptor using the EJB QL statement as mapped by the <ejb-ql> element. The abstract persistence schema in the deployment descriptor also specifies the relationship ScheduleBean has with ScheduleManagerBean, which calls its business methods.

Entity Beans with Local Interfaces versus Dependent Value Objects

The use of entity beans or Java classes as dependent value classes to model fine-grained logic has no significance in EJB 2.0. Via the remote and local interfaces in EJB 2.0, developers can implement coarse-grained business logic with remote interfaces and fine-grained business logic with local interfaces, receiving all the benefits of EJBs with minimal drawbacks. This doesn't mean that the dependent value class is no longer necessary. There are instances where dependent value objects are useful—for example, for efficiently passing data as a serialized object between components and clients.

Summary

Migrating from EJB 1.1 to EJB 2.0 depends on several factors—the complexity of the existing application, the bean developer's knowledge of EJB 2.0, and the time factor. The examples in this chapter were designed to highlight the basic approaches and the changes necessary for the migration, the difficulty involved, and the efforts required, which are proportional to the complexity of the application. Using EJB 2.0, developers can deploy EJB 1.1 applications in EJB 2.0 containers, potentially having the luxury of selectively phasing in migration without disrupting service to customers.

ASSEMBLING THE J2EE ONLINE REGISTRATION APPLICATION

Chapter 18

In Part 2 of this book, we focused our attention on understanding and implementing different types of EJB components. In the earlier chapters of Part 3, we discussed advanced concepts such as transactions, security, and design patterns. In this chapter, we won't cover any new concepts; instead, we'll refactor the individual components we developed in Part 2 and create one seamless application, the J2EE Online Registration Application (JORA). This process will include:

- discussing design goals
- applying design patterns
- refactoring existing EJBs
- assembling the EJB and deploying the application

Design Goals

There are three design goals that we'll address in this chapter. The first goal is to create an application from previously implemented EJB components and apply design patterns appropriately in the application. The application takes previously developed EJB components, refactors them as necessary, and implements new components to provide these application functions:

- search for classes
- use the shopping cart to hold classes

- register for classes
- enter addresses
- get a list of the courses for which the student is registered
- get a list of students' addresses

The second goal is to minimize coupling between different tiers by applying design patterns. Reducing coupling between different tiers provides more flexibility, so that developers can add new features to the components without breaking the application.

The third goal is to reduce network traffic and improve performance of the application by localizing fine-grained object interaction within the tier.

Applying Design Patterns

In this chapter, we'll also implement five EJB design patterns. Please refer to Figure 18-1 on page 584, which illustrates the assembled applications consisting of EJB design patterns, EJB components, and their interactions. We'll also discuss one design pattern from Chapter 6.

- `ServiceLocatorEJB`—stateful session bean (Service Locator design pattern)
- `ServiceLookUp`—Java class (Service Locator design pattern)
- `StudentFacadeEJB`—stateful session bean (Session Facade design pattern)
- `ServiceDelegate`—Java class (Business Delegate design pattern)
- `ScheduleDAO`—serializable Java class (Data Access Object design pattern)
- `AddressVO`, `RosterVO`, and `ScheduleVO`—Java class (Value Object design pattern)

Service Locator Design Pattern

While implementing the EJBs in the sample application, you might have noticed that the EJB components and clients usually end up performing one or more JNDI lookups before a client can invoke any business logic. In most business production environments, there's usually a central repository, most likely an LDAP directory server (with fail-over capabilities), where all objects are stored. Every time an EJB performs a JNDI lookup, it executes a remote call. Reducing the number of remote JNDI calls by caching remote objects improves the performance of the application. The Service Locator design pattern discussed in Chapter 16 accomplishes this; two variants of the pattern are implemented in the application.

The `ServiceLocatorEJB` implements the Service Locator pattern as a stateful session bean. The bean performs a lookup on behalf of the JNDI caller and then caches the home object. Subsequent requests for the particular home object from any caller return the home object from the cache, thus avoiding a remote call to the LDAP server. The remote home interface, `ServiceLocatorHome`, has a single mandatory `create()` method. The remote component interface, `ServiceLocator`, has one business method, `getHomeObject()`, which takes as an argument a JNDI name that references the remote home object and returns the home object.

```
public interface ServiceLocator extends EJBObject {

    public EJBHome getHomeObject(String jndiName) throws RemoteException;
}
```

The `ServiceLocatorEJB` is a fairly simple implementation using Hashtable to cache the home objects. The `getHomeObject()` method first checks whether the home object is available in the cache. If it finds the home object, it returns the home object and avoids a remote call. If the home object isn't available in the cache, it performs a JNDI lookup, saves it in the cache, and returns the home object to the client.

```
public void ejbCreate() {
    System.out.println(" -- ServiceLocatorEJB -- ejbCreate() ---");
    try {
    // Create the hashtable and an initial context for handling JNDI
        homeObjCache = new Hashtable();
        context =  new InitialContext();
    } catch (Exception e) {
        System.err.println("Error creating Service Locator: " + e);
    }
}

.....................
public EJBHome getHomeObject(String jndiName) {
    try {
        // Look in the homeObjCache for a matching name.
        // Return the associated EJBHome object if found in hash table
        if (homeObjCache.containsKey(jndiName)) {

            System.err.println("Returning existing Home Object for " + jndiName);
            return (EJBHome)homeObjCache.get(jndiName);
        }
        //if not found, get it and add it to the cache
        System.err.println("Creating new Home object for " + jndiName);
        Object ejbRef = context.lookup("java:comp/env/ejb/"+jndiName);
```

```
    EJBHome ejbHome = (EJBHome)PortableRemoteObject.narrow(ejbRef,
EJBHome.class);
    homeObjCache.put(jndiName, ejbHome);
    return ejbHome;
    } catch(Exception e) {
    System.err.println("Error getting home object: " + e);
    return null;
    }
}
```

The `ServiceLocatorEJB` is a very simple, but effective, implementation of the
Service Locator pattern for retrieving remote home objects. The clients that use
remote objects must perform one remote JNDI lookup to access the services of the
`ServiceLocatorEJB`.

The non-EJB implementation of this pattern, `ServiceLookUp`, is a Java class
implementation of the Service Locator pattern. It uses a singleton pattern to
provide a single service lookup object in the JVM. Note that we've strayed from
the pure Service Locator design pattern by implementing counter methods to
provide the address and roster ID numbers for `AddressEJB` and `RosterEJB`.
This simplistic approach to retrieve unique IDs solves a problem in the sample
application. You should use a more robust solution for generating a unique ID.

The `ServiceLookUp` also uses the Hashtable to cache data. It then uses
`getLocalHomeObject()` to return a local home object in the cache before
performing a JNDI lookup.

```
public ServiceLookUp()
  {
    try {
        homeObjCache = new Hashtable();
        ctx = new InitialContext();
        rosterCount = 100;
        addressCount = 1000;
    } catch (Exception e) {
        System.err.println("Error creating service lookup : "+e);
  }
}

public static ServiceLookUp getInstance()
{
    if (slookup == null)
        slookup = new ServiceLookUp();
    return slookup;
}
```

```
....................
public EJBLocalHome getLocalHomeObject(String jndiName)
{
    EJBLocalHome ejbLocalHome = null;
    try {
    if (homeObjCache.containsKey(jndiName)) {
        System.out.println(" -- returning existing Local Home object
="+jndiName);

        return ((EJBLocalHome)homeObjCache.get(jndiName));
    } else {

    System.out.println(" -- creating new home object jndi name ="+jndi-
Name);
    try {
        Object ejbRef = ctx.lookup("java:comp/env/ejb/"+jndiName);
        ejbLocalHome = (EJBLocalHome) ejbRef;
        homeObjCache.put(jndiName, ejbLocalHome);
    } catch (NamingException ne) {
        System.out.println(" Naming exception ="+ne.getMessage());
....................................... . . .
        return null;
    }
}
...........
public String getRosterCount()
{
    int count = rosterCount++;
    return (new Integer(count)).toString();
}
```

Using the Service Locator pattern reduces the JNDI lookup code replication requirements and centralizes lookups in one location, making it easier to maintain code and reducing the number of remote calls.

Session Facade Design Pattern

A desirable strategy is to reduce the dependencies between a client and the business objects and hide the complexity of the interactions between interdependent objects. Hiding the low-level calls between the client and business object reduces the coupling and brittleness of the application. Implementing a Session Facade design pattern helps achieve that objective. StudentFacadeEJB is a stateful session bean implementation of the Session Facade; it provides a coarse-grained business method to create student accounts, addresses, and/or get schedule lists. StudentFacadeEJB shields the clients from the changes in the method calls of the entity beans, namely StudentEJB, AddressEJB, and RosterEJB.

The StudentFacadeHome interface has a single create() method. StudentFacade has several coarse-grained business methods declared, as shown in the next code snippet. The methods createStudent() and createAddress() create student and address entities, while getAddresses() and getScheduleList() return a list of addresses and schedule value objects. The getStudent() method returns a student value object, while the enroller() method takes a list of class schedules and inserts them into the roster table. We've used value objects extensively to encapsulate data and ease the transfer of data between various components.

```
public interface StudentFacade extends EJBObject
{
    public void createStudent(StudentVO student) throws Remote-
Exception;
    public void createAddress(AddressVO address, String studentID)
throws RemoteException;
    public StudentVO getStudent(String studentID) throws RemoteEx-
ception;
    public Vector getAddresses() throws RemoteException;
    public Vector getScheduleList() throws RemoteException;
}
```

The code snippet from SessionFacadeEJB that follows illustrates the implementation of the createStudent() method. It uses a ServiceLookUp instance to retrieve the LocalStudentHome object and create a student entity. It also uses the StudentVO to extract the necessary arguments for the create method declared in the LocalStudent interface. The createAddress() method is similar to createStudent(), but the pertinent code snippet is not shown here.

```
public void createStudent(StudentVO studentVO)
{
    try {
    //use student bean to create an account.
    LocalStudentHome studentHome = (LocalStudentHome) lookUp.getLo-
calHomeObject("StudentRef");
    LocalStudent student = studentHome.create(studentVO.getStuden-
tID(), studentVO.getFirstName(), studentVO.getLastName());
    } catch (Exception e) {
        System.out.println(" exception e "+e.getMessage());
    }

}
```

The enroller() method is used to create roster entities; it depends on the
ServiceLookUp to access the LocalRosterHome object and then invokes the
create() method. Note that the method iterates through a list of scheduleIDs
and uses the getRosterCount() method to retrieve the roster ID necessary to
create a row in the roster table.

```
public void enroll(Vector vlist, String studentID)
{
    //use RosterBean to enroll students.
    try {
    LocalRosterHome rosterHome = (LocalRosterHome) lookUp.getLocal-
HomeObject("RosterRef");

    for (int i=0; i< vlist.size(); i++)
    {
        String rosterID = lookUp.getRosterCount();
        String scheduleID = (String) vlist.get(i);
        LocalRoster roster = rosterHome.create(rosterID, sched-
uleID, studentID);
    }
        } catch (Exception e) {
        lookUp.setRosterCount(rosterCount);
        System.out.println(" exception e "+e.getMessage());
    }

}
```

The last method reviewed in the SessionFacadeEJB class is the
getScheduleList() method, which uses ServiceLookUp to retrieve the
LocalStudentHome object. It then uses the findByPrimaryKey() method to
find the studentID and invokes the business method in LocalStudent to get
an ArrayList of LocalStudent objects. It then extracts the scheduleIDs, creates
a vector, and returns it to the caller. If we returned an ArrayList of LocalStudent
objects (as in the Chapter 11 example) instead of a vector of studentIDs, the client
would have to extract the LocalStudent object. The client would then make a
fetchScheduleID() method call from the presentation tier. By extracting the
scheduleIDs and providing them as a vector, the client doesn't have to make the
fetchScheduleID() method calls on the LocalStudent interface.

```
public Vector getScheduleList(String studentID) throws FinderException
{
Vector rosterVOList = new Vector(20);
    LocalStudentHome studentHome = (LocalStudentHome) lookUp.getLo-
calHomeObject("StudentRef");
    LocalStudent student = studentHome.findByPrimaryKey(studentID);
    ArrayList rosterList = student.getRosterList();
```

```
Iterator it = rosterList.iterator();
while (it.hasNext()) {
    LocalRoster rost =(LocalRoster)it.next();
    rosterVOList.add(rost.fetchScheduleID());
}
return rosterVOList;
}
```

Note that a client calling SessionFacadeEJB doesn't need to know about the implementation or about relationships between the CMP 2.0 entity beans.

Business Delegate Design Pattern

For the application to provide the functionality mentioned previously, the servlet in the presentation tier must interact with several EJBs. The complexity of the servlet code increases with the number of objects with which it needs to interact. Additionally, changes in the EJB interfaces result in changes in the servlet code; if these changes aren't made, the application can break. The Business Delegate design pattern solves the problem of tight coupling between the presentation tier clients and the business objects, hides the underlying implementation details of the services, and reduces the network traffic.

The servlet component should only handle the presentation logic; it shouldn't have to know how to access the various business services. By delegating the task of invoking business services to the Business Delegate, the Web components are easier to maintain and aren't affected by the changes in the EJB components. ServiceDelegate is a Java class implementation of the Business Delegate design pattern. It hides the JNDI lookup functions from the Web components (as shown by the ServiceDelegate() constructor that instantiates ServiceLocatorEJB) and makes the service available to the business methods.

```
public ServiceDelegate() throws ServiceDelegateException
{
    try {
    // Bootstrapping - we need to do this once to create the Service
Locator!
        Context ctx = new InitialContext();
        Object ejbLocatorRef = ctx.lookup("java:comp/env/ejb/Locator-
Ref");
        ServiceLocatorHome ejbLocatorHome = (ServiceLocatorHome)Porta-
bleRemoteObject.narrow(ejbLocatorRef, ServiceLocatorHome.class);
        ejbLocator = ejbLocatorHome.create();
    } catch(NamingException ne) {
    ............................ .
    }
}
```

The `StudentClient` invokes a simple `addItem()` method, but notice that the implementation of `addItem()` in the `ServiceDelegate` object includes performing a JNDI lookup for a `ShoppingCart` bean instance, creating a shopping cart instance if it's the first time, or retrieving an instance (if one already exists) by the use of the `getCart()` method. The `addSchedule(schedVO)` method then adds the schedule value object, uses the `getMyScheduleList()` method to retrieve the current list of items in the cart, and returns the list.

```
public Vector addItem(ScheduleVO schedVO)
{
    Vector cartList = new Vector(20);
    try {
        ShoppingCart cart = getCart();
        cart.addASchedule(schedVO);
        cartList = cart.getMyScheduleList();
    } catch (RemoteException re) {
        re.printStackTrace();
    }
    return cartList;
}
```

An example of a coarse-grained method that hides the `ServiceDelegate` implementation details from the servlet is the `makeStudentAccount()` method. This method performs the following functions: It conducts a JNDI lookup for the `StudentFacadeHome` object, creates an instance of the `StudentFacadeEJB` object, and then creates a student account before an address can be created. An address entity cannot exist with a student account; this logic is hidden from the servlet. Once the student account and address are created, the method uses a JMS client to send a list of class schedules as a message to a message-driven bean, `RosterMDB`, which inserts the schedules into the roster table.

Data Access Object Design Pattern

As discussed in Chapter 6, the main goal of the DAO (data access object) design pattern is to separate the business logic in the EJBs from the data access logic implementation. It not only makes the business logic portable across different database types but also helps with maintenance of the code. Notice that when the `ScheduleEJB` calls `ScheduleDAO`, it calls the `searchByCourseTitle()` method and passes the course title string argument. It doesn't have to worry about the details of the SQL query statements, extracting fields in the rows from the `ResultSet`, creating a schedule value object, or creating a vector to return the results. The details are hidden from the business logic of the `ScheduleEJB`; if the underlying database changes, only the `ScheduleDAO` class needs to be modified.

```
public Vector searchByCourseTitle(String courseTitle) throws Sched-
uleDAOException
{
    Statement stmt = null;
    ResultSet rset = null;
    Vector scheduleList = new Vector(20);
    Connection conn = this.getConnection();

    String queryString ="SELECT sid, courseid, locationid, city,
state, country, startdate, enddate, status, title, instructorID,
price, maxenrollment, currentenrollment FROM ScheduleEJBTable s,
CourseEJBTable c,  LocationEJBTable l  where courseid = c.id AND
locationid = l.id AND  title LIKE '%"+courseTitle+"%'";

    try
    {
    stmt = conn.createStatement();
    rset = stmt.executeQuery(queryString);

    while(rset.next())
    {
    ScheduleVO schedule = new ScheduleVO(
    rset.getString("sid"), rset.getString("courseid"), rset.get-
String("locationid"),
    rset.getString("city"), rset.getString("state"),  rset.get-
String("country"),
    rset.getDate("startdate"), rset.getDate("enddate"),
    rset.getString("status"),rset.getString("title"),
    rset.getFloat("price"), rset.getInt("maxenrollment"),
rset.getInt("currentenrollment")
    );
    scheduleList.addElement(schedule);
    }
    } catch(SQLException se) {
        throw new ScheduleDAOException(" Query exception "+se.get-
Message());
    } finally {
        closeResultSet(rset);
        closeStatement(stmt);
        closeConnection(conn);
    }
        return scheduleList;
    }
```

Refactoring Existing EJBs

The cooperating EJBs, Web components, and helper objects included in the J2EE Online Registration Application are illustrated in Figure 18-1. The figure shows the following previously developed EJB components:

- ScheduleEJB—stateless session bean (Chapter 6)
- ScheduleDAO—data access object (Chapter 6)
- ShoppingCartEJB—stateful session bean (Chapter 7)
- StudentEJB, AddressEJB, RosterEJB—CMP 2.0 entity beans (Chapter 11)
- RosterMDB—message-driven bean (Chapter 13)

Because we've already discussed these EJBs in detail in their respective chapters, we'll give a brief summary and indicate whether the bean class had to be factored. Please refer to the appropriate chapters for in-depth discussions on implementation details for the sample applications.

Stateless Session Beans

ScheduleEJB is a stateless session bean that makes it possible for students to search the listing of Java courses. State information doesn't need to be maintained between searches. Students are expected to perform lots of searches; stateless session beans are ideal for providing a fast and scalable solution. ScheduleEJB depends on the Data Access Design pattern to perform the actual search using the JDBC APIs. ScheduleEJB and ScheduleDAO don't have to refactored to work with the registration application.

Stateful Session Beans

Shopping carts are typically implemented as stateful session beans, as they need to track interaction between method calls. ShoppingCartEJB is implemented as a stateful session bean that keeps track of courses as students add or delete from their shopping list. There are no changes required for the ShoppingCartEJB stateful session bean.

CMP 2.0 Entity Beans

The application needs to track persistent data such as students, addresses and registration information; entity beans are designed to handle such persistent entities. AddressEJB and RosterEJB were refactored to use the ServiceLookUp object to find references to the StudentEJB home object.

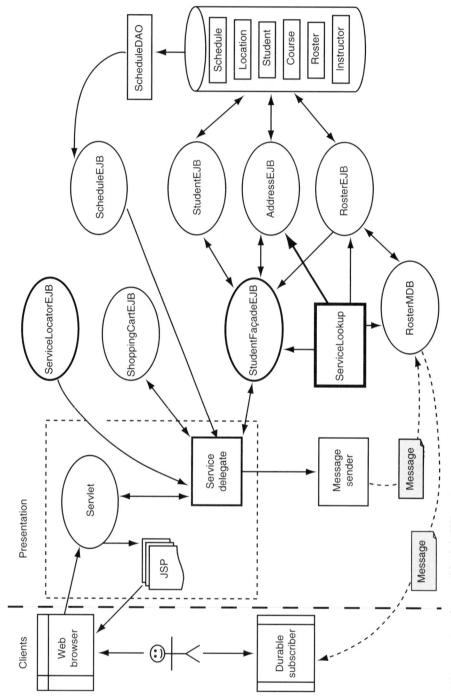

Figure 18-1 Assembled J2EE online registration application

584

Message-Driven Beans

The message-driven bean, RosterMDB, receives messages asynchronously from the servlet once the student pays, and the bean instance enrolls the student by updating the roster table, which holds the registration information. RosterMDB was refactored to also use the ServiceLookUp object to locate the RosterEJB home object.

Servlet Client

The servlet client, StudentClient, has been refactored, and all of the JNDI lookup and invocation code to various EJBs have been removed. This has resulted in cleaner and simpler client code that only handles presentation logic. The StudentClient delegates the task for lookup and access to the EJB to ServiceDelegate, a business delegate design pattern object. The Service Delegate object hides all logic and the EJB methods from the client and exposes a simple interface.

The init() method in the StudentClient servlet creates the ServiceDelegate object and is then used later to invoke coarse-grained business methods.

```
public void init() throws ServletException
{
    try {
      super.init();
      delegate = new ServiceDelegate();
    } catch (Exception e) {
      System.out.println(" == Servlet - init() --"+e.getMessage
());
    }
}
```

Notice that the business method on the ServiceDelegate object is invoked by the client.

```
try
{
    schedList = delegate.searchByTitle(searchToken);
    System.out.println(" == Servlet After calling ScheduleEJB ");
}catch(Exception e) {
    System.out.println(" SearchByCourseTitle exception  ="+e.getMes-
sage());
}
```

Assembling and Deploying the Application

The J2EE Online Registration Application consists of the following:

- EJB components
  - `ScheduleEJB` (SLSB)
  - `ShoppingCartEJB` (SFSB)
  - `StudentEJB` (CMP 2.0)
  - `AddressEJB` (CMP 2.0)
  - `RosterEJB` (CMP 2.0)
  - `RosterMDB` (MDB)
- Design pattern objects
  - `ScheduleDAO`
  - `ServiceLookUp`
  - `ServiceLocatorEJB`
  - `ServiceDelegate`
  - `StudentFacadeEJB`
  - `RosterVO`
  - `AddressVO`
  - `ScheduleVO`
- Clients
  - `StudentClient`
  - `MessageSender`
  - `DurableSubscriber`
- JSP files
  - `ShowSearchResult`
  - `ShowShoppingCart`
  - `GetAddressInfo`
  - `ThankYou`
  - `SearchStudent`
- HMTL page
  - `shop.htm`

Most of these EJBs were packaged and/or deployed in previous chapters. Because you now have experience in packaging and deploying several EJBs, in this chapter we'll highlight the pertinent steps with the help of screen captures only.

1. In the deployment tool, open a new Enterprise Application (ear) file named `JORA1App.ear` and begin by packaging the JAR files.

2. Start with `ScheduleEJB`; name the file `ScheduleJAR`.

3. Add the `ScheduleEJB.class`, `ScheduleHome.class`, and `Schedule.class` to the jar file, and specify the `jdbc/JCampDS` data source. (Refer to packaging and deployment section of Chapter 6.)

4. Open a `ShoppingCartJAR` file to package `ShoppingCartEJB.class`, `ShoppingCartHome.class`, `ShoppingCart.class`, and `ScheduleVO.class`. (Refer to the section on packaging and deployment in Chapter 7.)

5. Open a `CMPJAR` to package the three CMP 2.0 entity beans—`AddressEJB`, `StudentEJB`, and `RosterEJB`—along with a stateful session bean, `SessionFacadeEJB`. Also include the `ServiceLookUp` helper class in addition to following value objects: `StudentVO`, `ScheduleVO`, `AddressVO`, and `RosterVO`. (Refer to the packaging and deployment sections of Chapter 11.)

6. Because `AddressEJB` and `RosterEJB` reference `StudentEJB` in the code, specify the `ejb/StudentRef`, entity, local, `LocalStudentHome`, and `LocalStudent` values in the EJB reference window. The stateful session bean `StudentFacadeEJB` references all three entity beans, so it must specify the references to the entity beans (see Figure 18-2).

7. This example packages the `ServiceLocatorEJB` separately, requiring the developer to open `ServiceLocatorJAR`. Specify the EJB references for the home objects for which the `ServiceLocatorEJB` provides the JNDI lookup service. In this case, specify references to the `ShoppingCart`, `Schedule`, and `StudentFacade` home objects (see Figure 18-3).

8. To package the `RosterMDB`, open an `MDBJAR` file and specify the Queue and Topic factory and the respective destination (see Chapter 13). In this case, enter **ejb/RosterRef**, entity, local, `LocalRosterHome`, and `LocalRoster` to specify the EJB reference to `RosterEJB`. (Refer to the packaging and deployment sections of Chapter 13.)

9. In addition, package `DurableSubscriber` as an application client. Enter the complete path of the interface, for example:

```
javacamp.developoingEJB.chapter18.cmp.LocalRosterHome
```

10. Package the components in the presentation tier into one Web archive, `Client2WAR`, including the servlet, JSP, `ServiceDelegate`, and `MessageSender`. Although the `ServiceDelegate` interacts with the shopping cart, schedule, and student facade beans, you should only provide an EJB reference to the `ServiceLocatorEJB` to retrieve the home objects of the EJBs. All of the JSP files are included in the war file.

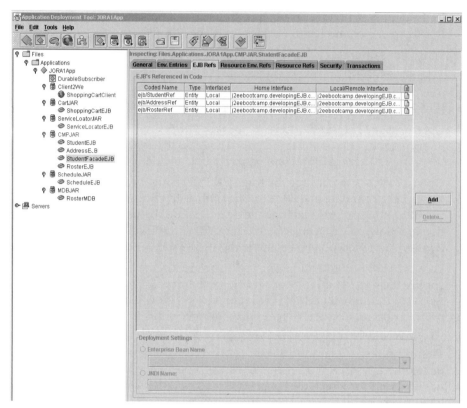

Figure 18-2 Specifying local EJB references

11. Set shop.htm as the default welcome file. Once packaging is complete, the deployment tool resembles Figure 18-4.

12. To deploy the application, click the JORA1App icon. Select Tools, deploy. The application is deployed.

13. Open the browser and enter the URL **http://localhost:8000/shop/**. Note the start page of the application (see Figure 18-5).

14. Enter **Java** and submit. The search result is shown in Figure 18-6.

15. Select one course at a time. Note that the shopping cart tracks the courses along with the running total cost (see Figure 18-7).

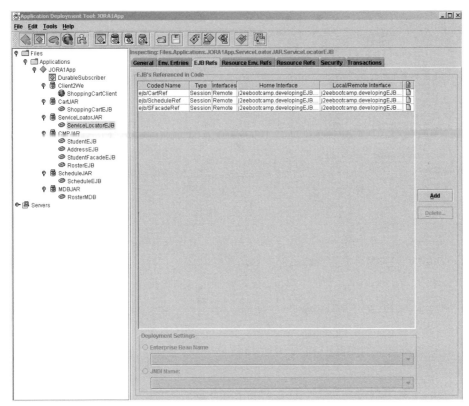

Figure 18-3 Specifying EJB references to the ServiceLocatroEJB

16. Remove a course, empty the shopping cart, or check out. Selecting a checkout button returns a student and credit card information page (see Figure 18-8).

17. Enter the information, and the application will create the student account. When the student creates an address and registers for all the courses in the shopping cart, a thank you page is displayed. The application doesn't authenticate the information provided.

18. Check for the student, address, and registration by invoking the Search-Student.jsp, which lists the student first name, last name, address, and courses for which the student is registered.

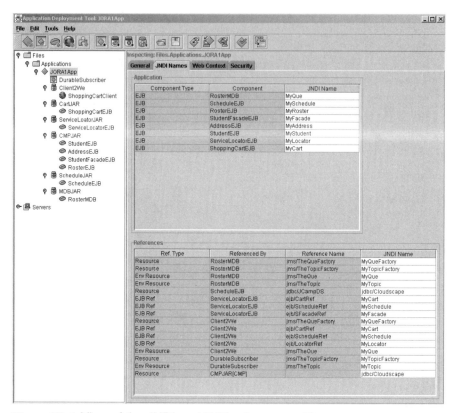

Figure 18-4 View of the JNDI and EJB reference settings

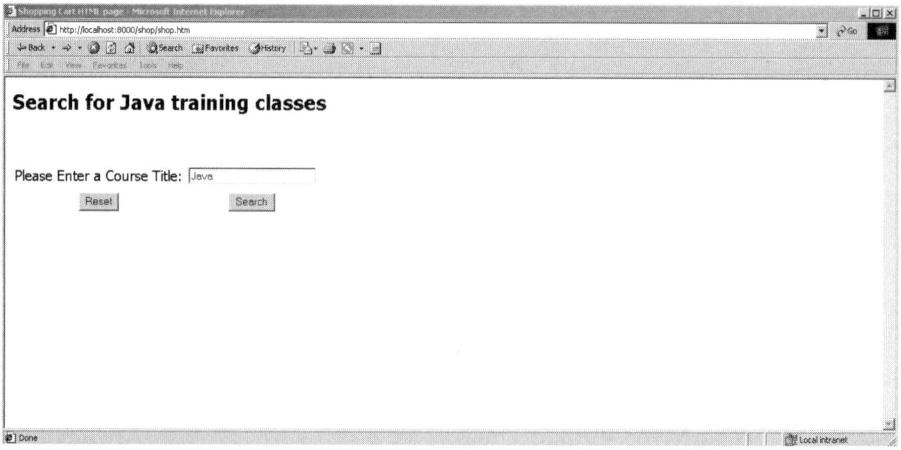

Figure 18-5 Example start page search page

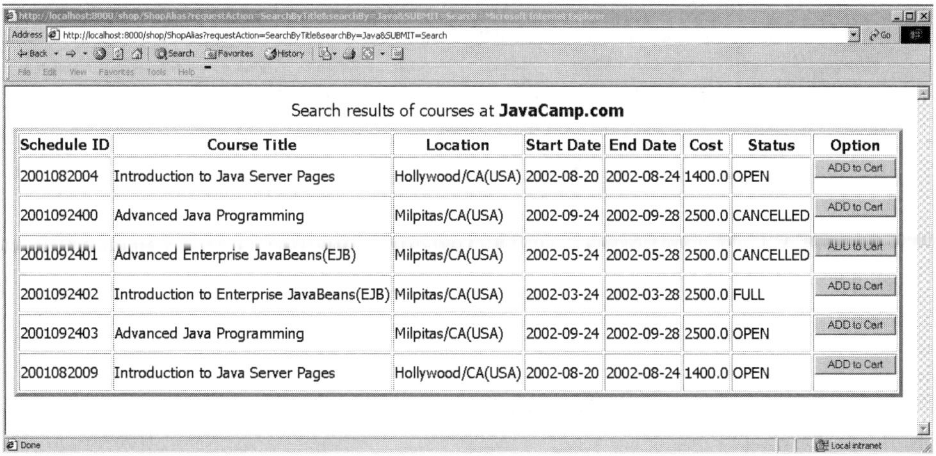

Figure 18-6 Result of the search

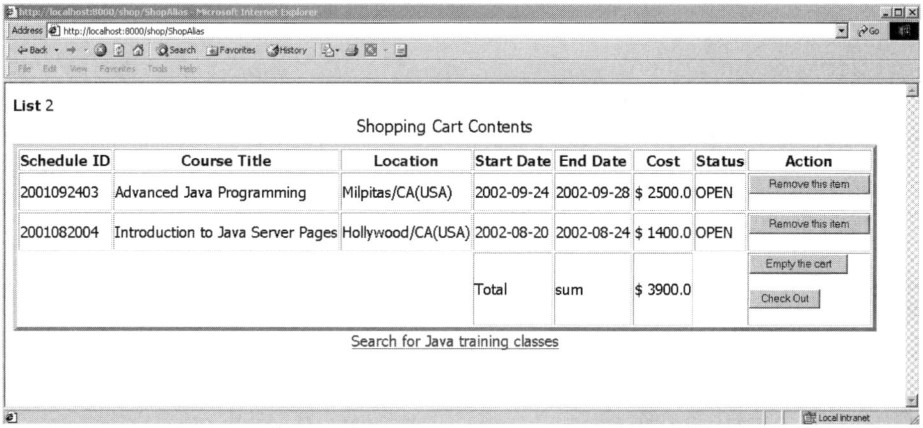

Figure 18-7 Contents of the shopping cart

Summary

In this chapter, we applied our implementation knowledge of EJBs and design patterns to assemble an application, J2EE Online Registration Application, consisting of previously implemented EJBs and several design patterns. We implemented the following design patterns: Service Locator (`ServiceLocatorEJB`,

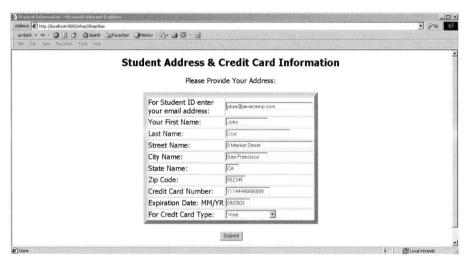

Figure 18-8 Submitting student and credit card information

`ServiceLookUp`), Data Access Object (`ScheduleDAO`), Session Facade
(`StudentFacadeEJB`), Value Object (`RosterVO`, `ScheduleVO`, and
`AddressVO`), and Business Delegate(`ServiceDelegate`).

We concluded the chapter with steps for the packaging, deployment, and testing
of the application.

Final Thoughts

As you come to the end of the chapter and the end of this book, I hope you have
found it helpful in your quest to master EJB. Learning how to encapsulate and
implement session, entity, and message-driven bean applications, and how to
package, assemble, and deploy them successfully is the easy part. The hard part is
actually implementing EJB in the real world. I hope that this book has equipped
you with the necessary knowledge and that this knowledge, combined with your
talents, has prepared you for any conceivable EJB implementation challenge.
Please feel free to send me e-mails (pvt@j2eebootcamp.com) with your comments
and any EJB development experience you'd like to share. Please visit the book's
companion Web site at http://www.j2eebootcamp.com/ for the latest
information on source code and bug fixes and to give your feedback.

Enjoy—and best of luck!

Appendix

INSTALLING AND RUNNING SUN REFERENCE IMPLEMENTATION J2SKDEE 1.3

This appendix instructs you on how to download, install, and run the J2SDKEE 1.3.1 reference implementation. J2SDKEE 1.3.1 is supported on the Solaris SPARC 7 and 8, Windows NT 4.0, Windows 2000 Professional, and Linux Redhat v. 6.2 operating systems. The information provided here applies only to the Windows 2000 platform. The appendix covers setting up the development environment and the application environment and preparing the J2SDKEE for operation.

Installation Requirements

The target system must meet specific requirements regarding software, disk space, and available RAM memory.

Software Requirements

To install and implement J2SDKEE 1.3.1 successfully, the target system must have the following software available:

- Java Software Development Kit (JDK 1.3.1)
- Java 2 Enterprise Edition, Software Development Kit (J2SDKEE 1.3.1)
- Windows 2000

Drive Space Requirements

The system on which J2SDKEE is to be installed requires approximately 250 MB of free drive space. That amount can be broken down as follows:

JDK 1.3.1 Installation

- JDK 1.3.1 installer: 33.6 MB
- JDK documentation and APIs: 22.57 MB
- Uncompressed and installed JDK 1.3.1 plus documentation: 166 MB

J2SDKEE 1.3.1 Installation

- J2SDKEE installer : 14.9 MB
- J2SDKEE 1.3.1 uncompressed and installed: 61.8 MB

Note: *The drive space values mentioned refer to the Windows 2000 platform; actual file sizes vary, and actual drive space requirements are platform dependent.*

Memory Requirements

The minimum amount of RAM memory recommended for the implementation is 128 MB.

Installation Overview in Brief

Three processes are involved in installing and implementing the J2SDKEE 1.3.1: setting up the development environment, setting up the application environment, and preparing the JSDKEE for operation.

Setting up the Development Environment

Here, in brief, are the steps involved in setting up the development environment:

1. Download and install JDK1.3.1.
2. Download and install J2SDKEE 1.3.1.
3. Set up environment variables.
4. Perform any additional setup that may be required for J2SDKEE 1.3 on the target system.
5. Test the environment.

Setting up the Application Environment

Setting up the application environment involves the following steps:

1.   Establish a source directory.

2.   Set up a database.

3.   Set up resources for JMS.

4.   Create a J2EE user account.

Preparing J2SDKEE for Operation

Steps specific to preparing J2SDKEE for operation include:

1.   Start the J2EE server.

2.   Shut down the J2EE server.

3.   Troubleshoot erratic behavior.

4.   Locate the logs file.

5.   Specify an alternative to the GUI deploytool.

Setting up the Development Environment

To set up the development environment:

1.   Download and install jdk1.3.1 from http://java.sun.com/j2se/. Then, double-click the jdk1.3.1 file, and the installer will prompt you for the location of the root directory. (Note that this step is necessary only if JDK 1.3.1 is not already installed on the target system.)

2.   Download and install the j2sdkee 1.3.1 from http://java.sun.com/j2ee/ download.html. Then, click the j2sdkee1.3.1 installer and specify the location of the target directory. The installer must be able to locate an installed version of JDK 1.3.1 before the installation will proceed. (Note that J2SKDEE 1.3.1 requires jdk version 1.3.1 or higher. If you experience problems at this stage, refer to the J2SDKEE 1.3 FAQ URL at http:// java.sun.com/j2ee/sdk_1.3/faq.html. Also, look at http://java.sun.com/ j2ee/sdk_1.3/install.html for detailed installation steps.

3.   Set up four environment variables: JAVA_HOME, J2EE_HOME, PATH, and CLASSPATH. These must set up correctly in order for the reference implementation to run. There's an additional variable (SRC) that must be set to run the sample application from the book. There are two options for setting up your environment so you can run the examples:

   • *Option 1: Using the system control panel*—This affects the account environment. Select Start I Settings I Control Panel I Systems I Advanced

| Environment Variables, and in the user variable window, click the New button to add the variable name and variable value. For the variable name, enter **JAVA_HOME** plus the root location of the JDK 1.3.1 (for example, **d:\jdk1.3.1**), as shown in Table A-1.

Table A-1   Environment Variables (System Control Panel Method)

Variable Name	Variable Value	Description
JAVA_HOME	D:\jdk1.3.1	JDK1.3.1 root directory
J2EE_HOME	D:\j2sdkee1.3.1	J2sdkee1.3.1 root directory
SRC	D:\ejbbook\sourceCode	Location of sample code
PATH	;%JAVA_HOME%\bin;%J2EE_HOME%\bin	Adds the bin directories for jdk and j2ee to the PATH
CLASSPATH	.;%SRC%;%J2EE_HOME%\lib\j2ee.jar	Needed by the Java compiler to find the class libraries

- *Option 2: Using the batch files*—In case you prefer not to tamper with the default user variables, setting up the environment via a batch file is a practical option. Go to the D:\j2sdkee1.3.1\bin directory, open the userconfig.bat file, and set JAVA_HOME=D:\jdk1.3.1 and J2EE_HOME=D:\j2sdkee1.3.1. From that point onward, whenever you run any J2SDKEE utility, it will read the userconfig.bat file and find the necessary executables and files in your environment.

4.   Test the environment. If you're using the system control panel method for setup, open a DOS terminal by selecting Start | Run. Enter **cmd**, and a terminal window will popup. When you enter **java–version**, the system should return Java version 1.3.1. When you enter **j2ee–version**, the system should return Java 2 Enterprise Edition version 1.3.1. If you're using the batch file method for setup, start a cmd terminal window, then run the **userconfig.bat** command before entering **java–version** and **j2ee–version**. In either case, the system should return the correct version.

Setting up the Application Environment

To set up the application environment after setting up the development environment successfully:

1.   Set up the example source directory. The source of all the code in this book is downloadable from the companion Web site,

http://www.J2EEBootCamp.com/developingEJB/. So that you can download and compile the sample examples, I suggest that you create a source directory named D:\ejbbook and have the SRC name in your environment point to it. If you do this, then when you unzip the files in the SRC directory you can compile without running into package and path problems. Note that here the examples have the package names `j2eebootcamp.developingEJB.chapterN.XXX`, where *N* corresponds to the chapter number and *XXX* corresponds to the specific component subdirectory name.

2.   Set up the Cloudscape database. The code examples in this book use the Cloudscape database, which is included with the J2SDKEE 1.3.1 reference implementation. Start cloudscape, then switch to the %SRC%\j2eebootcamp.developingEJB\database\cloudscape directory and execute **cloudIJ batch** to connect to the cloudscape database. Then, enter the command **run 'createSampleTables.sql'** in the terminal window, and Cloudscape will create all the necessary tables and populate them with data for the sample applications.

3.   Create a j2ee user account. We're using user account **j2ee** and password **j2ee** for all our sample applications. To create a user account, the deploytool must be running; select Tools | Server Configuration. When the Configuration Installation window pops up, click the User icon under the J2EE Server icon, then click the Add User button and enter **j2ee** as both the username and password, as shown in Figure A-1. Click Apply.

4.   Set up factories and destinations resources for JMS. You need to set up Connection Factories and Destinations for both the Queue and Topic messaging models. Select Connection Factories, click Add, enter **MyQueFactory** in the JNDI Name column, and from the pull-down menu, select Queue in the Type column. For the Topic messaging model, repeat the same steps, but select MyTopicFactory under JNDI name, and under Type, select Topic, as shown in Figure A-2.

5.   Next, click the Destination icon under JMS, and then add MyTopic under JMS Topic Destination and MyQueue under JMS Queue Destination, as shown in Figure A-3. Then, click OK. The Configure Installation window should disappear.

6.   Now, the J2EE server is set up to run the sample application. Shut down the deploytool, J2EE server, and Cloudscape, and restart them as described next.

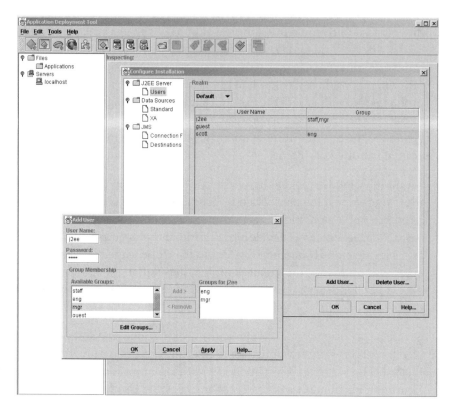

Figure A-1 Creating a user name and password

Preparing the J2SDKEE for Operation

To prepare the J2SDKEE for operation, you need to start the J2SDKEE RI, shut it down again, locate the logs file, and optionally specify an alternative to the GUI tool.

Starting the J2SDKEE RI

1. Start the J2SDKEE 1.3.1 Reference Implementation. Assuming that the environment variables have been set up correctly, you need to run Cloudscape, J2EE server, and the deployment tool. The startup sequence is important. So open three terminal windows and change to the D:\j2sdkee1.3.1\bin directory on all three windows. To start Cloudscape, execute **cloudscape–start**. If you're successful, you should see the result shown in Figure A-4.

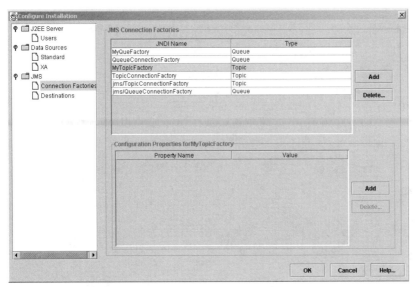

Figure A-2   Specifying Topic and Queue factories

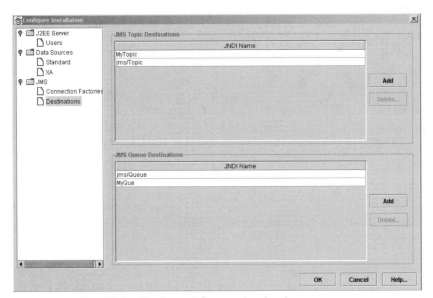

Figure A-3   Specifying Topic and Queue destinations

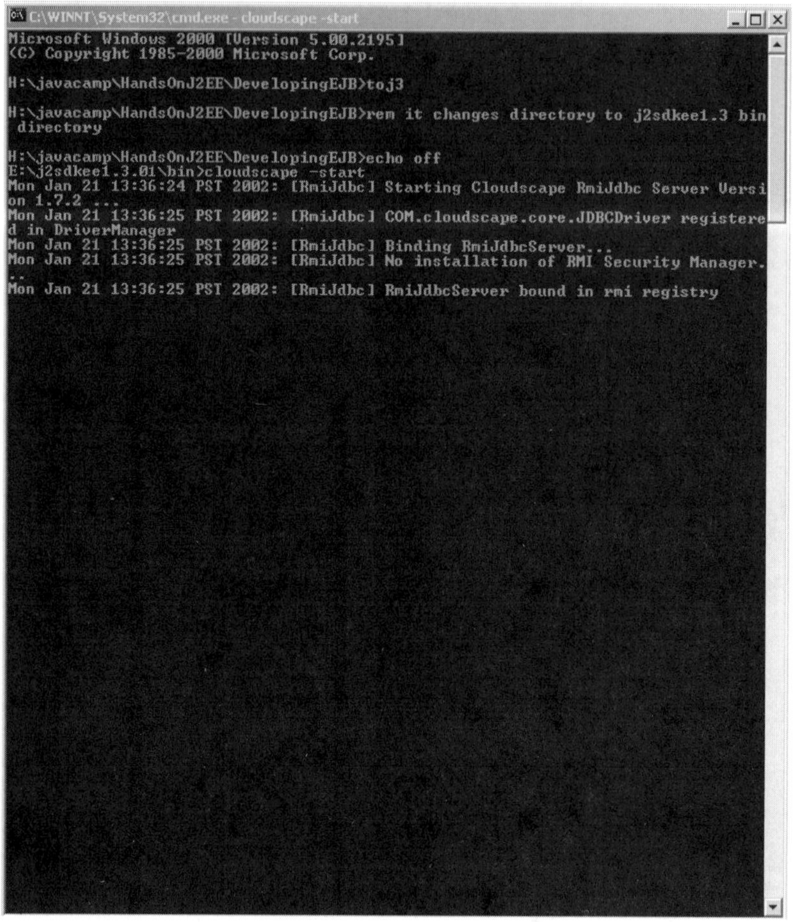

Figure A-4 Output of cloudscape startup

2. To start the j2ee server, go to the second open terminal window and execute **j2ee–verbose**. After a moment, you should see the results shown in Figure A-5.

3. Finally, you need to start the deployment tool. In the third open window, execute **deploytool**, and an Application Deployment tool should pop up, as shown in Figure A-6. Make sure the J2EE server is fully running—the `J2EE server startup complete` message should appear before you attempt to start the deploytool, or else the tool will be unable to connect to the J2EE server.

Figure A-5 Output of the J2EE server startup

Shutting Down the J2SDKEE RI

To shut down properly, first shut down the deploytool, then the J2EE server, and finally, Cloudscape. In the deploytool window, select File | Exit to close the window. Then, in the terminal window, enter **j2ee –stop** to shut down the J2EE server. You can then enter **cloudscape–stop** to shut down the Cloudscape server.

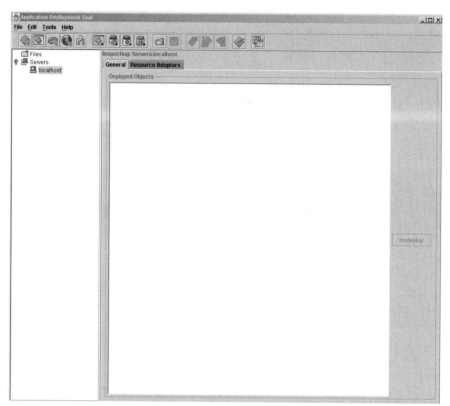

Figure A-6 Output of the deploytool startup

Troubleshooting Erratic Behavior by J2SDKEE 1.3.1

At times, the deploytool might yield bogus errors, or after you make changes and redeploy, the changes might not be visible to the J2EE server. In such a case, undeploy the current application, exit out of the deploytool, shut down the j2ee server, and then run the **cleanup.bat** file in the j2sdkee1.3.1\bin directory. The cleanup batch files delete old class files that the j2ee server is referencing. Then, restart the j2ee server and the deploytool in sequence, and finally, deploy your application.

Log Files and Troubleshooting

There are three log files (audit, log, and output) where the J2EE server saves information. These log files can be found in the j2sdkee1.3.1\logs\Your-HostName\j2ee\j2ee directory. The error file is highly informative.

In addition, at times the J2EE server will create files containing information about anomalous behavior during the deployment and execution phase; these are usually saved in the temp directory. When these types of unusual errors occur, the tools will indicate the relevant filename and location. Be sure to look at the log files, as they yield valuable information that will help you pinpoint possible bugs or incorrect settings related to your implementation.

Specifying an Alternative to the GUI Deploytool

We used the GUI deploytool to assemble and deploy all of our sample applications, mainly because it's easier to use than other methods. You should, however, be aware of command-line tools that provide the same functionalities. These command-line tools can accomplish the same results. You could, for example, use the admintool to create and delete user name, password, JMS factories, and destinations. The command-line package utility makes it possible for developers to package EJB and Web components and create jar, war, and ear files. The command-line verifier utility lets the developer test and verify the validity of the applications by performing numerous checks. Finally, even the deploytool (with certain options specified) can used to deploy applications on the command line. All these utilities are available the in j2sdkee1.3.1\bin subdirectory.

Index